BEYOND IMAGINATION?

The January 6 Insurrection

Mark C. Alexander
Arthur J. Kania Dean and Professor of Law, Villanova University Charles Widger School of Law

Michèle Alexandre
Dean and Professor of Law, Stetson University College of Law, Counsel to the President for Strategic Initiatives and Operations

Erwin S. Chemerinsky
Dean and Jesse H. Choper Distinguished Professor of Law, University of California, Berkeley School of Law

Danielle M. Conway
Dean and Donald J. Farage Professor of Law, Penn State Dickinson Law

Anthony W. Crowell
Dean and President, and Professor of Law, New York Law School

Garry W. Jenkins
Dean and William S. Pattee Professor of Law, University of Minnesota Law School

Kevin R. Johnson
Dean and Mabie-Apallas Professor of Public Interest Law and Chicana/o Studies, University of California, Davis, School of Law

Jennifer L. Mnookin
Dean and Ralph and Shirley Shapiro Professor of Law, UCLA School of Law

Kimberly Mutcherson
Dean and Professor of Law, Rutgers Law School

Andrew M. Perlman
Dean and Professor of Law, Suffolk University Law School

Carla D. Pratt
Dean and Professor of Law

Theodore W. Ruger
Dean and Bernard G. Segal Professor of Law, University of Pennsylvania Carey Law School

Daniel P. Tokaji
Fred W. & Vi Miller Dean and Professor of Law, University of Wisconsin Law School

Robert K. Vischer
Dean and Mengler Chair in Law, University of St. Thomas School of Law (MN)

WEST ACADEMIC PUBLISHING

444 Cedar Street, Suite 700
St. Paul, MN 55101
1-877-888-1330

Printed in the United States of America

ISBN: 978-1-63659-874-1

INTRODUCTION: *BEYOND IMAGINATION?*

The rule of law is the foundation of America's constitutional democracy. It is the principle by which all individuals and institutions are accountable to laws that are enacted publicly and lawfully, enforced equally, and subject to independent judicial review. While our nation has always been a work in progress, the rule of law serves as the guide to achieve the promise of equal justice under law. Throughout our nation's complex history, the rule of law and our carefully balanced constitutional system has allowed the nation to confront and successfully navigate many unique existential threats. Throughout its history, our nation has faced many significant threats, including a Civil War. And, one of the most significant threats in modern times, growing for many years from the propagation of politically polarizing and destructive disinformation, was realized on January 6, 2021.

On that day, a violent and deadly mob of insurrectionists stormed the U.S. Capitol building. The Congress was meeting in a joint session to perform the essential, yet largely ceremonial, task of counting the ballots from the Electoral College to declare the winner of the presidential election. That task has occurred without much attention for 200+ years, but this time it was different. Americans were transfixed as events unfolded, with a huge range of emotions.

Earlier in the day, President Donald Trump, who had lost his re-election bid, held a rally where he and others urged people to go to the Capitol to "stop the steal." Spurred by the President's urgent language, the mob moved *en masse* down Pennsylvania Avenue to the Capitol grounds. The insurrectionists—predominantly white men—set upon the Capitol, intending to disrupt the certification of the election and a peaceful transition of power, and they did. Once there, they destructively invaded the legislative chambers of our national government. In doing so, they broke windows and doors. They flew the Confederate flag, as well as the losing candidate's political campaign flags, pledging loyalty to the man who lost re-election, but not to the U.S. government. They beat police officers with zeal. They stole a wide range of property. Several people lost their lives, including a member of the Capitol Police. They threatened Vice President Mike Pence and called for his hanging. They ransacked the Office of the Speaker of the House. Senators and Representatives and their staffs were forced to shelter for their lives, protected by an outnumbered cadre of police, Secret Service, and other law enforcement officers. Throughout the siege, the President was mesmerized by what was taking place, albeit pleased by what he was seeing. This was demonstrated by his refusal to stand up in defense of our nation's Capitol, and thus his refusal to defend the rule of law.

Following that day's destruction, Congress quickly reconvened and worked well into the night to fulfill their constitutional duty and adhere to the rule of law, certifying the election results in the early morning of January 7. And, to this day, the now former President still maintains a false narrative that the election was stolen and fraudulent.

In the United States, we have long prided ourselves on the peaceful transfer of power after elections. Every four years we hold a presidential election, resulting in a winner. Dissenting voices may object, but the winner is accepted, and the loser moves on. Truth matters, and perhaps more here, in the context of free and fair elections, than in any other. This is the American way. Anything less should be beyond our imagination.

In the immediate aftermath of the events of January 6, the deans of American law schools came together to assess the situation. After much discussion, we decided to write an open letter, which was signed by almost every dean—171 of the approximately 200 deans in this country. We each have our own institutions to run, and while we may agree on many things, we almost never gather our collective will to speak out as clearly as we did in that letter.

Our message reads as follows:

Law Deans' Joint Statement on the 2020 Election and Events at the Capitol

We are deans of a diverse range of law schools across the country. We do not use our positions to advance our individual views. But we do have an obligation to support the rule of law and preserve the integrity of the legal profession. On rare occasions, despite our differing situations and views, that obligation requires us to speak as one to defend the fundamental commitments of our profession. This is such a moment.

The violent attack on the Capitol was an assault on our democracy and the rule of law. The effort to disrupt the certification of a free and fair election was a betrayal of the core values that undergird our Constitution. Lives were lost, the seat of our democracy was desecrated, and our country was shamed.

Many lawyers and judges worked honestly and in good faith, often in the face of considerable political pressure, to ensure the 2020 election was free and fair. However, we recognize with dismay and sorrow that some lawyers challenged the outcome of the election with claims that they did not support with facts or evidence. This betrayed the values of our profession. Our profession demands that when lawyers pursue legal action, they must bring claims in good faith, grounded in facts and evidence, and demonstrate respect for the legal system. Only then can lawyers fulfill their responsibilities as lawyers and public citizens to promote public confidence in the rule of law and the justice system—duties that extend to all professional activities, whether lawyers are representing a client or not. The rule of law is as much a touchstone of our profession as it is of our Constitution.

As law deans, our mission is to train the next generation of leaders to uphold the core values of our profession and sustain the rule of law. This should be a moment of reflection for legal educators and members of the legal

> *profession. A sustained effort will be necessary to repair and preserve our precious democratic institutions. As legal educators and lawyers ourselves, we must redouble our efforts to restore faith in the rule of law and the ideals of the legal profession. We have enormous faith in the law's enduring values and in our students, who will soon lead this profession. We call upon all members of the legal profession to join us in the vital work ahead.*

Why does this mean such a great deal to us as deans of American law schools? Because we train the next generation of lawyers, we are obligated to examine these seditious acts, with an eye on the lawyers involved, the rule of law, and our system of laws and government. As lawyers, we also must act according to certain standards of conduct, which reflect the great trust placed upon all members of our noble profession. Through this period of time, some lawyers excelled and earned that trust, while others debased themselves and consequently, our profession.

Upon becoming a member of the bar, every new lawyer swears an oath. These oaths are unique to each jurisdiction, but they all require those taking them to support the Constitution of the United States. They mean something about who we are as lawyers and about our obligations to society. As deans, we are proud to be lawyers, and to train lawyers, in part because of the oaths we have taken and the responsibilities that come with those oaths. As lawyers and legal educators, the ongoing legitimacy of our nation's republic requires us all to engage. As we train the next generation of lawyer-leaders, many of whom we ask to take these same oaths when they start law school, we must take stock and double down on the rule of law. This work will not be easy, and we decided to write a book, as part of the effort.

This book is not a partisan undertaking. Our cause is the rule of law; our loyalty is to the Constitution of the United States. We support the American people, not one candidate, elected official, or individual. We have attempted to strike a balance and draw some lines. While we are confident that we have presented a fair reading, we are also certain that not everyone will fully agree with every chapter, or every page within every chapter. We are united in this project, but we still have discrete disagreements among ourselves in each individual chapter. We want to challenge you, the reader, and we sincerely hope that our work contributes to exposing the problems that allowed us to suffer collectively on January 6, and then to promote healing. We speak for ourselves, not for our institutions. We hope we are speaking up *for* many people and speaking *to* our entire society about what once was and should always have been beyond imagination, but which no longer is.

Fourteen of us have collaborated on this work as co-authors, with the help of many other colleagues, family, and friends. It has been a labor of love and an exercise in collegiality, as we came together to quickly write something meaningful, putting in extra hours in our already-filled days. We each decided to write a chapter—relatively short and accessible, but still erudite. We have written in a way designed to appeal to many, without the typical heaviness that can weigh down academic writing. We write from our perspectives as legal scholars, as deans of our institutions, and as individuals who have been engaged in leadership in various ways, primarily (but not exclusively) in the law. We hope that all may be interested in reading this book as an exercise in civics. We hope to inspire our students, and we have agreed to donate royalties from the book to support students and/or programs at our respective law schools. We encourage our colleagues to use the material in teaching the next generation of lawyers as they make their way through law school. And we also encourage all lawyers to engage with the text and hope they find this important work to serve as a sober reminder of the weight and responsibility that attends the oaths we have taken to uphold the Constitution and the rule of law.

In alphabetical order (and with our institutions listed merely for identification purposes), we are:

- Mark Alexander, Villanova
- Michèle Alexandre, Stetson
- Erwin Chemerinsky, UC-Berkeley
- Danielle Conway, Penn State Dickinson Law
- Anthony Crowell, New York Law School

- Garry Jenkins, Minnesota
- Kevin Johnson, UC-Davis
- Jennifer Mnookin, UCLA
- Kimberly Mutcherson, Rutgers
- Andrew Perlman, Suffolk
- Carla Pratt
- Theodore Ruger, Penn
- Daniel Tokaji, Wisconsin
- Robert Vischer, St. Thomas, Minnesota

Each of us has contributed one chapter and supported one another along the way. Each chapter complements every other chapter to form a series of perspectives on what happened on January 6. Each can be read separately, or all can be read together in order; there is no one preferred or right way to read the book. After this Introduction, the book is organized in three parts and 14 chapters as follows:

Part 1: Lawyers and Leadership

Andrew Perlman: An astounding number and variety of lawyers promoted 2020 election conspiracy theories. While several filed election-related lawsuits, others—such as politicians and news commentators—did so outside of traditional lawyer roles. Dean Perlman's chapter explores the potential consequences that these lawyers could face because of their actions.

Michèle Alexandre: Dean Alexandre discusses the collective leadership that arose among law school faculty during the unprecedented election cycle. Her essay is a cautious narrative detailing the progress made in the legal community in the past 18 months.

Garry Jenkins: Dean Jenkins' chapter discusses leadership. In nearly all aspects of public and private life, leadership matters. Leadership is part of the story of the January 6, 2021 Capitol attack, part of the cause, and part of the solution. Dean Jenkins notes that lawyers and the legal profession have long demonstrated their capacity to respond to challenges of the day, and law schools can help lawyers reassert their importance going forward.

Danielle Conway: Dean Conway's chapter provides one perspective on the rise and the influence of the decanal collective voice that led to the Law Deans' Joint Statement addressing the 2020 election and the Capitol insurrection. In her chapter, Dean Conway emphasizes that with this collective voice, law schools pledged to stand together to uphold these obligations and to work alongside our elected officials and democratic institutions to repair the damage that has been done to our American democracy.

Jennifer Mnookin: Dean Mnookin's chapter discusses the importance of law schools training lawyers fundamentally committed to taking evidence and facts seriously. Further, her chapter discusses the importance of training lawyers who will recognize their pledge to uphold our democratic processes. Dean Mnookin notes that law schools must prepare graduates so they may bring claims in good faith, grounded in facts and evidence, and demonstrate respect for the legal system.

Theodore Ruger: Dean Ruger examines the impact of electoral politics on our system of checks and balances, in the context of the Insurrection and its aftermath. He looks at the actions of the states' Attorneys General and asks whether they are the living embodiment of James Madison's concerns about the power of ambition, the lure of electoral success, and the impact on the rule of law and our democracy. Because we are not and never will be governed by "angels," he asks whether our political structure is sufficient as a check against ambition.

Part 2: Roots of American National Identity

Robert Vischer: Dean Vischer examines the role Christian nationalism played in the insurrection. He defines and describes the Christian nationalism phenomenon while carefully distinguishing it from Christianity itself. He also theorizes on how to create a healthy Christian dialogue within politics.

Kimberly Mutcherson: Dean Mutcherson writes about the insurrection and its ties to racism. In her chapter, Dean Mutcherson calls for legal educators and students to focus their attention on teaching and approaching the law through a more scrutinizing lens, underlining the importance of acting as proponents for change.

Carla Pratt: Dean Pratt's chapter analyzes the foundations of white supremacy and its continuing effects on our nation. Delving into historical events and modern statistics, Dean Pratt urges the reader to pursue an "honest analysis of our history," as part of striving towards truth, fairness, and justice.

Erwin Chemerinsky: Dean Chemerinsky dedicates his chapter to an examination of democracy, with an emphasis on the history of our elections and, in particular, the 2020 election. Relatedly, Dean Chemerinsky discusses legal education and its role in preserving our democracy.

Part 3: Looking Forward/Pursuit of Truth and Solutions

Kevin Johnson: Dean Johnson's chapter contends that the nation's recent experience with President Trump demonstrates the importance of law schools re-dedicating themselves to teaching rigorous factual and legal analysis in legal education and devotion to the rule of law. A rigorous analytical approach can be beneficial to any thoughtful analysis of pressing public policy issues currently facing the nation. Dean Johnson argues that the legal travails of the Trump administration should reinforce the understanding that legal analysis is a sound approach when addressing legal problems and pressing public policy issues.

Anthony Crowell: Dean Crowell recounts the fluctuating emphasis on civics education throughout history. He posits that many of the current issues facing our country stem from a de-emphasis on civics, something that has resulted in what he calls *civic anemia*. Accordingly, he calls on law school communities to rethink and revamp civics education for the legal community.

Daniel Tokaji: Dean Tokaji argues that the legal method can help save American democracy. He describes the underappreciated strengths that the electoral system showed during the 2020 election, as well as the deeper weaknesses in constitutional democracy that it revealed, contending that the critical thinking skills taught in law schools could help address these problems.

Mark Alexander: Dean Alexander addresses how to move forward after the Insurrection, to pursue our more perfect Union. He calls for us to recognize certain values and commitments at the core of public discourse. He suggests that we must commit to a full, robust, wide-open, uninhibited debate going forward, based in universal values, in order to protect against such insurrection again—or any attempts to subvert and destroy our nation. He closes this book by arguing that we can return from this dangerous point in our history with a commitment to engage in the essential hard work at the heart of American democracy.

We never imagined the insurrection of January 6, 2021 and all the horrific actions and events of that day. But now it is our reality, part of our nation's history. The wounds inflicted on our nation are deep and painful, and they will take a long time to heal fully. Even then, we will forever bear scars reminding us of that awful day. We offer our thoughts in these collected chapters as a part of the healing process, a start of a conversation, and a call to action. We will remain engaged in this process for the long run for our great country, and we hope this book can help us all move forward as a nation.

TABLE OF CONTENTS

PART 3. LOOKING FORWARD/PURSUIT OF TRUTH AND SOLUTIONS

BEYOND IMAGINATION?

The January 6 Insurrection

PART 1

LAWYERS AND LEADERSHIP

CHAPTER 1

THE LEGAL ETHICS OF LYING ABOUT AMERICAN DEMOCRACY

Andrew M. Perlman[1]

Numerous lawyers contributed to the disinformation campaign that led to the storming of the U.S. Capitol on January 6, 2021. Some of the lawyers filed lawsuits that questioned the legitimacy of the presidential election, and others spread falsehoods while acting as legislators or in similar high-profile roles. This chapter explores the potential disciplinary consequences of their behavior and the larger implications of their conduct for American democracy.

One theme of this chapter is that, when lawyers make claims about elections, the consequences of misinformation are severe and threaten to undermine trust in our democratic institutions. Given the stakes, the legal profession should apply well-established procedures and rules to discipline lawyers who cross ethical lines in the context of election-related litigation. In contrast, discipline is far more complex, both legally and politically, for lawyers who serve in public roles and do not represent clients, such as lawyer-legislators who lied about the election. Instead of seeking to discipline these lawyers with traditional sanctions, the profession should speak with one voice and across the political spectrum to condemn them for lying about core features of our democracy.

The risks here are enormous. Lawyers play a critical role in supporting and lending legitimacy to bedrock political institutions, such as the judiciary and the electoral system. When lawyers lie or offer misleading information about those institutions, they create an existential threat to democracy itself. The disciplinary system can help to encourage appropriate behavior at the margins, but even with these professional guardrails, it is an open question whether lawyers will exercise

1 Dean & Professor of Law, Suffolk University Law School.

the kind of professional integrity that democratic institutions need.

A. THE LEGAL PROFESSION'S CONTRIBUTIONS TO SOCIAL PROGRESS AND DYSFUNCTION

Throughout history, the legal profession has contributed to some of the world's greatest social achievements. Lawyers have established enduring democracies, extended civil rights, expanded opportunities for the underrepresented, and advanced the rule of law. They also have offered voices for the voiceless, provided access to legal services for those unable to afford them, and generally ensured the proper functioning of numerous essential political institutions.

At the same time, lawyers have contributed to a wide range of scandals and disgraces, both while representing clients and serving in nonrepresentational public roles (e.g., elected officials and advisors to political leaders). To take a particularly horrific non-U.S. example, lawyers played a significant role in Nazi Germany's development and implementation of the laws that led to the Holocaust.[2] Within the U.S., lawyers have engaged in many instances of shameful (albeit obviously less heinous) behavior. For example, not only was President Richard Nixon himself a lawyer, but many of the high-level public officials who participated in the Watergate scandal were lawyers as well.[3] The earlier Teapot Dome scandal, which saw the first instance of a former Cabinet secretary go to prison, featured a lawyer. And President Bill Clinton, who was impeached for lying under oath during another prominent American scandal, was a lawyer.

Other examples, both recent and most distant, are plentiful, but the point is that lawyers are often at the center of society's greatest social achievements and failures. The rest of this chapter focuses on the latter and specifically on whether

---

[2] *See, e.g.*, Cynthia Fountaine, *Complicity in the Perversion of Justice: The Role of Lawyers in Ending the Rule of Law in the Third Reich,* 10 ST. MARY'S J. LEGAL MALPRACTICE & ETHICS 198 (2020).

[3] *See, e.g.*, Mark Curriden, *The Lawyers of Watergate: How a '3rd-Rate Burglary' Provoked New Standards for Lawyer Ethics*, ABA J. (Jun. 1, 2012, 10:20 a.m.), https://www.abajournal.com/magazine/article/the_lawyers_of_watergate_how_a_3rd-rateburglaryprovokednewstandards.

discipline is appropriate for lawyers who contributed to a social disgrace that has profound implications for the survival of American democracy: the spreading of misinformation that led to the seditious storming of the U.S. Capitol on January 6, 2021.

B. LAWYER DISCIPLINE AND THE 2020 ELECTION

The American system of lawyer discipline treats misconduct (such as making false statements) differently depending on whether lawyers are acting within their professional roles or in other contexts. The ABA Model Rules of Professional Conduct, which have been adopted in significant part in every U.S. jurisdiction, clearly apply to lawyers while they are representing clients. The rules, however, offer only a few options for disciplining lawyers in nonrepresentative public roles (LINPRs), such as lawyers who serve as elected officials. When assessing whether lawyers should be disciplined, it can be helpful to consider four possible categories of behavior.

Possible Bases for Lawyer Discipline

	Conduct is Unlawful[4]	Conduct is Lawful[5]
Conduct occurs while the lawyer is acting in a representational role	The rules of professional conduct apply to the behavior.	The rules of professional conduct apply to the behavior.
Conduct occurs while the lawyer is acting in a nonrepresentational role	A limited number of rules of professional conduct apply to the behavior, typically Rules 8.4(b) and (c).	?

[4] "Unlawful" means that the conduct either constitutes a crime or violates a civil law, rule or regulation other than the applicable rules of professional conduct.

[5] "Lawful" means that it is not a crime and does not constitute a crime or violate a civil law, rule, or regulation other than the rules of professional conduct.

The goal of this chapter is not to assess whether discipline is appropriate for any particular lawyer. Rather, the goal is to offer a framework for understanding the possible bases for discipline and explain when discipline would be appropriate.

1. Disciplining Lawyers for Conduct in a Representational Role

The top row of the table concerns behavior that occurs while lawyers are representing clients. In that context, it is uncontroversial that lawyers are subject to discipline for their unlawful behavior (the middle of the upper row) and for conduct that is otherwise lawful but violates the applicable rules of professional conduct (the upper-right corner). The only question in these contexts is whether the behavior actually violates well-established rules.

a. Alleged Unlawful Conduct in the 2020 Election Litigation

The lawyers who filed lawsuits challenging the results of the 2020 presidential election were acting in their role as lawyers and had to comply with the applicable rules of civil procedure (among other legal standards) when filing documents in court. Those rules require lawyers to certify that the factual allegations in their court documents have evidentiary support or are likely to have evidentiary support after an opportunity for investigation or discovery.[6] Lawyers also must not use their filings for any improper purpose, such as to harass or cause unnecessary delay.[7] If a lawyer's factual contentions fail to comply with this requirement, the lawyer can be subject to sanctions under the rules of civil procedure as well as discipline under the rules of professional conduct.[8]

Several lawyers have been accused of violating these standards. For instance, Sidney Powell joined several other lawyers in filing lawsuits around the country that alleged massive election fraud and related conspiracies. A disciplinary

---

[6] *See, e.g.*, FED. R. CIV. P. 11(b)(3).

[7] *See, e.g.*, FED. R. CIV. P. 11(b)(1).

[8] *See* MODEL RULES OF PRO. CONDUCT r. 3.1 (AM. BAR ASS'N, 2013) (prohibiting lawyers from initiating proceedings, "unless there is a basis in law and fact for doing so. . .").

complaint against the lawyers claims that many of their allegations lacked evidentiary support and were unlikely ever to have any.[9] As an example, it has been argued that Powell failed to have sufficient support for the provocative claim that Dominion Voting Systems, Inc. (the company that provided voting systems and services in dozens of states) was "founded by foreign oligarchs and dictators to ensure computerized ballot-stuffing and vote manipulation to whatever level was needed to make certain Venezuelan dictator Hugo Chávez never lost another election."[10]

Several related allegations rested on the opinion of an anonymous "U.S. Military Intelligence expert," who asserted (for instance) that Dominion "allowed foreign adversaries to access data and intentionally provided access to Dominion's infrastructure in order to monitor and manipulate elections, including the most recent one in 2020."[11] That expert, however, may never have served in military intelligence and supposedly did not pass the entry-level training course in that area.[12]

In August 2021, a Michigan court imposed sanctions against Powell and eight other lawyers as a result of their filings in that state.[13] In a 110-page opinion that catalogued the lawyers' failings, the court ordered that the lawyers pay the fees and costs incurred by the defendants in the case and complete continuing legal education courses in the areas of election law and pleadings standards. The court also referred the lawyers to the authorities responsible for disciplining lawyers in both Michigan and the other states where the lawyers were licensed to practice.

---

9 Defs. Mot. for Sanctions 1–56, ECF No. 78, https://www.courtlistener.com/recap/gov.uscourts.mied.350905/gov.uscourts.mied.350905.78.0.pdf (providing overview of numerous statements alleged to be false in Michigan case).

10 Complaint for Declaratory, Emergency, & Permanent Injunctive Relief, King v. Whitmer, Civil Case No. 20-13134 (E.D. Mich. Aug. 25, 2021) at 3.

11 *See id.* ¶ 74.

12 Emma Brown, Aaron Davis & Alice Crites, *Sidney Powell's Secret 'Military Intelligence Expert,' Key to Fraud Claims in Election Lawsuits, Never Worked in Military Intelligence*, WASH. POST (Dec. 11, 2020 at 6:29 p.m.), https://www.washingtonpost.com/investigations/sidney-powell-spider-spyder-witness/2020/12/11/0cd567e6-3b2a-11eb-98c4-25dc9f4987e8_story.html.

13 King v. Whitmer, Civil Case No. 20-13134 (E.D. Mich. Aug. 25, 2021), https://www.michigan.gov/documents/ag/172_opinion__order_King_733786_7.pdf.

Lawyers typically deserve some leeway when filing cases involving matters of great public importance, such as election-related litigation, but courts should not hesitate to discipline lawyers who cross legal and ethical lines, especially when their allegations threaten trust in our democracy. Here, the lawyers' claims were widely reported and contributed to the false belief among President Trump's supporters that the election was stolen and illegitimate. Although these conspiracy theories were already circulating on social media and elsewhere, the lawyers added their professional credibility to the theories by placing them in court filings. In doing so, they gave the public an additional reason to believe that the claims might be true. As the court said in sanctioning Powell and her colleagues, "[T]his case was never about fraud—it was about undermining the People's faith in our democracy and debasing the judicial process to do so."[14]

Other lawyers have been similarly accused of making misleading allegations about the election and undermining trust in the outcome. For instance, a group of state attorneys general asked the United States Supreme Court for leave to file a Bill of Complaint in which they asserted that "[t]he probability of former Vice President Biden winning the popular vote in the four Defendant States—Georgia, Michigan, Pennsylvania, and Wisconsin—independently given President Trump's early lead in those States as of 3 a.m. on November 4, 2020, is less than one in a quadrillion, or 1 in 1,000,000,000,000,000."[15]

This allegation by prominent lawyers received considerable public attention. For instance, President Trump's senior advisor and former press secretary Kayleigh McEnany repeated the statistical claim on Fox News.[16] (Notably, McEnany also happens to be a lawyer.) The claim reinforced the belief among

---

[14] *Id.* at 3.

[15] Motion for Expediated Consideration of the Motion for Leave to File a Bill of Complaint & for Expedition of Any Plenary Consideration of the Matter on the Pleadings if Plaintiffs' Forthcoming Motion for Interim Relief is Not Granted, Texas v. Pennsylvania, No. 20A at 8, (U.S. Dec. 7, 2021), https://www.supremecourt.gov/DocketPDF/22/22O155/163048/20201208132827887_TX-v-State-ExpedMot%202020-12-07%20FINAL.pdf [hereinafter Motion for Leave].

[16] Phillip Bump, *Trump's Effort to Retain Power Is Powered by Inaccurate and Nonsensical Jargon*, WASH. POST (Dec. 10, 2020 at 1:53 p.m.), https://www.washingtonpost.com/politics/2020/12/10/trumps-effort-retain-power-is-powered-by-inaccurate-nonsensical-jargon/.

many supporters of President Trump that he could not have lost the election. As with Powell, the lawyers lent their professional credibility to the idea that the election was stolen.

The problem is that the statistical assertion was largely based on a declaration (a legal statement created by a supposed expert at the request of the lawyers) that rested on two obviously flawed assumptions. First, the declaration compared voting patterns from the 2016 and 2020 presidential elections and appeared to assume that the percentage of voters supporting Hillary Clinton and Joe Biden should have been the same in both elections. For instance, in Georgia, the expert concluded that "the increase of Biden over Clinton is statistically incredible if the outcomes were based on similar populations of voters supporting the two Democrat candidates."[17] In other words, if the same percentage of the electorate in Georgia favored Biden and Clinton, there is no way that Biden could have won. This assertion is true as far as it goes—Donald Trump would clearly have prevailed if the electorate voted for Biden and Clinton in the same percentages in both elections. But the whole point of an election is to give people an opportunity to change their minds or to vote when they did not do so in a previous election.

The second problem with the expert declaration is that it assumed that the ballots included the same proportion of votes for Biden as Trump, both before and after 3:00 a.m. on the morning after the election. The expert explained that he "compared and tested the significance of the change in tabulated ballots earlier in the reporting to subsequent tabulations. For both comparisons [he] determined the likelihood that the samples of the outcomes for the . . . two tabulation periods were similar and randomly drawn from the same population."[18] This analysis also was flawed because the ballots counted later in the reporting period were primarily absentee ballots, and those votes were not expected to be "similar." They were expected to favor Biden because Republican voters reported that they were considerably more likely to vote in person on election day.[19]

---

17 *Motion for Leave*, *supra* note 15, ¶ 13.

18 *Id.* ¶ 7.

19 Phillip Bump, *Trump's Effort to Steal the Election Comes Down to Some Utterly Ridiculous Statistical Claims*, WASH. POST (Dec. 9, 2020 at 2:49 p.m.), https://www.

Again, the goal of this chapter is not to determine whether any particular lawyer who engaged in post-election litigation crossed ethical or legal lines. Instead, the goal is to describe where those lines are and explain why lawyers who cross them should be disciplined. Specifically, false contentions in this arena risk contributing to distrust about an existentially important feature of our democracy and stoking the kind of fervor that resulted in the storming of the Capitol. As noted earlier, lawyers deserve deference when litigating high-stakes public issues, but they must be held accountable if they engage in unlawful conduct, especially when the consequences of the conduct threaten the institutions that make the rule of law possible.

b. Lawful, but Potentially Unethical, Conduct Related to the 2020 Election

Lawyers are also subject to discipline for misconduct that is otherwise lawful but occurs while representing a client (i.e., the upper-right corner of Table 1). For instance, while representing President Trump's legal interests (i.e., while acting in their roles as lawyers), Sidney Powell, Rudy Giuliani, and John Eastman made numerous comments outside of court, such as at press conferences, on social media, and on television, that some have alleged were knowingly false but did not necessarily violate any legal responsibilities outside of the rules of professional conduct.

With regard to Powell, she asserted that Dominion had provided a "back door" that allowed officials to "take a certain percentage of votes from President Trump and flip them to President Biden."[20] She went on to claim that the software was designed "to rig elections" and that this was a "massive criminal

---

washingtonpost.com/politics/2020/12/09/trumps-effort-steal-election-comes-down-some-utterly-ridiculous-statistical-claims/; *see also* Eric Litke, *Fact Check: Statistical Analysis Supporting Pro-Trump Supreme Court Case is 'Ludicrous,'* USA TODAY (Dec. 10, 2020 at 4:30 p.m.), https://www.usatoday.com/story/news/factcheck/2020/12/10/fact-check-ludicrous-statistical-analysis-supporting-pro-trump-case/3877743001/ (explaining the spurious nature of the statistical claims).

[20] Aaron Blake, *Lou Dobbs, and The Most Problematic Claims Trump Allies Made About Voting Machines,* WASH. POST (Feb. 6, 2021 at 8:24 a.m.), https://www.washington post.com/politics/2021/02/05/most-legally-problematic-claims-trumps-allies-made-about-voting-machines/.

voter fraud."[21] She also suggested that state officials got kickbacks and bribes to install these systems.[22]

In response to a subsequent defamation suit by Dominion, Powell's counsel suggested that many of Powell's public statements in connection with the case were not intended to be statements of fact and should not have been taken seriously.[23] Specifically, her lawyers argued that, "even assuming, *arguendo*, that each of the statements alleged in [Dominion's] Complaint could be proved true or false, no reasonable person would conclude that the statements were truly statements of fact."[24]

Similarly, in a recent order suspending Rudy Giuliani from practice, a New York court concluded that he made numerous knowingly false statements, including:

- "false statements that there were 600,000 to 700,000 fabricated mail-in ballots [in Pennsylvania], which were never sent to voters in advance of the election"[25]
- false statements "that dead people 'voted' in Philadelphia in order to discredit the results of the vote in that city"[26]
- "numerous false and misleading statements regarding the Georgia presidential election results,"[27] such as false statements related to voting by underage voters, felons, and dead people and

[21] Complaint and Demand for Jury Trial, at ¶ 78, King v. Whitmer, Civil Case No. 20-13134 (E.D. Mich. Jan. 8, 2021), https://www.michigan.gov/documents/ag/118_Defs_Whitmer.Bensons_mtn_for_lv_for_supp_briefing_721667_7.pdf.

[22] *Id.* ¶ 181(g).

[23] Memorandum of Law in Support of Defendant's Motion to Dismiss at 32, U.S. Dominon. v. Powell, Civ. Action No. 1:21-cv-00040-CJN, (U.S.D.C. Mar. 22, 2021), https://storage.courtlistener.com/recap/gov.uscourts.dcd.225699/gov.uscourts.dcd.225699.22.2_3.pdf.

[24] *Id.* at 27.

[25] In re Rudolph W. Giuliani, No. 2021-00506, slip op. at 10 (N.Y. Sup. Ct. App. Div. filed May 3, 2021), http://www.nycourts.gov/courts/ad1/calendar/List_Word/2021/06_Jun/24/PDF/Matter%20of%20Giuliani%20(2021-00506)%20PC.pdf [hereinafter In re Giuliani].

[26] *Id.* at 14.

[27] *Id.* at 16.

false statements concerning Dominion and illegal vote counting[28] and

- numerous false statements about illegal voting by undocumented residents of Arizona[29]

In various other interviews, Giuliani suggested (as Powell did) that Dominion had manipulated the election. For example, he said that "this company [Dominion] has tried-and-true methods for fixing elections by calling a halt to the voting when you're running too far behind. They have done that in prior elections."[30]

Another lawyer—Professor John Eastman of Chapman University's Fowler School of Law (a former dean of that school)—made similar remarks while representing President Trump's legal interests. At the January 6, 2021 rally immediately before the seditious storming of the Capitol, Professor Eastman said:

> We know there was fraud, traditional fraud that occurred. We know that dead people voted. But we now know because we caught it live last time in real time how the machines contributed to that fraud. . . .They put those ballots in a secret folder in the machines, sitting there waiting until they know how many they need. And then the machine, after the close of polls, we now know who's voted and who hasn't. I can now match those unvoted ballots with an unvoted voter, and put them together in the machine. . . .We saw it happen in real time last night [in the context of the Georgia Senate runoff on January 5, 2021], and it happened on November 3rd as well.[31]

---

[28] *Id.* at 17–21.

[29] *Id.* at 22–25.

[30] Glenn Kessler, *Giuliani's Fantasy Parade of False Voter-Fraud Claims*, WASH. POST (Nov. 16, 2020 at 3:00 a.m.), https://www.washingtonpost.com/politics/2020/11/16/giulianis-fantasy-parade-false-voter-fraud-claims/.

[31] Clip of John Eastman and Rudy Giuliani at the Rally on Electoral Vote Certification, at 6:13–8:00 (Jan. 6, 2021), C-SPAN, https://www.c-span.org/video/?c4933578/user-clip-rudy-giuliani-professor-john-eastman. Professor Eastman also has been accused of engaging in other conduct that could be construed as "lawful but potentially unethical." For instance, Professor Eastman offered advice to President Trump and Vice President Pence concerning the Vice President's authority to overturn the outcome of the election. Memorandum from John Eastman on the Electoral Count Act to the White House (Dec. 2020), https://s3.documentcloud.org/documents/21066248/eastman-

The comments by Eastman, Giuliani, and Powell did not violate the rules of civil procedure because they were not made in the form of court filings. When such statements are made to the press and the public, however, those statements potentially violate Model Rule 4.1(a). That Rule provides that, in the course of representing a client, a lawyer shall not knowingly make "a false statement of material fact or law to a third person." Arguably, the public is a "third person" for purposes of the rule. Indeed, the New York court that suspended Giuliani from practice cited Rule 4.1(a) and Giuliani's out-of-court statements to the public as one of the primary bases for the suspension.[32]

There is some debate about whether Rule 4.1(a) can be constitutionally applied to a lawyer's knowingly false statements in the public domain, even when those statements are made in the context of the lawyer's ongoing representation of a client.[33] Public statements trigger First Amendment protections, and the Constitution offers considerable freedom to comment (even falsely) on public matters. On the other hand, the United States Supreme Court has upheld various kinds of restrictions on a lawyer's expression that would otherwise run afoul of the First Amendment, especially when lawyers are acting within their professional roles (e.g., statements to judges or to parties in litigation).[34] In fact, the Court has suggested that lawyers can be disciplined for statements to the press under limited circumstances.[35] The precise line, however, between

memo.pdf. Some have argued that the advice was unethical because Eastman knew it was unlawful. Letter from Ambassador Norman Eisen (ret.), U.S. Democracy Ctr., et al. to George S. Cardona, Off. of Chief Trial Couns., State Bar of Ca., Concerning a Request for the Investigation of John C. Eastman (Oct. 4, 2021), https://statesuniteddemocracy.org/wp-content/uploads/2021/10/10.4.21-FINAL-Eastman-Cover-Letter-Memorandum.pdf. Model Rule 1.2(d) prohibits lawyers from "assist[ing] a client. . .in conduct that the lawyer knows is criminal or fraudulent."

[32] In re Giuliani, *supra* note 25, at 14–25.

[33] Bruce Green & Rebecca Roiphe, *As the Giuliani Case Goes Forward, Courts Should Think Deeply About The First Amendment*, WASH. POST (July 6, 2021 at 5:32 p.m.), https://www.washingtonpost.com/opinions/2021/06/25/suspend-giulianis-law-license-dont-chill-free-speech/.

[34] *See generally* Rodney A. Smolla, *Regulating the Speech of Judges and Lawyers: The First Amendment and the Soul of the Profession*, 66 FLA. L. REV. 961 (2014).

[35] Gentile v. State Bar of Nevada, 501 U.S. 1030, 1074 (1991) (explaining that "the speech of lawyers representing clients in pending cases may be regulated under a less demanding standard than that established for regulation of the press").

First Amendment freedoms and the legal profession's ability to regulate lawyer speech in a case like this one remains unclear.

Again, the point here is not to offer an assessment of whether Eastman, Powell, Giuliani, or any other lawyer involved in election-related litigation should ultimately be disciplined for their out-of-court statements. In ordinary circumstances, the profession should hesitate to discipline lawyers for discussing matters of great public interest, including (and perhaps especially) with the press. But given the institutional stakes here and assuming the constitutionality of the basis for discipline, the profession should not be reluctant to impose discipline when lawyers knowingly spread misinformation in the course of litigation that undermines the legitimacy of our democracy.

To be clear, most of the lawyers who represented President Trump did not engage in such behavior. Many of the president's lawyers litigated claims on his behalf without making any problematic assertions or factual contentions, either in court documents or statements to the public. In fact, some lawyers for the president withdrew from representing him, presumably because they ultimately determined that their claims were inconsistent with their ethical and other legal obligations. The point is that the mere representation of President Trump in the context of the post-election litigation was not itself ethically or legally problematic.

Our legal system actually benefits enormously when lawyers take on difficult, unpopular, and questionable claims, even claims that the lawyers themselves do not believe will or should ultimately prevail. If claims and factual contentions in highly contentious matters satisfy ethical and procedural requirements, society benefits from a full airing of the best arguments that can be made on each party's behalf. In the particular case of the post-election litigation, the public benefited from knowing that judges (several of whom were appointed by President Trump) rejected the president's election-related fraud claims. If judges had not had the opportunity to rule on those claims, some members of the public may have had additional reasons to question the legitimacy of the election's outcome.

That said, there is an important line between, on the one hand, taking on unpopular or challenging cases to ensure a fair hearing and, on the other hand, making allegations about core features of our democracy that are either knowingly false or are unlikely ever to have evidentiary support. Some of President Trump's lawyers appeared to conclude that this line had been crossed and admirably withdrew. Moreover, some lawyers in the administration who were serving in lawyerly roles (but did not represent President Trump personally) reportedly pushed back on efforts to peddle false narratives to the public.[36] In other words, there were many lawyers who worked in the administration or represented President Trump personally who fulfilled their legal and ethical responsibilities. A small number of lawyers, however, can do substantial damage, and the profession should not hesitate to discipline them when they engage in misconduct.

2. Disciplining Lawyers for Conduct in Nonrepresentational Roles

The more difficult cases, both legally and politically, are those that fall in the bottom row of the table. In that context, lawyers are acting in nonrepresentational roles, and the basis for discipline is more limited. This is by design. For the most part, the rules of professional conduct address behavior that tends to be problematic only in the particular context of lawyering, such as matters relating to advertising, conflicts of interest, and conversations with represented parties. There is usually no reason to apply those rules to lawyers when they are acting outside of their professional roles. Another reason to limit the scope of the rules is that conduct occurring outside of the professional role is typically irrelevant when assessing whether someone has the competence and character to practice law.

There are, however, two important exceptions. One is when a lawyer engages in misconduct that is so egregious that we question the lawyer's fitness and character for law practice. Model Rule 8.4(b) provides that "[i]t is professional misconduct for a lawyer to. . .commit a criminal act that reflects adversely

---

36 George T. Conway III, *America Owes Thanks to Trump's Lawyers—Even William Barr,* WASH. POST (Jun. 28, 2021 at 2:46 p.m.), https://www.washingtonpost.com/opinions/2021/06/28/george-conway-trump-barr-lawyers/.

on the lawyer's honesty, trustworthiness or fitness as a lawyer in other respects. . . ."

A related provision allows for discipline when lawyers engage in significant instances of dishonesty. Specifically, Model Rule 8.4(c), provides that it is professional misconduct for a lawyer to "engage in conduct involving dishonesty, fraud, deceit or misrepresentation. . . ." As with Model Rule 8.4(b), the thought here is that LINPRs may engage in conduct that is so lacking in integrity that we may not be able to trust them to perform their professional duties.

a. Disciplining the Lawbreaking LINPR

The clearest case for disciplining lawyers for conduct occurring outside their professional roles is when they engage in unlawful conduct (the middle of the bottom row of the table). Consider, for example, the Watergate lawyers. Several of them broke the law while acting outside of their representational roles, such as by engaging in "campaign finance fraud, obstruction of justice, lying to federal agents and Congress, and conspiring to violate the constitutional rights of citizens."[37] Discipline, including disbarment, was appropriate even though some (but not all) of the lawyers were acting outside of their representational roles when they broke the law.[38]

Disciplining lawyers for this kind of unlawful, nonrepresentational conduct makes good sense. After all, if a lawyer breaks the law in a way that reflects on that lawyer's trustworthiness and character or if the lawyer otherwise engages in unlawful conduct involving dishonesty, fraud, deceit or misrepresentation, there should be a mechanism for discipline and disbarment.

b. Disciplining the Law-Abiding LINPR

The bottom right corner of the table is the most fraught and controversial. In this context, lawyers are not only acting outside of their capacity as lawyers, but they are engaging in conduct that is, by definition, otherwise lawful.

---

[37] Curriden, *supra* note 3.

[38] Kathleen Clark, *The Legacy of Watergate for Legal Ethics Instruction*, 51 HASTINGS L. J. 673 (2000).

Consider the statements of a number of high-profile lawyers who claimed that the 2020 presidential election was fraudulent, stolen, or otherwise illegitimate.

- Congressman Mo Brooks said that "this is the worst election theft in the history of the United States."[39]
- Congressman Louie Gohmert claimed that there was "massive multi-state electoral fraud committed on Biden's behalf that changed electoral results in Arizona and in other states such as Georgia, Michigan, Pennsylvania and Wisconsin."[40]
- U.S. Senator Lindsey Graham told Fox News's Sean Hannity that "Philadelphia elections are crooked as a snake. . .Why are they shutting people out? Because they don't want people to see what they're doing."[41]
- In a letter to the U.S. Attorney General, a group of 37 House members (some of whom were lawyers) said that "there are a number of anomalies, statistical improbabilities and accusations of fraud that bring the election results in several states into question."[42]
- U.S. Senator Tom Cotton alleged that poll watchers were impermissibly prohibited from observing the counting of ballots, and he went on to claim that "Democrats will try to steal this election."[43]

[39] Celine Castronuovo & Juliegrace Brufke, *Mo Brooks Planning to Challenge Electoral College Votes,* HILL (DEC. 2, 2020 AT 4:25 p.m.), https://thehill.com/homenews/house/528446-mo-brooks-planning-to-challenge-electoral-college-votes.

[40] Chris Canipe & Jason Lange, *The Republicans Who Voted To Overturn the Election,* REUTERS (Feb. 4, 2021), https://graphics.reuters.com/USA-TRUMP/LAWMAKERS/xegpbedzdvq/.

[41] Katie Shepard, *GOP Splits Over Trump's False Election Claims, Unfounded Fraud Allegations,* WASH. POST (Nov. 6, 2020 at 10:09 a.m.), https://www.washingtonpost.com/nation/2020/11/06/republicans-split-trump-election-fraud/.

[42] Letter from Michael Cloud et al., U.S. House of Representatives to the Honorable William Barr (Dec. 1, 2020) https://allen.house.gov/uploadedfiles/12.1.20_election_integrity_letter_to_attorney_general_barr.pdf.

[43] Michael Crowley, *Trump's False Election Fraud Claims Split Republicans,* N.Y. TIMES (Nov. 6, 2020), https://www.nytimes.com/2020/11/06/us/politics/trump-election-republicans.html.

- Eleven U.S. Senators, four of whom were lawyers (Ted Cruz, Bill Hagerty, John Kennedy, and Cynthia Lummis), asserted in a joint statement that, "[b]y any measure, the allegations of fraud and irregularities in the 2020 election exceed any in our lifetimes."[44]
- U.S. Senator Josh Hawley claimed that some states, particularly Pennsylvania, had "failed to follow their own election laws," even though multiple courts had already rejected that claim. Hawley was also the first Senator to say that he would challenge the election results based on the allegations of fraud.
- Kayleigh McEnany, in addition to embracing the frivolous statistical claim referenced earlier, also accused Democrats of "welcoming" fraud and illegal voting."[45]

Assuming for the sake of discussion that these lawyers made statements that they knew or should have known were either false or misleading, can they be disciplined?

The law on this question is remarkably unclear. One scholar recently observed that "there is scant authority about the ethical obligations of government lawyers outside the traditional settings of the practice of law and whether, and to what extent, ethics rules apply to the many lawyers who work in government"[46] Some scholars have argued that the ethics rules should be applied to law-abiding LINPRs and have even gone so

---

[44] Joint Statement from Senators Cruz, Johnson, Lankford, Daines, Kennedy, Blackburn, Braun, Senators-Elect Lummis, Marshall, Hagerty, Tuberville, U.S. Senator for Texas Ted Cruz (Jan. 2, 2021), https://www.cruz.senate.gov/?p=press_release&id=5541. Unlike the other statements, this one was at least carefully crafted to focus on the unprecedented nature of the "allegations" rather than to assert baldly that fraud had occurred. Nevertheless, the statement misleadingly implies that the election was fraudulent.

[45] Morgan Chalfant, *Fox Cuts Away from McEnany Press Conference,* HILL (Nov. 9, 2020 at 5:49 p.m.), https://thehill.com/homenews/media/525205-fox-cuts-away-from-mcenany-press-conference.

[46] Ellen Yaroshefsky, *Regulation of Lawyers in Government Beyond the Representation Role,* 33 NOTRE DAME J. L. ETHICS & PUB. POL'Y 151, 162 (2019).

far as to file disciplinary charges against one.[47] Other scholars have rejected this idea.[48]

There are several possible legal bases for discipline in this context, but they are ultimately quite thin. One option can be found in Comment [6] to the Preamble to the Model Rules, which says that:

> a lawyer should further the public's understanding of and confidence in the rule of law and the justice system because legal institutions in a constitutional democracy depend on popular participation and support to maintain their authority. . . .[49]

The Preamble, however, does not provide a basis for discipline. It speaks only to what lawyers should strive to achieve, not what is prohibited for purposes of punishment.

Another option is Model Rule 8.4(c), which (as noted earlier) provides that "[i]t is professional misconduct for a lawyer to. . . engage in conduct involving dishonesty, fraud, deceit or misrepresentation." This language implies that LINPRs can be disciplined for dishonesty that is otherwise lawful. Comment [2], however, elaborates on the meaning of Model Rule 8.4(c) and refers to the need to discipline lawyers for "illegal conduct," strongly implying that lawful conduct should not be a basis for discipline.

Comment [7] suggests a similar conclusion. That Comment says that "[l]awyers holding public office assume legal responsibilities going beyond those of other citizens. A lawyer's abuse of public office can suggest an inability to fulfill the professional role of lawyers." The Comment's reference to "legal responsibilities" once again implies that the Rule is not intended to reach a LINPR's entirely lawful behavior. In addition, the reference in the subsequent sentence to an "abuse of public

---

47 Letter from Abbe Smith, Professor of Law, Georgetown Law, to Off. of Disciplinary Couns. Dist. Of Columbia Court of Appeals (Feb. 20, 2017), https://s3.documentcloud.org/documents/3474086/Read-the-misconduct-complaint-sent-by-law.pdf.

48 *See, e.g.,* Steven Lubet, *In Defense of Kellyanne Conway,* SLATE (Feb. 27, 2017 at 9:22 a.m.), https://slate.com/news-and-politics/2017/02/the-misconduct-complaint-against-kellyanne-conway-is-dangerously-misguided.html.

49 MODEL RULES OF PRO. CONDUCT, Preamble, (AM. BAR ASS'N, 2013).

office" appears to amplify the prior sentence's point about "legal responsibilities" and suggests that Model Rule 8.4(c) is not intended to be a basis for disciplining LINPRs for otherwise lawful conduct.

There are nevertheless a handful of cases where courts have disciplined lawyers for nonrepresentational conduct that is otherwise lawful. For example, a few older cases involved the discipline of lawyers who made knowingly false statements during political campaigns,[50] and there are more recent cases involving lawyers or prospective lawyers who (lawfully) expressed racist or similarly pernicious views.[51] Although it is debatable whether these cases would be resolved the same way today,[52] there is at least some precedent and scholarly commentary supporting the idea that LINPRs can be disciplined for conduct that is otherwise lawful.

In sum, there is disagreement about the extent to which LINPRs can be disciplined for lawful conduct, such as the expression of knowingly false statements about an election. The disagreement about the current state of the law, however, masks a more fundamental question: *should* LINPR's be disciplined for otherwise lawful behavior?

C. POSSIBLE APPROACHES TO THE LYING LINPR

The legal profession can address lying LINPRs in at least two ways that are not mutually exclusive: (1) develop a rule or clarifying comment that would expressly allow for the discipline of LINPRs when they make knowingly false statements concerning matters of great public importance and (2) publicly condemn LINPRs for those statements. For the reasons offered below, the profession should rely only on the latter approach.

---

[50] *See, e.g.,* State v. Russell, 610 P.2d 1122 (Kan. 1980), *cert denied* 449 U.S. 983 (1980); Neb. State Bar Ass'n v. Michaelis, 316 N.W.2d 46 (Neb. 1982), *cert. denied,* 459 U.S. 804 (1982); In re Baker, 542 P.2d 701 (Kan. 1975).

[51] *See, e.g.,* Jana DiCosmo, *Racism in the Legal Profession: A Racist Lawyer is an Incompetent Lawyer,* N.L.G. REVIEW https://www.nlg.org/nlg-review/article/racism-in-the-legal-profession-a-racist-lawyer-is-an-incompetent-lawyer/.

[52] MODEL RULES OF PRO. CONDUCT r. 8.4(g) (AM. BAR ASS'N, 2016). Rule 8.4(g) makes it professional misconduct to engage in harassment or discrimination "related to the practice of law," so it does not appear that the rule would currently support discipline over a lawyer who made discriminatory comments outside the practice of law. *Id.*

1. A Disciplinary Solution

One possibility is to discipline LINPRs for lying about central features of our democracy. One argument for doing so is that LINPRs are in a position to do more harm to our governing institutions than the typical public official who lies. Specifically, a LINPR's claims about those institutions are more likely to be taken seriously by non-experts and given more credence precisely because LINPRs are lawyers. A second reason for disciplining the lying LINPR is to take a principled stand against socially corrosive falsehoods. Namely, we should expect lawyers to rise above our society's increasing willingness to embrace and spread baseless conspiracy theories.

For these consequentialist and principled reasons, one could imagine a narrowly tailored rule or clarifying comment that makes clear that LINPRs have an obligation to avoid knowingly false statements on matters about which lawyers should have a special duty, such as those involving elections, the electoral system, and the judiciary. Here is one possible formulation of such a Rule:

> A lawyer serving as a public official shall not knowingly make a false statement about democratic institutions, elections, or the judiciary, even when the lawyer is acting outside of the representation of a client.

The particulars of the rule are less important than the overall idea that discipline could be targeted to reach LINPRs who engage in socially destructive (but otherwise lawful) conduct outside of the representation of a client.

Putting aside any First Amendment objections to this approach (which are likely to be considerable),[53] attempts to discipline LINPRs for knowingly false statements have a few serious problems. First, the consequentialist argument (i.e., that LINPRs may do particular harm because of their status as lawyers) is debatable. The reality is that most of the public is not particularly aware of which politicians have a license to practice law.

---

[53] *See* Yaroshefsky, *supra* note 46, at 169–72 (summarizing opposing arguments).

Second, any rule that targets public officials for their comments creates a risk that the disciplinary process will be used in politically motivated ways. Nearly every lawyer-politician could at some point be found to violate a rule that prohibits public officials from making knowingly false statements about democratic institutions, elections, or the judiciary. Politicians in both major parties are notorious for such statements, and turning those falsities into potential disciplinary offenses would open the door to politically motivated disciplinary proceedings.

For instance, 11 Republican U.S. Senators asserted that the "allegations of fraud and irregularities in the 2020 election exceed any in our lifetimes." Did this statement cross the line? On the one hand, the "allegations of fraud" did, indeed, "exceed any in our lifetimes," so the statement is true as written. On the other hand, the clear intent of the statement was to imply that the Senators believed that the election was fraudulent. Although the statement was morally reprehensible, efforts to discipline the Senators for these statements would open the door to disciplinary proceedings against Democratic legislators for making similarly misleading statements in the future. A damaging politicization of the disciplinary process would be inevitable.[54]

A third and related problem is that a LINPR rule could put the legal profession in the untenable position of having to resolve the truth of contentious political disagreements. Bar disciplinary authorities would be asked to parse the public statements, tweets, news conferences, media interviews, etc., of politician-lawyers to determine whether their comments were knowingly false and, if so, whether they involved matters that were sufficiently related to core democratic institutions to warrant discipline. Such determinations are unlikely to be resolved in a way that would be generally accepted within the politically diverse legal profession.

Another problem is that disciplinary proceedings against LINPRs for lawful conduct would only heighten the sense that

[54] *See generally* James Moliterno, *Politically Motivated Bar Discipline*, 83 WASH. U. L. Q. 725 (2005) (reviewing the history of politically motivated efforts to discipline lawyers).

already exists in some quarters that the legal profession has a political bias. As dangerous as it is for LINPRs to make false claims about democratic institutions, it may be more dangerous for the legal profession itself to be viewed as taking sides in partisan disagreements involving lawful public statements. Whatever remaining credibility lawyers have in the public's eye would be jeopardized if the legal profession began to arbitrate the truthfulness of highly politicized statements by public figures.

A final problem is that the rule could make lawyers reluctant to serve as LINPRs in the first place. There are a great many political matters that involve the judiciary, elections, and democratic institutions. Given the inevitable exaggerations and truth shading that are commonplace in those arenas, lawyers may make the reasonable calculation that becoming a LINPR presents too great a risk to their professional livelihood. The result is unlikely to be more honesty in politics; the result is that the dishonesty will simply occur among legislators who are not licensed to practice law. Rather than the disinformation from lawyer-legislators, we will simply have more lying legislators who are not lawyers. Not only will we gain nothing in terms of political honesty, but we will lose out on the longstanding benefits that lawyers bring to our political institutions.

In sum, it seems wise to limit discipline under Model Rule 8.4(c) to those circumstances where a LINPR has engaged in conduct that is unlawful. At the same time, it is important to acknowledge that lying LINPRs present a real threat to American democracy, and we should try to hold LINPRs accountable for their mendacity.

2. Public Condemnation

The absence of a disciplinary solution does not mean that the profession has no recourse when LINPRs spread knowingly false information about critical features of our democracy and judicial system. Another option exists: public condemnation.

Shortly after the attack on the Capitol on January 6, 2021, the overwhelming majority of the nation's law school deans issued the joint statement printed in the introduction to this book. Reflecting the views of politically diverse deans at a cross-section of public and private law schools from around the country, the statement denounced the role that lawyers played in fomenting the unrest that led to the seditious attack. Other groups issued conceptually similar statements around the same time.[55]

One benefit of such statements is that we can set a high threshold of bipartisanship before issuing them. For example, there were earlier discussions among the deans about a possible joint statement, but there was inadequate consensus at the time to release one. By waiting until we had a very strong consensus among deans with different political viewpoints, we were able to ensure that the moment was the right one and that the statement would not reasonably be perceived as political posturing. In contrast, a disciplinary process typically involves only a small number of people, making it more susceptible to partisan sentiments.

Such statements are an important articulation of ideals, but their value should not be overstated. The reality is that they do not provide much of a disincentive to LINPRs or others. In some instances, the condemned LINPRs might even use such statements as a badge of honor, arguing to supporters that the condemnation proves the LINPR's anti-elitist bona fides. (For that matter, professional discipline could be used similarly.) In other words, the prospect of condemnation or discipline might not be a deterrent to a populist-minded LINPR. It could be an incentive.

At the same time, saying and doing nothing is problematic as well. The legal profession should not remain silent while its prominent members spread misinformation about existentially important democratic institutions. Doing so risks a decline into nihilism for both the profession and the nation. Condemnation may not have much of a practical impact, but it is a critical statement of ideals.

The unfortunate reality is that the legal profession has little power to address the lawful yet socially corrosive efforts of its

---

[55] Valerie Strauss, *Thousands of Law School Alumni and Students Push for Disbarment of Sens. Hawley and Cruz*, WASH. POST (Jan. 10, 2021 at 11:54 a.m.), https://www.washingtonpost.com/education/2021/01/10/thousands-law-school-alumni-students-push-disbarment-sens-hawley-cruz/.

own members. Discipline is unlikely to be effective and could undermine the legal profession's claim to political neutrality. Condemnation offers a useful statement of values, but it is also unlikely to alter behavior and may even have the perverse effect of bolstering support for populist LINPRs who spread misinformation.

D. CONCLUSION

To protect our democratic institutions, there is difficult work to be done that transcends any question of lawyer discipline or professional integrity. An effective salve for the steadily declining state of our democracy will require a wide range of efforts, from more effective civics education (see Chapter 12) and bold election reforms to more effective leadership training of future lawyers (see Chapter 3) and addressing systemic inequalities that are fueling animosity towards elites and established institutions.

As much as we will need these wide-ranging approaches to salvage our democracy, we must acknowledge the critical role that lawyer will have to play in those efforts. When they lie about core political institutions, the risks to democracy are significant and real. The storming of the Capitol is a notable example, perhaps even the canary in the coal mine, of what can happen when lawyers lend their professional credentials to conspiracy theories. Our nation was originally founded by lawyers, and lawyers continue to have the power and credibility to ensure our democracy's survival. The jury is out on whether we are up to the task.

CHAPTER 2

THEY WHO ARE CALLED TO SERVE

Michèle Alexandre[1]

"There is a vague popular belief that lawyers are necessarily dishonest. I say vague, because when we consider to what extent confidence and honors are reposed and conferred upon lawyers by the people, it appears improbable that their impression of dishonesty is very distinct and vivid. Yet, the impression is common, almost universal."[2]

Abraham Lincoln, Notes for a lecture on law, c. July 1850 THE WIT AND WISDOM OF ABRAHAM LINCOLN

A. INTRODUCTION

Lawyers lead in diverse ways through their duties as agents of law. They unveil the facts in issues related to family, business, governmental structures, foreign affairs, and many other social contexts. For that reason, law schools are charged to teach the importance of leadership. It takes initiative to unearth the facts in a case, to steer courts and jurors to understanding the issues at play. Those leadership qualities, excitement for knowledge, appreciation for other people, the ability to connect with others to solve problems, are instrumental regardless of the role a lawyer plays.

In my classes, as an introduction, I take a few minutes to illustrate the ways law serves as backbone to society. From equitable conservatorship to fair housing, to basic access to loans, to partnerships like marriage, law permeates all aspects all life.

---

[1] Dean and Professor of Law, Counsel to the President for Strategic Initiatives and Operations, Stetson University College of Law (2019–Present), previously Associate Dean for Faculty and Intellectual Life at the University of Mississippi School of Law.

[2] JAMES C. HUMES, THE WIT AND WISDOM OF ABRAHAM LINCOLN, page 18 (1999) (notes for a lecture Abraham Lincoln gave on the law in July 1850).

As a result, legal education carries a high burden to shape lawyers with the skills and comportment of good leaders. This duty was put to the test as the intersecting challenges of the pandemic and national unrest unfolded in 2020. Legal education faced its most urgent call to apply its teachings to fast-paced, life altering events. As these events took shape, law schools' vulnerability and interconnectedness loomed large.

As with other sectors, law schools had to move quickly as the pandemic and political tensions flared. The national reckoning sparked by the death of George Floyd during the summer of 2020, coupled with the raging pandemic, caused a renewed focus on human connection, on learning from one another and on the importance of service. In other words, we all had to become more vulnerable and open. The collective disbelief at the actions surrounding January 6, 2021[3] intensified that need for courageous vulnerability and candor.

Students played an instrumental role in helping bring out courageous vulnerability in law schools. They watched intently as law schools navigated a global pandemic, rampant racial tension, fear mongering, economic stressors.[4] They inquired of their professors and administrators about a blueprint and role models for negotiating racial and political polemics.

Law schools are the site of critical thinking. Students expect classroom discussions to raise tough questions about governance, the nature of rights, the rule of law and the structure of American democracy. They migrate to practical applications of the laws they study in the classroom.

---

[3] *January 6: Inside The Capitol Siege*, NATIONAL PUBLIC RADIO (Jan. 15, 2021, 9:32 PM ET), https://www.npr.org/2021/01/15/957362053/january-6-inside-the-capitol-siege ("Jan. 6, 2021 was supposed to be the day that Joe Biden became the certified winner of the 2020 presidential election. Instead, Jan. 6 will now be known as the day that a violent mob stormed the U.S. Capitol.").

[4] *See Demonstrations & Political Violence in America New Data for Summer 2020*, The Armed Conflict Location & Event Data Project (Sept. 2020), https://acleddata.com/2020/09/03/demonstrations-political-violence-in-america-new-data-for-summer-2020/ ("The United States is at heightened risk of political violence and instability going into the 2020 general election. Mass shootings hit a record high last year . . ., violent hate crimes are on the rise . . ., and police killings continue unabated, at 2.5 times the rate for Black men as for white men . . . [,] [t]he COVID-19 pandemic has killed well over 180,000 . . . and disrupted the economy, while George Floyd's death in police custody has sparked a massive wave of protest across the country.").

And, as students watched the events of January 6, 2021, amplified consternation and concern rose regarding the role of law in American democracy in the aftermath of these events.

These sorts of palpitations, to be frank, loomed before the pandemic. In my experience in and out of classrooms in recent years, students have routinely agonized over the dismal state of discourse in the country. The issue comes up often in class discussions. With fast changing political landscape, students couldn't help but inquire as to whether ideals and practical realities matched.

They sought a vision of the future that could guide them to fruitful professional paths and delineate their potential contributions to society.[5]

It is then not a coincidence that, when students felt conflicted by the examples they saw in the media, they turned to law schools to confirm lawyers' professional responsibility. They understood the classroom as the ideal setting for that type of inquiry. Our rules of professional conduct require that we train our future lawyers to emulate ethical leadership and service to justice.[6]

B. A CALL TO ACTION

This demand from students motivated deans of American law schools to join forces. As early as March 2020,[7] it became evident that collective leadership, not rugged individualism, would be the best antidote to the conditions presented by the earthshattering global crisis. Deans from the two hundred and

---

5 *See* Hannah Hayes, *Law Schools Vow to Address Structural Racism*, AMERICAN BAR ASSOCIATION (Sept. 25, 2020), https://www.americanbar.org/groups/diversity/women/publications/perspectives/2021/september/law-schools-vow-address-structural-racism/ ("[s]tudents want to see their country changed[ ]" after the murder of George Floyd and Breonna Taylor).

6 ABA Standards and Rules of Procedure for Approval of Law Schools 2020–2021 §§ 301(a), 302(c), 303(a)(1) (American Bar Association 2020).

7 By Ivan Pereira and Arielle Mitropoulos, *A year of COVID-19: What was going on in the US in March 2020*, ABC NEWS (Mar. 6, 2021, 10:06 AM), https://abcnews.go.com/Health/year-covid-19-us-march-2020/story?id=76204691 ("While the novel coronavirus had been in the country for at least a month, in March case began to jump at alarming rates as did the hospitalizations and deaths. Former President Trump and other federal leaders initially claimed that the virus would not be a major problem, but many changed their stance by the end of the month and the virus was declared a national emergency.").

seven law schools began to collaborate in a way they had never before. Putting aside hierarchies, they leant into the needs of the moment, developing a vulnerability and service centered approach to problem solving. This led to a form of a service-based collaborative leadership.[8] It is a form of leadership focused on finding solutions capable of serving the common good and fulfilling mission. Through dialogue and open connections, law schools collectively implemented the tenets of compassion taught, but often hard to emulate[9]

This was not pure altruism. The future of the legal profession depended on mutual vigilance. Were law schools not intentional about reinforcing principles of professionalism and collaboration to students, they risked graduating generation of lawyers ambivalent about their duties to society. Legal education was vulnerable. And, as Author Brené Brown advises, embracing that vulnerability became an essential ingredient in directing our organizations.[10] Vulnerability, our ability to connect across wounds, to open ourselves to one another without the baggage of shame, made the difference[11]

It is significant that this service-based collaboration among law deans took place at a time when universities had appointed at a historic rate women and people of color to lead law schools.[12]

---

[8] Brian Tait, *Traditional Leadership Vs. Servant Leadership*, FORBES (Mar. 11, 2020, 8:40 AM EDT), https://www.forbes.com/sites/forbescoachescouncil/2020/03/11/traditional-leadership-vs-servant-leadership/?sh=6be87292451e ("A servant leader focuses on the people that are directly below them, rather than the company as a whole. In servant leadership, the leader ensures that the followers are growing in all areas—their profession, knowledge, autonomy and even their health and physical development.").

[9] *See* Palena Neale, *Why Servant Leadership Is More Important Than Ever*, FORBES (May 26, 2020, 7:00 AM EDT), https://www.forbes.com/sites/forbescoaches council/2020/05/26/why-servant-leadership-is-more-important-than-ever/?sh=624f141a 2861 (detailing what servant leadership is and how important it is in a pandemic).

[10] BRENÉ BROWN, DARE TO LEAD 17–165 (2018).

[11] *See* Karen Sloan, *Law Schools Have an 'Obligation' to Help End Racism and Injustice, Deans Argue*, LAW.COM (June 02, 2020, 2:45 PM), https://www.law.com/2020/06/02/law-schools-have-an-obligation-to-help-end-racism-and-injustice-deans-argue/?slreturn=20210602115120 ("Law schools are hosting open forums for students and staff to discuss recent police killings of minorities and systemic inequality, as well as workshops on policing and other relevant legal issues.").

[12] *See* Cynthia L. Cooper, *Women Ascend in Deanships as Law Schools Undergo Dramatic Change*, AMERICAN BAR ASSOCIATION (July 09, 2016), https://www.american bar.org/groups/diversity/women/publications/ perspectives/2016/summer/women_ascend_deanships_law_schools_undergo_dramatic_change/ ("As of July 31, 2016, 61 women—a solid 30 percent—hold the position of law dean in ABA-approved law schools,

As the crises reached their peak, women and persons of color were asked to step in to correct longstanding structural issues.[13] Collective leadership was needed to confront the daunting tasks at hand.[14]

This chapter explores key benefits that resulted from this service-based collaborative leadership. It is divided in the following parts: 1) the shift; 2) clarity of vision; 3) ability to navigate without a roadmap; 4) balance of service-based leadership and historic demands; and 5) vigilance against attempts at erasure.

At its core, this book from law deans has focused on the transformational impact of the first eighteen months of the pandemic. It has explored, particularly, the difficulty that law schools faced regarding educating the community on the rule of law in the aftermath of January 6, 2021.

This specific chapter, however, focuses less on the substantive debate regarding the rule of law and law schools' role during that period. Rather, it focuses on the imperatives that can motivate a collective service-centered leadership model. As we write this book, the pandemic and national angst continue to storm; with new mutations of the COVID-19 virus, seething, creating an uncertain end to the pandemic. A service-based collaborative leadership, fueled by courageous vulnerability, is needed more than ever.

It is consequential that the pandemic prompted leadership that is service-centered collaboration. For more than a decade now, law schools, and higher education in general, have been called to fulfill added roles to its constituencies, students,

---

and the number is likely to increase by the start of the next academic year. Since 2006, the number of women law deans has doubled, and it has more than quadrupled since 1997 when only 14 women held the title of law dean."); *See also* Karen Sloan, *'It's the Moment for This': An Unprecedented Number of Black Women Are Leading Law Schools*, LAW.COM (May 13, 2021, 2:55 PM), https://www.law.com/2021/05/13/its-the-moment-for-this-an-unprecedented-number-of-black-women-are-leading-law-schools/.

[13] *See* Ayanna Alexander, *Black Women Law Deans to be Honored for Antiracism Efforts*, BLOOMBERG LAW (Nov. 13, 2020, 12:14 PM), https://news.bloomberglaw.com/social-justice/black-women-law-deans-to-be-honored-for-antiracism-efforts ("five black women law school deans will be recognized for their efforts to reshape legal education and provide law students and young lawyers with the tools needed to combat racism[ ]" following the death of George Floyd).

[14] *See* Neale, *supra*.

faculty, staff, alumni, and community partners. By function of the intersectional nature of law and changing demographics, law schools are called more pointedly than other areas of higher education to serve all fully, abashedly, and comprehensively. The current challenges have highlighted opportunities to do this in meaningful ways. Those lessons apply beyond the pandemic.[15]

1. The Shift

The term service-based leadership is used in this chapter to mean a servant who collaborates with constituencies to help extract the best out of people and the institution.[16] Such servant leaders play pivotal roles in times of social change as fear, resistance, and vulnerability peak.[17]

Service and care for society and institutions are what rules of professional conduct imagine when they admonish future lawyers to serve justice. The Preamble of the Florida Bar states, for example:

> As a public citizen, a lawyer should seek improvement of the law, access to the legal system, the administration of justice, and the quality of service rendered by the legal profession. As a member of a learned profession, a lawyer should cultivate knowledge

---

[15] Gianpiero Petriglieri, *The Psychology Behind Effective Crisis Leadership*, HARVARD BUSINESS REVIEW (Apr. 22, 2020), https://hbr.org/2020/04/the-psychology-behind-effective-crisis-leadership (detailing the limitations of visionary leadership especially "in times of crisis, uncertainty, or radical change[ ]" and advocating for servant leadership to ensure long term stability).

[16] *See* Neale, *supra* ("In *Leadership: Theory and Practice*, Peter G. Northouse describes 10 characteristics of servant leadership: listening, empathy, healing, awareness, persuasion, conceptualization, foresight, stewardship, commitment to the growth of people and building community.").

[17] *See* Artika Tyner, *Nelson Mandela and the Transformative Power of Service*, HUFFPOST (July 30, 2015, 3:43 PM ET), https://www.huffpost.com/entry/nelson-mandela-and-the-transformative-power-of-service_b_7903478 ("[Nelson Mandela's] leadership focused on the importance of community-building and empowering others to lead social change"); *See also* James Perry, *Martin Luther King, Jr: A True Servant Leader*, HUFFPOST (Mar. 20, 2010, 5:12 AM ET), https://www.huffpost.com/entry/martin-luther-king-jr-a-t_b_427417 (detailing how Martin Luther King acted as a servant leader during the Civil Rights Movement); *See also Lincoln as a Servant Leader*, The Abraham Lincoln Institute For The Study of Leadership and Public Policy at Lincoln Memorial University (May 31, 2011, 11:48 AM), https://lincolninstitute.wordpress.com/2011/05/31/lincoln-as-a-servant-leader/ ("The American Civil War provided a platform for Abraham Lincoln to demonstrate servant leadership. . . Lincoln's commitment to serve the greater good for the most people both revolutionized and forever changed a nation for the generations that have followed.").

> of the law beyond its use for clients, employ that knowledge in reform of the law, and work to strengthen legal education. In addition, a lawyer should further the public's understanding of and confidence in the rule of law and the justice system, because legal institutions in a constitutional democracy depend on popular participation and support to maintain their authority. A lawyer should be mindful of deficiencies in the administration of justice and of the fact that the poor, and sometimes persons who are not poor, cannot afford adequate legal assistance. Therefore, all lawyers should devote professional time and resources and use civic influence to ensure equal access to our system of justice for all those who because of economic or social barriers cannot afford or secure adequate legal counsel. A lawyer should aid the legal profession in pursuing these objectives and should help the bar regulate itself in the public interest.[18]

When applied to legal academia, this definition attaches to all who touch legal education. The work of shaping future lawyers requires partners across disciplines and roles. And the baseline of that work centers on law schools. At no time did this become more apparent than during the global pandemic.

It was March 2020, law schools had been monitoring the virus' impact for a couple of months, then in collaboration with their respective universities. Everyone was vigilant. Yet, no one envisioned that our industry could move as fast as it did.

We were called to build a new world that spring: an academic enterprise capable of continuing to challenge students and serve the profession regardless of the gargantuan hurdles placed by public health restrictions and physical threats.[19]

---

[18] Rules of Professional Conduct Chap. 4 Preamble (The Florida Bar 2019).

[19] Gabriel Kuris, *The Impact of the Coronavirus on Legal Education*, U.S. NEWS (June 14, 2021), https://www.usnews.com/education/blogs/law-admissions-lowdown/articles/the-impact-of-the-coronavirus-on-legal-education (detailing law school's adaptions in the Spring of 2020 such as moving classes online, canceling activities and events, restricting facilities, and switching to pass/fail); Sameer Rao, *3 Takeaways On COVID-19's Impact On Law School Faculty*, LAW 365 PULSE (May 25, 2021, 4:56 PM EDT), https://www.law360.com/pulse/articles/1387560/3-takeaways-on-covid-19-s-impact-on-law-school-faculty (detailing how law schools had to adapt to COVID-19).

Like medical schools in a sense, law schools could not afford to cut corners or shortchange the curriculum. They had to deliver students capable of ethically and effectively serving their clients.

So, these institutions, until then known as the bastion of hierarchy, did something unexpected. They united.

From the first week, deans of law schools began to band together in a way that hierarchical, class and racial barriers had formerly prevented. Further, they collaborated with bar associations and industry partners, the ABA,[20] the AALS,[21] LSAC and other entities to ensure that decisions would be vetted in real time through the varied lenses of the profession.[22]

Collaboration was pivotal for both safety and innovation. Moreover, the 207-member decanal group was able to diagnose and gather data on rapidly evolving issues like the challenges of the bar exam during the pandemic and the hurdles to progressing inclusion in times of racialized tensions. Through it all, the characteristics of collaborative leadership continued. Law deans met weekly, called, and consulted with each other, mined data for the collective benefit. Increased communication and trust helped garner consensus across difference.

2. Clarity of Vision

This experience working across geographical lines, beyond individual mission and rank demonstrates the key role that clarity in purpose plays in effective service-based collaborative leadership. The law deans knew that vison and clarity are cornerstones of institutional leadership. Yet, nurturing a collective vision can prove difficult, prey to the specific pitfalls of each organization's DNA.

---

[20] *See Coronavirus resources and information for law students*, AMERICAN BAR ASSOCIATION, https://www.americanbar.org/groups/young_lawyers/career-tools/coronavirus-resources-for-law-students/.

[21] *See Legal Education in the Time of COVID-19*, ASSOCIATION OF AMERICA LAW SCHOOLS, https://www.aals.org/faculty-staff-resources/covid19/ ("AALS has organized documents, resources, and information related to legal education and the legal profession to help law faculty, students, and staff plan for classes and operations during the coronavirus pandemic.").

[22] *See Helping You Navigate Law School Admission During the Coronavirus Crisis*, Law School Admission Counsel, https://www.lsac.org/covid-19-resources-law-school-candidates (containing general tools and resources for law school applicants).

On the flip side, long gone are the days where an individual could ram their singular vision into their organization. In law schools particularly, the interconnected complexity of the enterprise makes collaboration crucial. Still, hierarchical differences and national divisions risked endangering this goal.

Before the pandemic and the historic work among law schools, top tier law schools barely engaged with lower ranked schools. Tensions between faculty and staff presented hurdles to effective management and advancement of goals.[23] On any given day, so much attention would be dedicated to specific minor hierarchy-based personality conflicts that greater work remained endangered. Important issues like the disproportionate impact of bar passage standards nationally were primarily relegated to the purview of administration in many schools. It was far from an industry-wide issue as it now is.

As the pandemic hit, however, and as law deans migrated to collaborative leadership, they implemented key principles of collaboration that sped the process: "no one person is ever the smartest person in the room" and "individual schools are only as strong as the legal profession as a whole, no matter how highly ranked." Because the crisis presented a reality no one had prepared for and for which no blueprint had been created, every dean came to the table eager to learn and co-lead.

Deans' groups began to meet as a collective nearly every week. Smaller groups met more frequently as troubleshooting bodies or vetters/task forces focused on specific issues. Deans within a number of states, for example, joined together with their colleagues to safeguard their graduates from the horrific administration of the summer 2020 bar exams. Similar efforts took place to protect students in career placement and externships.

---

[23] *See Law Schools and the Global Pandemic New Research*, Thomas Reuters Institute 4–5 (2020) (44% of the administrations surveyed by Thomas Reuters found resistant and uncooperative faculty challenging; the top challenges for law school faculty surveyed included "inability to influence administrators decision making" and "Inadequate communication from law school administrators").

Then came the summer of 2020. The killing of George Floyd and the advent of a renewed civil rights movement.[24] This new turmoil came had at a point where everyone was already on edge. It challenged the new and fragile collaboration the law deans' group had created.

They were faced with a choice. They could run and hide behind platitudes and placations as had been done in law schools on the issue of race before the pandemic. Or they could join together to sharpen a collective understanding of law schools' responsibility on the issue of racial justice. They chose to rise to the moment.[25]

Despite the pandemic being then in its apogee, law schools leant into more opportunities to effectuate change for the benefit of the profession. From the Clearing House Project on anti-racism,[26] collective and individual anti-racist statements, by

---

[24] *See The 2020 United States Civil Rights Movement*, THE NATIONAL TRIAL LAWYERS TOP 100 (July 31, 2020), https://thenationaltriallawyers.org/2020/07/the-2020-united-states-civil-rights-movement/; Lauren Mattiuzzo, *From the Courtroom to the Streets: A Timeline of the Civil Rights and Black Lives Matter Movements*, HEIN ONLINE BLOG (July 20, 2020), https://home.heinonline.org/blog/2020/07/from-the-courtroom-to-the-streets-a-timeline-of-the-civil-rights-and-black-lives-matter-movements/; Valarie Strauss, *'This is my generation's civil rights movement'*, THE WASHINGTON POST (June 6, 2020), https://www.washingtonpost.com/education/2020/06/06/this-is-my-generations-civil-rights-movement/.

[25] *See* Alexander, *supra* ("This summer, the deaths of George Floyd and others sparked demands for systemic reform, including in the legal profession. And law schools were among the institutions that jumped at the opportunity."); *See also* Sara Rimer, *Angela Onwuachi-Willig among Five Black Women Law Deans Honored for Efforts to Bring Antiracist Reform to Legal Education*, BU TODAY (Jan. 12, 2021), http://www.bu.edu/articles/2021/angela-onwuachi-willig-honored-for-efforts-to-bring-antiracist-reform-to-legal-educations/ ("some schools have already taken steps to add antiracist pedagogy to the curriculum, recruit more faculty of color, and bring greater diversity to their student bodies—future members of a profession that remains overwhelmingly white[ ]").

[26] Hayes, *supra* ("Law Deans Antiracist Clearinghouse Project, a website co-curated by five women-of-color law school deans . . . collected and posted antiracist statements and encouraged others to "listen" as a first step."); Pearl Stewart, *Law Schools Respond to the Movement for Social Justice*, DIVERSE EDUCATION (Apr. 12, 2021), https://diverseeducation.com/article/210890/ ("response to Floyd's brutal death came from five Black female deans who founded the Law Deans Antiracist Clearinghouse Project, which provides antiracism resources and information on the Association of American Law Schools' website[ ]").

schools,[27] to the creation of the Florida 12 law schools Consortium on Racial Justice,[28] they led with their heart.

This is what Brené Brown calls "courageous vulnerability" in action.[29] Law schools and their collaborators modeled a love for the profession that inspired trust and cooperation within their constituencies as well as across other industries and university departments of higher education.

3. Navigation Without a Roadmap

Leading courageously, it turns out, was the only choice. In the pandemic, lead or perish was an implicit motto. Still, like all leaders at that time, law schools operated without a roadmap, facing endless urgent demands from multiple constituencies. The moment asked all to grow and stretch to become something better than they were when the crisis started.[30]

The fact that the legal profession found itself at the forefront of this call to grow is not surprising considering that the theme of the last twenty months whether speaking of the pandemic,

---

[27] Hayes, *supra* ("law school deans began issuing statements vowing to fight racism within their institutions"); Sloan, *supra* ("[d]eans nationwide are sending messages . . . that they support the protesters"); Keeshea Turner Roberts, *Law Schools Push to Require Anti-Racism Training and Courses*, AMERICAN BAR ASSOCIATION (Dec. 14, 2020), https://www.americanbar.org/groups/crsj/publications/human_rights_magazine_home/rbgs-impact-on-civil-rights/law-schools-push/ ("Many law schools . . . issued powerful statements condemning the rise in racial injustice.").

[28] *See Florida's Law Schools Come Together to Address Racial Justice*, THE FLORIDA BAR (July 1, 2020), https://www.floridabar.org/the-florida-bar-news/floridas-law-schools-come-together-to-address-racial-justice/; Jill Baker, *New York City-Area Law Schools Form Law School Anti-Racism Consortium*, LAW.COM (Jan. 29, 2021, 10:45 AM), https://www.law.com/newyorklawjournal/2021/01/29/new-york-city-area-law-schools-form-law-school-anti-racism-consortium/; *See also ABA collaborates with law schools on legal issues in policing, public safety*, AMERICAN BAR ASSOCIATION (Oct. 12, 2020), https://www.americanbar.org/news/abanews/aba-news-archives/2020/10/aba-collaborates-with-law-schools-on-legal-issues-in-policing--p/ ("the consortium will advance the widespread adoption of model police practices and initiate other projects designed to support effective policing, promote racial equity in the criminal justice system and eliminate tactics that are racially motivated or have a disparate impact based on race[ ]").

[29] BRENÉ BROWN, DARE TO LEAD (2018).

[30] *See* Hayes, *supra* ("While discussions tend to be polarized, they have also raised deeper structural issues that law schools are in a unique position to address."); Kuris, *supra* ("lawyers are more needed than ever in a post-COVID-19 world. America's triple crises of illness, economic downturn and racial injustice have exposed structural problems requiring legal solutions, from health care disparities to police reforms to the fragility of small businesses[ ]"); Sloan, *supra* ("law students and lawyers have a key role to play in promoting justice and ending inequality[ ]").

racial justice or the economy, could be summed up in one word: inequity. Cities witnessed protests across the country.[31] At the same time, constituencies turned to law schools to demand a greater commitment to equity.[32] If law schools could or would not engage in justice work, who would?

In the midst of a centennial global crisis, social upheaval, and anxiety was rampant. Add to that a volatile political context, constituencies' sense of belonging risked evisceration.

As this all took shape, a reality became clear for law schools. The demands on them could not be resolved by one institution or one person. We had to be all in.

That is when law schools doubled down on the meaning of service. Their actions showed a fierce type of love for the craft and constituencies they served. As Brené Brown states:

"To love someone fiercely, to believe in something with your whole heart, to celebrate a fleeting moment in time, to fully engage in a life that doesn't come with guarantees—these are risks that involve vulnerability and often pain. But I'm learning

---

[31] The Armed Conflict Location & Event Data Project, *supra* at 3 ("Floyd's death prompted a surge of demonstrations associated with the Black Lives Matter (BLM) movement that quickly spread from Minneapolis throughout the country. Between 26 May, the day after Floyd's death, and 22 August, ACLED records over 7,750 demonstrations linked to the BLM movement across more than 2,440 locations in all 50 states and Washington, DC.").

[32] *See* Harvard Black Law Students Association, *Harvard's Black Law Student Association's Letter to the Administration Regarding Black Lives* (June 25, 2020), https://orgs.law.harvard.edu/blsa/2020/06/05/harvards-black-law-student-associations-letter-to-the-administration-regarding-black-lives/; Areeba Jibril, McKayla Stokes, and Mariah Young, *Students take to Twitter to demand racial equality*, AMERICAN BAR ASSOCIATION FOR LAW STUDENTS (July 1, 2020), https://abaforlawstudents.com/2020/07/01/students-take-to-twitter-to-demand-racial-equality/ (The conversation this month may have been sparked by our deans' failure to speak out, but the blame is not theirs alone. Administrators and faculty must recognize their role in harming BIPOC students, professors, and staff. They must understand that studying racial bias, litigating civil rights cases, or generally having "good intentions" does not prevent them from being racist. They must say, without pause and fear of repercussions, that Black Lives Matter. Then, they must prove it."); Karen Sloan, *This Is the Civil Rights Movement of My Lifetime': Black Law Students Demand Action*, LAW.COM (June 18, 2020, 03:40 PM), https://www.law.com/2020/06/18/this-is-the-civil-rights-movement-of-my-lifetime-black-law-students-demand-action/ ("In open letters to classmates and deans, [students] argue that statements in support of the protests that have followed the killing of George Floyd, hastily arranged town hall meetings and panels centered on racism, and shared reading lists about the experience of black people in America and in the justice system fall woefully short at this critical moment.").

that recognizing and leaning into the discomfort of vulnerability teaches us how to live with joy, gratitude and grace."[33]

This is a principle of love in action. It looks deceptively simple, but requires dedicated time and a commitment to interconnection. To implement this principle, law schools created public conversations to educate the public about the rule of law, round table discussions, action items to implement for the benefit of rectifying past wrongs, reading groups to facilitate uncomfortable conversations, raised funds to support justice causes, etc.[34]

Schools compiled data on the disproportionate impact of the bar exam on vulnerable groups and led the charge to stem the tide of hate and assaults on human dignity. Schools also undertook to interrogate their internal structures and remedy historical shortcomings. The Law Deans Antiracist Clearinghouse Project hosted by the AALS[35] and the anti-racism statements and commitments authored by a number of law schools are two examples of this.

And, more importantly, law schools worked to be more proximate to their students. They listened and learned more deeply about needs across the spectrum of their population, as well as advocated for additional resources.

Through it all, law school leaders also had to navigate the difficult task of modeling difficult conversation across the political schisms in the most incendiary context of the last fifty years. What do you do when one word taken out of context could lead to a political crisis at the institution? There was not a one-size-fits-all-answer. Balancing interests and bracing against pitfalls, we crafted approaches designed to support students and other constituencies while remaining consistent to our educational mission.

---

[33] BRENÉ BROWN, THE GIFTS OF IMPERFECTION 73 (2010).

[34] *See* Sloan, *supra* ("Law schools are hosting open forums for students and staff to discuss recent police killings of minorities and systemic inequality, as well as workshops on policing and other relevant legal issues.").

[35] https://www.aals.org/about/publications/antiracist-clearinghouse/.

4. The Balance of Service-Based Leadership and Historic Demands

Coincidentally, during this period law schools underwent the greatest surge in application and enrollment in over a decade.[36] Time will tell as to the real cause of this increase. Suffice it to consider, however, that with the advent of fast media and continued coverage of legal issues, law schools and the work that takes place there are more relevant and necessary than ever.

Thus, teaching abstractly about justice in law schools is no longer enough. Students are demanding clarity of purpose at a time where the world has become more complex for everyone.[37]

Similarly, staff, faculty and alumni yearn to be in close proximity and collaboration with one another and with leadership.[38] In times of uncertainty, constituencies need more support. Much of that support takes the form of emotional and concrete resources. That places leaders in a particularly demanding position. They find themselves pulled in all directions, called to provide and anticipate all things from all constituencies. In the long-term, that is not sustainable.

Hence the importance of a service-based collaborative leadership in law schools. As we look back to the past months, examples abound that show the power of collective problem solving, data mining and solution crafting on specific issues. From pass/fail to the pitfalls of bar exams, to collective anti-

---

[36] Kuris, *supra* ("For law schools and applicants alike, the past year has been the most competitive and stressful admissions season in recent memory. According to LSAC data, as of June 10 the number of law school applicants this cycle is up about 17% from the previous year and up about 15% from the year before. The number of applications submitted by those applicants is up nearly 30% from last year and about 27% from the year before."); Karen Sloan, *2021 Law School Applicant Pool Shaping Up to Be the Largest in a Decade*, LAW.COM (Apr. 19, 2021, 2:38 PM), https://www.law.com/2021/04/19/2021-law-school-applicant-pool-shaping-up-to-be-the-largest-in-a-decade/ (the national law school applicant pool already has 10,723 more people than it did at this time last year. If that trend holds steady in the final weeks of the cycle, law schools will end the year with approximately 76,000 applicants. That would be the single-largest applicant pool since 2011, which represented the beginning of a sustained downturn in law school applicants.").

[37] *See* Kuris, *supra* ("lawyers are more needed than ever in a post-COVID-19 world. America's triple crises of illness, economic downturn and racial injustice have exposed structural problems requiring legal solutions, from health care disparities to police reforms to the fragility of small businesses.").

[38] Thomas Reuters, *supra*.

racist work, to pivotal responses to new ABA standards, law schools were efficient and responsive to the needs of a variety of constituencies.

5. Law Schools and Prevention of Erasure

2021 has seen a record period of inclusive leadership across law schools. Leaders who identify as women, persons of color and LGBTQIA were appointed in numbers higher than ever before.[39] There is a long way to go. However, in a profession known to be slow to change, this is notable.

In light of that fact and the pressures discussed above, legal education and university partners must seriously guard against retrenchment and dilution of these important gains. This cautionary principle is important to record at the onset. Regression in the face of progress has occurred after nearly each major event in American history: Reconstruction,[40] the modern

---

[39] *See Legal Scholar and Law School Leader Kimberly Mutcherson Named Co-Dean of Rutgers Law School*, RUTGERS (Jan. 2, 2019), https://law.rutgers.edu/news/legal-scholar-and-law-school-leader-kimberly-mutcherson-named-co-dean-rutgers-law-school ("When her appointment took effect on Jan. 1, 2019, Mutcherson became the first woman, the first African American, and the first LGBT law dean at Rutgers, The State University of New Jersey."); *See* Dallas Duncan, *Emory Law Names School's First LGBTQ Female Dean*, GEORGIA VOICE (July 3, 2019), https://thegavoice.com/news/atlanta/emory-law-names-schools-first-lgbtq-female-dean/; *See also* Anna Timmons, *'American Dream' dean Anthony Varona heads UM Law School*, THE MIAMI HURRICANE (Nov. 13, 2019), https://www.themiamihurricane.com/2019/11/13/american-dream-dean-anthony-varona-heads-um-law-school/ ("Varona has made history in his newest position at the University of Miami; he is the first Hispanic and openly gay dean of the Law School."); *See also* Kevin Truong, *Golden Gate University law school dean fights homophobia and fear (Video)*, SAN FRANCISCO BUSINESS TIMES (June 14, 2018), https://www.bizjournals.com/sanfrancisco/news/2018/06/14/ggu-law-school-dean-fights-homophobia-fear.html (Anthony Niedwiecki Dean, Golden Gate University School of Law was "one of the nation's only openly gay law school deans[ ]").

[40] *E.g.*, *Reconstruction Timeline*, AMERICAN EXPERIENCE (last visited July 12, 2021), https://www.pbs.org/wgbh/americanexperience/features/reconstruction-timeline/ (after Lincoln's death "President Johnson shows growing leniency toward the white South: he orders the restoration of land to its former owners, including the land provided to freed slaves" and "starts aligning himself with the Southern elite[.]" In addition, "President Johnson declares the reconstruction process complete. . . [m]ore than sixty former Confederates arrive to take their seats in Congress[,]" he withdraws Union soldiers from the south, he vetoes bills that would extend protection to southern blacks, "black elected officials are ousted from" state legislatures, and "Southern legislatures begin drafting 'Black Codes' to re-establish white supremacy"); *Civil Rights Movement*, HISTORY (Oct. 27, 2009), https://www.history.com/topics/black-history/civil-rights-movement ("To marginalize Black people, keep them separate from white people and erase the progress they'd made during Reconstruction, 'Jim Crow' laws were established in the South beginning in the late 19th century.").

civil rights movement, of the 1960s,[41] etc.[42] What is more, efforts at inclusion by institutions are often accompanied by limited or non-existent support to those appointed, causing inevitable strains with the oft entrenched and hostile power structure.

Nearly two years into the pandemic, the world and institutions are itching to get back to normal. It is natural. This past year has been the most destabilizing event in a century. The staggering death toll from the pandemic defies past war casualties. We all yearn for the familiar.

Still, it is that very impulse toward a proverbial normalcy that proves dangerous. If the pandemic has taught us anything, it is that we have much work to do to remedy the gaping inequalities with which society had previously made peace. Mercilessly, the virus laid bare the countless lives that we left behind during so-called normal times.

---

41 *See* Jason Whitlock, *America's race-relations regression*, ABC NEWS (Mar. 11, 2015, 5:10 PM), https://abcnews.go.com/Sports/americas-race-relations-regression/story?id=29566289 ("The racial tension at the University of Oklahoma paints the latest picture of the trouble brewed by 50 years of backlash to Martin Luther King Jr.'s courageous 'We Shall Overcome' movement."); *see also* Sharon Austin, *Black Americans mostly left behind by progress since Dr. King's death*, THE CONVERSATION (Feb. 7, 2018, 6:26 AM EST), https://theconversation.com/black-americans-mostly-left-behind-by-progress-since-dr-kings-death-89956 (detailing the progress black people have been able to make since the Civil Rights Movement, and conversely detailing the ways in which "we've barely budged as a people[ ]"); *see also* Jeremy D. Mayer, *LBJ Fights the White Backlash: The Racial Politics of the 1964 Presidential Campaign*, NATIONAL ARCHIVES (2001), https://www.archives.gov/publications/prologue/2001/spring/lbj-and-white-backlash-1.html (white backlash after the Civil Rights Act's passage almost lost President Johnson the 1964 presidential nomination to "George Corley Wallace, a segregationist governor of Alabama" famous for the phrase "segregation today, segregation tomorrow, segregation forever!").

42 John Blake, *This is what 'whitelash' looks like*, CNN (last updated Nov. 19, 2016, 9:09 PM EST), https://www.cnn.com/2016/11/11/us/obama-trump-white-backlash/index.html ("Reconstruction in the 19th century was followed by a century of Jim Crow. The civil rights movement of the 1950s and '60s was followed by President Ronald Reagan and the rise of the religious right[,]" and after President Obama's election, the country had a surge of white backlash); Patrik Jonsson, *After Obama's win, white backlash festers in US*, THE CHRISTIAN SCIENCE MONITOR (Nov. 17, 2008), https://www.csmonitor.com/USA/Politics/2008/1117/p03s01-uspo.html ("[w]e're not looking at a race war or anything close to it, but . . . what we are seeing now is undeniably a fairly major backlash by some subset of the white population," in the wake of President Obama's election).

Families were torn apart. First responders held hands with patients who hated them until the last breath. Homelessness runs rampant and the social safety net is nonexistent.[43]

So, as we think of "normalcy", what lessons may we take to create a new world? We need only look at the last hundred years for edification. Post-World War II, for instance, sheds light on our impulses to rush to put tragedy behind us.

Much like now, World War II triggered a previously untapped workforce, made up of women and people of color, to stabilize society. And, tragically after the war, the erasure of their work begun. This act of erasure of women and people of color are well documented after World War II.

> If the Allies' fight for "freedom" meant personal independence, then American women had embraced it in the early 1940s. Of the "Four Freedoms" articulated by President Roosevelt in 1940, "freedom from want" and "freedom from fear" went a long way in explaining why some American women enjoyed the financial, social, and emotional rewards of the war years. The large number of those who developed skills and carried out new work, who put on military uniforms, married quickly, engaged in sexual activity freely, or moved several hundred miles away from home—or all of these—did so inside the grander framework of national and global crisis. Out of crisis, the most meaningful transformations emanated from the confidence they developed and the independence they felt and exercised. Many feared these would fade or be retracted after the war, and their fears were justified. From popular culture to social commentary to political leadership, powerful voices urged women to "go back home to provide jobs for service men," despite the fact that the jobs many held were not available to servicemen before

[43] *See* Pam Fessler, *HUD: Growth Of Homelessness During 2020 Was 'Devastating,' Even Before The Pandemic*, NATIONAL PUBLIC RADIO (Mar. 18, 2021, 6:01 AM ET), https://www.npr.org/2021/03/18/978244891/hud-growth-of-homelessness-during-2020-was-devastating-even-before-the-pandemic; *New Report Shows Rise in Homelessness in Advance of COVID-19 Crisis*, NATIONAL ALLIANCE TO END HOMELESSNESS (Mar. 18, 2021), https://endhomelessness.org/new-report-shows-rise-in-homelessness-in-advance-of-covid-19-crisis/.

> the war and that many returning servicemen had not worked for wages regularly in the 1930s. Numerous surveys and polls of female workers found that most wanted to remain in the work force rather than return to their prewar employment conditions. Efforts to "contain" women during the late 1940s and convince them to embrace a middle-class dream where they would play starring roles as domestic goddesses in their own homes eventually backfired. Their wartime experiences combined with collective memory not only affected their daughters . . ."[44]

One primary lesson of post-war rehabilitation effort is simple: institutions must not rewrite the vital reliance placed on women and people of color during crises. As a light shines at the end of the tunnel now, a familiar temptation connects the current period to World War II. The tendency is emerging at the margins: the diminishment and devaluation of the massive work and support shouldered by women and persons of color.

The dominant structure has begun to rearrange itself in various ways to craft a narrative of normalcy that may mirror this pattern. Still, after twenty months of co-dependent and collaborative service to one another, erasing the work of vital contributors would not only be harmful to the institutions, it is impossible. The marks are everywhere.

C. CONCLUSION

In the Law School Survey on Student Engagement (LSSSE) retrospective, the Changing Landscape of Legal Education, students report that "law schools are playing larger roles in contributing to their understanding of people from different racial and ethnic backgrounds, developing personal codes of values and ethics, and complex problem solving."[45] These results illustrate the important role that law schools play in students' lives and their professional development. Gone are the days of

---

[44] Melissa A. McEuen, *Women, Gender, and World War II*, AMERICAN HISTORY (June 9, 2016), https://oxfordre.com/americanhistory/view/10.1093/acrefore/9780199329175.001.0001/acrefore-9780199329175-e-55.

[45] *The Changing Landscape of Legal Education a 15-Year LSSSE Retrospective*, The Law School Survey on Student Engagement 16 (2020).

the Paper Chase and other law schools' horror stories.[46] Students and law schools are partners in a sacred and significant professional endeavor: building the next generation of well rounded, justice seeking, ethical and thoroughly prepared lawyers.

[46] The Paper Chase (20th Century Studios 1973) (depicting the struggles of a first-year law student at Harvard Law School who is repeatedly humiliated by his contracts professor).

CHAPTER 3

REPAIRING DEMOCRACY: ON LAWYERS, TRUST, AND LEADERSHIP

Garry W. Jenkins[1]

In nearly all aspects of public and private life, leadership matters. Leadership is part of the story of the January 6, 2021 Capitol attack: part of the cause, and part of the solution. On January 6th, an armed mob invaded the U.S. Capitol building to interrupt the peaceful transfer of power from one administration to the next. This was no standard act of political protest but rather an insurrection that resulted in injuries, death, and vandalism. Our national security was risked. The horrifying and indelible images of sedition, violence, and mayhem placed in sharp relief the long-term impact of a sitting U.S. President's persistent assaults on the rule of law, relentless attacks on the norms of good governance, and purposeful efforts to mislead through false statements and gross exaggerations over four years in office. The consequences of Donald Trump's weaponized rhetoric and his followers' beliefs in manipulative lies manifested themselves in an unprecedented mob attack by American citizens incited by their leaders. More specifically, they were incited by the lies of Donald Trump, Rudy Giuliani, and other political leaders who embraced baseless claims about the 2020 election.[2]

If we wish to move forward as a nation, we must first comprehend and confront the circumstances that culminated in

---

[1] Dean and William S. Pattee Professor of Law, University of Minnesota Law School (2016–present). He was previously associate dean, professor, and the founding co-director of the Program on Law and Leadership at The Ohio State University Moritz College of Law.

[2] *See* Alan Feuer & Nicole Hong, *We Just Followed Trump's Cue, Several Accused in Rioting Say*, N.Y. TIMES, Jan. 18, 2021, at A1; Sam Levine, *How Republicans Came to Embrace the Big Lie of a Stolen Election*, GUARDIAN (UK) (June 13, 2021), https://www.theguardian.com/us-news/2021/jun/13/republicans-big-lie-us-election-trump; Jim Rutenberg et al., *77 Days: Trump's Campaign to Subvert the Election*, N.Y. TIMES, Feb. 1, 2021 at A1.

the lethal attack on the Capitol. What made so many so receptive to the lies that led to their breaking into the Capitol and threatening members of Congress? Surely, there was a complicated mix of motivations. But two of the many truths revealed by the attack are the existence of substantial underlying fissures and divisions between those perceived to be losing ground and those gaining ground and a deep distrust in the democratic institutions, processes, systems, and people charged with serving our democracy. While the strife and distrust culminating in the ransacking of the Capitol may have been stoked by President Trump along with his aides and political allies, the fundamental origins of discontent can be traced back to significant changes in our society.

Interviews and background profiles of the individuals who participated in that violent Capitol takeover suggest that the root causes of the deadly siege were a pervasive sense of fear, loss, and uncertainty in some parts of American society. These emotions stem from growing economic inequality and precarity, changing racial demographics, and a perceived loss of power and status.[3] Moreover, President Trump uniquely validated their sense of victimhood and provided an outlet for them to channel it into action.

As the forces of globalization and interconnectedness take hold, America is no longer a singular power. Rather, our interests are increasingly integrated with and affected by events in other parts of the world. Our national economic model is now driven by knowledge and services, which prioritize education and complex skills. We are also experiencing a widening gap between the rich and the poor. Meanwhile, census demographic population projections show that the nation will shift from predominantly white to a majority of the population being "minorities" or "people of color" by 2045.[4] In addition, heightened

---

[3] *See* Todd C. Frankel, *A Majority of the People Arrested for Capitol Riot Had a History of Financial Trouble*, WASH. POST, Feb. 10, 2021.

[4] *See* SANDRA L. COLBY & JENNIFER M. ORTMAN, U.S. CENSUS BUREAU, PROJECTIONS OF THE SIZE AND COMPOSITION OF THE U.S. POPULATION: 2014 TO 2060: POPULATION ESTIMATES AND PROJECTIONS (P25–1143) 9 (March 2015), https://www.census.gov/content/dam/Census/library/publications/2015/demo/p25-1143.pdf; U.S. CENSUS BUREAU, PROJECTING MAJORITY-MINORITY NON-HISPANIC WHITES MAY NO LONGER COMPRISE OVER 50 PERCENT OF THE U.S. POPULATION BY 2044, https://www.census.gov/content/dam/Census/newsroom/releases/2015/cb15-tps16_graphic.pdf. *But see* Richard Alba, Morris Levy & Dowell Myers, *The Myth of a Majority-Minority*

levels of partisan politics, the spread of online news disinformation and false narratives, and the undermining of the mainstream press have mixed to form a toxic brew of fear, anxiety, and anger in large segments of the American public. These forces have combined to sow exceptional levels of distrust in government, degrade democratic institutions, and place our democracy in a vulnerable position. We reaped the horrors on January 6, 2021.

The growing democratic disillusionment, as evidenced by the willingness of millions of Americans (and scores of federal and state officials) to undermine free and fair elections, presents a fundamental threat to the rule of law and free-market capitalism. But repairing our democracy requires addressing the underlying problems, the high levels of institutional distrust, and the leadership failures that have resulted in events like January 6th. It is not enough to simply assert that the presidential election was legitimate. We need thoughtful interventions from various sectors of society, including lawyers, that seek to tackle deep schisms in America, to build bridges and connections, to demonstrate efforts to improve people's lives, and to reverse the inequality that is at the root of so much distrust and discontent. Far too many people no longer believe the system works for them: they see an uneven playing field, they have little faith in institutions and the people that run them, and thus they are willing to believe false narratives and even take action. Generating a cycle of distrust. The storming of the Capitol is just one example of how dangerous a lack of trust in democratic institutions can be.

Even though President Trump no longer holds office, the anger and distrust that led to the Capitol attack remain. And things can get much worse if we let them. Not only is our political system at risk, but also our economic and social systems are vulnerable as well. Make no mistake, this loss of faith in our

---

America, ATLANTIC, Jun. 13, 2021 ("The majority-minority narrative contributes to our national polarization. Its depiction of a society fractured in two, with one side rising while the other subsides, is inherently divisive because it implies winners and losers. It has bolstered white anxiety and resentment of supposedly ascendant minority groups, and has turned people against democratic institutions. . . . By rigidly splitting Americans into two groups, white versus nonwhite, it reinvents the discredited 19th-century 'one-drop rule' and applies it to a 21st-century society in which the color line is more fluid than it has ever been.").

democratic institutions amounts to a catastrophic leadership failure. We cannot possibly find our way back to each other without addressing trust, and we cannot do that without good leadership. We need sound and effective solutions and leaders to help us through these challenging global governance issues. We must build community and bring people together—this is a pressing issue of leadership. Indeed, this new normal demands a new kind of leader.

As a law school dean and a scholar of law and leadership studies, I keep returning to two interwoven ideas: first, there is a crisis of trust in our nation's institutions and leaders and second, law schools play a critical role in educating future leaders. These realizations spark the following questions: what are we going to do to boost trust in and for the next generation of leaders, specifically lawyer-leaders? How can lawyers, armed with a sophisticated understanding of the art and science of leadership, help mend democracy? Would a law school culture committed to developing leadership capacities help strengthen our democratic institutions? The present moment seems especially propitious for improving the capacity for leadership in the legal profession and supporting efforts of lawyers to rebuild the trust necessary to support our fragile democracy.

Recognizing that this crisis goes deeper than Donald Trump, this chapter argues that we cannot move on from January 6th without focusing on root problems, including the erosion of trust and failures of leadership. It begins by drawing the connections between trust and leadership. Then it examines the troubling levels of trust in our institutions, in our politics, and in one another. It further posits that leaders—all kinds of leaders, including lawyers—are needed to rebuild trust and engage in the everyday work of democratic repair. Accordingly, then, law schools should prepare lawyers to be those kinds of leaders, to help them begin developing the tools they will need to lead and revive institutions. Finally, it concludes that if there is any hope for our country to come together and build trust, then good, effective lawyer-leaders (as well as other leaders) will need to step in and step up. And we need to proactively create them. Otherwise, as we have seen, unscrupulous political leaders can all too easily turn distrust into rage.

A. THE ROLE OF TRUST IN LEADERSHIP

Trust is an essential element of leadership. While many assume that the traditional leadership narrative is about command, singular vision, power, or perhaps charisma, today's leadership is actually more grounded in collaboration, participation, integration, and culture creation. In other words, leadership is about developing—not controlling—others. At the heart of effective leadership is a connection and relationship between leaders and followers. As James MacGregor Burns wrote in his seminal book, *Leadership*, "transforming leadership is a relationship of mutual simulation and elevation that converts followers into leaders and may convert leaders into moral agents."[5] Recognizing that the leader-follower relationship is a voluntary exchange, trust then becomes a critical currency for a leader.

James MacGregor Burns and others have helped us move our understanding of leadership beyond the perspective of the individual heroic leader to the leadership relationship. We find in examining different philosophies, frameworks, and models of leadership that each contains various attributes; but if the relationship between the leader and followers is at the center of the matter, then trust cannot be far behind. Trust is the glue that binds leaders and followers together and fuels leadership success.

The connection between trust and leadership pervades the leadership literature. For example, in their leadership classic *The Leadership Challenge*, scholars James Kouzes and Barry Posner wrote that "collaboration is the critical competency for achieving and sustaining high performance[, and] . . . at the heart of collaboration is trust. It's the central issue in human relationships within and outside organizations. Without trust you cannot lead."[6] This is consistent with Gilbert Fairholm's description of trust as "the prime mechanism for group cohesion. Indeed, no organization can take place without interpersonal trust, and no organizational leader can ignore the powerful

---

5 JAMES MACGREGOR BURNS, LEADERSHIP 4 (1978).

6 JAMES M. KOUZES & BARRY Z. POSNER, THE LEADERSHIP CHALLENGE 242–44 (3rd ed. 2002).

element of trust."[7] And in a recent *Harvard Business Review* article entitled "Begin with Trust," Frances Frei and Anne Morriss outlined their model of empowerment leadership in which trust provides the foundation for the practice of leadership.[8]

In making the case for the importance of trust, scholar Mirta Martin reached a similar conclusion:

> The most important characteristic for a leader/follower relationship to flourish is trust. Furthermore, the trust most needed is that which is earned and then cherished. Being trusted is motivating, energizing and exciting.
>
> The development of trust is a never-ending process. . . . Once the trust relationship has been established, a transformation process begins that integrates the goals of the individuals with the goals of the organization, thus inspiring a self-led follower. As the self-led follower begins to accomplish the goals of the organization, ownership of responsibilities becomes inevitable, and a new leadership based on mutual trust emerges.[9]

This connection between trust and leadership has also been borne out by several empirical research studies. For example, Zenger Folkman, an international management and organizational consultancy firm, recently conducted a study of a broad set of leadership practices and team member trust. In a study of more than 75,000 organizational leaders and 400,000 of their direct reports, the researchers examined how levels of trust interact with sixteen different leadership competencies to impact employee engagement. The data revealed that adding a high level of trust to each competency improved employee engagement by an average of 23 percentage points. In the case of all sixteen competencies in the study, high trust (rather than low trust) moved engagement to the 70th percentile or higher. Interestingly, not all the competencies alone were correlated with increased engagement—but mixing trust with any of them

---

7 GILBERT W. FAIRHOLM, LEADERSHIP AND THE CULTURE OF TRUST 96 (1994).

8 Frances X. Frei & Anne Morriss, *Begin with Trust*, HARV. BUS. REV., May–June 2020, at 112.

9 Mirta M. Martin, *Trust Leadership*, 5 J. LEADERSHIP & ORGANIZATIONAL STUD. 41, 43 (1998).

improved engagement significantly. The researchers concluded from their study that "trust changes the way people respond to a leader."[10]

When it comes to building and developing trust, leaders play a primary role. Much of the leadership literature suggests that effective leaders create and earn trust through authentically caring about others, displaying honesty and integrity, sharing information, and acting predictably and consistently.[11]

Regardless, we know that leadership and organizational change are hard. Organizations and people are resistant to change, even when it is required. Consequently, trust is a prerequisite for any leader seeking to innovate, shift culture, or inspire others. Vision setting and developing buy-in require trust. Trust fosters cooperation, cultivates creativity, and nourishes commitment. Trust eases pathways for teams and organizations, especially when tasks are complex and unstructured or require high levels of interdependence, cooperation, or information sharing.[12] The one thing any successful leader understands is that one cannot compel trust or expect it easily: it must be given by followers and engendered by leaders over time.

B. MAKING SENSE OF TRUMP'S FOLLOWERSHIP

One cannot help but note that in the case of President Trump, he has forged a visceral connection with his set of followers. They seem to have trusted him and his lies about the election; this perhaps suggests that their perception of his caring about them, their concerns, and their interests transcends all other factors. In his book *The Trust Trifecta*, business executive Jordan Berman emphasized the risks of assuming that competence automatically will generate trust. Instead, he

---

[10] Joe Folkman, *Understanding Trust: The Salt of Leadership*, FORBES (Jul. 28, 2020), https://www.forbes.com/sites/joefolkman/2020/07/28/understanding-trust-the-salt-of-leadership/?sh=6f3908f109ed.

[11] *See, e.g.*, FAIRHOLM, *supra* note 7, at 108–110; Patrick A. Duignan & Narottam Bhindi, *Authenticity in Leadership: An Emerging Perspective*, 35 J. EDUC. ADMIN. 195, 195 (1997).

[12] *See* Nicole A. Gillespie & Leon Mann, *Transformational Leadership and Shared Values: The Building Blocks of Trust*, 19 J. MANAGERIAL PYSCH. 588, 588 (2004).

argued, people trust when they feel they know you and that you are being "straight" with them.[13] For better or worse, perhaps Trump's followers felt both things; all while he provided a bullhorn for their grievances.

But, despite having devoted followers, Trump did not come close to building the broad levels of trust required for effective leadership. In fact, some scholars distinguish between leaders and power-holders, with the former seeking to satisfy higher community needs and the latter seeking to advance their own motives.[14] Others have used the term misleadership to describe those leaders who actually undermine the conditions for communal flourishing. Ethics scholars Al Gini and Ronald Green, in writing about misleadership, noted that "[s]ome misleaders are simply pathetic egocentric scoundrels, or selfishly vain adolescent narcissists, full of bluster and pomposity. . ." They further identified multiple living and historical examples of misleaders, including then-television personality Donald Trump,[15] several years before he even announced his candidacy for the U.S. presidency.

We should also remember that some followers, too, can be bad—becoming enablers and supporters of bad leadership.[16] In her book *Followership*, Barbara Kellerman argued that "bad leaders depend absolutely on bad followers to sustain them."[17] Consider the physical violence of January 6th, the deplorable displays of Confederate flags and other indicia of white supremacy in "the citadel of democracy," the prominent role of white-nationalists and right-wing extremists and militants (i.e., Proud Boys, Oath Keepers, Three Percenters, Aryan Brotherhood), the open brandishing of Tasers and plastic zip-tie restraints to take hostages, and the throngs of red "Make

---

[13] JORDAN BERMAN, THE TRUST TRIFECTA: A LEADER'S GUIDE TO HITTING THE TRUST JACKPOT 9 (2020).

[14] *See, e.g.*, BURNS, *supra* note 5, at 4, 17.

[15] Al Gini & Ronald M. Green, *Bad Leaders/Misleaders*, 117 BUS. SOC'Y REV. 143, 150 (2012).

[16] To be clear, not all Trump voters or supporters are deserving of condemnation (or should be considered "bad followers"). However, in my view, that moniker may be used appropriately for members of the insurrectionist mob that showed up at Donald Trump's behest and stormed the U.S. Capitol, as described in the text accompanying notes 17–20 below, and those who encouraged and supported them.

[17] BARBARA KELLERMAN, FOLLOWERSHIP: HOW FOLLOWERS ARE CREATING CHANGE AND CHANGING LEADERS 233 (2008).

America Great Again" hats being worn by middle-class, middle-aged everyday citizens, marking their loyalty to Trump[18] while hurling racial slurs and abuse at Capitol police.[19] As Kellerman observed, bad followers can become caught up in "contagious craziness that leads to political violence and to the bureaucracies that support it."[20] In this case, their passions were, as former President George W. Bush described, "inflamed by [Trump's] falsehoods and false hopes."[21]

Irrespective of Trump's popularity among his followers, two things are certain. First, to the extent Trump's "Stop the Steal" lies undermine trust, those lies weaken societal leadership and democracy; trust and leadership are intertwined. Second, the fact that a leader has followers does not mean that the leader is good, sound, or moral. There are leaders who may treat their own followers well but engage in corrupt practices and damaging behavior that harm the institutions they lead.[22]

Good leaders are responsible leaders. "That means they focus on doing the right thing, not winning at all costs . . . [they] leave the team, the organization, or the nation better off than they found them."[23] In this instance, the promotion of inchoate lies that promote a favored election outcome, without any evidence, clearly exhibits self-interest and harms democracy. Good leaders work to engender a general level of trust in an organization or society across divides—even seeking to reach those with whom they may disagree. Recognizing that even in a highly pluralistic society like ours that "[s]ome measure of cohesion and mutual tolerance is an absolute requirement of

---

18 *See* Robert A. Pape & Keven Ruby, *The Capitol Rioters Aren't Like Other Extremists*, ATLANTIC, Feb. 2, 2021.

19 *See* Luke Broadwater & Nicholas Fandos, *Beaten, Tased and Crushed by Rioters at Capitol*, N.Y. TIMES. Jul. 28, 2021, at A1.

20 KELLERMAN, *supra* note 17, at 232–233.

21 *See* Press Release, George W. Bush Presidential Center, Statement by President George W. Bush on Insurrection at the Capitol (Jan. 6, 2021), https://www.bushcenter.org/about-the-center/newsroom/press-releases/2021/statement-by-president-george-w-bush-on-insurrection-at-the-capitol.html.

22 *See* KELLERMAN, *supra* note 17, at x; JOHN W. GARDNER, ON LEADERSHIP 67 (1990). *See also* JEAN LIPMAN-BLUMEN, THE ALLURE OF TOXIC LEADERS: WHY WE FOLLOW DESTRUCTIVE BOSSES AND CORRUPT POLITICIANS—AND HOW WE CAN SURVIVE THEM (2006).

23 Ronald E. Riggio, *Power, Persuasion, and Bad Leadership*, in WHY IRRATIONAL POLITICS APPEALS: UNDERSTANDING THE ALLURE OF TRUMP 71, 73 (Mari Fitzduff ed., 2017).

social functioning," John W. Gardner wrote that effective leaders strive to reduce conflict rather than escalate it.[24] In contrast to Trump's leadership approach as well as others who only cater to their political tribe, Gardner argued that "all our leaders must spend part of their time dealing with polarization and building community . . . In fact, the leader willing to combat polarization is the braver person . . . ."[25] Accordingly, Gardner also saw raising the level of trust as essential to the work of leadership.[26]

C. THE CRISIS OF TRUST IN AMERICAN SOCIETY

Despite the significance of trust, by many accounts our levels of trust in our institutions, each other, and democratic connections are extraordinarily low. According to the 2021 Edelman Trust Barometer,[27] fewer than half (48%) of Americans trust U.S. institutions (government, NGOs, the media, and business), a five-point decline from 2020. Of the twenty-seven countries studied, only six fared worse (Argentina, South Korea, Spain, United Kingdom, Japan, and Russia). With respect to government specifically, fewer than half (42%) of Americans say they trust their government. Trust in media and NGOs was similarly low at 45% and 50% respectively. Furthermore, government was viewed as both least ethical and least competent compared to business, NGOs, and the media. Not surprisingly, overall institutional trust was significantly lower among Trump voters than Biden voters, with a 13-percentage-point gap. For government and the media, the trust gaps were a cavernous 15 and 39 percentage points, respectively, between Biden and Trump voters. The Edelman study also revealed a trust gap between the informed public and the mass population of the United States of 18 percentage points, one of the largest in the study. Furthermore, across all categories, white Americans are less trusting of all institutions than their Black, Latinx, or Asian-American counterparts.

---

24 *See* GARDNER, *supra* note 22, at 16.

25 *Id.* at 17.

26 *Id.*

27 EDELMAN, EDELMAN TRUST BAROMETER 2021, https://www.edelman.com/sites/g/files/aatuss191/files/2021-01/2021%20Edelman%20Trust%20Barometer_U.S.%20Country%20Report_Clean.pdf.

Likewise, there is a strong sense among Americans that distrust has grown over time. A 2019 Pew Center research study[28] reported that 76% of Americans believe trust in the federal government has declined in the past twenty years. In addition to concerns about low and declining levels of trust in government, many Americans are anxious about the level of confidence citizens have in each other. Some 71% of Americans think that interpersonal confidence has worsened in the past twenty years as well, according to the same Pew study.

This pervasive lack of trust translates into a lack of confidence in leadership.[29] For example, the Edelman report indicated that a majority of Americans do not trust government leaders (33%), CEOs (47%), or journalists (48%) "to do what's right." Not surprisingly, Biden and Trump voters again had huge disparities in their responses regarding having trust in government leaders (17 percentage points) and journalists (42 percentage points). Yet most seem to agree that political and ideological polarization is an extreme problem (57%), and 62% believe that government leaders actively engage in spreading lies and misinformation.

Trends such as these have distressing consequences for the state of our democracy. Simply put, when people believe that the system and its rules are fundamentally just, they tend to engage in constructive behaviors and follow rules and norms, even if they do not agree with them. When they do not believe in the system—when they lose faith and lose trust—everyone looks out for only themselves, and collective society suffers. When people distrust, they withhold, censor, distort, and conceal information.

Without deep and genuine trust in our leaders or our democratic system, we are left with weak or failing institutions. Our social relations and social capital are threatened by the lack of trust. Weak institutions are more vulnerable when disaster strikes and are ill-equipped to recover in the aftermath. The

---

[28] Lee Rainie, Scott Keeter & Andrew Perrin, Pew Rsch. Ctr., *Trust and Distrust in America* (July 22, 2019), https://www.pewresearch.org/politics/2019/07/22/trust-and-distrust-in-america/.

[29] *See* JOSEPH S. NYE JR., THE POWERS TO LEAD ix (2008); Matthew Harrington, *Survey: People's Trust Has Declined in Business, Media, Government, and NGOs*, HARV. BUS. REV. DIGITAL (Jan. 15, 2017), https://hbr.org/2017/01/survey-peoples-trust-has-declined-in-business-media-government-and-ngos.

erosion of trust creates a void that increases the likelihood of dysfunction "associated with a lack of cooperation, lower satisfaction and commitment, and possibly even retribution and actively hostile behavior"[30] in actors. The Capitol attack is just one example of what can happen when people stop trusting leaders and institutions.

D. LAWYER-LEADERS AS BROKERS OF TRUST

While many legal experts and political scientists who seek to cure these ills have focused on proposals involving policy design (substantive, formal, rule-oriented, institutional-minded reforms)—such as electoral system reform, term limits, regulation of technology and technology companies, expansion of national service, etc.—we may also need to consider interpersonal, relational work that can be carried out, on the ground, only through principal institutional agents (e.g., elected officials, community groups, activists, public administrators, and heads of public departments) engaged in proactive leadership. In practice, this will involve such leaders proactively working to restore broken trust and resourcefully connecting citizens to democratic institutions and processes using classic leadership tools of influence, trust-building, persuasion, empathy, communication, relationship management, collaboration, story-telling, and empowerment, among others. Accordingly, society needs leaders, including lawyer-leaders, of the first order. Leaders with the capacity to promote communication and connections among diverse constituencies, experiment with new models of engagement, work for the greater good (not for themselves), and reinforce the integrity of our democratic fabric. That kind of deliberate leadership engagement is essential to advance what political scientist Carolyn Hendriks and her colleagues call "democratic mending":

---

[30] *See* Roy J. Lewicki & Edward C. Tomlinson, *Distrust*, BEYOND INTRACTABILITY PROJECT (Guy Burgess and Heidi Burgess, eds.), Conflict Information Consortium, University of Colorado, Boulder (Dec. 2003), http://www.beyondintractability.org/essay/distrust.

the intentional, ordinary democratic practices that, through connection, seek to renew and repair trust.[31]

Thankfully, effective leadership can have a multiplier effect. Because leaders are responsible for the decisions of others as well as their own, they can dramatically impact the amount of good they do by encouraging positive action. In addition, in our pluralistic society leadership is widely dispersed throughout various segments and sectors—government, business, nonprofit associations, the professions, communities, and so on. The norms and decisions set by leaders influence numerous people and organizations.

Thus, the troubled state of our democratic polity that ultimately resulted in the January 6th attack has also given rise to new needs and demands from our educational system, including law schools. The legal profession long has been perceived by the public as comprising problem-solvers and leaders, especially in public life. Given the importance of lawyers to our society and the powerful role legal education plays in personal and professional development at a critical stage, academic leaders and faculties have a responsibility to be attentive to society's needs with the utmost seriousness. The next generation of great lawyers must be not just superb legal practitioners but also highly capable leaders ready to operate in a constantly changing, interconnected, and interdependent world. Leadership education complements and enhances legal expertise.

For a long time, a law degree has been regarded as a golden ticket, offering entrée to prestigious, high-profile positions in a wide variety of sectors and fields. Lawyers constitute a disproportionately high proportion of our political leaders, business leaders, and civil society leaders. In fact, no other profession has accounted for more leaders in the public sector. We know that law school graduates will serve in positions of influence at the global, national, regional, local, and even neighborhood level. Whether it be advising international businesses, serving as an officer of a national organization, sitting on a city council, holding elective office, staffing a

---

[31] *See* CAROLYN M. HENDRIKS, SELEN A. ERCAN & JOHN BOSWELL, MENDING DEMOCRACY: DEMOCRACY REPAIR IN DISCONNECTED TIMES (2020).

government office, running a corporation, or administering a government agency: these are all positions of leadership and trust.

Of course, leaders—like anyone else—may behave badly or conduct themselves with distinction. In other words, leaders can behave in ways that are positive and constructive or negative and destructive. In his book *Dangerous Leaders*, Anthony C. Thompson argued that a lack of understanding of leadership may make lawyers dangerously ill-prepared to perform their duties when they reach key decision-making roles.[32] He contended that "lawyers who misunderstand the need to learn how to lead in today's environment will likely . . . engage in dangerous behaviors"[33] associated with bad leaders. We see bad leaders misapplying power, abusing subordinates, covering up mistakes, lying when it suits their purposes, surrounding themselves with sycophants, and distorting reality as a leadership tool. At worst, bad leaders can easily exhibit behaviors—from rigidity and callousness to corruption and cruelty to short-term focus and self-promotion—that lead them to be ineffective or unethical or both.[34] Unethical leadership makes institutions unfair, and people's belief in those institutions diminishes. Ineffective leadership weakens institutional performance and undermines people's confidence in the competence and judgments exercised by the institution.

Leadership education in law schools is critical because it is a fallacy to assume that leadership education and training happens in organizations and institutions. Successful technical or functional experts—like lawyers—are frequently tapped for leadership positions based on their individual contributions and technical competence. However, moving from the role of technical expert to organizational leader is a challenge that, in practice, is complex. Too often new organizational leaders are figuratively thrown into the deep end to sink or swim—to either prove that they are a "natural leader" or to fail miserably and never again try a leadership role. Such an approach is woefully

---

[32] ANTHONY C. THOMPSON, DANGEROUS LEADERS: HOW AND WHY LAWYERS MUST BE TAUGHT TO LEAD (2018).

[33] *Id.* at 149.

[34] *See generally* BARBARA KELLERMAN, BAD LEADERSHIP: WHAT IT IS, HOW IT HAPPENS, WHY IT MATTERS (2004).

outdated and troublesome. Because "the days [of] when a single individual, however gifted, can solve our problems are long gone. The problems we face today come at us so fast and are so complex, that we need groups of talented people to tackle them, led by gifted leaders, or even teams of leaders."[35]

If lawyers are going to continue to step into leadership roles, they must be prepared to provide the kind of leadership our institutions need—to carry out their work in ways that mend democracy by focusing on fairness, equity, reciprocity, and accountability. They must understand that leadership is something beyond individual ambition. Both law and leadership are moral activities, not merely pragmatic exercises in raw power in furtherance of a personal agenda. And they must understand trust sits at the center. As a society, we cannot effectively recommit to our institutions without lawyers leading the way.

E. EDUCATING LAWYERS FOR LEADERSHIP

Virtually all top law schools say they want to develop leaders, whether in a marketing brochure or a stirring commencement address. But intentional, strategic, substantive efforts to do so are still rare. If the curriculum demonstrates what an institution deems most important in an educational program, then it is clear that law schools are not embracing their opportunity to prepare lawyers to be effective leaders. While business schools and public policy schools have long recognized the need to integrate leadership into the core educational program, legal education has largely ignored leadership as a serious subject of study.

Leadership education just might help law students transition into lawyers with the skills, mindset, and orientation to deliver the leadership we so urgently need. As a long-time scholar and teacher of law and leadership, I see five objectives for leadership development in legal education.

First, law students should be made aware of the historic and central roles lawyers have played (and can play) as leaders in a

---

[35] WARREN BENNIS, ON BECOMING A LEADER xviii (2nd ed. 2003).

variety of contexts and sectors. Such case studies can serve as models of how to exercise their own abilities and responsibilities to lead in the future. They also remind us that leaders come in many diverse forms and styles.

Second, students should acquire an understanding of some basic frameworks about effective leadership, become conversant in the dynamic process of leadership, question assumptions about leadership, and begin to see the ways in which it can be a tool to advance justice and serve others rather than just an exercise of power. Such an understanding enables students to both elevate their own leadership competencies and capacities and become better consumers and analyzers of the leadership skills exercised by others.

Third, students should be prompted to consider their professional leadership identities. (What kind of leader do you want to be? How will you show up as a leader? How will you use your talent and skills as a leader?) As part of this activity, students may become inspired to embark on career paths that lead to positions of authority in which they can use their skills, capacities, habits, and desire to serve the common good.

Fourth, a leadership development program should highlight the ethical dimensions of leadership, raising values to a higher level of consciousness and enhancing awareness of how a leader's behavior influences others. (How do you balance personal ambition with fundamental ethics? Are you concerned with what benefits your community/others or in what benefits your prestige/ego? Why do leaders unconsciously overlook serious wrongdoing if it benefits them or their organization?) All too often, professional responsibility in law school focuses almost exclusively on the lawyer-client relationship, ignoring other settings in which lawyer-leaders might face ethical dilemmas.

Finally, leadership development education should foreground developing strong inner character—becoming the kind of person who understands their own guiding principles, who has a deep sense of purposefulness, who exercises self-control, and who stands for personal and institutional integrity.

Understanding these five things helps (at least some) early-career professionals who dream of leadership develop values and habits associated with good leadership, learn to think in institutional terms, and perhaps even begin to develop the character and muscles to exercise courage when the moment calls. It can also equip them with a more sophisticated view of leadership that enables them to see through leaders who exploit distrust, play on bigotry and prejudice, and take society down paths that weaken us.

To be clear, leadership education need not solely be a political goal or one that is limited to lawyers who aspire to work in the public sector. Understanding core elements of thoughtful, productive leadership benefits all who may be entrusted to lead, whether in a law firm, corporation, nonprofit, or government office. Furthermore, an understanding of inspiring a shared vision, fostering collaboration, empowering others, embracing diversity in all its forms, transforming vision into reality, turning obstacles to innovation, forming coherent solutions to genuine problems, and acting with moral courage do not presuppose a preference for any particular government policies or political party. At its core, the law is dependent on a healthy and robust democracy, and academic leaders have a duty to students and society to try to preserve and reinforce the foundational elements essential to our system of government.

Progress in this area cannot be accomplished by simply waving a magic wand over existing courses and saying the word "leadership." It requires law schools to commit to experimentation, to embrace their role in building a sense of purpose and professional identity that includes "leader," and to more broadly develop leadership along with other soft skills and integrate those skills with technical ones. Law schools play an especially important role in helping young lawyers shape their professional identities, but not all educators agree that or understand how law schools can or should undertake the aforementioned responsibilities. Faculties often discount or take for granted legal education's role in leadership development. They assume that such skills cannot be taught, that they are better learnt "in the real world," or that they are acquired naturally alongside the discussion of legal concepts. Yet corporations, the military, and other parts of the academy (e.g., business and public policy schools) have long embraced leadership development as a part of their education and training. Based on my years of experience teaching leadership, I believe that progress in leadership development is possible for any student willing to take the work seriously.[36]

Although higher education is often slow to change, some law schools are acknowledging the need to intentionally expose tomorrow's lawyers to leadership development. For more than fifteen years now at both The Ohio State University and the University of Minnesota law schools, I have led pioneering efforts to integrate leadership education into the law school experience.[37] Yet, a recent study by Professor Leah Witcher Jackson Teague of Baylor Law School revealed that only approximately two dozen of the 200+ U.S. law schools have formally incorporated leadership education into their curricula.[38] Perhaps this latest democratic crisis—which surely won't be the last—will serve as a catalyst for additional schools to consider new, innovative efforts to educate and support lawyers as leaders so we can look to lawyers to help mend our democratic fabric.

Fortunately, if law schools accept the compelling case for leadership development's essential contribution to a comprehensive legal education, it can fit into the curriculum in numerous ways. In fact, there are many diverse and creative examples of curricular approaches and pedagogy, including skills-based, case study, literature, professional responsibility, organizational dynamics, gender and leadership, and many other approaches. In addition, law firms, bar associations, and other professional organizations should join efforts to bring leadership education to lawyers already in practice.

Whatever the future brings, one thing is certain: Trump being out of office will not be nearly enough to restore trust. The changes necessary to achieve it must begin with all citizens and

---

36 *See* Garry W. Jenkins, *Educating Lawyer-Leaders: The Mechanics and Artistry of Case Study Teaching and Discussion Leadership*, 83 TENN. L. REV. 729 (2016). *See also* SHARON DALOZ PARKS, LEADERSHIP CAN BE TAUGHT: A BOLD APPROACH FOR A COMPLEX WORLD (2005).

37 *See* Jenkins, *supra* note 36.

38 *See* Leah Witcher Jackson Teague, *Training Lawyers for Leadership: Vitally Important Mission for the Future Success (and Maybe Survival) of the Legal Profession and Our Democracy*, 58 SANTA CLARA L. REV. 633, 665–72 (2018).

sectors. The underlying conditions that gave rise to January 6th are not going away without thoughtful intervention from various sectors, law included.

F. THE WAY FORWARD

Unfortunately, it seems that trust is easier to shatter than to construct. Without strong leadership, I am not convinced we can find a path forward. Unquestionably, social distrust was a serious problem well before Trump's presidency, but it is also most certainly the case that Trump, especially in the aftermath of the 2020 political campaign and the "Stop the Steal" movement, has made the situation worse. Even more disheartening, Trump has provided a playbook for politicians willing to use distrust to manipulate and activate their bases, one that often involves trading in prejudices and racial hostility, tapping into fears and resentment. So, the consequences of January 6, 2021, may very well haunt us in many ways and for many years to come. While we cannot undo the damage from the deadly Capitol siege, we can either take proactive steps to restore trust across government, business, and civic institutions or succumb to more chaos and conflict. Efforts to address the trust deficit can and must come from many quarters. As a potent pipeline of diverse, talented leaders able to participate in governance, business, and civic life, the legal profession must acknowledge the problem of social trust, understand it, and take steps to remedy it.

Better leadership education in higher education alone cannot prevent mob attacks or rebuild the tears in our democratic fabric. But the gradual loss of public trust does require more attention and more action from those with an interest in democratic institutions and society in general. Without sustained and thoughtful intervention from many directions, public attitudes will likely only worsen. During the global pandemic of 2020–21, society highlighted the role of "essential workers"; lawyers are the essential workers of our democracy. In the 1830s, Alexis de Tocqueville recognized that American lawyers are the protectors of the rule of law in a system of democracy.[39] Perhaps we might benefit if we were to provide these essential guardians of our democracy with a sophisticated understanding of what it means to lead effectively so that we can begin to regain the public's trust in our democratic institutions.

Ultimately, the nation's democratic backsliding reflected in the horrific events of January 6, 2021 highlight many different types of failures, including leadership failures. Accordingly, the development of more and better leaders is important. While such an effort will not magically eradicate all bad leaders or bad followers, I believe it can result in having more of our leaders prioritizing the common good over power and self-interest. It can give us a real chance to strengthen our democratic institutions and diminish the likelihood of future catastrophic leadership failures that culminated in the fatal January 6th Capitol attack. And if those types of events were to happen again, more voices will stand up against them. Just as Watergate pushed the profession and legal education to reconsider how legal professionals are socialized and educated about ethics,[40] perhaps January 6th will prompt us to reconsider how legal professionals are socialized and educated about leadership.

Educating more people about leadership and how it works will make it less likely that our society will be susceptible to leaders who seek to benefit from distrust. Early career leadership education can help law students, in particular, to begin to practice and refine the skills and habits they will need over the course of their careers. In fact, creating leaders who can address trust deficits starts with higher education—it begins with us. Leadership is important not just to our students and their careers but to every organization, societal sector, and community. We need more effective leaders, and we need them now more than ever. Lawyers and the legal profession have long demonstrated their capacity to respond to challenges of the day, and law schools can help them reassert their relevance.

---

[39] 1 ALEXIS DE TOCQUEVILLE, DEMOCRACY IN AMERICA 272–80 (Henry Reeve trans. & Phillips Bradley ed., Vintage Books 1990) (1835).

[40] *See* Deborah L. Rhode, *Ethics by the Pervasive Method*, 42 J. LEGAL EDUC. 31, 39 (1992).

CHAPTER 4

THE RISE OF THE DECANAL COLLECTIVE VOICE

Danielle M. Conway[1]

A. INTRODUCTION

On January 6, 2021, we, as law school deans, found ourselves in an unprecedented moment. The members of the decanal ranks, diverse in every way, collectively experienced insurrection, impeachment, and inauguration—in what will become known undoubtedly as the Three Wednesdays that shuddered American Democracy. This chapter explains one perspective on the rise and the influence of the decanal collective voice that led to the law deans joint statement addressing the 2020 election and the events that took place at the Capitol, which resulted from a shared belief that the rule of law was under assault. This collective voice emerged from shared experiences in the global pandemic, the protests against racial inequality and the relationship-based coalition response to systemic inequality, and the perils of leadership during tumultuous times. This collective voice is a result of the growth in trust relationships between and among deans, the embrace of loyalty to a new vision for the legal profession, and a sense of shared compassion and empathy for one another. In writing about the intimate relationship members of the decanal ranks have developed in this moment, I propose that law school deans

---

[1] Dean and Donald J. Farage Professor of Law at Penn State Dickinson Law. Dean Conway is the co-recipient of the inaugural Association of American Law Schools' (AALS') Impact Award, which honors individuals who have had a significant, positive impact on legal education or the legal profession. Dean Conway received this recognition for her work in establishing the Law Deans Antiracist Clearinghouse Project. Launched in June 2020, the project is a webpage for law deans, faculty and staff, and the public that contains resources and information related to addressing racism in law and legal education. Dean Conway also serves as one of three co-chairs of the Select Penn State Presidential Commission on Racism, Bias, and Community Safety. Dean Conway has been a member of the American Law Institute since 2004. She is a member of the AALS Executive Committee and a member of the Board of Directors of AccessLex Institute. Dean Conway retired from the U.S. Army in the rank of lieutenant colonel after 27 years of combined active, reserve, and national guard service.

speaking in one voice on issues most pressing in our society is, individually and collectively, part of our obligation as lawyers and leaders in the legal academy and in the profession.

The American law school dean is a relatively modern figure in higher education history, as are law schools themselves. Scan any number of law school websites and you will find that individual law schools essentially pay tribute to their respective founders and leaders who have served at the helms of their law schools in only general and often cursory ways. Implicit in this observation is that these leaders have rarely conjured the image of members of a coalition working together, interdependently, in service to the legal academy and the legal profession.

Instead, one can draw on the experiences of the law school dean—prior to the formation of the Association of American Law Schools's (AALS's)[2] Law Deans Steering Committee and the AALS Executive Committee circa 2014—as a siloed venture in which maybe a shifting and changing collection of deans interested in addressing discrete issues impacting their respective institutions formed, at best, transactional, short-lived alliances to achieve desired outcomes. This is not surprising as the law school dean, especially in the latter part of the 20th Century to this very moment, would be wise to remain keenly focused on the all too seemly sole indicator of success—law school rankings, inclusive of median LSAT and uGPA data, employment data, and peer and reputation rankings, to name a few.

The start of the second decade of the 21st Century was met by cataclysmic, calamitous events that created upheaval within the legal academy, the legal profession, and the larger society. These events—a pandemic, the murder of Black and Brown bodies, an assault on facts in a fraught election cycle, and the

[2] *See* About AALS, available at https://www.aals.org/about/ (last visited July 31, 2021). The Association of American Law Schools (AALS) is a nonprofit association with 176 member and 17 fee-paid law schools. "Founded in 1900, the mission of AALS is to uphold and advance excellence in legal education. In support of this mission, AALS promotes the core values of excellence in teaching and scholarship, academic freedom, and diversity, including diversity of backgrounds and viewpoints, while seeking to improve the legal profession, to foster justice, and to serve its many communities—local, national, and international." "[The] AALS has the dual responsibility of serving law schools and their deans as their institutional membership organization, and individual law school faculty and administrators as their learned society."

Capitol insurrection brought on by the specter of white supremacy—upended what many understood the traditional role of the law school dean and, by definition, the entire decanal community to be—the intellectual leader of the law school. With little or no notice, the changes were thrust upon the majority of law school deans who had anticipated nothing more than a traditional tour of duty in the decanal ranks. For a distinct segment of the decanal ranks, however, these types of cataclysmic events amounted to known and knowable subterranean lived experiences that formed part of being racialized, subordinated, oppressed. and othered in America.

For the Black law dean, the events leading up to the Capitol insurrection were no surprise. Why? These events mirrored the racialized backlash of the post-Civil War Reconstruction Era, the many riots fomented by white people such as the 1906 Atlanta Massacre and the 1921 Tulsa Race Massacre, and the state-sponsored racialized violence against the Civil Rights Movement in the 1950s and 1960s, illustrated by "Bloody Sunday" at the Edmund Pettus Bridge in Selma, Alabama. In the hours during the Capitol insurrection, *all* law school deans saw, heard, and understood the role that White America's racism and its tolerance of white supremacy were playing in fueling an attack on America's democratic institutions and the rule of law.

For purposes of unearthing the decanal collective voice it is less important at this juncture to focus on the different paths on which we walked, which have been, up to now, largely as individual, siloed administrators. Now, it is more important to focus on what we all experienced on January 6, 2021, distinct from how we all experienced it. Even more crucial, our collective experience transformed many of us from administrators to leaders armed with a newly found collective power, a newly acknowledged collective obligation, and a newly experienced collective voice, all of which combine to present the potential for a metamorphosis for the legal academy, the legal profession, and for our society.

The intersecting crises of a global pandemic, which continues to disproportionately impact Black and Brown people;[3] a full-throated social movement demanding racial equality following 2020's cascade of murders of, among others, Ahmaud Arbery, Breonna Taylor, George Floyd, and, most recently in 2021, the murder of Daunte Wright by police impunity;[4] and voter suppression efforts across the nation have accelerated the need to address systemic inequities hampering the legal academy's and the legal profession's ability to deliver on the power and the promise of the rule of law to realize the vision of equal justice for all.[5] Law school deans had visceral, individual reactions to these traumatic events and many questioned their responsibility as lawyers and leaders to speak out on behalf of their teaching and learning communities, the larger demos, and on behalf of democracy itself.

Compellingly, these events also caused members of the decanal ranks to look deeply within their respective law schools to discern the role of their own institutions and the role of the legal academy in producing and perpetuating the systemic inequities at the root of the crumbling democratic infrastructure. Specifically, the events of 2020, alone, have given law school deans a stark example of the complicity of law in propping up white hierarchy, structural racism, subjugation, oppression, and inequality. Discussing the landscape of subordination and oppression, generally, and racial inequality, specifically, have been necessary predicates on the road to understanding and appreciating the steps that law deans can take to move their respective law schools away from edifices of structural inequity and toward equity focused institutions.

Each dean's active and interdependent participation in a coalition based on relationships that deploy the power of the decanal collective voice contributes to the transformation of the legal academy, writ large, towards the democratic goal of systemic equity. With a collective voice centered on equity and

---

3 *See* WORLD HEALTH ORGANIZATION, Director-General's opening remarks at the media briefing on COVID-19—11 March 2020, https://www.who.int/director-general/speeches/detail/who-director-general-s-opening-remarks-at-the-media-briefing-on-covid-19---11-march-2020 (last visited Jan. 29, 2021).

4 *See* Larry Buchanan, Quoctrung Bui & Jugal K. Patel, *Black Lives Matter May Be the Largest Movement in U.S. History*, N.Y. TIMES (July 3, 2020), https://www.nytimes.com/interactive/2020/07/03/us/george-floyd-protests-crowd-size.html.

5 *See* Jeffrey Toobin, *Protecting the Vote*, NEW YORKER (Sept. 28, 2020), https://www.newyorker.com/magazine/2020/10/05/ending-trumps-assault-on-the-rule-of-law.

justice, law school deans can focus on the rebuilding of democratic institutions and the strengthening of the rule of law.

B. THE ORGANIC FORMATION OF THE COLLECTIVE VOICE

Shortly after I began my deanship in 2015, I was fortunate to be invited to serve on the AALS Law Dean's Steering Committee. The composition and work of the committee are defined succinctly as being "comprised of 15 law school deans, [ ] charged with addressing the national impact of topics affecting law schools." The type of service I observed and participated in was collegial, yet predominantly transactional. I describe it as transactional largely because the work and even the consensus to act together was done to accomplish a task, respond to a particular challenge, or to address and attempt to resolve a specific issue. In the sense that the governing body of deans joined together as a group seeking consensus, that consensus was to either maintain a status quo or to achieve some incremental advantage for the majority of the law schools within the academy. If I were to give a name to describe the relationship of these law deans vis-à-vis the issues that came before the steering committee, I would land on the term "transactional coalition."[6]

I would define a transactional coalition as a group of members or organizations assembled for a discrete purpose to pursue a mutually beneficial goal or objective. In a transactional coalition, members or organizations often represent different

---

6 *Compare* Tiziana Casciaro, Amy C. Edmondson, and Sujin Jang, *Cross-Silo Leadership*, May–June 2019 HARV. BUS. REV. 130–139 (discussing the importance of breaking down silos to help people collaborate across boundaries by, among other things, valuing horizontal interface collaborations that encourage members of diverse teams to proactively take on the perspectives of others) *and* Arthur T. Himmelman, *On Coalitions and the Transformation of Power Relations: Collaborative Betterment and Collaborative Empowerment*, 29, 2 AM. J. CMTY. PSYCHOL. 277, 278, 284 (opining that transformation from collaborative betterment coalitions to collaborative empowerment coalitions could occur by reformulating coalition power relationships, by providing opportunities for members to practice becoming more powerful in a democratic manner and growing comfortable with the responsibility and accountability to others that democratic power requires) *with* MARIAME KABA, WE DO THIS 'TIL WE FREE US: ABOLITIONIST ORGANIZING AND TRANSFORMING JUSTICE pp. 175, 178–80 (stating "[c]ommunity matters. Collectivity matters. . . . If we can't get along with each other, then what the hell are we doing? If anybody is listening to this . . . please be part of the community of folks who are building an accountable community with each other. . . because what matters is . . . developing stronger relationships.").

interests; yet members, after performing a cost benefit analysis, make determinations that the net interests to them or their organizations are best served by joining with others to pursue a specific outcome. With a transactional coalition, the probability is high that certain members will leave the coalition or become passive in their advocacy at that point when such members achieve their respective purpose for joining the coalition. This point on the coalition spectrum can be referred to as the point of inflection when interest convergence ceases, and members are faced with a decision matrix that places themselves or the institutions they represent before the interests of the coalition.

Another view of a transactional coalition is the use of coalition resources to address a specific issue impacting only a segment of the membership of the coalition. What separates this approach to coalition building and maintenance from a more personal, more invested coalition—what I will introduce later in this chapter as a relationship-based coalition—is a long-view commitment to a transformational vision of change for all coalition members and the institutions they represent. Relationship-based coalitions rely on transformational leadership of a collective in which each member is invested in achieving, not their own objectives exclusively, but the objectives of other members in the coalition. Consequently, some members of the coalition may commit relationally, while other members of the coalition will only commit transactionally. This renders the entire coalition minimally transactional in nature once the coalition efforts reach the point of inflection. It is equally possible that members can move in and out of a transactional coalition based on the specific task or issue, but this kind of plug and play partnership has the potential to minimize trust between and among coalition partners, reduce the effectiveness of advocacy on task-related efforts not to mention transformational change efforts, and delimit future progress when coalition action is most necessary.

One example of transactional coalition building was the work of the deans steering committee in response to the California Task Force on Admissions Regulation

Recommendations.[7] The State Bar of California proposed an additional requirement for admission to the California Bar, specifically competency training that would require applicants to have 15-credit hours of specified experiential learning. The Deans Steering Committee expertly responded to the recommendations that would have impacted California law schools as well as students attending law school outside of California but who would be required to meet the proposed requirement if they intended to seek admission to the California Bar.

I refer to this advocacy as transactional along the coalition continuum because the deans steering committee was not speaking for all law deans and their respective institutions in responding to the specific issue of a competency training requirement in California. As well, while the requirement likely could have had negative impacts on non-California deans and their institutions, there was not a call from the whole of the legal academy to support the California deans in their advocacy directed at reconsideration of the competency requirement for admission. Within the deans steering committee itself, however, a camaraderie was palpable and inspirational.

These deans were dialed in to layers of information that allowed them to discern the ramifications that the California admissions recommendation would have on innovation in the legal academy, the career choices of students and graduates, and the overall access to justice and rule of law implications for the larger society. That said, this information was not being accessed by the entire community making up the decanal ranks, either because some law schools were regional in their focus, while other law schools may have already transitioned their curriculum to a similar requirement, or because some law schools were focused on merely surviving through deficit existences caused by the recession of 2008 and the negative impact of the national downturn in admissions. Far from casting aspersions on law deans and their institutions for not moving beyond a transactional coalition stance, this example exposes far

---

[7] *See* AALS Deans Steering Committee Issues Statement on the California Task Force on Admissions Regulation Recommendations, available at https://www.aals.org/tfarr-statement/ (last visited, May 30, 2021).

greater issues that lent themselves to a relationship-based approach to collective action on behalf of the entire academy—namely the relentless assault on law schools during and after the 2008 recession.

The beginning of 2020 was like most others for the legal academy. Faculty and Deans gathered at the AALS annual meeting in Washington, D.C. and engaged intellectually and operationally on the standard issues du jour. The time leading up to the full appreciation of the pandemic in March 2020 still did not change that posture significantly. Most deans were thrown into the deep water of responding to the unknowns of the pandemic and how this soon to be revealed long-term crisis would impact their respective programs of legal education. The AALS and several deans, faculty, and staff members authored a website and a report that "organized documents, resources, and information related to legal education and the legal profession to help law faculty, students, and staff plan for classes and operations during the coronavirus pandemic."[8] The act of pulling these resources together was one of important service to the legal academy to assist law schools in remaining current on the effects of the pandemic on teaching and learning, specifically providing information "regarding admissions tests, the bar exam, college reopening, federal aid, online teaching, and student loans."[9]

Without question, the work pulling these resources together was critical in supporting deans as they led their respective law schools during the beginning of the pandemic. Equally without question, law school leaders experienced many of the same challenges across the board owing to the universal nature of the harm and disruption caused by the pandemic and the national leadership response thereto, but the work of the law deans remained generally an individual exercise falling short of even a transactional approach to responding to the pandemic. One

[8] *See* AALS Legal Education in the Time of COVID-19, available at https://www.aals.org/covid19/ (last visited May 31, 2021).

[9] *See* AALS Adds News & Information Related to COVID-19, available at https://www.aals.org/about/publications/newsletters/aals-news-spring-2020/aals-adds-news-information-related-to-covid-19/ (last visited May 31, 2021).

exception though was the cross-siloed collaboration[10] between the authors of the "The Bar Exam and the COVID-19 Pandemic: The Need for Immediate Action."[11] In this work, the authors saw an immediate and looming challenge to one of the most significant functions of the partnership between the legal academy and the legal profession—the administration of the high-stakes, gatekeeping function that is the bar examination. The authors rightly assessed that "[a]ttempting to administer the bar examination to hundreds of test-takers in a single room would endanger the test takers, staff administering the exam, and the public health."[12] This joint work and the attention that it garnered offered a glimpse at the potential for law deans to move beyond siloed leadership through and possibly past a transactional coalition.

On the heels of the nascent stages of this work to move from siloed leadership to something more, a Black man, a father, a life partner, a brother, and a community member named George Floyd was killed by Minneapolis police officer Derek Chauvin. The world witnessed this murder, as it was clearly captured by mobile phone video. We relived the 9 minutes and 29 seconds through continuous news cycles, protest rallies, social media engagements, documentaries about disproportionate police contact with Black and Brown communities, and during the criminal prosecution of Derek Chauvin. What was different about this murder of a Black man was context, both past and present. The past contexts, of course, were the many Black bodies slain before George Floyd's murder. Just two and one-half months before, Breonna Taylor was killed after police entered her apartment under color of a no-knock warrant and began firing their weapons in the premises. This horrific incident took place on the same day that President Trump finally announced a pandemic lock down in the United States.

---

[10] *See* Tiziana Casciaro, Amy C. Edmondson, and Sujin Jang, *Cross-Silo Leadership*, available at https://hbr.org/2019/05/cross-silo-leadership (last visited May 31, 2021).

[11] *See* Claudio Angelos, et al., *The Bar Exam and the COVID-19 Pandemic: The Need For Immediate Action*, available at https://papers.ssrn.com/sol3/papers.cfm?abstract_id=3559060 (last visited, May 31, 2021).

[12] *See id.* at 1.

The Black Lives Matter (BLM) social movement against racial inequality seemed to catalyze around these events, bringing sharp focus to police plunder of Black and Brown bodies, which came to a head on May 25, 2020. After George Floyd's murder, people from all walks of life joined BLM in protesting racial inequality. Knowledge that the pandemic was having a disproportionate impact on Black and Brown bodies coincided unmistakably with the disproportionate police contact that these same Black and Brown bodies had long been experiencing. Many people have asked why this was the time that drew attention to this data. I postulate that the pandemic's isolation effects drew us farther into social media use and that the capture of the murder of George Floyd pulled us deeper into the vortex of the reality of the harms of structural inequality (the disproportionate impact of the pandemic on oppressed and subordinated people) and systemic inequality (murder of Black bodies by police under the color of law).

Law deans were among the groups of people who bore witness to this plunder. As one very special set of leaders in the legal profession, law deans individually felt the weight of the American system of laws' hand in what was unfolding after George Floyd's murder. Several of us felt the pangs of law's complicity in these cascading tragedies. I recall feeling both sick and betrayed by yet another on the long list of Black bodies stolen from this world too soon and too horrifically. As well, I recall feeling oddly vindicated for legitimately loathing the acts of those who would manipulate the rule of law that is, in theory, meant to belong to all of us, especially those most vulnerable in our society.

Upon learning about George Floyd's murder, I, as a Black woman, felt keenly my own sense of vulnerability. I also felt paralyzed in my grief and by my fear for my family, specifically for my Black husband and Black son. In that grief, I reached out to four of my dean colleagues—Angela Onwuachi-Willig, Kim Mutcherson, Carla Pratt, and Danielle Holley-Walker—Black women who were living my experience. The first of many of our conversations that weekend were about our shared disgust over the killing of yet another Black body. We listened to one another's grief, sorrow, anger, fear, and outrage over yet one more body piled on top of thousands of bodies in graves, hanging from trees, dragged by chains, shot in the back, beaten, dismembered, and disfigured. And then our attention turned to our positions as deans of law schools and the odd task we were being asked to perform—the "message to community."

The five of us on that weekend call pondered and pushed back on whether and how to approach the seemingly dreaded task of drafting a message to our respective communities about the murder of George Floyd, the death count in the wake of the pandemic, and the path forward for our next moments, not to mention the next month, and the remainder of the year. As the weekend closed and Monday morning loomed, we each knew we as leaders had to marshal the strength and courage to address with our respective communities the breaches of humanity to which we were all being subjected. We wrote our messages to our communities, not just Black women law deans but the overwhelming majority of all law deans. Whether prompted by whomever wrote first, second, or third, the messages to community surfaced.

During the surfacing of these messages to community, I continued to feel unmoored by the events that seemed to be overtaking all of us. I reached out to a trusted leader, LSAC President and CEO Kellye Testy. We were just checking on each other and she asked me how I was doing. Well, my anguish poured out of me. I shared the disgust I felt over the racialized killings of Black men, women, and children. I shared the disgust of having to write messages to my law school community about the law's role in ensuring equal justice for all when what was really on display was law's complicity in propping up systemic inequality and oppression. I shared the disgust of attempting to make sense of the dismantling of our democratic institutions to justify what we were teaching in our respective programs of legal education. At almost the same time, I had inquired on our deans' listserv how we might come together as law deans to attempt to address, collectively, the harms that we were all experiencing, including the racialized killings, the loss of life from the pandemic, and the assault on civil rights and our democratic institutions. The immediate response from my query to the deans' listserv was the trickling in of copies of individual messages from deans about "the message" each wrote to their communities, which I must admit was off-putting.

With empathy and compassion, Kellye Testy advised me to speak with AALS Executive Director Judy Areen about my visceral and negative reactions to the messages that were being posted. Judy Areen also listened with empathy and compassion and toward the end of the call she asked me if I would consider developing a website that could possibly catalogue the deans' messages to community. I said I would take up the task. In an almost instinctive reflex, I began to scope out a draft presentation to share with the four Black women law deans whom I had been commiserating with the week before. What I now realize I was doing was creating a coalition among these Black women law deans to begin a process of regaining my strength, power, and voice by trusting others enough to expose my vulnerabilities to them. Within two days of meeting, sharing, trusting, collaborating, crying, and laughing together, the five of us—Black women law deans—conceived of something much more than a collection of web accessible resources meant to address racism, oppression, and subordination.

Out of our grief, pain, and anguish, we found the strength to develop the AALS Law Deans Antiracist Clearinghouse Project.[13] I would mark the publication of this Project as the first real step in pushing past siloed leadership and transactional coalitions to forging a path toward relationship-based coalitions. Such relationship-based coalition building was and is made possible by a new understanding of our interdependence as leaders of law schools.

The distinctiveness of the AALS Law Deans Antiracist Clearinghouse Project lay in its scope to encompass every law school dean in the process of moving the entire legal academy away from complicity in propping up systemic inequity by maintaining a status quo that privileges white people and disadvantages people of color. The goal of the Project was to establish a baseline for action as opposed to being merely an archive to house messages to law school communities about the visible injustice of the murder of George Floyd. In this way, the

---

[13] *See* AALS Law Deans Antiracist Clearinghouse Project, available at https://www.aals.org/antiracist-clearinghouse/ (last visited June 2, 2021).

approach to the Project created a pathway for explicitly acknowledging the collective power of the decanal voice. Specifically, it was one thing to individually write to one's community about the violation of George Floyd's civil and human rights yet quite another thing to acknowledge our role as lawyers and leaders pledging action to both eradicate racialized violence and to actively commit the resources of our institutions to promote antiracist teaching and learning.

It was this moment that crystallized for me that law is itself a construct, which depends on human beings to draw out its power to protect people and communities from injustices. Without a relationship-based collective, especially within the legal profession, to leverage that power for the common good, the next generation of lawyers and leaders will inherit the same social maladies, such as systemic racism and white supremacy, that currently plague our democratic institutions. The insurrection of January 6, 2021, and the social unrest we experienced in 2020 forced law school deans and the AALS to reckon with the unmistakable connection between structural racism, white supremacy, and the attack on the rule of law. Like it or not, law school deans are on the front lines of the battle for a stronger rule of law, a battle that is far more significant than law school rankings and one that is crucially dependent on a relationship-based coalition among decanal colleagues to preserve the democratic institutions that are our law schools, the training ground for future lawyers and leaders.

I was encouraged in my belief that a relationship-based coalition was possible among my decanal colleagues when I saw an overwhelming majority of them embracing the teaching and learning embedded in the AALS Law Deans Antiracist Clearinghouse Project. Specifically, based upon feedback from the AALS, the Clearinghouse Project has been the most visited page on the AALS website. When law school deans engaged the iterative process of the AALS Law Deans Antiracist Clearinghouse Project—listening, learning, leading, audit reporting, and iterating solutions—many implicitly acknowledged and supported the democratic principle of equality, as manifested in the form of antiracism. Law school deans activated their collective voice by shepherding faculty and institution antiracist resolutions to adoption, endorsing the Project by transforming their respective messages to community into messages of solidarity for antiracism, and committing their institutions to actively engaging in antiracism teaching and learning by performing one or more of the five steps set forth by the Project. The Clearinghouse Project captures the shift from siloed leadership to an embrace of the collective voice and a commitment to relationship-based coalition building with this following passage:

> By creating a space for our collective voices as leaders of law schools to engage our institutions in the fight for justice and equality, we strive to focus our teaching, scholarship, service, activism, programming, and initiatives on strategies to eradicate racism.
>
> To engage as Antiracists, we must listen and learn from each other's experiences, lead our communities by example, audit our schools to ensure progress toward racial equality (with an understanding that race cannot be neatly segregated from socioeconomic class), influence policy, and iterate our commitment to the fight for racial equality, all to demonstrate our resolve to eradicate racism in the United States.[14]

The actions of the law deans clearly fall into the category of collective action because so many of our decanal colleagues acted on behalf of others, for example, standing in solidarity with students especially those negatively impacted by the murder of George Floyd, standing with faculty colleagues who've been negatively impacted by the pandemic, and standing with decanal colleagues through the exercise of deference, support, and solidarity as these colleagues established a leadership stance that offered one example of the kind of antiracist response that could come from the legal academy. The relationship-based coalition building by and among these decanal colleagues across the inequality-equality, disadvantaged-privilege, and nonexclusive-elite spectra brought into focus how we as leaders could work across institutional affiliations to address the universal role of the legal academy and the legal profession to

[14] *See id.*

uphold fundamental democratic ideals for all and reimagine our obligation to contribute to society by transforming our own institutions to be more just and more equitable.

C. EXTENDING THE COLLECTIVE VOICE

On January 6, 2021, our Temple of Democracy was besieged and defiled by lawless mobs and rioters. They terrorized fellow Americans, public servants, and Capitol police officers. I watched over and over the video of a Black Capitol police officer exercising heroic restraint in not brandishing his weapon on the mob of white men chasing him up the stairs of the Capitol. It was later confirmed that he was leading the mob away from the Chamber in which our elected officials were barricading themselves inside for protection from the insurrectionists. This scene and the many other criminal acts committed at the Capitol that day represent an inexcusable breach of our social contract, a debasement of our system of laws, and a violation of our shared humanity. As Republican Senator Pat Toomey stated: "[This is what happens when] [m]en in power refuse to acknowledge the truth."[15]

The insurrection at the Capitol stood in stark contrast to the peaceful voter turnout for the November 2020 election cycle. While voter suppression tactics were deployed throughout the year, there was no mistaking the historic voter engagement of the American populace during this election cycle. It cannot go unrecognized the role that Stacey Abrams, a lawyer and a leader, and the voters in Georgia played in decisively bending the arc of justice toward universal suffrage in furtherance of our democracy. We must applaud the long-term vision of attorney Stacey Abrams in leading the effort to transform Georgia into a competitive purple state. From these efforts, Reverend Raphael Warnock became the first African-American man from the State of Georgia to be elected to the United States Senate. Thomas Jon Ossoff, a former intern of the late Congressman John Lewis, became only the second Jewish candidate to win a statewide election in Georgia. We must recognize the thread that runs

---

[15] *See* Associated Press, *Romney: 'The best way we could show respect for the voters who are upset is by telling them the truth,'* available at https://www.abc4.com/news/politics/romney-the-best-way-we-could-show-respect-for-the-voters-who-are-upset-is-by-telling-them-the-truth/ (last visited July 31, 2021).

through these Americans—an unwavering commitment to guarantee the voting franchise for all and to upholding our democracy. These voters and elected officials have breathed new life into American democracy by demonstrating how to *lawfully* resist voter suppression, systemic inequality, subordination, and oppression.

Frederick Douglass, when writing about his part in discerning and affecting history during the final road to disunion (1859–1861) said that "nations are taught less by theories than by facts and events."[16] Each of us lived through the facts and events that took place on January 6, 2021, and we cannot dis- or mis-remember them. Our obligations as lawyers, leaders, and American citizens require that we take stock of the facts and events that unfolded on January 6 and draw our line in the sand. On January 12, 2021, the overwhelming majority of law school deans did just that. Using the power of the relationship-based coalition formed earlier in the year, law school deans—171 strong—released a joint statement addressing the 2020 election and the events that took place at the Capitol.[17] The joint statement marks a rare occasion: it is unusual for such a diverse group of law deans to come together to speak as one on an issue that falls outside the specific ambit of legal education. Be it rare, having previously taken a stand in support of racial justice, law school deans reaffirmed their commitment to a relationship-based coalition to lead our academy and, to some extent, our profession in transforming our democracy, especially because legal education plays such a significant role in forming the identity of lawyers who are in positions that have an outsized impact on our democracy. Law school deans chose truth, freedom, democracy, and humanity. Using our collective voice, we stated, and I quote, in part:

> We are deans of a diverse range of law schools across the country. We do not use our positions to advance our individual views. But we do have an obligation to support the rule of law and preserve the integrity of the

---

[16] *See* DAVID W. BLIGHT, FREDERICK DOUGLASS: PROPHET OF FREEDOM, p. 310 (Simon & Schuster, 2018).

[17] *See* Law Deans' Joint Statement on the Election and Events at the Capitol, available at Microsoft Word—Law Deans Joint Statement, 1.12.21 final.docx (yale.edu) (last visited, June 2, 2021).

> legal profession. On rare occasions, despite our differing situations and views, that obligation requires us to speak as one to defend the fundamental commitments of our profession. This is such a moment.
>
> The violent attack on the Capitol was an assault on our democracy and the rule of law. The effort to disrupt the certification of a free and fair election was a betrayal of the core values that undergird our Constitution. Lives were lost, the seat of our democracy was desecrated, and our country was shamed. . . .
>
> As law deans, our mission is to train the next generation of leaders to uphold the core values of our profession and sustain the rule of law. This should be a moment of reflection for legal educators and members of the legal profession. A sustained effort will be necessary to repair and preserve our precious democratic institutions. As legal educators and lawyers ourselves, we must redouble our efforts to restore faith in the rule of law and the ideals of the legal profession. We have enormous faith in the law's enduring values and in our students, who will soon lead this profession. We call upon all members of the legal profession to join us in the vital work ahead.[18]

My truth is embedded in this collective statement. I am an American, a patriot, and a military veteran who watched in disgust the shamefulness of the events that transpired on January 6, 2021. In spite of those shameful acts, I remain an American. I am emboldened to breathe my patriotism and the patriotism of my ancestors into our nation. I commit to being a part of the collective to beat back this coup by embracing even more fiercely the power and the promise of the rule of law. I do this, in part, to honor my colleagues and friends who comprise our relationship-based coalition. As always, my duty is to defend the United States Constitution, to promote the rule of law, and to represent the most vulnerable among us. I look forward to continuing to serve this coalition as we join others to rebuild and transform our American democracy.

---

[18] *See id.*

D. EPILOGUE TO THE INSURRECTION

Regardless of where we lead, where we teach, where we learn, or where we live, the acts of violence that ensued at the United States Capitol on January 6, 2021, have affected all of us. What we experienced with the Capitol insurrection and calamitous crises in 2020 serve as a hard lesson to all law school deans that the once siloed nature of our positions as leaders should be seriously considered when guiding our actions and decision-making. While we are leaders of our individual institutions, we have a duty to know where we must land on the coalition-building spectrum and when we must act together in solidarity to face crucible events that threaten our democratic institutions, the legal profession, and the rule of law.

As law school deans, we used our collective voice to issue a call to action to all lawyers and law students to defend the values of the legal profession after the Capitol insurrection. We spoke as one because we were and remain committed to a relationship-based coalition to restore faith in the rule of law. We spoke as one because we recognized that it is an honor to teach about the power and the promise of the rule of law, the lawyer's obligation to defend the United States Constitution, and our solemn obligation to represent and serve the most vulnerable among us. With our collective voice, we pledged to stand together as law students, members of the legal academy, members of the legal profession, and members of the judiciary to uphold these obligations and to work alongside our elected officials, our communities, and our democratic institutions to repair the damage that has been done to our American democracy.

Law has the power to protect individuals and their communities by drawing on core values such as liberty, equality, equity, inclusiveness, and fairness. With a focus on these core values, the fundamental purpose of the law—to foster an organized, civilized society—offers one of the best opportunities for collective community engagement and progress. There is much work to be done by the members of our relationship-based coalition. We must support one another in coalition, and we must grow this relationship-based coalition by continuing to promote the value of the rule of law to every member of our society.

CHAPTER 5

REFLECTIONS ON THE POST-2020 ELECTION CHALLENGES: ON THE CRITICAL IMPORTANCE OF GOOD FAITH AND EVIDENCE

Jennifer L. Mnookin[1]

On January 12th, 2021, more than 170 law school deans came together to issue a brief, but strongly worded statement about the 2020 election and its aftermath, including the many legal challenges to the election and the January violent attack on the United States Capitol.

This statement read, in part:

> Many lawyers and judges worked honestly and in good faith, often in the face of considerable political pressure, to ensure the 2020 election was free and fair. However, we recognize with dismay and sorrow that some lawyers challenged the outcome of the election with claims that they did not support with facts or evidence. This betrayed the values of our profession. Our profession demands that when lawyers pursue legal action, they must bring claims in good faith, grounded in facts and evidence, and demonstrate respect for the legal system. Only then can lawyers fulfill their responsibilities as lawyers and public citizens to promote public confidence in the rule of law and the justice system—duties that extend to all professional activities, whether lawyers are representing a client or not. The rule of law is as much a touchstone of our profession as it is of our Constitution.

---

[1] Dean and Ralph and Shirley Shapiro Professor of Law, UCLA School of Law. Thanks to Dean Mark Alexander both for leading this project and for very thoughtful comments and suggestions. I also thank UCLA law librarian Rachel Green, Phillip Raucci and Juan Dawson for helpful research assistance.

> As law deans, our mission is to train the next generation of leaders to uphold thc core values of our profession and sustain the rule of law. This should be a moment of reflection for legal educators and members of the legal profession.[2]

In this short essay, I write as both a law school dean and evidence scholar, to take up the invitation of our joint deans' statement that we make these election lawsuits and the collective responses to them a moment of reflection for legal educators. Unlike some of the essays in this volume, I do not focus directly on the insurrection attempt on January 6th, 2021 and the attack on the Capitol. My focus, instead, is primarily on the lawsuits and disinformation campaign that largely preceded (and enabled) it, and continued on well-afterwards as well.

The specific sentences from our letter that spur my reflections are: "that some lawyers challenged the outcomes of the election with claims that they did not support with facts or evidence," and that "our profession demands" that lawyers "bring claims in good faith, grounded in facts and evidence."

Surely we need a commitment to "good faith, grounded in facts and evidence," to be a core principle for the lawyers who bring cases to court and for the judges who rule on them, and we need it to be equally central within our classrooms as we try to help our students learn to 'think like lawyers' and forge their professional identities. In some sense this seems obvious, almost trivially so; it is foundational to the idea of rule of law.

But what does it mean to bring good faith—and evidence—to one's engagement with law and the legal system, whether as a litigant, a judge, or a student of law? And how do we even know if someone is engaging in good faith? More specifically, with respect to the numerous post-2020 presidential election challenges, in particular, how do we distinguish between a weak but legitimate lawsuit, and a case brought in troubling bad faith? And more generally, as legal educators, how do we help our students understand the difference between the two?

---

2 *Law Deans Joint Statement on the 2020 Election and Events at the Capitol* (Jan. 12, 2021), https://law.yale.edu/sites/default/files/documents/pdf/law_deans_joint_statement_1.12.21_final.pdf. I was one of the 170+ deans who signed the statement.

It would be easy—but in my view, quite mistaken—to believe that the post-election lawsuits were brought in something other than good faith simply because they virtually all lost. Not so. There is a place for bringing suits or claims not at all likely to win. In addition, there are plenty of times when judges' rulings may be, quite simply, wrong. The bare fact of losing, and even consistent, unambiguous legal losses across multiple jurisdictions, ought not to be treated as strong evidence that the litigants were acting in bad faith, nor even that their arguments and evidence are lacking in merit and that their losses are justified.

And yet, in what follows, I *do* want to suggest that these post-election cases were almost entirely lacking in merit. The issue is not that they all lost, but rather, that in most instances, the plaintiffs failed to mount any genuinely serious effort at even trying to persuade the judges of their position. While this essay will not endeavor to unpack the more-than-five-dozen cases in great detail, I will illustrate that a number of these lawsuits made disingenuous, blatantly self-serving efforts to modify election policies that had gone into effect well before the election itself (and to which the plaintiffs lodged no objection until after the election occurred). Perhaps worse, most of these lawsuits went forward with a shocking absence of grounded, plausible, evidence, an almost unfathomable absence of evidence considering the gravity of accusations made and remedies requested. And a legal case brought in good faith ought to have some plausible basis in evidence.

The good news is that judges from all over the political spectrum—including several Trump nominees to the federal courts—squarely rejected these unfounded and substanceless claims. For anyone who takes an extreme legal realist view that judicial reasoning is literally nothing but politics and individual preferences, that judges' holdings simply express those preferences and that their so-called reasoning is nothing more than an after-the-fact justification of those preferences, these cases and their unanimity thus pose something of a challenge. (Or they at least reveal that our nation's judges of virtually any and every political bent appear to be more committed to some basic, rudimentary rule-of-law values (perhaps we can even call them 'good-faith' values?), such as 'evidence is required,' than exclusively to their first order political preferences.)

The less good news is that delving into the details of these cases (and the judicial responses to them) invites the clear and overwhelming inference that they truly were not brought in good faith—that is to say, not born of sincere efforts to persuade the courts to take the action requested.[3] And I say this as someone temperamentally rather loathe to make accusations of bad faith—indeed, I deeply believe that just as students of law need to understand that judges can be wrong, and must learn to find weaknesses, logical gaps and motivated reasoning within a judicial opinion, they also, simultaneously, need to learn to read opinions sympathetically, trying to understand how and why the judge justifies her conclusion, even, perhaps especially, when that conclusion seems legally or morally or factually wrong.

And yet, loathe though I may be as a general matter to leap to ascribe bad faith to legal actors with whom I disagree, in these post-election lawsuits, the label fits. For in these cases, it seems as if the real audience for the lawsuits was not even primarily the courts at all, but rather the public, or at least a significant swath of Trump voters (and, most likely, Republican electoral and legislative officials too). The lawsuits themselves were so very weak, in both legal basis and evidentiary foundation, that read collectively, they invite the inference that their real purpose was not their ostensible one. It seems quite plausible that they were brought less out of any sincere hope of achieving the actual, requested legal remedies, and more for the purpose of sowing further public distrust and doubt about the fundamental legitimacy of the election and our voting systems. These lawsuits were thus continuing a dangerous, false narrative that President Trump had been seeding for many months, a narrative that helped spur the storming of the Capitol on January 6th.

---

[3] I recognize I am using the phrase 'bad faith' somewhat loosely, and further, that by using it at all, I am participating within a long tradition and practice of believing that those with whom we disagree strongly are operating in bad faith. For a thoughtful exploration of bad faith and what it means in Constitutional Law, *see* David Pozen, *Constitutional Bad Faith*, 129 HARV. L. REV. 885, 917 (2016) (exploring the lack of focus on bad faith and its meaning within constitutional law doctrine, while recognizing that it is a "time-honored tradition of American constitutionalism that nearly every sect believes the other sects are operating in bad faith.").

Before we turn to the spate of post-election lawsuits themselves, we need to go back to earlier in 2020 and trace some of the rhetoric that preceded the election. Recall that many months prior to the 2020 election, then-President Trump repeatedly attacked mail-in voting in tweets, at his rallies, and in interviews. Back in May 2020, for example, he tweeted, "There is NO WAY (ZERO!) that Mail-In Ballots will be anything less than substantially fraudulent. Mail boxes will be robbed, ballots will be forged & even illegally printed out & fraudulently signed."[4] He called mail-in voting a "catastrophic disaster" that he claimed opened the door to foreign influence in the election.[5] He falsely asserted that states like Nevada do not require any signature verification on mail-in ballots, and that unsolicited ballots were going to be sent by states like California even to non-citizens.[6] As the election drew closer, the drumbeat of these assertions grew in intensity. Trump frequently proclaimed that the only way he would lose the election is if it were "rigged" or "stolen" because of fraud. He tweeted that the upcoming election "will be the most INACCURATE & FRAUDULENT Election in history." In the weeks and months going into the election, the President of the United States repeatedly emphasized the supposed dangers of mail-in-voting (never mind that he used it himself!),[7] voicing regular and insistent doubts about whether the 2020 election could be "honest," calling mail-in ballots "a disaster" and "a whole big scam."[8] He also refused to commit to

---

4 Even Fox News noted in reporting on this tweet that he cited no evidence for his claim. Paul Steinhauser, *Trump Charges Voting by Mail Will Result in "Rigged Election,"* FOX NEWS (May 26, 2020), https://www.foxnews.com/politics/trump-charges-voting-by-mail-will-result-in-rigged-election.

5 Tara Subramaniam & Holmes Lybrand, *Fact-Checking Trump's Continued Assault on Mail-In Voting and Suggestions of Delaying the Election*, CNN (July 30, 2020), https://www.cnn.com/2020/07/30/politics/trump-delay-election-fact-check/index.html.

6 Eugene Kiely & Rem Rieder, *Trump's Repeated False Attacks on Mail-In Ballots*, FACTCHECK (Sept. 25, 2020), https://www.factcheck.org/2020/09/trumps-repeated-false-attacks-on-mail-in-ballots/.

7 *See, e.g.*, Jordan Fabian, *Trump, First Lady Cast Votes by Absentee Ballot for Midterms*, HILL (Nov. 2, 2018), https://thehill.com/homenews/administration/414549-trump-first-lady-cast-votes-by-absentee-ballot-for-midterms; Eric Lutz, *Trump: Mail-In Voting Is "Horrible" Except When I Do It*, VANITY FAIR (Apr. 8, 2020), https://www.vanityfair.com/news/2020/04/trump-mail-in-voting-is-horrible-except-when-i-do-it.

8 Trump made all of these comments in August or September of 2020. *See* Nick Niedzwiadek, *The 9 Most Notable Comments Trump Has Made About Accepting the Election Results*, POLITICO (Sept. 24, 2020), https://www.politico.com/news/2020/09/24/trump-casts-doubt-2020-election-integrity-421280.

a peaceful transfer of power after the election. And he asserted, fully six weeks before the election occurred, that he expected the election to end up in the Supreme Court, presaging his pre-election anticipation of post-election lawsuits should the ballots not go his way.[9]

The broader context in which his messaging took place, of course, included the widespread belief that mail-in ballots would likely tilt Democratic rather than Republican, given both party demographics and the fact that this election was to occur in the midst of a global pandemic which had itself been significantly politicized along party lines—and with a postal service facing its own challenges.

Now, fast forward to election night. In several swing states, including, Georgia, Florida, Michigan, Pennsylvania and Wisconsin, Trump had an 'early lead' as returns came in. Were these voting patterns representative of the state's electorate as a whole, or would they instead turn out to be 'red mirages,' the appearance of greater electoral strength by the Republicans than the total results would provide? (To be clear, there can be 'blue mirages' as well—the point is simply that early results do not necessarily accurately forecast the overall state total.)

It is worth noting that in the latter three of these states, Republican state legislators had blocked recent bills that would have permitted pre-election day processing of mail-in votes, a practice already in place in a number of other states, and viewed by many across the political spectrum as a sensible idea, especially given the expectation of a substantially greater quantity of mail-in ballots due to the pandemic.[10] This procedural decision to prohibit the processing or counting of high volumes of mail-in votes until after the polls closed all but ensured that early vote counts in these states would tilt more heavily Republican than those processed later, and,

---

[9] Michael Crowley, *Trump Won't Commit to 'Peaceful' Post-Election Transfer of Power*, N.Y. TIMES (Sept. 23, 2020), https://www.nytimes.com/2020/09/23/us/politics/trump-power-transfer-2020-election.html.

[10] Eric Cortellessa, *Republicans Are Slowing Down Mailed-In Vote Counts in Key Swing States*, WASH. MONTHLY (Sept. 30, 2020), https://washingtonmonthly.com/2020/09/30/republicans-are-slowing-down-the-counting-of-mailed-in-votes-in-key-swing-states/.

furthermore, that complete vote counting would take considerable time beyond election day.

In the wee hours of the morning following election day, Biden said he was "on track" to win the Presidency, but that the public needed "to be patient until the hard work of tallying votes is finished."[11] Meanwhile, Trump asserted "We are up BIG but they are trying to STEAL the election,"[12] and asserted in a speech that "we did win this election," but claimed there was "fraud on the American public." He also again said he would be going to the US Supreme Court.[13]

By the morning after the election, Trump had been called as the winner in Florida, and still had a lead in Pennsylvania and Michigan.[14] But as the vote counting continued in these swing states—and especially as the mail-in ballots were gradually included—then-Democratic-candidate-and-now-President Joe Biden won both Pennsylvania and Michigan, along with Wisconsin and Georgia. The final electoral college result was 306 for Biden, 232 for Trump (precisely the same margin of victory Trump had declared a 'landslide' four years earlier). Biden won more than 81 million votes, more than 7 million more than Trump, in what turned out to be the highest-turnout election ever in terms of votes cast, and the highest by participation percentage in more than a century.[15]

But as we all know, that was not at all the end of the story. For many Trump supporters well-primed to feel distrust of mail-in ballots, already dubious about the fairness of the election, and alert to the possibility of potential fraud, this significant shift in

---

[11] Anita Kumar, *Trump's Supreme Court Vow Was What He Planned All Along*, POLITICO (Nov. 4, 2020), https://www.politico.com/news/2020/11/04/trump-plan-contest-election-434014.

[12] Marianna Spring, *"Stop the Steal": The Deep Roots of Trump's "Voter Fraud" Strategy*, BBC (Nov. 23, 2020), https://www.bbc.com/news/blogs-trending-55009950.

[13] Philip Rucker, Toluse Olorunnipa & Annie Linskey, *Presidential Election Hangs in Balance as Trump Falsely Asserts Fraud and Makes a Claim of Victory*, WASH. POST (Nov. 4, 2020), https://www.washingtonpost.com/politics/presidential-election-hangs-in-the-balance-in-a-country-convulsed-by-crisis/2020/11/04/c2a3ec26-1e17-11eb-90dd-abd0f7086a91_story.html.

[14] Christina Wilkie, *What's Behind Trump's Early Leads in Michigan and Pennsylvania*, CNBC (Nov. 4, 2020), https://www.cnbc.com/2020/11/04/whats-behind-trumps-leads-in-michigan-and-pennsylvania-.html.

[15] James M. Lindsay, *The 2020 Election by the Numbers*, COUNCIL ON FOREIGN RELS. (Dec. 15, 2020), https://www.cfr.org/blog/2020-election-numbers.

voting results after election night, and the move from Trump to Biden in several states, felt highly suspicious.

And sure enough, in the days, weeks and even months after the election—and continuing even now, as I write this essay many months later—claims of fraud were loud and insistent, both from Trump himself and from a great many supporters in the conservative media and beyond.[16]

On November 7th, when Biden claimed his victory, Trump refused to concede.

The next move by Trump and some of his supporters and surrogates? Surely no surprise, given this state of affairs and Trump's relentless pre-election messaging; cue the lawsuits. Indeed, the first post-election suits had already been filed by the Trump campaign on November 4th, primarily focusing on poll watchers and observer access to the count. And over the next week and well beyond, the Trump campaign and Republican party officials and activists filed multiple lawsuits in multiple states, many of them attempting to block certification of the results in states like Pennsylvania, Georgia and Wisconsin, alleging irregularities and intimating fraud, or challenging voting procedures put into place prior to the election, or attempting to prevent the counting of some portion of the mail-in votes, or attempting to decertify results already reached.[17]

And what happened to these numerous lawsuits?

One after another, they completely fizzled. In some instances, the plaintiffs voluntarily withdrew the cases. In a great many others, they were dismissed on procedural grounds, for lack of jurisdiction, lack of standing, or mootness. And in a number of instances, the cases were squarely rejected on the merits. Over and over and over, with only one minor exception (involving the deadline to provide missing proof of identification

---

[16] As one example among a great many, *see* Glenn Kessler, *Fact-Checking Trump's Cellphone Rant of Election Falsehoods*, WASH. POST (Nov. 26, 2020), https://www.washingtonpost.com/politics/2020/11/26/fact-checking-trumps-cellphone-rant-election-falsehoods/.

[17] For a helpful website describing the many lawsuits and linking to relevant documents, *see In the Courts*, DEMOCRACY DOCKET, https://www.democracydocket.com/case_type/post-election/ (last visited July 28, 2020).

for a small sub-group of mail-in voters in Pennsylvania),[18] the courts rejected the plaintiffs' claims. State courts, federal courts, and yes, even the United States Supreme Court, all dismissed or ruled against these suits.

Surely this seems, at a minimum, to be strong prima facie evidence that there was no significant election fraud in the 2020 Presidential election. After all, there were more than 60 lawsuits challenging various aspects of the election, presided over by judges of various political stripes in many different states as well as numerous members of the federal judiciary (some of them appointed by Trump), all reaching the conclusion that the suits lacked legal merit.

Can't we stop there? Isn't it obvious? Doesn't the avalanche of judicial opinions dismissing the cases dispositively establish that there wasn't any substantial fraud, that the election wasn't rigged or stolen, and that those who say otherwise are spouting nonsense?

It's tempting. But no, as legal educators, we definitely cannot stop there. . .

Why not? Why can't we take the fact of virtual judicial unanimity in these five dozen cases—especially in our polarized, partisan moment in which this much agreement across political divides is rare indeed—as compelling proof establishing that Trump's lawsuits are meritless?

The short answer is: because judges—even when operating in all good faith—really can be wrong, both in the individual case and even as a collective.

My son is not (yet) in law school—who knows, perhaps someday?—but I've tried to teach him this point already. When he was young, he didn't much like to hike. We would nonetheless periodically drag him on family hikes, sometimes in the canyons of Los Angeles, sometimes farther afield. To pass the time and distract him we'd often play games. One of our family favorites was what we came to call "The Case Game." This involved my describing, briefly, the facts of a legal case. Sometimes these

---

[18] Donald J. Trump for President, Inc. v. Boockvar, No. 602 M.D. 2020 (Pa. Commw. Ct. Nov. 12, 2020) (order enjoining respondents from counting certain ballots), https://www.pacourts.us/Storage/media/pdfs/20210604/020642-file-10440.pdf.

were major cases currently before the Supreme Court; other times they might be 19th century torts cases or evidence cases I'd taught in class. I'd briefly describe the facts and the basic legal issue before the court, usually in just a few sentences. And then I would ask my son what he thought the judge should do. He loved proposing answers, in matters ranging from whether there should be marriage equality for LGBT people (that one was an easy yes for him) to whether Helen Palsgraf should be able to recover from the railroad when she was injured on the platform because a passenger, while being pulled into the train by railroad employees, dropped his package, which then exploded and thereby caused the nearby scales to fall on Palsgraf and injure her. (My son said no, the railroad shouldn't have to pay, or at least they shouldn't have to pay her a whole lot, as her injuries were too unconnected from the railroad's actions—intuiting the notion of proximate cause in torts—but he noted that it sure would be nice if they would at least help with her hospital bills). Sometimes he'd ask for additional information, but usually, he would eagerly share his moral intuition about what he thought the outcome of the case should be.

Then he'd look at me and ask expectantly, "Did I get it right? Did I?"

And I'd look back at him and ask, "Well, I don't know. What do you mean by 'getting it right' "?

"Mom," he would say, looking a little exasperated. "Did I get the same answer as the real judge?" And, assuming it was a case that had already been decided, whether *Palsgraf v. Long Island Railroad*,[19] *Obergefell v. Hodges*,[20] or an order by a trial court judge about the admissibility of a piece of evidence, I'd answer him, telling him a little about the court's reasoning in whatever case I'd cribbed from. He'd look satisfied and happy when his reasoning or conclusion more or less matched the judge (or the majority opinion) and disappointed when not.

But then I'd ask: "Hold on, how do you know that the judge was right? Maybe the judge got it wrong."

---

[19] 162 N.E. 99 (NY 1928).

[20] 576 U.S. 644 (2015).

"No mom," he told me more than once. "He's the *judge*. The judge gets to decide."

"True enough," I said (ignoring the possibility of appeal). "The judge has the *power* to decide the outcome. But that still doesn't mean she or he is necessarily *right*."

I remember an 'aha' moment for him in one of these conversations, when he looked at me and said something like, "Oh . . . I get it. So the judge really might be wrong? Even though they're the judge and even though they get to determine what actually happens?"

In that moment he recognized that just because a court—potentially even the highest court of the land—said something, that didn't necessarily make it right or true or well-reasoned or even the best reading of the evidence. It made it the legal outcome, to be sure, but the judge-made legal answer was not necessarily the right answer, assessed in moral terms, nor even as a matter of factual accuracy.

This is perhaps an obvious point—yes, of course a judge can be wrong. Obvious, perhaps, but nonetheless important. Law students need to learn to find the flaws in a judicial opinion, their hidden assumptions, faulty inferences, and places where judicial reasoning goes astray. (To be sure, while some law students struggle with this insight, for others, this point is learned almost too easily; those students need to work especially hard to be serious and sympathetic readers of judicial opinions that reach conclusions with which they disagree. It is and should be a dialectical process, learning to see and evaluate both the strengths and the weaknesses of an opinion, and developing this set of skills is and should be a key component of a legal education.)

Returning to the point at hand: Judges can surely be mistaken, yes, but what does this point have to do with the post-election cases as a whole? Here, we have a great many cases, not one; we are not talking about a single, potentially mistaken judge, or a single appellate court. In these cases, judge after judge consistently reached the conclusion that the post-election lawsuits before them did not warrant relief. Surely that is different. Isn't it therefore fair to assume that the near unanimity establishes that the judges' collective conclusions are right?

Perhaps, but not necessarily. And this is an issue rather close to my heart. As a scholar, I've spent a considerable amount of time thinking and writing about forensic pattern evidence. I have been a critic of a number of long accepted forms of evidence routinely used in criminal cases, like fingerprint identification, firearms identification, bitemark identification and the like. All of these techniques have been widely accepted by courts over many decades (indeed, in the case of fingerprint identification evidence, for more than a century), in case after case, over and over, by many judges in many jurisdictions.

And yet I, along with a small group of other scholars, have argued that these forms of forensic pattern matching in fact largely lack scientific validation.[21] Pattern identification experts regularly make scientifically unjustified claims, asserting that they are 100 percent certain about a match, or that they've never made a mistake in identification, or that their matching technique field has an error rate of zero when done properly. In fact, these fields, though frequently labeled 'scientific,' largely depend on the expert's unconstrained, experience-based judgment about what level of similarity warrants finding a 'match.' And these forensic techniques lack clearly specified quantitative methodologies, or formal statistical models, or validated probability assessments to determine the likelihood that two patterns share a common source. Nor do we know nearly enough about how often experts make mistake in their judgments about identification—and what we do know suggests that mistakes are not especially rare.

Truth be told, until the last decade or two, these fields were subject to remarkably little scientific scrutiny. And in my view, there are good and quite persuasive arguments that none of

[21] My work on forensic science includes: Jennifer L. Mnookin, *The Uncertain Future of Forensic Science*, 147 DAEDALUS 99 (2018); Jennifer L. Mnookin et al., *The Need for a Research Culture in the Forensic Sciences*, 58 UCLA L. REV. 725 (2011); Jennifer L. Mnookin, *The Courts, the NAS, and the Future of Forensic Science,* 75 BROOK. L. REV. 1209 (2010), Jennifer L. Mnookin, *The Validity of Latent Fingerprint Identification: Confessions of a Fingerprinting Moderate*, 7 J.L., PROBABILITY & RISK 127 (2008), as well as DAVID FAIGMAN, EDWARD CHENG, JENNIFER L. MNOOKIN, ERIN E. MURPHY, JOSEPH SANDERS & CRHISTOPHER SLOBOGIN, MODERN SCIENTIFIC EVIDENCE: THE LAW AND SCIENCE OF EXPERT TESTIMONY (2019–2020 ed.).

these forms of evidence comfortably meets the current standards for the legal admissibility of expert and scientific evidence.[22] I am not alone in holding these views; indeed, in addition to a small group of legal scholars who have also worked in this area, a number of eminent scientists have also recognized that longstanding forms of pattern evidence regularly used in court lack adequate proof of scientific validity. Both a National Academy of Sciences report issued back in 2009[23] and a report by the President's Council of Advisors on Science and Technology in 2016[24] offered serious and detailed critiques of numerous kinds of widely-used pattern evidence. Furthermore, faulty, misleading or false forensic evidence is a significant contributing cause to a great many wrongful convictions.[25]

And yet, for the most part, courts consistently reject defense efforts to curtail or exclude the use of these forensic techniques. Occasionally, judges faced with admissibility challenges do express genuine concern about the surprising lack of scientific evidence. Sometimes they even restrict or exclude the most dramatic overstatements by experts, but the bottom line is that they almost always allow forensic pattern techniques into evidence, notwithstanding the paucity of evidence establishing scientific validity.[26] Some judges refuse even to grant a preliminary hearing to consider the question of admissibility—viewing any such hearing as a waste of time and resources, given that so many other judges have so consistently allowed the same kind of evidence.

For our purposes, the key point is that across many different jurisdictions, judges continue, consistently, to say that these

---

[22] This generalized conclusion is, to be sure, a bit overbroad: fingerprint evidence, for which there has been somewhat more research over the last decade, is a close question on that score, whereas bitemark identification is so flawed and its accuracy so utterly unproven that its exclusion from evidence in most instances ought to be obvious.

[23] COMM. ON IDENTIFYING THE NEEDS OF THE FORENSIC SCIS. COMTY., NAT'L RSCH. COUNCIL OF THE NAT'L ACADS., STRENGTHENING FORENSIC SCIENCE IN THE UNITED STATES: A PATH FORWARD (2009), https://www.ojp.gov/pdffiles1/nij/grants/228091.pdf.

[24] PRESIDENT'S COUNCIL OF ADVISORS ON SCI. & TECH., FORENSIC SCIENCE IN CRIMINAL COURTS: ENSURING SCIENTIFIC VALIDITY OF FEATURE-COMPARISON METHODS (2016), https://obamawhitehouse.archives.gov/sites/default/files/microsites/ostp/PCAST/pcast_forensic_science_report_final.pdf.

[25] *See, e.g.*, BRANDON GARRETT, CONVICTING THE INNOCENT (2011).

[26] There is one exception: courts are (finally!) beginning to recognize the profound weaknesses in bitemark identification evidence.

forms of evidence are valid and reliable. So, if judicial nose counting were enough to establish the correctness of judicial outcomes, there is no question that one—or more pointedly, that *I*—would have to conclude that admitting these forms of evidence was indeed the right answer. And yet, in my view, that would be a significant mistake. Though it can sometimes feel quixotic to keep trying to draw judicial attention to the limitations of forensic science, and the efforts of scholars and scientists have not (yet) had a terribly substantial influence on courts in this domain, the continuing judicial consensus has certainly in no way persuaded *me* that the judges are correct. (I would say that many of these opinions are wrong; at the same time, for the most part I would *not* say that they are written in bad faith. And I would hope that even those judges who have refused to grant a preliminary hearing to a defense challenge to a forensic science technique, would not claim that the challenge had been brought in bad faith either.)

While this excursus into the judicial reception of forensic science techniques might seem to have taken us far afield, in fact it relates quite directly to the 60+ cases arising from the 2020 Presidential election. The point is a simple but important one: While it might be tempting to insist that these cases' results speak for themselves, almost like the notion of *res ipsa loquiter* in tort law, I posit that a commitment to evidence means that we need to resist that conclusion. Even repeated, firm dismissal by so many judges in multiple jurisdictions does not inherently establish the illegitimacy or frivolity of these lawsuits.

As legal educators, we therefore need to recognize that it is at least *possible* that, notwithstanding an overwhelming judicial consensus, the judges have gotten it wrong, just as they often have with forensic science pattern evidence, as just one example.

My pedagogic point is that students need to learn the law, but we also need to provide space where they can recognize and name when the law, or particular legal outcomes, aren't justified, even if well-accepted by many. I want my students to appreciate that a judge—or even a widespread judicial consensus—can simultaneously be authoritative and wrong. Even groups of judges within or across jurisdictions who are nearly unanimous on a given point, can sometimes be quite wrong—and if this is true vis-à-vis, say, firearms identification evidence or bitemarks, then the near unanimity of the judicial decisions in dismissing the post-election lawsuits does not, as a bare fact, prove in good faith that the suits have no legitimate basis.

We thus cannot simply take the judges' consistent conclusions that these lawsuits lacked merit as dispositive evidence that these lawsuits lacked merit, nor, standing alone, even as persuasive evidence that there was no election fraud.

And yet, to be clear, as I indicated at the outset of this essay, my own view is that these judges who threw out the 60+ post-election cases were absolutely right to do so, and that these cases indeed profoundly lacked both evidentiary grounding and legal merit. My point here is not (yet) about substance, but rather a pedagogic one: that it is important to recognize (and to help students see and understand) that the mere fact that judges from across the political spectrum all reached consistent conclusions cannot be taken as dispositive evidence that they are right.

That necessarily requires a deeper dive into the evidentiary substance supporting the claims made, the arguments leveled by the parties, and the conclusions, analysis, and reasons given by the judges. It requires engaging in reasoned debate about the plausibility of the claims made, not just counting outcomes or judicial noses.

And so let us turn now to the opinions themselves. What is most striking in reading these opinions as a group, is how woefully unpersuasive the plaintiffs' claims seem to be. In many instances, they seem so utterly ungrounded and lacking in plausible evidence or even carefully constructed legal arguments or procedurally plausible claims that it invites the inference that they were not even fully *intended* to be serious legal efforts to persuade the judges before whom they were brought. As one judge notes dryly about the lack of plausible evidence presented in a case brought in Arizona, "Allegations that find favor in the public sphere of gossip and innuendo cannot be a substitute for earnest pleadings and procedure in federal court."[27]

[27] Bowyer v. Ducey, 506 F. Supp. 3d 699, 724 (D. Ariz. 2020).

Indeed, when reading the post-election opinions, it begins to feel that the plaintiffs' goals and purposes might well have been directed precisely—and distressingly—at the "public sphere of gossip and innuendo" rather than at the judges whose burden it was to assess the merits and rule accordingly.

And if so—if the machinery of the courtroom, and the judges' time, effort and engagement, in more than 60 cases across the country, were really just unwitting props for a performance on another stage—well, this would indeed be a bad faith use of our legal processes.

To be sure, this short essay is not the place to explore in great depth the array of post-election lawsuits filed (and I am an evidence scholar, not an election law scholar). But for illustrative purposes, I will briefly explore two aspects of a number of these cases, to attempt to capture how legally weak and unpersuasive they were found to be.

First, several cases attempt to base claims for dramatic relief on aspects of the election procedures that were established and put in place well before the election itself—and to which legal objections, if sincerely-held, could easily have been made much earlier, but were not. To give one simple example from one of the lawsuits in Arizona, one claim was based on the use of voting centers rather than precincts for this election. But this was a decision that had been made in Arizona before the Presidential primaries, and well before the general election. As the court notes, the plaintiff could have filed eight or nine months earlier, or any time prior to the general election—and this post-election lawsuit was therefore brought "far too late"[28] to be taken seriously. In another case, the plaintiff challenged a settlement agreement reached a year before the election in Georgia, regarding how absentee ballot signatures would be evaluated and under what circumstances could be rejected for not matching the signatures on file. The settlement agreement was executed in March 2020—and yet it was, as the court pointed out, "nearly eight months later—and *after* over one million voters cast their absentee ballots in the General

[28] Arizona Republican Party v. Fontes, No. CV2020-014553, slip op. at 8 (Ariz. Super. Ct. Dec. 21, 2020) (order affirming dismissal), https://www.clerkofcourt.maricopa.gov/home/showpublisheddocument/2024/637441633456370000.

Election" that the plaintiff challenged the agreement as unconstitutional, a delay for which he offered "[no] reasonable justification."[29]

Similarly, in one of the federal lawsuits filed, the Trump campaign sued the Wisconsin Elections Commission (WEC) and several Wisconsin officials, complaining of several aspects of election guidance that the WEC had provided, regarding matters like how to handle absentee ballots with missing addresses, how to make use of absentee ballot drop boxes, and how to define what was required for a voter to meet the standard of "indefinitely confined." Election workers relied on this guidance—some of which dated back to 2016, some of which was put forward in spring or fall 2020, prior to the election—and as a result there were more than five hundred drop boxes used throughout the state, and approximately 240,000 voters granted absentee ballots because they defined themselves as "indefinitely confined." The plaintiffs claimed that the WEC lacked the authority to issue the guidance that it had promulgated, and thus violated Wisconsin law and the federal Constitution by failing to have the election proceed in the "manner" designated by the legislature and required by the Constitution. The plaintiff requested, as a remedy, that the Court declare the Wisconsin general election void.

In this case, the judge rejected a number of procedural objections that some judges in other states found persuasive in similar cases elsewhere, regarding standing, mootness, and jurisdiction, and proceeded to address the merits. The Court swiftly swatted down the plaintiff's argument that Wisconsin's procedures violated the constitution's strictures about the "manner" of the election as "contrary both to the plain meaning of the Constitutional text and common sense," given that the dispute and claims were not about the fundamental manner of the election, but about much more modest dimensions of election administration. And the Court found that even if "manner" were interpreted more broadly, the WEC guidance did not reveal any deviation from the legislature's directives substantial enough to be a violation of the Electors Clause, and besides, the claims

[29] Wood v. Raffensperger, 501 F. Supp. 3d 1310, 1324 (N.D. Ga. 2020) *aff'd*, 981 F.3d 1307 (11th Cir. 2020).

could well have been made earlier but were not. The court concluded, "This is an *extraordinary* case. A sitting president who did not prevail in his bid for reelection has asked for federal court help in setting aside the popular vote based on disputed issues of election administration, issues he plainly could have raised before the vote occurred. This Court has allowed plaintiff the chance to make his case and he has lost on the merits. In his reply brief, plaintiff 'asks that the Rule of Law be followed.' It has been."[30]

On appeal, the 7th Circuit affirmed the district court's judgment, finding that the plaintiff's claims fell short on the merits, and highlighting still more emphatically the unreasonableness of the timing of the suit: "The President had a full opportunity before the election to press the very challenges to Wisconsin law underlying his present claims. Having foregone that opportunity, he cannot now—after the election results have been certified as final—seek to bring those challenges." Perhaps worth noting: all three judges on the 7th circuit panel were appointed by Republicans, and one of the three was appointed by Donald Trump, as was the district court judge.

In these cases and others, the lawsuits complain of electoral administration decisions made well before the election, for which the plaintiffs seek drastic remedies afterwards because they do not like the results. The idea that we unmake the results of an election because of procedures—even if imperfect—promulgated well beforehand, to which timely objection could have been made but was not, strains credulity, and as one judge said, "smacks once again of political gamesmanship . . . ."[31] And indeed, such efforts persuaded absolutely none of the judges of either party who heard such claims.

Second, and perhaps even more critically, a number of judges forcefully condemn the tremendous failure to provide plausible or persuasive evidence of claims made. As one Arizona judge states, "The plaintiff offered only suspicion of wrongdoing,

30 Trump v. Wis. Elections Comm'n, 506 F. Supp. 3d 620, 639 (E.D. Wis. 2020), *aff'd*, 983 F.3d 919 (7th Cir. 2020).

31 Wis. Voters All. v. Pence, No. 20-3791, 2021 WL 686359, at *2 (D.D.C. Feb. 19, 2021) (order referring counsel to the Committee on Grievances), https://drive.google.com/file/d/1b_ig9lDaPT5Ril4964EL18WIqUjqa4in/view.

in a situation that required it to plead specific, facially credible facts backed by 'the most credible, positive, and unequivocal evidence' of fraud or malfeasance. The plaintiff here did not even allege facts that cast doubt on the reliability of the hand count audit, let alone the outcome of the election or the honesty of the officials who administered it."[32] In another case, the judge describes the "supplemental evidence" offered to suggest tampering with ballots as multiple level inadmissible hearsay—consisting primarily of an affidavit from someone claiming that some other unnamed poll worker told her still other poll workers instructed her to make changes to the ballot dates. Such evidence is, as the judge rightly says, "inadmissible hearsay within hearsay," and furthermore, the plaintiffs offered no hearsay exception to justify considering it.[33] In another Michigan case, the court calls the plaintiffs' claims that many ballots have been changed or falsified "mere speculation" and concludes that "plaintiffs have made only a claim but have offered no evidence to support their assertions."[34]

In another Arizona case, the court writes, "Advancing several different theories, Plaintiffs allege that Arizona's Secretary of State and Governor conspired with various domestic and international actors to manipulate Arizona's 2020 General Election results allowing Joseph Biden to defeat Donald Trump in the presidential race. The allegations they put forth to support their claims of fraud fail in their particularity and plausibility. Plaintiffs append over three hundred pages of attachments, which are only impressive for their volume. The various affidavits and expert reports are largely based on anonymous witnesses, hearsay, and irrelevant analysis of unrelated elections."[35] The court goes on to describe the evidence as nothing more than "innuendoes," and describes as "concerning to the Court" that the plaintiff's " 'expert reports' reach implausible conclusions, often because they are derived from

[32] Arizona Republican Party v. Fontes, No. CV2020-014553, slip op. at 12 (Ariz. Super. Ct. Dec. 21, 2020) (order affirming dismissal), https://www.clerkofcourt.maricopa.gov/home/showpublisheddocument/2024/637441633456370000.

[33] Donald J. Trump for President, Inc. v. Benson, No. 20-000225-MZ, 2020 WL 6594903, at *2 (Mich. Ct. Cl. Nov. 6, 2020).

[34] Stoddard v. City Election Comm'n of the City of Detroit, No. 20-014604-CZ, slip op. at 4 (Mich. 3d Jud. Cir. Ct. Nov. 6, 2020).

[35] Bowyer v. Ducey, 506 F. Supp. 3d 699, 721 (D. Ariz. 2020).

wholly unreliable sources," like a secondhand report of a "survey of unknown size and to unknown persons" allegedly given in multiple states.[36] "The sheer unreliability of the information" in this survey, the Court says, "cannot plausibly serve as a basis to overturn a presidential election, much less support plausible fraud claims . . . ."[37] In other evidence offered, the Court notes "a lengthy collection of phrases beginning with the words 'could have, possibly, might,' and 'may have,' " and which in aggregate, "have not moved the needle for their fraud theory from conceivable to plausible," which is necessary to state a claim.[38]

In another Pennsylvania case, one of the key cases brought by the Trump campaign, and indeed argued by Rudy Giuliani himself, the judge describes the case thus:

> In this action, the Trump Campaign . . . seek[s] to discard millions of votes legally cast by Pennsylvanians from all corners . . . . In other words, Plaintiffs ask this Court to disenfranchise almost seven million voters. This Court has been unable to find any case in which a plaintiff has sought such a drastic remedy in the contest of an election, in terms of the sheer volume of votes asked to be invalidated. One might expect that when seeking such a startling outcome, a plaintiff would come formidably armed with compelling legal arguments and factual proof of rampant corruption, such that this Court would have no option but to regrettably grant the proposed injunctive relief despite the impact it would have on such a large group of citizens.
>
> That has not happened. Instead, this Court has been presented with strained legal arguments without merit and speculative accusations, unpled in the operative complaint and unsupported by evidence. In the United States of America, this cannot justify the disenfranchisement of a single voter, let alone all the

---

36 *Id.* at 722.

37 *Id.* at 723.

38 *Id.*

> voters of its sixth most populated state. Our people, laws, and institutions demand more.[39]

On appeal, Judge Stephanos Bibas, another Trump appointee, writing for a panel on the Third Circuit, takes up only a very narrow question: whether the district court abused its discretion in refusing to allow the Campaign to modify its complaint a second time. The court answers 'no,' but also elects to comment pointedly on the lack of evidence: "Free, fair elections are the lifeblood of democracy. Charges of unfairness are serious. But calling an election unfair does not make it so. Charges require specific allegations and then proof. We have neither here."[40]

Even this brief, somewhat whirlwind excursion into the judicial opinions arising from these post-election challenges is, I hope, revealing. We can see, in aggregate, a group of cases in which the judges find virtually no plausible evidence to support the plaintiffs' claims of misconduct, error, or fraud. We see a variety of instances in which the legal claims seem farfetched at best. And in many instances, the procedures or practices that plaintiffs argue violated the law were in place well before the election (and yet the plaintiffs raised concerns about these procedures and practices only *after* their preferred candidate lost).

So yes, judges may be wrong, and even a substantial collection of judges may be wrong. But in these election lawsuits, it does not look like there is any credible argument that these judges were wrong to dismiss these suits. On the contrary, many of the cases were so weak and unpersuasive that perhaps the better question is why so many of these lawsuits were brought at all.

---

39 Donald J. Trump for President, Inc. v. Boockvar, 502 F. Supp. 3d 899, 906 (M.D. Pa 2020). The judge in this case also analogized one of the plaintiff's theories of the case to "Frankenstein's Monster," because it was "haphazardly stitched together from two distinct theories in an attempt to avoid controlling precedent" *Id.* at 910.

40 Donald J. Trump for President, Inc. v. Sec'y of Pennsylvania, 830 F. App'x 377, 382 (3d Cir. 2020). Bibas later notes that while the campaign alleges discrimination, in order to generate a federal claim out of already-rejected questions of state law, "its alchemy cannot transmute lead into gold. The Campaign never alleges that any ballot was fraudulent or cast by an illegal voter. It never alleges that any defendant treated the Trump campaign or its votes worse than it treated the Biden campaign or its votes. Calling something discrimination does not make it so." *Id.* at 391.

Perhaps the primary audience for these suits was not the judges themselves before whom the cases were brought, but the set of Trump supporters who had already been primed by the relentless pre-election messaging about the dangers of the election. As Biden campaign advisor Bob Bauer suggested, a week after the election in a post-election legal briefing, these cases were in fact "theatrics, not lawsuits."[41]

And *this* is precisely what is so disturbing about the post-election lawsuits as a group—not that courts uniformly rejected them, but that in a great many cases they so failed to pass muster as serious or plausible challenges that it seems likely they were not even intended to be taken seriously by the judges who heard them. (As election law scholar Justin Levitt quipped, "A lawsuit without provable facts showing a statutory or constitutional violation is just a tweet with a filing fee."[42])

Serious, good-faith legal disagreement is entirely legitimate, even when one view has few adherents or has little practical chance of winning, given existing precedent or the dominant legal paradigm. But using the courts and our system of justice as a prop in a public relations campaign is not. Filing lawsuits not out of a serious desire to persuade the court, but instead to purvey a frenzied, false narrative of widespread fraud and the illegitimacy of the election outside the courtroom is antithetical to both the rule of law and to democratic governance—this is indeed The Big Lie.

Indeed, several of the judicial opinions themselves come very close to explicitly naming this terribly dangerous game, the judicial equivalent of an actor breaking the third wall. For example, in a federal case in Wisconsin, the judge writes,

> The election that preceded this lawsuit was emotional and often divisive. The pleadings that have been filed over the past week are passionate and urgent. People

[41] Biden Campaign, *Post-Election Legal Briefing*, PERISCOPE (Nov. 10, 2020), https://www.pscp.tv/KamalaHarris/1jMJgpgYqMlxL?t=14s, *quoted in* Jennifer Rubin, Opinion, *The Election Can't Be 'Stolen.' But Something Worse Is Happening*, WASH. POST (Nov. 11, 2020), https://www.washingtonpost.com/opinions/2020/11/11/you-can-deplore-republicans-nothing-is-being-stolen-its-far-worse.

[42] *Quoted in* Ian MacDougall, *If Trump Tries to Sue His Way to Election Victory, Here's What Happens*, PROPUBLICA (Nov. 4, 2020), https://www.propublica.org/article/if-trump-tries-to-sue-his-way-to-election-victory-heres-what-happens.

> have strong, deep feelings about the right to vote, the freedom and opportunity to vote and the value of their vote. They should. But the legal question at the heart of this case is simple. Federal courts have limited jurisdiction. Does a federal court have the jurisdiction and authority to grant the relief this lawsuit seeks? The answer is no.
>
> Federal judges do not appoint the president in this country. *One wonders why the plaintiffs came to federal court and asked a federal judge to do so. After a week of sometimes odd and often harried litigation, the court is no closer to answering the "why."* But this federal court has no authority or jurisdiction to grant the relief the remaining plaintiff seeks. The court will dismiss the case."[43]

Why indeed . . .? Might it not be to continue pushing forward, outside of the courtroom, the narrative that the election was stolen?

Similarly, take, for example, *King v. Whitmer*, in which the plaintiffs, Republican nominees for Presidential Electors, claimed "widespread fraud in the distribution, collection, and counting of ballots in Michigan . . . ."[44] In this case, the court finds a number of procedural reasons not to reach the underlying merits, including, for example, that much of their requested relief is moot (because the Michigan election had already been certified), and also finds that as they could have brought the case earlier but did not, so the doctrine of laches applies.

However, notwithstanding the multiple procedural grounds upon which to deny plaintiffs' motion for injunctive relief, Judge Linda Parker elected also to assess the merits. And here, as in so many other cases, the court finds the plaintiffs' evidence to be "nothing but speculation and conjecture . . . ."[45]

But then, in a rather extraordinary conclusion, she names outright the deeply troubling concern that the lawsuit was not

---

[43] Feehan v. Wis. Elections Comm'n, 506 F. Supp. 3d 596, 600 (E.D. Wis. 2020) (italics added).

[44] 505 F. Supp. 3d 720, 726 (E.D. Mich. 2020).

[45] *Id.* at 738.

even brought out of a genuine interest in the remedy requested. She writes, "In fact, this lawsuit seems to be less about achieving the relief Plaintiffs seek—as much of that relief is beyond the power of this Court—*and more about the impact of their allegations on People's faith in the democratic process and their trust in our government.* Plaintiffs ask this Court to ignore the orderly statutory scheme established to challenge elections and to ignore the will of millions of voters. This, the Court cannot, and will not, do. The People have spoken."[46]

This judge thus names explicitly that, in her view, the real purpose of the lawsuit is to foment distrust in the democratic process and doubts about the election.

In another case, decided just days before Congress was set to count the electoral votes on fateful January 6th, D.C. District Court Judge Jeb Boasberg critiques the troubling bad faith of the lawsuit before him even more explicitly, rebuking one of the plaintiff's theories as "somewhere between a willful misreading of the Constitution and fantasy."[47] He further writes,

> In addition to being filed on behalf of Plaintiffs without standing and (at least as to the state Defendants) in the wrong court and with no effort to even serve their adversaries, the suit rests on a fundamental and obvious misreading of the Constitution. It would be risible were its target not so grave: the undermining of a democratic election for President of the United States.[48]

As in numerous other post-election suits, Judge Boasberg expresses skepticism about the timing—in this case, the plaintiffs are, in part, claiming unconstitutional statutes that are decades old. And he concludes, incisively and directly,

> It is not a stretch to find a serious lack of good faith here. . .
>
> Yet even that may be letting Plaintiffs off the hook too lightly. Their failure to make any effort to serve or formally notify any Defendant—even after reminder by

[46] *Id.* at 739 (italics added).

[47] Wis. Voters All. v. Pence, 514 F. Supp. 3d 117, 119 (D.D.C. Jan. 4, 2021).

[48] *Id.* at 119.

> the Court in its Minute Order—renders it difficult to believe that the suit is meant seriously. Courts are not instruments through which parties engage in such gamesmanship or symbolic political gestures.[49]

We see here something quite extraordinary; these judges are not simply detailing the weaknesses of the claims made and the lack of evidence. They are implying—and in some cases saying absolutely outright—that these lawsuits are a frightful joke, brought by plaintiffs with "a serious lack of good faith," brought not from a genuine belief in the claims they are making or with a sincere hope of gaining the remedy requested, but to undermine confidence in the election and in our democratic process.

Indeed, it seems entirely plausible to believe that the actual purpose behind many of these lawsuits was not to try to resolve a good-faith legal dispute by turning to the courts, but rather, something quite performative, an act intended to play out on a stage entirely outside the courtrooms themselves. Put bluntly, these lawsuits were, at least in significant part, performances primarily designed to further the *outside*-the-courtroom swirling story of fraud and a stolen election.

Perhaps among those who filed these cases there were hopes that some conservative judges would be so loyal to Trump and party as to ignore or paper over the substantive weaknesses of the claims being made. If so, those hopes were—fortunately!—resoundingly dashed. We can therefore feel some degree of appreciation or relief that when suits aiming to overturn major election results were based, at most, on underspecified conjecture and unproven speculation, judges' rule-of-law norms really did trump (yes, trump) political preferences. While reasonable disagreement might exist about precisely the degree to which ideology, political preferences, cognitive biases and personal beliefs shape judicial outcomes, these cases illustrate that second-order commitments to the rule of law do, at least in clear-cut cases, influence and bound judicial decisionmaking.

But evaluated in aggregate, the post-election lawsuits were so substantively weak that it seems almost certain that they

---

49 *Id.* at 121.

were part of a deeply troubling strategy to intensify the commitments of Trump's base to a false narrative of election fraud. In the heated days and weeks after the election, as Trump refused to concede, the lawsuits were designed to further light the fires burning through social media and the Trump loyalist press, falsely affirming that, precisely as Trump had already preached over and over prior to the election, the election was rigged.

The suits did not persuade any judges that the presidential election was rigged, unfair or fraudulent. But they nonetheless helped further the false narrative begun months earlier, suggesting that the only way Trump could lose was via fraud. If a supporter believed (a) that Trump would surely win unless the election were stolen, and (b) that Democrats were actively trying to rig the election, and finally, (c) that Trump appeared to have lost the election, then concluding (d) that the election was in fact illicitly stolen becomes a simple and necessary deduction, a consequence of syllogistic reasoning from the distorted premises that Trump and his allies seeded among his supporters long before the vote itself. And the drama of bringing the lawsuits and proclaiming the need for them was, itself, the point—not actually to overturn the election in court, but further to delegitimize the Democrats' win. Yes, Bob Bauer had it precisely right: "theatrics, not really lawsuits."

From one perspective, the fact that virtually all the lawsuits challenging the Presidential election were decisively thrown out by judges from all across the political spectrum, might be seen as a fairly successful, albeit limited, 'pressure test' of the judiciary. And indeed, the heightened scrutiny produced by dozens of legal cases finding no credible evidence of fraud can be seen as a powerful defense of the fundamental accuracy of the election results.

Furthermore, it is worth noting, especially given the intense partisanship of the situation, that quite a number of the judges who ruled against the Trump Campaign and its allies were Republicans, including a number of Trump appointees to the bench. And these judges—thank goodness—chose their oaths of office and professional commitment to the core values of rule of law and judicial independence over loyalty to the President who put them in office.

Perhaps there should be no surprise, even in our currently polarized moment, at a set of cases that, in aggregate, reveal judges of all political persuasions taking the rule of law—however they understand it—most seriously. To put it differently, judicial unanimity is not altogether surprising when plaintiffs fail to make claims that are even facially plausible. And when the evidentiary basis and legal claims are especially weak, we would expect that ideology, politics, judicial philosophy, implicit bias and the danger of motivated reasoning are all likely to have less impact on judicial assessment, as compared to cases where the legal or evidentiary claims are stronger and more contestable.

At the same time, we should nonetheless name, recognize and appreciate that in a period of genuine crisis—and even an attempted insurrection—the courts largely stood firm as a bulwark protecting core values of the rules of law, including the critical need for claims to have a grounding in actual evidence, not fantastic and unsupported speculation.

Given the almost shocking flimsiness of the suits, that these cases played out this way is both a relief and something that ought to be able to be taken as expected, a given, part and parcel of a basic commitment to the rule of law. For those who fear that our partisan divide has become so thorough as to leave no space for shared understandings, the post-election cases potentially reveal otherwise.

Yet the shared understandings achieved here can provide only small comfort. First, they emerged, one fears, only because of the extraordinary lack of legal and factual foundation to undergird the plaintiffs' claims. It may be that judges from across the political spectrum can agree to this degree only when the cases are so weak that they ought not to have been brought at all. These cases may tell us almost nothing about what some of these same judges would and will do if faced with weak-but-somewhat-more-legally-plausible efforts to undermine election law or an unwelcome election outcome.

In addition and quite distressingly, these many, decisive judicial rejections of the false claims made by the President and his allies seemed to have had extraordinarily little impact on the views of large segments of the public. Well after the election, a great many people continued to believe (or at least to espouse) the false narrative of fraud, not only including those who stormed the Capitol on January 6, 2021 in an attempted insurrection, but also many congressional leaders and Attorneys General from Republican states.

Indeed, even now, as I write this essay more than six months beyond the election, a significant segment of the public continues to espouse The Big Lie, that President Biden's victory was due to fraud. For example, a June 2021 poll reported that thirty-two percent of respondents continue to say that Biden won because of fraud. And this percentage has remained extraordinarily 'sticky,' with virtually identical percentages coming out of several separate polls conducted by Monmouth over the past six months.[50]

In other words, it seems that the decisive rejection of Trump's claims in courts all over the country by judges of all political stripes changed virtually no one's mind. One might have hoped, or even expected, that these many legal opinions would have caused some substantial number of those who believed in electoral fraud to pause and at least consider whether they *might* be mistaken. Instead, filing the suits and fighting them (both in the courts and in the Trump-allied media) gave Trump and his supporters still more fodder for conspiracy theories, somehow providing additional atmospherics, and sustaining rather than tamping down the widespread Republican belief in what they refer to as "the steal."

This seeming irrelevance of facts, evidence, and multiple decisive judicial determinations illustrates the rise of a worryingly large 'evidence-free zone,' where for many, including a distressing number of congressional leaders and lawyers, there

[50] Max Greenwood, *One-Third of Americans Believe Biden Won Because of Voter Fraud: Poll*, HILL (June 21, 2021), https://thehill.com/homenews/campaign/559402-one-third-of-americans-believe-biden-won-because-of-voter-fraud-poll; Monmouth University Polling Institute, *Public Supports Both Early Voting And Requiring Photo ID to Vote*, MONMOUTH U. (June 21, 2021), https://www.monmouth.edu/polling-institute/reports/monmouthpoll_us_062121/.

seems to be little relationship between actual facts and the distorted stories people are prepared to spin.

This is tremendously dangerous territory for our polis, as well as for legal education. For the operation of the rule of law, and for the functioning of our democracy, we need to have a core, shared commitment to factfinding, to the idea that evidence and truth matter, both inside and outside the courtroom.

To be sure, a commitment to evidence and to truth-seeking, does not mean that all our truths will be the same, or that we will all agree entirely even on the methods by which truth should be determined. 'Truth' can be elusive, contested, messy, and hard to pin down. Facts can be reasonably and legitimately and passionately disputed, and certainly do not speak for themselves. We can, in absolute good faith, disagree too about what kinds of evidence warrant belief, or about how a piece of evidence should be interpreted and understood.

But the core premise—that the facts of the matter need to *matter*—should not be up for debate. It is important to recognize that in the aftermath of the 2020 presidential election, there were officials of both parties who worked with enormous integrity, and who stayed true to the facts as they understood them, sometimes withstanding tremendous political pressure in the process. But there were also far too many people—and far too many lawyers—who participated in spreading false claims out of court, and still worse, within the courtroom too.

As a core matter of legal ethics, it is a familiar precept that lawyers are required to have a good faith basis in law and fact to bring a lawsuit in the first place.[51] It is tremendously hard to believe that the post-election lawsuits meet that standard—again, not because the cases decisively lost, but because they were, in many instances, so legally weak and without any credible or substantial evidentiary support. Furthermore, if the primary reason for bringing them was to further fan partisan flames and delegitimize President-elect Biden—if they were indeed as much "gamesmanship or symbolic political gesture,"

[51] "A lawyer shall not bring or defend a proceeding, or assert or controvert an issue therein, unless there is a basis in law and fact for doing so that is not frivolous, which includes a good faith argument for an extension, modification or reversal of existing law." MODEL RULES OF PRO. CONDUCT r. 3.1 (AM. BAR ASS'N 2020).

in Judge Boasberg's words, as legal claim—that surely warrants condemnation and sanction.

Indeed, in the aftermath of these legal cases, Rudy Giuliani's law license has been suspended, and as I write this essay, there are hearings underway to consider whether to discipline some of the attorneys who participated in the post-election lawsuits for having committed grave ethics violations.[52]

Sanctions on lawyers who act in clear bad faith are important for the legal profession's legitimacy and ethical grounding. To be sure, sanctions are problematic if overused; they risk chilling controversial suits brought in good faith, But in the aftermath of these post-election lawsuits, one might well worry more about the opposite danger. If lawyers can bring evidence-free suits aiming to unmake and undermine a legitimate democratic election, without consequence or sanction, it threatens further to erode trust in our collective commitment to rule-of-law values, and could well generate still more frequent frivolous suits, in the election law space and beyond. Unfortunately, like the lawsuits themselves, sanctions are distressingly unlikely to dislodge the beliefs of those who continue to adhere to The Big Lie.

As legal educators, we are left with important questions as we think about training the next generation of legal professionals. Looking forward, how do we go about training

[52] Just as I complete final edits on this essay, Magistrate Judge N. Reid Neureiter imposed sanctions on a set of plaintiffs who brought a class action in December 2020, an "enormous conspiracy theory" alleging constitutional violations of their right to vote as well as alleging RICO violations. O'Rourke v. Dominion Voting Sys., Inc., No. 20-cv-03747, 2021 WL 3400671, at *2 (D. Colo. Aug. 3, 2021). Judge Neureiter writes, "Albeit disorganized and fantastical, the Complaint's allegations are extraordinarily serious, and, if accepted as true by large numbers of people, are the stuff of which violent insurrections are made." *Id.* at *3. While plaintiffs' counsel insisted that they truly believed what they were arguing, Neureiter is not persuaded; even if so, he says, "an 'empty-head' but 'pure-heart' is no justification for patently frivolous arguments or factual assertions," and in this case, the plaintiffs made zero efforts to critically assess, or evaluate the materials they introduced, including materials they cut and pasted from other earlier failed post-election lawsuits. Id. at *11 (quoting Collins v. Daniels, 916 F.3d 1302, 1320 (10th Cir. 2019)). After this essay was completed (but before page proofs were finalized), another judge, Linda Carter, imposed sanctions on a set of plaintiffs as well, noting that the case was an effort at "undermining the People's faith in our democracy and debasing the judicial process to do so," and asserting that they had "scorned their oath, flouted the rules, and attempted to undermine the integrity of the judiciary along the way." *See* King v. Whitmer, ___ F. Supp. 3d ___, 2021 WL 3771875 at *1, *2. Judge Carter also referred the plaintiffs to the Michigan Attorney Grievance Commission for potential disciplinary consequences. *Id.* at *42.

lawyers and leaders who will have a fundamental commitment to taking evidence and facts seriously? And how do we train lawyers who will recognize that their commitment to our democratic processes must take primacy over their commitment to their politically preferred outcome?

In addition, what do we do when false beliefs become a matter of faith that cannot be dislodged? This is a frightening concern for our democracy and our ability to engage across difference, and yet the widespread continued adherence to The Big Lie reveals the importance of the question. I do recognize that perhaps some of those who continue to assert in their answers to poll questions that Biden was elected by fraud do not truly believe it. For some respondents, it might be, at this point, more an assertion of solidarity with their preferred candidate or political outlook than a genuinely-held belief. It might be a gestural assertion marking them as belonging to 'Team Trump,' rather than a factual claim.

But if we take the polls at face value, they suggest that a great many of Trump's supporters continue to believe that widespread fraud marred the 2020 presidential election. If so, it appears that for a non-trivial group of Americans, there is no evidence to the contrary, no process of sifting and adducing proof, no engagement with the facts of the matter that could or would persuade them otherwise. In our highly polarized and partisan times, I do recognize that there may also be shibboleths taken equally on faith by those on the other side of the political aisle too, though I do not believe there is an equivalent to The Big Lie in terms of scale or scope or danger to our democracy.

We thus have our work cut out for us. As deans and legal educators, we must work to train all of our graduates so that, whatever their political perspective, they recognize, as we deans put it in our joint letter, that "Our profession demands that when lawyers pursue legal action, they must bring claims in good faith, grounded in facts and evidence, and demonstrate respect for the legal system." This expectation does not seem like it should be so terribly difficult, or even up for question, and yet, the events of the past year reveal all too clearly that it absolutely cannot be taken as a given.

As a starting point, we need to engage our students in the best of faith, and we need to imbue in them a deep sense of responsibility to take evidence seriously. Evidence can surely be highly contestable, and facts do not speak for themselves. A shared meta-commitment to evidence will by no means prevent profound disagreements of many kinds. But it can, if pursued in good faith, likely somewhat narrow the spaces of disagreement, and, if taken seriously, it would put the lie to notions like The Big Lie. We need to train lawyers who are fierce advocates, yes, but who also recognize a core and non-negotiable professional responsibility to make arguments grounded in evidence. For the good of both our country and our profession, we must ensure that we and our students remain collectively and deeply tethered to the idea that that the "facts of the matter" matter deeply.

CHAPTER 6

THE PRIMACY OF ELECTORAL POLITICS AND OUR OUTDATED CHECKS AND BALANCES

Theodore W. Ruger[1]

A. INTRODUCTION

In the months following the November 2020 election, many Americans watched with increasing dismay and disbelief as the then-President of our nation refused to accept the reality of those election results even after over sixty federal judges, including many appointed by Donald Trump himself, rejected as completely baseless all claims of a "stolen" election. After the Supreme Court ruled unanimously and decisively against him on December 11, 2020, the President and his private attorneys ratcheted up his baseless grievances and his incendiary rhetoric, breaching our fundamental constitutional tradition that the loser of a valid, lawful election must leave office peacefully and honor our democracy's smooth transition of power. President Trump did the opposite, rallying his most extreme supporters to the Capitol on January 6 by intensifying his lies about election fraud, and then encouraging them to use any means necessary, including violent occupation of the Capitol building, to thwart Congress from performing its constitutional duty to certify the valid election results.

These events, and the substantial number of public officials, attorneys, and others who enabled and advanced President Trump's specious claims, have generated the ample concern among the legal profession and the legal academy that forms the subject of this book. The events following the November 2020 election have strained our democracy and shattered many people's confidence in the legal ethics and civic morality of the lawyers and others who occupy high office and/or represent those

---

[1] Dean & Bernard G. Segal Professor of Law, University of Pennsylvania Carey Law School.

who do. Many have appropriately called on law schools and the broader profession to redouble our efforts to produce and enforce a culture of ethical and law abiding and inclusive lawyering, and I support all of those efforts. Other chapters in this book creatively and effectively advance ideas for reforms and measures that would enable law schools and the profession to strengthen our teaching of civic ethics and professional responsibility.

While I hold these impulses and applaud these efforts at curricular and professional reform, this chapter takes a different point of emphasis, namely exploring how our democracy can protect itself from lawyer-leaders who have not, and perhaps cannot, internalize the prevailing norms of legal ethics and civic duty that we would have them aspire to. Later in the chapter I explore the fact that while almost all elected Republican state Attorneys General signed on to a tendentious, perhaps frivolous, brief led by the Texas Attorney General supporting President's Trump's theory of election fraud, almost all of the appointed Republican AGs, even in deeply "red" states, declined to join the politicized briefing effort. Two other Republican AGs who declined to join the Trump effort, Kentucky's Daniel Cameron and Idaho's Leslie Wasden, hold office by election but are for unique reasons insulated from the sharp discipline of Trump-affiliated GOP primary voters: Cameron by his close affiliation and political sponsorship of Senator Mitch McConnell, the leading force in Kentucky Republican politics, and Wasden since he had already won five prior elections and held the AG's office since 2003. Taken together, the litigation behavior of the nation's Republican Attorneys General provide a clear glimpse into the heavy sway that Republican primary politics plays in shaping, perhaps distorting, the choices that public officials made following the November 2020 election. That such influences operated on Attorneys General—all members of the Bar and all holding an office that calls for public-regarding "rule of law" decision-making—is both striking and concerning. Research and reform ought focus on how to insulate and protect such officials, and perhaps others in the federal and state government, from the most extreme operation of electoral pressure.

This attention to structural safeguards is needed because no regime of education or ethics will ever perfectly screen out self-serving or unethical public officials. No matter how strong our educational institutions, and how careful our professional ethical standards, lawyers and elected officials will slip through who fall far short of those ideals. From the earliest days of our constitutional democracy, framers and theorists have struggled with this fundamental duality. We seek to train and promote and reward individuals of high moral integrity into public service; all the while knowing that public office simultaneously attracts others sheerly for ambition and desire for raw power. Such insights about our government and its structure were held by James Madison and other architects of our Constitution. Their writings and the design choices they made inform our current predicament even as the limitations of those original structural protections against intentional lawlessness were laid bare by Trump and his attorneys following the 2020 election.

For James Madison and other framers of the Constitution, one of the imperatives of the new federal institutional design was the cultivation of a better caliber of public servant, one more free of "faction" and other vices.[2] He wrote and thought deeply about the importance of civic virtue in leadership, and in the obligation of a wise and virtuous electorate in selecting leaders who upheld their sense of ethics. In a speech to the Virginia ratifying convention, he argued:

> I go on to this great Republican principle, that the people will have virtue and intelligence to select men of virtue and wisdom. Is there no virtue among us? If there be not, we are in a wretched situation . . . . If there be sufficient virtue and intelligence in the community, it will be exercised in the selection of these men; so that we do not depend on their virtue. I put confidence not in our rules, but in the people who are to choose them.[3]

While advancing civic virtue, Madison was simultaneously aware of, and candid about, the limits of such aspirational norms and values, and was unwilling to trust the stable functioning of

---

[2] *See* Joseph E. Kobylka & Bradley Kent Carter, *Madison, 'The Federalist' & the Constitutional Order: Human Nature & Institutional Structure*, 20 POLITY 190 (1987).

[3] *See id.*, at 207–08.

American democracy entirely to the good faith and public ethics of those who would hold high office and those who would elect them. Hence our most effective constitutional traditions do not vest unvarnished trust in the maintenance of individual civic ethics or morality, but rather build structures to check, or blunt, even the most mendacious and venal aspects of human nature. As Madison wrote in Federalist 51, we are not and will never be governed by "angels," and so we need a political structure built for "ambition to counteract ambition."[4]

For Madison, as for many astute observers today, there will occasionally be ambitious demagogues like Donald Trump with a cadre of willing enablers and allies. The question regarding these actors is what can be done to structure governmental defenses against that? In classic Madisonian design thinking, these defenses are commonly referred to as "checks and balances," and inhere in the splitting of power and oversight between different branches of the federal government and between the national and state governments.

Most observers agree that our system of checks and balances is not as balanced as it once was, and is increasingly an inadequate check against Executive overreaching.[5] The weeks and months following the 2020 election laid bare the growing realization that the nation's intense partisan polarization has rendered several of the Constitution's separation-of-power checks ineffective at restraining an overreaching, or even lawless, Chief Executive. The causes of this separation of powers breakdown are complex and multifaceted, but the ability of strong Presidents to impose their will without serious congressional check when their party holds one or both houses of Congress is commonly attributed to the dramatically increased party discipline and ideological polarization that is visible both in Congress and in the nation's electorate and geographic voting map in recent years and decades.

Whatever the precise causes, the result is that imperatives of party identification driven by elected officials' desire for reelection or advancement into higher office, overwhelm the

---

4 THE FEDERALIST NO. 51 (James Madison, 1788).

5 *See generally* Daryl J. Levinson & Richard Pildes, *Separation of Parties, Not Powers*, 119 HARV. L. REV. 2311 (2006).

institutional loyalty that Madison thought members of Congress would assert as against the President. Members of a President's own party in the House or Senate are overwhelmingly likely to support the President's policy positions and basic claims to remain in office during impeachment trials or post-election, regardless of external views on the merits of those positions. To a certain extent this has long been true, as witnessed by the partisan judicial appointment battles that gave rise to *Marbury v. Madison*[6], and in Andrew Johnson's party line impeachment during Reconstruction.[7] But most observers, and this author, see the phenomenon as sharpening in the first two decades of the 21st-century. This is a deep problem in our constitutional democracy going forward, and there's no easy solution.

B. ELECTIONS NOT IDEOLOGY

Before exploring this problem in greater detail, it is worth pausing to note that perhaps our national rule of law problem is not as bad as it might be, or at least could have been, following the November 2020 election. What I mean by this perhaps counterintuitive suggestion is that support for President Trump's frivolous election claims following November 2020 was surprisingly and importantly lacking among many elite conservative and Republican actors and institutions. While almost every Republican in Congress or in the state attorneys general offices who faced imminent reelection before a Republican primary base sided with the President in late 2020 and early 2021, most Republican officials not facing electoral pressure did not align with Trumpist claims. A host of important and influential conservative and Republican individuals and institutions pointedly spoke against or even ruled against the President's claims. As such, it is most accurate to regard support for President Trump following his November 2020 loss as an *election-seeking imperative* rather than a core conservative or Republican ideological view. As I will show below, this is dramatically illustrated by the differential support of the president among Republican state Attorneys General, even in

---

[6] Marbury v. Madison, 5 U.S. 137 (1803).

[7] U.S. Senate: The Impeachment of Andrew Johnson (1868) President of the United States, https://www.senate.gov/artandhistory/history/common/briefing/Impeachment_Johnson.htm (last visited Aug 17, 2021).

deeply red states, who were appointed to their offices as opposed to the norm of standing for election.

Republicans and conservatives insulated from looming electoral pressure, in whatever institution where they were situated, tended to act and speak in accordance with democratic and rule of law values particularly after December 2020 when the US Supreme Court, itself filled with six Republicans and three Trump appointees, ruled decisively against the President. Over sixty judges on the federal bench and in the states, many of them Republicans and several appointed by Donald Trump himself, unanimously ruled against the President and his attorneys over a crucial three-month period. A high proportion of Republican Senators and House members who had previously announced that they were retiring in January 2021 or not seeking reelection in a subsequent senatorial round (e.g., Senator Pat Toomey of Pennsylvania) were similarly unwilling to support or vouch for the President's claims, and often (though belatedly, in the eyes of many) spoke out affirmatively against his efforts. Likewise, other national institutions such as the military and its leadership, led by men and women who may be Republican but did not serve in elected office, played an important role in our democracy's security by refusing to join the capital insurrection or other interventions suggested by some of Trump's team. Elite conservative thought makers such as the editorial pages of the *Wall Street Journal* and *National Review* were likewise extremely skeptical of the President's claims and critical of his failure to yield after the Supreme Court's December 2020 ruling.[8] And further, afield from government and into the professional ethical sphere, for all the hue and cry about the lawyers representing President Trump, he and his advisers had an increasingly difficult time eventually finding lawyers not named Rudy Giuliani. Major law firms, other attorneys who had originally represented the President, and the

---

[8] *See, e.g.*, Ed. Bd., *Trump's Embarrassing Electoral College Hustle*, WALL STREET JOURNAL (Dec. 30, 2020, 6:41 PM), https://www.wsj.com/articles/trumps-embarrassing-electoral-college-hustle-11609371708?page=22; Andrew C. McCarthy, *The Trump Campaign is Likely to Strike Out in Pennsylvania—Again*, NATIONAL REVIEW (Nov. 23, 2020, 11:09 AM), https://www.nationalreview.com/2020/11/the-trump-campaign-is-likely-to-strike-out-in-pennsylvania-again/.

overall bar seemed to resist supporting the most baseless of the President's claims.

All of this supports the point that many of our institutions and professional norms operated quite well under the dramatic strain of a lawless power seeker like President Trump. One can easily imagine a dramatically more extreme scenario had Trump-appointed judges ignored the law and ruled in his favor, and military leaders loyally supported his coup attempt. Something about our consensus rule of law norms *was* operating in the aftermath of the 2020 vote.

The problem, then, is less rule of law generally so much as it is a particular subpopulation's willingness to ignore rule of law and democracy values—those public officials who face upcoming elections to either hold their current post or ascend to a higher one. In the latest episode all those elected officials were Republican, but there is no claim here that Democratic elected officials are immune to the increasingly partisan pressures that apply to primary and general elections. Willingness to push past the limits of democratic traditions appears to be far more substantially correlated with the fact of standing for election or reelection than it does ideology. This makes the problem rather more limited, although it certainly does not make it small.

It is beyond the scope of this short chapter to offer a comprehensive solution to the failures of electoral politics in our current democracy, even if this author had such a solution. My aim is more limited, although points to an important set of questions that have been under-studied in the legal and political science academies. A relatively striking empirical fact emerged in November and December 2020 as the majority of the country's Republican Attorneys General signed on to a brief authored by Texas supporting the President's claims, containing legal arguments that the vast majority of academic observers regarded as illegitimate and frivolous.[9] Many readers will not be

---

[9] Mot. For Expediated Consideration of the Mot. For Leave to File a Bill of Compl. and for Expedition of Any Plenary Consideration of the Matter on the Pleadings if Pls.' Forthcoming Mot. For Interim Relief is Not Granted, 8, Dec. 7, 2021, https://www.supremecourt.gov/DocketPDF/22/22O155/163048/20201208132827887_TX-v-State-ExpedMot%202020-12-07%20FINAL.pdf; *See also* Alison Durkee, *17 States Agree The Supreme Court Should Overturn Biden's Win*, FORBES (Dec. 9, 2020 4:28 PM), https://www.forbes.com/sites/alisondurkee/2020/12/09/17-states-agree-the-supreme-court-should-overturn-election-biden-win-texas/?sh=327a03676452.

surprised that so many Republican Attorneys General joined such a brief, just as they would not be surprised if in some analogous future case if the majority of Democratic Attorneys General adhered to their party's leader and supported his or her national claims.

More interesting, and relevant to the notion of structural insulation from partisan politics, is the phenomenon of the handful of Republican Attorney's General who decided *not* to sign onto this bandwagon briefing by their GOP colleagues. When I looked at who they were, I was surprised initially that some of the non-signers came from some extremely "red" states, those that have gone for President Trump in 2016 and then again in 2020 often by 65% or more. Rather than baseline ideological polarity, the variable most associated with not joining the Texas brief was: <u>not</u> standing for contested reelection. A chart of these individuals along with each state selection mechanism and further analysis, comes later in the chapter. For now, I will briefly return to a bit more Madisonian theory and the general perception that our separation of powers regime is broken, before returning to the curious case of the Republican Attorneys General.

C. MADISON'S THEORY AND ITS LIMITS

In devising a democratic republic while holding deep fears of tyrannical overreaching, James Madison and other architects of the U.S. Constitution faced quandaries arising not just from governmental design but also from the realities of human nature of which they were well aware. For Madison and others, experience had proven that men were far from "angels" in terms of pure civic virtue, even those—perhaps especially those—who would seek and hold high public office. According to Madison, "[e]nlightened statesmen will not always be at the helm.[10] Personal ambition and appeal to base partisan instincts in the voting population, what the Framers called "faction", were clear and present dangers to be avoided in constitutional design. Much of the thought and debate during the Constitutional Convention, and the complexity and structure of the document that ultimately emerged, were driven by two fundamental

---

10 THE FEDERALIST NO. 51 (James Madison, 1788).

insights about structure and personal ambition and a desire to build a government that would dampen or thwart the influence of the latter. The problem is—by 2020 it was pretty clear that both structural checks on personal ambition were either ineffective or counterproductive, or both.

Madison's first hypothesis was that the unusually large scale of the new republic, which would only grow over the past two centuries, was itself a check on self-serving or faction-based politics. Larger voting pools—both statewide for the more deliberative U.S. Senate and even more so nationally for the exalted office of President—would blunt the force and corrupting influence of "faction" on the officials who held such national posts. *Quote about a big republic ensuring virtuous officials.*

Ironically, "bigness" may be block rather than salvation. Just like the parties subverting the structural checks and balances, drawing on Levinson and Pildes and others, the way media and social media and movements go viral and national enables rather than prevents a Donald Trump figure emerging nationally.

But Madison not content simply with predictive inculcation of civic virtue. He held the older notion that the perfectibility of human nature is fundamentally limited, such that good government sometimes must resort to structural counters—"checks and balances" in common parlance:

> Ambition must be made to counter ambition . . . . If men were angels, no government would be necessary. If angels were to govern men, neither external nor internal controls on government would be necessary. In framing a government which is to be administered by men over men, the great difficulty lies in this: you must first enable the government to control the government and in the next place obliged to control itself.[11]

Many historians and political scientists who have studied Madison and these writing attribute to him a pessimistic, even dismal, view of human nature. Exemplary of this attitude is Vernon Harrington's contention that Madison's overarching aim was to "overcome universal selfishness" through proper

[11] THE FEDERALIST NO. 51 (James Madison, 1788).

governmental structures.[12] Robert Dahl in summarizing Madison's Views of Human Ethics opined that,

> these axioms are Hobbesian in character and run something like this: men are instruments of their desires they pursue their desires to satiation if given the opportunity on such desire is the desire for power over other individuals, for not only is power directly satisfying but it also has great instrumental value because a wide variety of satisfactions depend on it."[13]

Subsequent history has demonstrated the soundness of the insight that human nature coupled with high office will occasionally produce and enable leaders who makes choices contrary to the public interest. The fundamental principle that "ambition must be made to counter ambition" is as important now as it was over two centuries ago. More modern structures, like strong and disciplined political parties and the rise of diffused and fragmented media culture, have strained traditional checks and balances almost to the breaking point. Traditional separation of powers devices are by themselves inadequate to check power; among elected officials partisan affiliation runs deeper than ever and induces behavior correlated with party identification rather than institutional affinity. What may be needed, particularly for elected "rule of law" officials like the Attorneys General in the various states, is insulation from the normal operation of electoral politics so their fidelity to office corresponds more closely to the original Madisonian insights that are under strain today.

D. LESSONS FROM STATE ATTORNEY GENERAL BEHAVIOR IN THE ELECTION AFTERMATH

The attorneys general of the 50 states or an increasingly important institutional office in our law and politics, and relative to their importance, dramatically understudied in legal academia. I notable exception to this dearth of scholarship is William Marshall's elegant essay in the Yale Law Journal fifteen years ago, and I will draw on Professor Marshall's description of

[12] Kobylka, *supra* note 2, at 202.

[13] *See id.* at 193.

the office and his insights in the following paragraphs.[14] Although the vast majority of states provide that their Attorney General is elected, enough states retain older models of appointed attorneys general similar to the federal model, that in late 2020 this variation provided a natural experiment in the salience of facing a Republican primary election and support of President trumps speeches election fraud claims. I will return to this differential voting behavior among Republican AGs in a few paragraphs, after a summary of the history of this office in the United States and its connection with rule of law values.

Professor Marshalls essay on the office of Attorney General provides a concise historical overview as well as citations to other literature on the office. To summarize, the office as it currently stands has roots that stretch back almost 800 years, when English kings appointed Royal attorneys to represent the ground in various regions.[15] Gradually English kings adopted the practice of appointing a single chief attorney, designated the Attorney General, to be the chief legal advisor to the royal executive. As the powers and duties of this office developed through the 17th and 18th centuries, the Attorney General was regarded as having a civic duty to defend the rule of law and public justice.[16] The National Association of State Attorneys General in the United States, aware of this rule of law pedigree, took pains to mention in a 1990 report that even the Kings' Attorney General was an independent rule of law official "responsible for justice."[17]

In the colonies in the new United States after 1789, states imported and retrenched the core aspects of attorney general authority in their own constitutions. From the beginning, according to Professor Marshall, states valued and granted more independent executive authority to their own Attorneys General then was embodied in federal constitutional text and practice. And this was true even though contrary to today, almost all states originally provided for a appointment of their attorney

[14] *See* William P. Marshall, *Break up the Presidency? Governors, State Attorneys General, and Lessons from the Divided Executive*, 115 YALE L.J. 2446 (2006).

[15] *See id.* at 2449.

[16] *See id.* at 2450.

[17] NASAG Report, 16.

general, rather than popular election.[18] The Minnesota supreme court in 1851 aptly summarized the checks and balances Rationale of enhanced a G authority in the states, writing:

> Rather than conferring all executive authority upon a governor, the drafters of our constitution divided the executive powers of state government among six elected officers. This was a conscious effort on the part of the drafters, who were well aware of the colonial aversion to Royal governors who possessed unified executive powers.

In our modern political matrix, state attorneys general do often provide legal and political counterweight to otherwise strong governors in many states. But just like congressional checks and balances, the distort tattoo of a fact of strong partisan politics on the structural checks provided by attorney general independence has diluted much of the good government protection. This was vividly illustrated in November and December 2020 as the vast majority of Republican Attorney General breached their rule of law judgment to join a patently frivolous brief failed by the Texas Attorney General. Importantly, the majority of Republicans Attorneys General who did not have to face popular election or were otherwise insulated, did not join the meritless Attorneys General brief.

Somewhat ironically yet unfortunately, this distorting effects of partisan politics are able to operate in most states on the office of Attorney General, because of what was thought to be a late 19th and early 20th century reform proposal, namely making attorneys general selected by direct election as opposed to buy gubernatorial or state Supreme Court appointment. From the middle of the 19th century forward, almost all new states joining the union provided for election of the Attorney General, and most existing states switched their state constitutions to mirror this electoral trend. The rationale for doing so was a good government checks and balances view resident with James Madison's Federalist 51. Open public elections were at the time thought to be less tainted by political and partisan influence than any of the available direct appointment regimes.[19] This has

---

18 *See supra* note 14 at 2451.

19 *See id.* at 2452; *see also id.* at FN 28.

contributed to a greater partisan polarization in this office originally imagined as a more neutral rule of law position.

I do not attempt to assess the overall merits or to merits of direct election of Attorneys General, a structure which is the prevailing norm in over 40 states. What is clear, however, in the context of the grassroots partisanship of the Trump election contestation, is that standing for a contested election correlated extremely highly among state Attorneys General with joining the tendentious Texas brief.

The following table lists the fill in the blank Republican Attorneys General in fall 2020, along with whether they joined the Texas lawsuit as well as the method by which they are appointed or retained in office.

1. GOP Attorneys General Not Joining

State	Attorney General	Manner of Selection[20]	Comments
Alaska	Ed Sniffen[21]	Gubernatorial Appointment	Appointed by Governor Mike Dunleavy in 2020.
Arizona	Mark Brnovich[22]	Popular Election	
Georgia	Chris Carr[23]	Popular Election	
Idaho	Leslie Wasden[24]	Popular Election	Took office in 2003.

[20] *How States Have Selected/and Select the Attorney General*, THE ALASKA STATE LEGISLATURE, http://www.akleg.gov/basis/get_documents.asp?session=28&docid=19896 (last visited May 19, 2021).

[21] *Ed Sniffen*, BALLOTPEDIA, https://ballotpedia.org/Ed_Sniffen (Last visited May 19, 2021).

[22] *Attorney General of Arizona*, BALLOTPEDIA, https://ballotpedia.org/Attorney_General_of_Arizona (Last visited May 19, 2021).

[23] *Attorney General of Georgia*, BALLOTPEDIA, https://ballotpedia.org/Attorney_General_of_Georgia (Last visited May 19, 2021).

[24] *Attorney General of Idaho*, BALLOTPEDIA, https://ballotpedia.org/Attorney_General_of_Idaho (Last visited May 19, 2021).

Kentucky	Daniel Cameron[25]	(Appointed)	Appointed by Governor Andy Bashear in 2019.
New Hampshire	Gordon MacDonald[26]	Gubernatorial Appointment	Subsequently nominated to the New Hampshire Supreme Court.
Ohio	David Yost[27]	Popular Election	
Wyoming	Bridget Hill[28]	Gubernatorial Appointment	Took office in 2020.[29]

2. GOP AGs Joining

State	Attorney General	Manner of Selection	Comments
Alabama	Steve Marshall[30]	Popular election	Term limited.
Arkansas	Leslie Rutledge[31]	Popular election	Term limited.

25 *Attorney General of Kentucky*, BALLOTPEDIA, https://ballotpedia.org/Attorney_General_of_Kentucky (Last visited May 19, 2021).

26 *Gordon MacDonald*, BALLOTPEDIA, https://ballotpedia.org/Gordon_MacDonald (Last Visited May 19, 2021).

27 *Attorney General of Ohio*, BALLOTPEDIA, https://ballotpedia.org/Attorney_General_of_Ohio (Last Visited May 19, 2021).

28 *Attorney General of Wyoming*, BALLOTPEDIA, https://ballotpedia.org/Attorney_General_of_Wyoming (Last Visited May 19, 2021).

29 *Bridget Hill*, NATIONAL ASSOCIATION OF ATTORNEYS GENERAL, https://www.naag.org/attorney-general/bridget-hill/ (Last visited May 19, 2021).

30 *Attorney General of Alabama*, BALLOTPEDIA, https://ballotpedia.org/Attorney_General_of_Alabama (last visited May 19, 2021); Ala. Const., amend. 282.

31 *Attorney General of Arkansas*, BALLOTPEDIA, https://ballotpedia.org/Attorney_General_of_Arkansas (last visited May 19, 2021).

Florida	Ashley Moody[32]	Popular election	
Indiana	Curtis Hill[33]	Popular election	Defeated in July 2020 primary.
Kansas	Derek Schmidt[34]	Popular election	No term limits. Running for governor in 2022.
Louisiana	Jeff Landry[35]	Popular election	
Mississippi	Lynn Fitch[36]	Popular election	
Missouri	Eric Schmitt[37]	Popular election	
Montana	Tim Fox[38]	Popular election	Term limited. Ran for governor in 2020.
Nebraska	Doug Peterson[39]	Popular election	

32 *Attorney General of Florida*, BALLOTPEDIA, https://ballotpedia.org/Attorney_General_of_Florida (last visited May 19, 2021); Fla const., art. VI, § 4b.

33 *Curtis Hill*, BALLOTPEDIA, https://ballotpedia.org/Curtis_Hill (last visited May 19, 2021).

34 *Attorney General of Kansas,* BALLOTPEDIA, https://ballotpedia.org/Attorney_General_of_Kansas.

35 *Attorney General of Louisiana*, BALLOTPEDIA, https://ballotpedia.org/Attorney_General_of_Louisiana (last visited May 19, 2021).

36 *Mississippi Attorney General*, BALLOTPEDIA, https://ballotpedia.org/Mississippi_Attorney_General (last visited May 19, 2021).

37 *Attorney General of Missouri*, BALLOTPEDIA, https://ballotpedia.org/Attorney_General_of_Missouri (last visited May 19, 2021).

38 *Tim Fox (Montana)*, BALLOTPEDIA, https://ballotpedia.org/Tim_Fox_(Montana) (last visited May 19, 2021).

39 *Attorney General of Nebraska*, BALLOTPEDIA, https://ballotpedia.org/Attorney_General_of_Nebraska (last visited May 19, 2021).

North Dakota	Wayne Stenehjem[40]	Popular election	In office since 2000.
Oklahoma	Mike Hunter[41]	Popular election	
South Carolina	Alan Wilson[42]	Popular election	
South Dakota	Jason Ravnsborg[43]	Popular election	
Tennessee	Herbert Slaterly[44]	State Supreme Court selection	
Texas	Ken Paxton[45]	Popular election	
Utah	Sean Reyes[46]	Popular election	
West Virginia	Patrick Morrissey[47]	Popular election	

Although individual attorneys general's choices might be driven by localized or idiosyncratic factors, taking as a whole, the national trend illustrated in the above tables is striking. Seventeen of the eighteen GOP state AGs who were on the Texas brief alleging far-fetched theories of election fraud took office through popular election. They exercised their legal judgment

40 *Attorney General of North Dakota*, BALLOTPEDIA, https://ballotpedia.org/Attorney_General_of_North_Dakota (last visited May 19, 2021).

41 *Attorney General of Oklahoma*, BALLOTPEDIA, https://ballotpedia.org/Attorney_General_of_Oklahoma (last visited May 19, 2021).

42 *Attorney General of South Carolina*, BALLOTPEDIA, https://ballotpedia.org/Attorney_General_of_South_Carolina (last visited May 19, 2021).

43 *Attorney General of South Dakota*, BALLOTPEDIA, https://ballotpedia.org/Attorney_General_of_South_Dakota (last visited May 19, 2021).

44 *Attorney General of Tennessee*, BALLOTPEDIA, https://ballotpedia.org/Attorney_General_of_Tennessee (last visited May 19, 2021).

45 *Attorney General of Texas*, BALLOTPEDIA, https://ballotpedia.org/Attorney_General_of_Texas (last visited May 19, 2021).

46 *Attorney General of Utah*, BALLOTPEDIA, https://ballotpedia.org/Attorney_General_of_Utah (last visited May 19, 2021).

47 *Attorney General of West Virginia*, BALLOTPEDIA, https://ballotpedia.org/Attorney_General_of_West_Virginia (last visited May 19, 2021).

about whether or not to join the Texas brief while facing the prospect of standing for reelection and/or running for higher office in future years, both instances in which they would be directly dependent on the support of a motivated and pro-Trump GOP primary base. It is implausible, based on these numbers, to avoid the implication that their political ambition inflected the choice they made as public attorneys regarding the Texas lawsuit. By contrast, half of the attorneys general who did not join this effort were appointed to their office, and even those elected had particular reasons that insulated them from the sharpest aspects of partisan politics in their home states. Leslie Wasden of Idaho, for instance, has held that state AG's office for almost 20 years, winning six competitive elections, thus building up an incumbency advantage that outweighs some effects of pure partisan primary voting. In Kentucky, Daniel Cameron is under the high-profile patronage of his former employer, Senator Mitch McConnell, who is a dominant force in the GOP politics of that state independent of President Trump and his supporters.

A simple probabilistic analysis underscores the above points. In December 2020, there were 21 GOP attorneys general who held their offices through election; 17 of them were on the Texas brief. Crudely speaking, being an elected Attorney General and a Republican produced a 81% likelihood of joining the far-fetched electoral claims that Texas asserted. Conversely, four of the five GOP attorneys general who were appointed to their posts decided in their legal judgment not to join the brief, meaning that being a Republican Attorney General and holding office through appointment made one only 20% likely to endorse the Texas claims. This insulation from electoral sanction perhaps applied even to the behavior of the nation's Attorney General, William Barr, who few outside the core GOP would have regarded as a bastion of pure neutrality during his controversial tenure in office. But at the end of his term, even AG Barr and other top Trump-appointed DOJ officials refused to endorse or pursue the President's ongoing and increasingly baseless claims of fraud. These were ideological allies of the President to their core, but the future prospects for Barr and others like him did not depend on their own standing for office in a GOP primary.

In sum, last year's episode provides a clear and vivid example of the distorting effects of elected Attorneys General on their function in promoting the rule of law. To the extent we think Attorneys General play a substantial rule of law function distinct from there being purely political actors. This in turn leads to a confident suggestion to the legal and political science academies as well as a much more tentative cluster of policy ideas to consider. From a research and scholarly point of view, Attorneys General are under studied in most respects, not the least of which has to do with the connection between their selection and reappointment mechanisms and the contested choices they would make an office. Their behavior surrounding the Texas brief and the 2020 election litigation does suggest that facing a primary electorate in the current Republican party correlates with behavior that many in the profession would consider to be a breach of the rule of law. My point here is structural and not ideological, and that the same distorted of influence from facing election good well occur for Democratic Attorneys General should a national controversy occur in future years.

My scholarly suggestion for members of the little legal and political science academies is to focus more carefully on the broad range of choices that state Attorneys Generals make, and develop studies with empirical rigor of whether contested political choices in the ordinary operation of state policymaking are inflicted by the way in which an attorney general is chosen. A voluminous body of empirical and descriptive scholarship exists with respect to state judges, comparing judicial decision making by different judicial selection mechanisms, and does show statistically significant differences in how judges decide cases with elections looming. We would predict a similar dynamic to apply to other rule of law officials such as Attorneys General. More research and granular tracking of the thousands of policy decisions and litigation choices made by the nations Attorneys General is necessary, however, before we have a clear sense of the scope of the issue or problem. But more and better academic research in the years ahead will help in this assessment, and might produce welcome policy reform.

As to the reforms themselves, there's no easy or obvious path. Most straightforward of course would be for the majority of states who currently elect their Attorneys General to consider reverting to the older model of appointed Attorneys General. This would solve one problem, but it might exacerbate another. Recalled that many of the states who adopted an electoral model for their Attorneys General did so precisely to insulate the AG from Gubernatorial control. Moving back to an appointed model would entail creative solutions such as having the attorney general perhaps appointed by the state Supreme Court or some other body which itself was normally insulated from direct political influence. But those structures invite complexity and contestation in the state constitutional convention is involved, and at the end of the day actual reforms are unlikely soon.

A more limited model of reform might except the fact that state Attorneys General are elected, and that disconnection to public opinion may even be a desirable model. Reforms might then inhere in the form of reducing incentives to seek multiple reelections or to seek higher state-wide or even national office. State constitutions could be structured to bar Attorneys General from running for any other state-wide office such as governor. The predictive effect of this would be to dilute incentives to pander to the most extreme aspects of either parties' primary base. More constitutionally suspect, but perhaps equally efficacious, would be efforts for states to amend their constitutions to prevent their Attorneys General from running for national office such a senator. While states probably could do this with a restriction on running for higher office for current Attorneys General, they probably could not do so for former office holders. But a proscription on current Attorneys General seeking higher state office, either as Governor or Senator or House Member, would do some work in blunting the incentive to higher office, or in Madisonian terms the "ambition" that many state Attorneys General displayed in the 2020 election litigation and other episodes.

For many readers, and perhaps even for this author, some of this seems almost fanciful given how deeply political The office of Attorney General has become in most states, and the tendency of popular Attorneys General in both parties to see higher office within their state or nationally. For a broadening perspective, however, a bit of judicial history is helpful. Following the Civil War and in the mid to late 19 century, many prominent judges at the state and federal level or often mentioned or promoted as candidates for Senate, or president, or governor, or other prominent and purely political offices. This trend was so salient that a counter movement arose, arguing the judges were so fundamental to the rule of law that they aren't either be barred, Or make it clear voluntary statement that they would not seek political office during or after their judicial tenure. A forceful speech to this effect was given by New York Supreme Court Justice W.W. Goodrich in 1903, protesting what he termed "the vicious invasion which is threatening the usefulness of the bench."[48] Justice Goodrich criticized to hypothetical "Judge who is listening with expectant ear to the beat of political preferment buzzing in his bonnet." In an evocative phrase that mini today would like to a tribute to our state and federal judges, just as good rich opined that "*the judicial office should be at once the cradle of duty and the grave of political ambition.*"[49] Although our courts today and judges are by no means completely free of ideology or occasional politicized voting, revealed behavior in the 2020 election litigation and other salient recent examples does suggest that judges today do embody at least a measure of good riches "cradle of duty" ideal. Republican-appointed judges in the months following the 2020 election repeatedly broke from their party, often even from the man who appointed them to the federal bench, to rule against President Trump and his frivolous claims.

As a thought experiment, how important is us to regard state Attorneys General, the top lawyer in every state charged with representing the public interest, as inhabiting an office that that is "at once the cradle of duty and the grave of political ambition." Because while the modern state attorney general's office may well have an ample quantum of public regarding duty associated with it, it is hardly the grave of political ambition. Indeed, in many states and for many ambitious and talented candidates who happen to be lawyers, the attorney general

48 Note, *A Judicial Protest Against Judges Running for Office*, 37 AM. L. REV. 1, 440 (1903).

49 *See id.* (emphasis added).

position yes quite strategically a launching pad to aspirations or actual achievement of higher political office. It may be that there is nothing inherently wrong with this, or even that the benefits outweigh the problems with such a system. But such political incentive structures do inflect and even distort performance in office and warrant further study and ought to catalyze discussion of reforms. Politics and the rule of law will always interact, and ought to in a democracy, but the past year illustrates the importance of building better structures to ensure they remain distinct in times of greatest crisis.

PART 2

ROOTS OF AMERICAN NATIONAL IDENTITY

CHAPTER 7

CHRISTIAN NATIONALISM AND THE RULE OF LAW

Robert K. Vischer[1]

Because so much of the "Stop the Steal" movement—culminating in the deadly attack on the U.S. Capitol on January 6, 2021—was covered with a veneer of Christianity, our response has to include a dimension grounded in an authentic Christian understanding of the world. Among the many heart-breaking images emerging from that day were the "Jesus Saves" banners being held by rioters entering the Capitol, right alongside the confederate flags, nooses, and Holocaust sweatshirts. This followed weeks of "Jericho marches," prayer meetings, and rallies premised on the idea that God ordained Donald Trump to serve eight years as President, and that those who stood in the way were attempting to thwart God's will for America.

Theologians can address Christian nationalists' claims about God, historians can contextualize their influence against the backdrop of earlier American fundamentalist movements, and sociologists can analyze the movement as a cultural phenomenon. But lawyers and law professors—particularly Christian lawyers and law professors—must use our expertise to help Americans understand how and why Christian nationalism distorts our faith and threatens the rule of law.

A. WHAT IS CHRISTIAN NATIONALISM (AND WHAT IS IT NOT)?

One unfortunate aspect of the American culture war is the tendency to deploy words in ways that stretch them beyond any semblance of their original meanings. Terms such as "woke," "PC" and "cancel culture" are now deployed to signal that something is bad without shedding meaningful light on the

---

1 Dean and Mengler Chair in Law, University of St. Thomas School of Law (MN). Thanks to Mark Alexander, Rick Garnett, Andy Perlman, and David Skeel for helpful comments on an earlier draft. I am writing this from my perspective as a Catholic and the dean of a Catholic law school.

reasons why it's bad. The latest term to meet this fate may be "Christian nationalism." Since the attack on the U.S. Capitol, it's showing signs of becoming an all-purpose condemnation of any effort to integrate Christian beliefs with civic engagement, even perfectly peaceful ones.[2]

So let's start by clearing away some confusion, which can lead to conversations about Christian nationalism simply enflaming our political tribalism: What is Christian nationalism not?

First, Christian nationalism is not patriotism. Love of country is a healthy aspect of being human, a reflection that the particularity of place matters to our identity and values. Patriotism becomes unhealthy when we reimagine our national identity as an expression of divine will, elevating our nation above others on some sort of God-ordained hierarchy.

Second, Christian nationalism is not Christian political engagement. We are not a "Christian nation" in the sense that Christian nationalists mean, but we are a nation in which our political discourse has long been shaped by Christian values, on both the left and the right. The civil rights movement was infused with Christian images and principles. The progressive push for immigration reform prominently features Christ's admonition about welcoming the stranger. On the issue that's been the most contentious over the past half-century, abortion, the most effective pro-life voices have been steeped in Christian principles. But the core of their arguments has been grounded in observations about fetal development and articulations of life's value in terms that are accessible beyond Christianity.

Third, Christian nationalism is not white evangelicalism. Though many Christian nationalists count themselves as white evangelicals, other non-evangelical Christians, and even some

---

[2] *See, e.g.*, Katherine Stewart, *The Supreme Court's Religious Persecution Complex*, THE NEW REPUBLIC, April 9, 2021 (arguing that the "real goal" of the Supreme Court's rulings on challenges to COVID restrictions brought by churches was "to reinforce a certain narrative—a narrative of Christian nationalism, as it happens—through a piece of courtroom theater") (https://newrepublic.com/article/161987/supreme-court-fulton-philadelphia-religious); Rachel Mikva, *Christian nationalism is a threat, and not just from Capitol attackers invoking Jesus*, USA TODAY, Jan. 31, 2021, https://www.usatoday.com/story/opinion/2021/01/31/christian-nationalism-josh-hawley-ted-cruz-capitol-attack-column/4292193001/ (arguing that Senator Ted Cruz "uses code words like 'religious liberty' to sustain Christian privilege and cultural authority.").

non-Christians, hold Christian nationalist beliefs, and many white evangelicals reject Christian nationalism.[3]

Fourth, Christian nationalist beliefs do not correspond to Christian religious practices. There is no evidence to suggest that our concern about the former should translate into concern about the latter. For example, the more one adheres to Christian nationalist views, the less willing one is to acknowledge police discrimination against Black Americans.[4] However, "as people more frequently attend church, pray, or read their sacred scriptures, they become more likely to recognize racial discrimination in policing."[5] The same pattern holds regarding attitudes toward immigration, the environment, refugees, and Muslims.[6] In light of the data, Andrew Whitehead and Samuel Perry conclude that it would be a mistake for "observers to conclude that 'religious commitment' necessarily inclines Americans to hold conservative political positions."[7] For the most part, researchers "find that the association between Christian nationalism and . . . attitudes toward racial and religious minorities tends to work in the opposite direction than the association between private religious practice and these same things."[8]

While Christian nationalists "seek to defend particular group boundaries and privileges using Christian language," that approach is not pervasive in American Christianity.[9] Christian nationalism and American Christianity are not the same thing. As Philip Gorski puts it, Christian nationalism "is political idolatry dressed up as religious orthodoxy."[10]

So what precisely is Christian nationalism? Paul Miller explains that Christian nationalism is a political ideology holding that "the American nation is defined by Christianity and that the government should take steps to keep it that way to

---

3 ANDREW L. WHITEHEAD & SAMUEL L. PERRY, TAKING AMERICA BACK FOR GOD: CHRISTIAN NATIONALISM IN THE UNITED STATES x (2020).

4 *Id.* at 21.

5 *Id.*

6 *Id.*

7 *Id.*

8 *Id.* at 155.

9 *Id.* at 21.

10 *Id.*

sustain and maintain our Christian heritage."[11] Whitehead and Perry provide the most comprehensive account of Christian nationalism, which they describe as "a complex of explicit and implicit ideals, values, and myths . . . through which Americans perceive and navigate their social world."[12] It "is a cultural framework that blurs distinctions between Christian identity and American identity, viewing the two as closely related and seeking to enhance and preserve their union."[13] If America was founded for a unique purpose by God, and the Constitution was divinely inspired, then displaying the American flag in church sanctuaries, for example, is not a blurring of American and Christian identity but a natural marker of faith.[14]

B. WHY SHOULD WE CARE?

Christian nationalism is not the primary threat to the rule of law globally—inequality, dislocation, polarization, and rapidly declining trust in government all loom large in the toxic stew that has seen a significant decline in fundamental rights, an erosion of checks on government power, and a rise in corruption in countries around the world.[15] Even in the United States, these other factors likely carry more explanatory weight than Christian nationalism. But Christian nationalism has contributed to the threat the rule of law faces in our nation. Its adherents may commit acts of political violence in extreme cases, as they did on January 6, but the more common threat will be

---

[11] Paul D. Miller, *What Is Christian Nationalism?*, CHRISTIANITY TODAY (Feb. 3, 2021), https://www.christianitytoday.com/ct/2021/february-web-only/what-is-christian-nationalism.html.

[12] WHITEHEAD & PERRY, *supra* note 3, at x.

[13] *Id.* at 15.

[14] Not everyone agrees that "Christian nationalism" is the appropriate term to describe what is happening: "What has passed for Christian nationalism in the United States is not Christian nationalism at all, but instead a revivalist folk religion massively overrepresented in so-called Evangelical, fundamentalist, and charismatic Protestantism. The very Americanism of what liberals and progressives have identified as Christian nationalism indicates that this is a rhetorical conflation done in service of openly partisan political aims." Miles Smith, *Would That It Really Were 'Christian Nationalism'*, THE AMERICAN CONSERVATIVE (Mar. 8, 2021, 12:01 AM), https://www.theamericanconservative.com/articles/would-it-really-were-christian-nationalism/.

[15] Ted Piccone, *The rule of law is under duress everywhere*, BROOKINGS (Mar. 17, 2020), https://www.brookings.edu/blog/order-from-chaos/2020/03/17/the-rule-of-law-is-under-duress-everywhere/; WORLD JUSTICE PROJECT, Rule of Law Index (WJP Rule of Law Index (worldjusticeproject.org)) ("Around the world [in 2020], more countries declined than improved in overall rule of law score for the third year running, continuing a negative slide.").

support for candidates who undercut the rule of law by attacking the institutions and traditions on which it depends.

And why is Christian nationalism so dangerous? Put simply, when we merge our identity as Christians with our identity as Americans, we invest political positions with a level of certainty and fervor traditionally reserved for matters of religious faith. We will do anything to ensure that our conception—or more accurately, our tribe's conception—of American interests prevails politically.

Christian nationalists are no longer debating ideas about which reasonable people can disagree; they are defending Christianity against its enemies. This is why noted evangelical author Eric Metaxas said, in reference to his claims of a stolen election, that it's "God's will" for America to keep spreading liberty around the world, and so, "Who cares what I can prove in the court?" Regardless of what the courts say about election fraud, "we need to fight to the death, to the last drop of blood because it's worth it."[16] Or the Minnesota pastor who, speaking from his church sanctuary three days after the violence at the Capitol, explained to his congregation how important it is for every town to have "patriots who are ready to arm up and be part of a citizens militia to protect our freedoms."[17]

When a particular political outcome becomes a tenet of my Christian faith, there's nothing left to argue about. And when there's nothing left to argue about, that's a very dangerous place for democracy to find itself.[18] The danger is exacerbated because the substantive claims of Christian nationalism are rooted in an us-versus-them mindset. The claims represent "something more than religion," as Christian nationalism "is as ethnic and

---

[16] Robert K. Vischer, *Getting serious (and precise) about Christian nationalism*, RELIGION NEWS SERVICE (Feb. 12, 2021), https://religionnews.com/2021/02/12/getting-serious-and-precise-about-christian-nationalism/; *see also* Rod Dreher, *What I Saw At The Jericho March*, THE AMERICAN CONSERVATIVE (Dec. 12, 2020), https://theamerican conservative.com/dreher/what-i-saw-at-the-jericho-march/ (quoting "Jericho March" speaker who urged crowd to "align our spirituality to our politics.").

[17] NPR, *Some Christians Feel It's A God-Given Mission To Fight On Trump's Behalf: NPR*, MORNING EDITION, at 5:04 AM (Jan. 18, 2021), https://www.npr.org/2021/01/18/957982008/some-christians-feel-its-a-god-given-mission-to-fight-on-trumps-behalf.

[18] This phenomenon is not unique to the United States, of course, and can be seen, to varying degrees, in the rise of religious fundamentalists in Israel, India, and various Islamic countries.

political as it is religious."[19] Proponents "have historically built their ideological foundation on a narrow, literalist interpretation of God's commands to Old Testament Israel, applying them to their contemporary national situation."[20]

Christian nationalists' calls to " 'take America back for God' are not primarily about mobilizing the faithful toward religious ends," but instead seek "to retain or gain power in the public sphere—whether political, social, or religious."[21] And the struggle reflects "a particular racialized understanding of national identity" that "allows those who embrace it to express a racialized identity without resorting to racialized terms."[22] Though the rhetoric of liberty pervades Christian nationalism, proponents tend "to promote defenses of authoritarian control, especially when the target population of that control is nonwhite."[23]

As a percentage of the population, Christian nationalists are in decline, but that can actually increase the danger they pose in the near term. Americans are leaving the Christian tradition, particularly Protestantism. Americans "who are not connected to a Christian tradition will be much less likely to be exposed to Christian nationalism," and "their social networks will offer much lower levels of social support for those beliefs in the event that they hold them."[24] However, the "committed core of true believers will most likely maintain their intensity of support for Christian nationalism, especially as they continue to see themselves as a persecuted minority."[25] More Americans are rejecting the notion that our nation should favor Christianity formally, and thus "the sizable portion of Americans who pine for Christianity's former prominence in American civic life feel threatened and marginalized."[26]

---

19 WHITEHEAD & PERRY, *supra* note 3, at 10. Christian nationalism is "often a stronger predictor of Americans' attitudes about race, gender, immigration, gun rights, Islam, and family/sexuality issues than political ideology." *Id.* at 13.

20 *Id.* at 13 (noting arguments by sociologist Phillip Gorski).

21 *Id.* at 15.

22 *Id.* at 16.

23 *Id.* at 17.

24 *Id.* at 49.

25 *Id.*

26 *Id.* at 4–5. Note that it's not necessarily an example of "Christian nationalism" to regret the fact that policies in a given area no longer reflect norms shaped by

Even as their ranks diminish, Christian nationalists still comprise a significant portion of Americans. As of 2017, 29% of Americans agreed that "the federal government should declare the United States a Christian nation," and as of 2013, nearly two-thirds of Americans agreed that "God has granted America a special role in human history."[27] Some observers predict that Christian nationalism has strong future prospects in American politics because it can cloak "inflammatory xenophobia in religious language that may be more broadly palatable."[28]

C. TOWARD A HEALTHY CHRISTIAN POLITICAL ENGAGEMENT

Against the tumultuous backdrop of Christian nationalism, this would be a good time for American Christians to step back and reflect on the role that our faith plays in our political engagement. If we're not happy with the voices that loudly proclaim direct knowledge of God's will for American politics (often arising on the right), and we're not ready to agree with the voices that insist faith has only a marginal role to play in our political discourse (often arising on the left), what's the path forward?

Christian nationalism has exemplified three characteristics that healthy Christian political engagement must avoid: our engagement must not be a conversation-stopper, a signal of self-righteousness, or driven by fear of "the other."

1. Christian Faith Should Not Be a Conversation-Stopper

Christians have long used religious language to advocate for particular policies, and there is nothing inherently wrong with doing so provided that the religious language is an entry point, not the entirety of the argument. "The Bible says it, I believe it,

---

Christianity. Americans can and should advocate for policies that they believe promote human flourishing, and their views will often be influenced by their faith traditions.

[27] *Id.* at 6. "If you define a Christian nationalist as anyone who believes the United States is currently or ever was a Christian nation, more than three out of every five Americans reside in this category. If it includes only those who currently see America as a Christian nation, the number is less than three in 10." *Id.* at 7.

[28] Eliza Griswold, *A Pennsylvania Lawmaker and the Resurgence of Christian Nationalism*, THE NEW YORKER (May 9, 2021) https://www.newyorker.com/news/on-religion/a-pennsylvania-lawmaker-and-the-resurgence-of-christian-nationalism.

that settles it" may be a pithy (and popular) bumper sticker, but it's not fertile ground for the dialogues on which our democracy depends. The rule of law requires that the law-giver offer reasons that are rationally accessible, even if not agreeable, to all. On both sides of the political spectrum, the most effective advocates convey the public relevance of Christian values in terms that are wide open to disagreement.

The problem arises when Christian nationalists merge their religious and political identities, offering religious conclusions in place of political arguments. In explaining a key aspect of democracies, Jurgen Habermas argued that "the justification of norms and commands requires that a real discourse be carried out."[29] His principle of "discourse ethics" holds that "[o]nly those norms may claim to be valid that could meet with the consent of all affected in their role as participants in a practical discourse."[30] It's the same reason judges take the time to explain the reasoning underlying their decisions—in a democracy, it's important that the exercise of power is grounded in terms that are accessible to those against whom it is wielded. References to God's will or divine judgment are not accessible; if you don't accept the underlying religious premises, there's no meaningful way to participate in the discourse. And if you embrace the religious premise, it can be difficult to dissuade you from whatever conclusion is presumed to follow.

Consider, for example, a refrain of Robert Jeffress, a megachurch pastor and a member of President Trump's evangelical advisory board: "we say without hesitation or apology that America was founded as a Christian nation, and our future success depends on our country being faithful to those eternal truths of God's word."[31] The truths proclaimed in the Bible are offered as governing principles for the nation, not based on their merits, but because "[t]he framers of the Constitution and the earliest jurists demonstrated a clear preference for Christianity," and "[t]hey did not hesitate to declare that America was a Christian nation."[32] According to

[29] JÜRGEN HABERMAS, MORAL CONSCIOUSNESS AND COMMUNICATIVE ACTION 68 (Christian Lenhardt et al. trans., 1990).

[30] *Id.* at 197.

[31] *Id.* at 57.

[32] *Id.* at 4.

Jeffress, we should be guided by our history, which reveals, in his view, that "the government can (and for more than 150 years did) show a preference for the Christian faith."[33]

Contrast this identity-driven boundary-drawing—i.e., our identity as a Christian nation compels obedience to what we assert as Christian political positions—with the humility of Abraham Lincoln's second inaugural address, delivered near the end of a brutal and bloody war. President Lincoln observed that both sides in the conflict "read the same Bible and pray to the same God and each invokes His aid against the other."[34] This was a simple recognition of our shared humanity and shared faith, even at a time when we were killing each other in a conflict over the deeply immoral practice of slavery. Lincoln did not accuse those fighting for the Confederacy of not being "real Christians," he did not claim that God had personally assured him that the Union's cause was just, and he did not assert that God's plan for civilization hinged on the outcome of the war. Instead, he recognized that those on the other side were just as sincere in their faith as he was.

Did Lincoln's humility weaken his resolve to win the war and end slavery? Not at all. Did his empathy for those supporting the Confederacy lead him to look the other way and ignore their support of a deeply unjust institution? Hardly. Humility and empathy shaped the way he engaged his opponents, not his commitment to the moral claims underlying the conflict.

The "Stop the Steal" movement was driven, at least in part, by Christian nationalists who embraced the religious assertion that God's will for America was to have Donald Trump serve two terms as President. After he lost the election, the emerging narrative wrapped the desired political objective in religious imagery and conspiracy theorizing that was immune from factual refutation. Trump was chosen by God, forces of evil were working to thwart God's plan, and good Christians must join the battle. Whether or not judges found evidence to support the assertion that Trump received more votes than Joe Biden was

---

[33] *Id.*

[34] Abraham Lincoln, Second Inaugural Address (Mar. 4, 1865), Lincoln's Second Inaugural Address—Lincoln Memorial (U.S. National Park Service) (nps.gov).

beside the point. As Eric Metaxas told an interviewer who asked about the election litigation, "I am thrilled to be too ignorant of the details to answer that question in any substantive way."[35] After all, "people I know and trust well have heard from God that Trump will have a second term."[36] The attack on the Capitol did not result from a careful weighing of the evidence of election fraud. Evidence is irrelevant once God has spoken. The chaos of January 6 did not lead Christian nationalists to rediscover humility or consider the possibility that their advocacy might have been misguided: evangelical leader Franklin Graham, for example, compared Trump's second impeachment—imposed after the President had stirred up his supporters by relentlessly promoting stolen election claims—to the betrayal of Jesus.[37]

The answer today is not, as some insist, to exclude commitments grounded in faith from our political discourse or to require that believers translate their moral claims into non-religious language before joining the debate. The answer is to articulate the public relevance of our faith commitments in terms that reflect humility and empathy. For example, Martin Luther King Jr.'s faith was inseparable from his public witness. Faith was not out of bounds for him, but his faith was not invoked to shut down dissent or signal an us-versus-them worldview. His opposition to segregation was grounded in his belief that "a just law is a man-made code that squares with the moral law, or the law of God."[38] However, he went on to explain that "an unjust law is a code that a majority inflicts on a minority that is not binding on itself."[39] King did not demand that his listeners embrace the religious foundations of his truth-telling; he asked them to embrace the resulting moral claims, regardless of how one arrived at them. He brought his faith into the public

[35] Dreher, *supra* note 16.

[36] *Id.*

[37] Phillip Gorski, *Trump's rise and fall unified the two most pernicious, racist myths about America*, NBC NEWS (Jan. 29, 2021), nbcnews.com.

[38] Martin Luther King Jr., *Letter From a Birmingham Jail* (1963), https://letter fromjail.com.

[39] *Id.*

square without a trace of embarrassment, but it was the beginning of the conversation, not the end of it.[40]

Today's Christian nationalists are hindered not only by their failure to engage in terms that are rationally accessible, but often by their failure to engage reality itself. In his recent encyclical *Fratelli Tutti*, Pope Francis writes that true community is possible only when it is built by those who "shoulder the inevitable responsibilities of life as it is."[41] Christian nationalists too often preclude meaningful conversations with those who disagree by failing to engage life "as it is." They are among the leading proponents of various conspiracy theories regarding the 2020 election, secret plots to put tracking devices into vaccines, climate change as a fraud, child-trafficking rings, and various far-fetched plots promulgated by the internet movement Q-Anon.[42] Christians are supposed to engage and minister to the world as it is in order to help bring about the world as it could be; Christians are not allowed to retreat to a fantasy world as an escape from human suffering or disorder. That requires us to invest time and effort in understanding reality, not a tribal narrative presented in You Tube videos and anonymous internet messages. The fact that Christians have a leading role in Q-Anon and other outrageous conspiracy theory movements is a scandalous departure from the dictates of our faith.[43]

Bringing faith into the political arena as a conversation-stopper—whether through political advocacy as a function of

---

[40] ROBERT K. VISCHER, MARTIN LUTHER KING JR. AND THE MORALITY OF LEGAL PRACTICE: LESSONS IN LOVE AND JUSTICE (2013).

[41] Francis, "Fratelli Tutti," The Holy See (Oct. 3, 2020), https://www.vatican.va/content/francesco/en/encyclicals/documents/papa-francesco_20201003_enciclica-fratelli-tutti.html.

[42] *See, e.g.*, Andrew Gardner, *Why are Christians so susceptible to conspiracy?*, BAPTIST NEWS GLOBAL, Aug. 31, 2020 (https://baptistnews.com/article/why-are-christians-so-susceptible-to-conspiracy/#.YPh6—hKiUk); *Why Do So Many Christians Buy Into Conspiracy Theories Like "Plandemic?,"* RELEVANT MAGAZINE, May 14, 2020 (https://www.relevantmagazine.com/current/why-do-so-many-christians-buy-into-conspiracy-theories-like-plandemic/).

[43] *Understanding QAnon's Connection to American Politics, Religion, and Media Consumption*, PRRI (May 27, 2021), https://www.prri.org/research/qanon-conspiracy-american-politics-report/ (reporting that 25% of White evangelical Protestants, 26% of Hispanic Protestants, and 18% of Mormons agree that "the government, media, and financial worlds in the U.S. are controlled by a group of Satan-worshipping pedophiles who run a global child sex trafficking operation").

religious identity or through a disregard of demonstrable facts—is not just a threat to democratic norms, it's a threat to our public witness. When the world sees Christians as gullible, naïve, and unwilling to do the hard work of critically evaluating information, Christians lose credibility on everything—including our assertions about the historical veracity of the Gospel. When Christians post a meme about Anthony Fauci or Bill Gates plotting to distribute the mark of the Beast through a vaccine, and then follow up with a post about eyewitness testimony regarding the life of Jesus, both will tend to meet the same response: this person is not a trustworthy source on questions that matter.

Christians believe that our minds are a gift from God. Like all good gifts, we are called to steward them wisely. Faith and reason have nothing to fear from each other. As Christian nationalism asserts power in American politics, we can't just roll our eyes as though we're accommodating an embarrassing uncle who drops by for holiday dinners. The Gospel speaks to the heart <u>and</u> the mind. If fellow Christians are short-circuiting reason-driven political debate or spouting wild conspiracy theories, Christians shouldn't just be scandalized; we should be motivated to reclaim the intellectual traditions of our faith. Faith commitments are important contributors to debates about the common good; they should never be conversation-stoppers.

2. Christian Faith Should Not Be a Rationale for Self-Righteousness

Christian nationalism employs rhetoric that promotes a sense of self-righteousness among adherents, which is in direct conflict with traditional Christian teaching. The emphasis on returning America to a (usually unspecified) era of greatness may not provide a practical policy roadmap, but it reassures proponents that new initiatives to tackle systemic injustices are unnecessary. The Christian nationalist narrative does not convey accountability—much less culpability—for a history of marginalization and oppression; it mythologizes U.S. history, turning it into a sentimental destination.[44] Political opponents

[44] "Christian Americanism, set out earlier in this report as the belief that: "America was founded to be a Christian nation governed by Bible-based laws"; "the country has tragically departed from its roots"; and "it should reclaim its Christian

are not merely separated by ideology; they are enemies engaged in spiritual warfare. If those who reject Christian nationalist aims are "demonic,"[45] then of course Christian nationalists enjoy the satisfaction of knowing that God is on their side.

Indeed, the prevailing narrative makes plain that Christian nationalists themselves are today's true victims of injustice. After years of conservatives mocking liberals for playing the victim, President Trump embraced the label wholeheartedly on behalf of his supporters. Consider the rally at which the President proclaimed, in conjunction with alleged election fraud, "We're all victims. Everybody here, all these thousands of people here tonight, they're all victims. Every one of you."[46] Surveys show that a majority of white evangelicals believe that Christians face discrimination in the United States and are more likely to face discrimination than Muslims.[47] As Paul Miller explains, "In the last 40 years, Christian nationalists tend to believe that Christians are under attack and are being persecuted."[48]

For Christians, self-righteousness is toxic on several fronts. If we refuse to recognize the possibility that our political tribe is capable of evil, we are denying the reality of sin. If our initial response to news of the January 6 attack on the Capitol was to conclude, "Antifa must have dressed up as Trump supporters and infiltrated the protest," we have lost sight of what the Bible

---

heritage," which typically involves giving Christian or biblical teaching preferential treatment in law and public policy." David R. Brockman, Christian Americanism and Texas Politics Since 2008 (bakerinstitute.org) (Mar. 2020) (quoting Mark A. Chancey, *Rewriting History for a Christian America: Religion and the Texas Social Studies Controversy of 2009–2010*, 94 J. OF RELIGION 325, 329 (2014)).

[45] *See, e.g.*, Nancy LeTourneau, *Why Christian Nationalism is a Threat to Democracy*, WASHINGTON MONTHLY (Nov. 26, 2019), https://washingtonmonthly.com/2019/11/26/why-christian-nationalism-is-a-threat-to-democracy/ (reporting exchange in which Franklin Graham and Eric Metaxas portray efforts to undermine President Trump as "demonic" and part of a "spiritual battle").

[46] Miles T. Armaly & Adam M. Enders, *New research shows the connection between political victimhood and White support for Trump*, WASH. POST, Jan. 13, 2021, https://www.washingtonpost.com/politics/2021/01/13/new-research-shows-connection-between-political-victimhood-white-support-trump/.

[47] Emma Green, *White Evangelicals Believe They Face More Discrimination Than Muslims*, THE ATLANTIC, Mar. 10, 2017, https://www.theatlantic.com/politics/archive/2017/03/perceptions-discrimination-muslims-christians/519135/.

[48] Morgan Lee, *Christian Nationalism is Worse Than You Think*, CHRISTIANITY TODAY (Jan. 13, 2021) (https://www.christianitytoday.com/ct/podcasts/quick-to-listen/christian-nationalism-capitol-riots-trump-podcast.html).

teaches us about human nature.[49] This was not a problem that just emerged out of the blue in January. When Donald Trump observed, at a campaign stop in 2016, that "I could stand in the middle of 5th Avenue and shoot somebody, and I wouldn't lose any voters,"[50] he was tapping into a human tendency seen clearly by Martin Luther King: the willingness to overlook our own tribe's evil because we seek to maintain our significance.

Dr. King did not speak in terms of victimhood. He shared powerful stories of injustice without focusing on his own suffering, much less exaggerating it. Even among his followers, Dr. King's exhortations did not leave much room for self-righteousness. He did not always make his own followers comfortable, as he challenged them to overcome their fears and refused the easy path of telling them what they wanted to hear. Even within the Black community of his own city, Dr. King showed that Christian faith stretches us beyond our comfort zone. Christians cannot presume that our own journey of moral growth is complete, or that justice requires nothing from us. King worked, for example, to motivate the community to organize and persist in the Montgomery bus boycott, and he encountered significant resistance to his efforts initially. He later wrote that the people, even though they were "exhausted by the humiliating experiences that they had constantly faced on the buses . . . came to see that it was ultimately more honorable to walk the streets in dignity than to ride the buses in humiliation."[51]

Christian political engagement is not a sure-fire path to popularity for those who practice it—it is not about telling people what they want to hear. It is not about affirming the righteousness of our followers. Witness King's willingness to speak hard truths, and the changing public reaction to him as a result. From August 1964 to August 1966, Gallup surveys showed that the percentage of Americans who viewed King

---

[49] *See, e.g.*, *Faith leaders react to mob at Capitol with prayers, calls for end to violence*, RELIGION NEWS SERVICE (Jan. 6, 2021), https://religionnews.com/2021/01/06/faith-leaders-react-to-mob-at-capitol-with-prayers-calls-for-end-to-violence/.

[50] Kristen East, *Trump: I could 'shoot somebody' and I wouldn't lose voters*, POLITICO (Jan. 23, 2016), https://www.politico.com/story/2016/01/donald-trump-shooting-vote-218145.

[51] MARTIN LUTHER KING JR., STRENGTH TO LOVE 151 (1963).

unfavorably jumped from 38% to 63%.[52] In the years leading up to 1964, King had led the Montgomery bus boycott, spoke at the funerals of the girls killed in the Birmingham church bombing, wrote his *Letter from a Birmingham Jail*, brought worldwide attention to Bull Connor's regime attacking peaceful protestors with police dogs and firehoses, and gave his "I Have a Dream" speech in which he envisioned a day when his children would one day be judged not by the color of their skin, but by the content of their character, and called out in particular the states of Georgia, Alabama, and Mississippi.

So what happened between 1964 and 1966? King publicly opposed the Vietnam War for the first time, which could explain part of the shift in public opinion against him. I think the bigger change, though, was that King shifted his gaze to northern cities. He moved to Chicago and launched his first civil rights campaign outside the deep South. In Chicago, he encountered what he described as the most hostile crowds of his life. Rather than target a southern society that advertised its segregation policies for all to see, he now protested deeply embedded real estate practices that kept blacks locked in northern ghettos. He spoke hard truths to white Americans who were accustomed to the self-righteousness that came from knowing they weren't refusing service to Black Americans at the lunch counter or turning police dogs loose on peaceful protesters. The Christian narrative does not easily facilitate self-righteousness, and King knew that.

King was influenced by the work of Reinhold Niebuhr, a leading figure in a Christian realist tradition that stretches back to Augustine. In King's words, "Niebuhr made me aware of the complexity of human motives and the reality of sin on every level of man's existence," including "the glaring reality of collective evil."[53] Niebuhr lamented modern society's failure to recognize that, no matter how impressive its achievements, "there is no level of human moral or social achievement in which there is not

---

[52] Jeffrey M. Jones, *Americans Divided on Whether King's Dream Has Been Realized*, GALLUP (Aug. 26, 2011) https://news.gallup.com/poll/149201/Americans-Divided-Whether-King-Dream-Realized.aspx?utm_source=alert&utm_medium=email&utm_campaign=syndication&utm_content=plaintextlink&utm_term=Politics.

[53] KING, STRENGTH TO LOVE., *supra* note 51, at 148.

some corruption of inordinate self-love."[54] We all have "a darkly unconscious sense" of our "insignificance in the total scheme of things," and we perpetually strive to compensate for that insignificance. Human conflicts arise from a person or group striving "to guard its power and prestige against the peril of competing expressions of power and pride."[55]

Under Niebuhr's influence, King was optimistic about the arc of history, but his optimism was not the sort that allowed him to sit back and watch society's natural tendencies work themselves out over time. King credited Niebuhr's work for helping him see liberalism's sentimentality and false idealism. He saw that humans have an uncanny ability to "use our minds to rationalize our actions,"[56] and he worked to keep the capacities for both good and evil in clear view. King knew that the capacity for good made his struggle for civil rights possible, but the capacity for evil made the struggle necessary.

Christianity's warning against self-righteousness applies far beyond Christian nationalism, of course. The pitfalls warned about by Niebuhr, King, and other leading voices from Christian history apply to liberals and conservatives alike. Indeed, when King wrote his "Letter from a Birmingham Jail," he was not writing to conservatives—he was writing to moderate liberal pastors. Those pastors supported many of the goals of King's movement, but they had urged King to be patient, to stop being disruptive, and to give white residents time to embrace the movement's goals gradually, over time. King called out the liberals for being unwilling to recognize reality: that white people would not change the deeply unjust system without disruption. Sin is a human issue, not a partisan one.

Rejecting self-righteousness means taking sin seriously; it does not mean abandoning the struggle for justice. Niebuhr, for example, cautioned that "[a] realism becomes morally cynical or nihilistic when it assumes that the universal characteristic in

---

[54] REINHOLD NIEBUHR, CHILDREN OF LIGHT AND CHILDREN OF DARKNESS 169 (1944).

[55] *Id.* at 171.

[56] Martin Luther King Jr., *Pilgrimage to Nonviolence* (1960), in A TESTAMENT OF HOPE, at 35, 36 (James Washington, ed. 2003).

human behavior must also be regarded as normative."[57] We can and should work to draw a person "out of himself" and save him "from the self-defeating consequences of self-love."[58] When Christian nationalists rely on a narrative that pins the blame for our nation's problems squarely on other groups (many of whom live on the margins of American society), and elevates themselves as victims of injustice, that is not the path toward overcoming the self-defeating consequences of self-love.

If political power is harnessed to a pervasive sense of self-righteousness (a malady that can infect more than Christian nationalists, to be sure), the accountability on which the rule of law is premised may soon be in jeopardy. When outraged Christian nationalists attacked the Capitol, they may not have seriously considered the possibility that President Trump and his media champions were exaggerating and fabricating reasons to doubt the election's outcome. Their example is a cautionary lesson for citizens across the political spectrum. Self-righteousness distorts our perception of reality and precludes the mutual recognition of fallibility on which the give-and-take of democracy depend.

3. Christian Faith Should Not Stoke Fear of the Other

In contrast to the radical "love thy neighbor" teachings of Jesus, the rhetoric of Christian nationalism engenders loyalty by stoking fear. Christian nationalism does not "involve a plea to live out transcendent Christian values of love, mercy, or justice."[59] By contrast, it entails "either a proprietary claim or a call to arms, always in response to a perceived threat."[60] In other words, Christian nationalism is about power—to be won and wielded against external threats. Relying on fear and finger-pointing as a political weapon creates an us-versus-them mindset. This threatens the rule of law, which aims to guarantee that all are treated fairly, that laws operate prospectively as guides to conduct, and that the application of laws is not contingent on a group's popularity. By building a political

---

[57] Reinhold Niebuhr, *Augustine's Political Realism*, in THE ESSENTIAL REINHOLD NIEBUHR 123, 130 (Robert McAfee Brown, ed. 1986).

[58] *Id.*

[59] PERRY & WHITEHEAD, *supra* note 3, at 86.

[60] *Id.*

movement on the scapegoating of particular groups, Christian nationalists' rhetoric creates tension with these guarantees.

Consider the "Jericho March," a nationwide series of "Stop the Steal" protests in which Christians gathered to "pray, march, fast, and rally for election integrity." Organizers called on God to "save the republic" by uncovering the election fraud that they claimed wrongfully deprived President Trump of a second term.[61] As Emma Green reported, "Just as God instructed Joshua to march around Jericho seven times with priests blowing trumpets," protesting Christians blew "shofars, the ram's horn typically used in Jewish worship, to banish the 'darkness of election fraud' and ensure that 'the walls of corruption crumble.' "[62] Additionally, organizers warned that "globalists, socialists, and communists" are set to "destroy our beautiful nation by sidestepping our laws and suppressing the will of the American people through their fraudulent and illegal activities in this election."[63] Several of the Jericho March speakers called for the President's political enemies to be jailed for attempting to steal the election.

Though Christian nationalism's scapegoating of others became more well-known during the election's aftermath, it has long been committed to a "social order in which the old hierarchies—native-born over foreigners, men over women, Christians over Jews and Muslims, whites over non-whites—are re-asserted and strengthened."[64] Christian nationalism does not stand simply for the merger of national and faith identities; the movement also roots the merged identity in an unmistakably us-versus-them mindset.

Take immigration, for example. Surveys show that "the percentage of Americans who affirm negative stereotypes about immigrants and believe the number of immigrants coming into

---

61 Emma Green, *A Christian Insurrection*, THE ATLANTIC (Jan. 8, 2021), https://www.theatlantic.com/politics/archive/2021/01/evangelicals-catholics-jericho-march-capitol/617591/.

62 *Id.*

63 Harry Bruinius, *Will 'stolen election become a new 'lost cause' for evangelicals?*, CHRISTIAN SCIENCE MONITOR (Dec. 16, 2020), https://www.csmonitor.com/USA/Politics/2020/1216/Will-election-become-a-new-lost-cause-for-evangelical-conservatives.

64 Timothy Keller, *A Book Review on the Topic of Christian Nationalism*, https://quarterly.gospelinlife.com/book-review-on-the-topic-of-christian-nationalism/.

the United States should be 'strongly reduced' correlates with how important they think being a Christian is to being 'truly American.' "[65] If one thinks being a Christian is important to being American, one also is more likely to agree that immigrants "undermine American culture" and "increase crime," and that immigration "should be reduced a lot."[66] Further, one is more likely to believe that "true Americans" are "those who are born here, lived here their whole lives, are able to speak English, and have American ancestry."[67]

And if we don't thwart the plans of our enemies—particularly non-believers and those on "the Left"—by turning back to God, "He will stop blessing America."[68] As Robert Jeffress recounted in a recent sermon, when "secular Sup Ct justices" removed prayer and Bible reading from public schools in the 1960s, we "allowed the secularists, the humanists, the atheists, the infidels to pervert our Constitution into something our founding fathers never intended."[69] It is time, Jeffress insists, "for Americans to stand up and say, 'Enough! We're not going to allow this in our Christian country anymore!' It is time to put an end to this."[70]

In sharp contrast to Christian nationalists, Dr. King famously preached and practiced love for his enemies. Loving the white segregationist was borne out of his recognition that the white man's personhood had been distorted by segregation, so love was in direct response to the white man's needs. King's invocation of faith made clear that even white segregationists were worthy of what he called "the beloved community." He protested against the perpetrators of injustice, of course, but his goal was not power to be wielded against "the other"—his goal was the restoration of relationships broken by segregation.

King proposed agape as the standard for Christians' engagement with the world. "Agape" appears in the Bible to signal sacrificial love, as distinguished from "phileo," which is a

---

65 PERRY & WHITEHEAD, *supra* note 3, at 92–93.

66 *Id.*

67 *Id.* at 99.

68 Keller, *supra* note 64.

69 PERRY & WHITEHEAD, *supra* note 3, at 57.

70 *Id.*

love based on one's feelings for another. King insisted that his followers love white segregationists, "not because we like them, not because their attitudes and ways appeal to us, but because God loves them."[71] Agape is a disinterested, unselfish love; it springs from the needs of the other person and is not based on "any qualities people possess."[72] Whatever perceived threats Christian nationalists fear, they would not be sufficient to lift our obligation to love, which extends, as King put it, to the enemy from "whom you can expect no good in return, but only hostility and persecution."[73] Agape insists "on community even when one seeks to break it"—it is "a willingness to go to any length to restore community.[74]

In *Letter from a Birmingham Jail*, King cited Martin Buber's "I-Thou" relationship in which one views another person as a "thou," rather than an "It," and thereby avoids relegating people to the status of things.[75] In loving others—friend or foe, black or white—King aimed to restore community. He worked to see the world through others' eyes, but he also insisted that others expand their view to develop a more authentic, less isolated understanding of their own well-being.

This is a theme that permeates the Christian tradition, as represented powerfully in the parable Jesus told of the Good Samaritan. As Pope Francis explains the lesson of that parable, "a community can be rebuilt by men and women who identify with the vulnerability of others, who reject the creation of a society of exclusion, and act instead as neighbours, lifting up and

---

[71] Martin Luther King Jr., *Nonviolence and Racial Justice* (1957), in A TESTAMENT OF HOPE, *supra* note 56, at 5, 8–9.

[72] Martin Luther King Jr., *An Experiment in Love* (1958), in A TESTAMENT OF HOPE, *supra* note 56, at 16, 19.

[73] "I'm very happy that [Jesus] didn't say like your enemies, because it is pretty difficult to like some people. Like is sentimental, and it is pretty difficult to like someone bombing your home; it is pretty difficult to like somebody threatening your children; it is difficult to like congressmen who spend all of their time trying to defeat civil rights. But Jesus says love them, and love is greater than like. Love is understanding, redemptive, creative, good will for all men. And it is this idea, it is this whole ethic of love which is the idea standing at the basis of the student movement." Martin Luther King Jr., *Love, Law, and Civil Disobedience*, in A TESTAMENT OF HOPE, *supra* note 56, at 43, 47.

[74] Martin Luther King Jr., *An Experiment in Love*, in A TESTAMENT OF HOPE, *supra* note 56, at 20.

[75] MARTIN BUBER, I AND THOU (1923).

rehabilitating the fallen for the sake of the common good."[76] We must always show compassion "for the sufferings of the man on the roadside."[77] The Christian practice of solidarity "finds concrete expression in service," which is "never ideological, for we do not serve ideas, we serve people."[78] Fear of "the other" is antithetical to this call.[79]

D. CONCLUSION

Understanding what healthy Christian political engagement looks like—and how Christian nationalism has fallen short—is important for law schools, which are tasked with training attorneys to be faithful stewards of the rule of law. Too often, we overlook the extent to which this stewardship must include a recognition of, and response to, religion's role in American politics. Becoming familiar with First Amendment case law is not sufficient.[80] Learning to "think like a lawyer" need not (and should not) preclude the meaningful exploration of faith, both because faith will often be among the lawyer's own deeply held and professionally relevant commitments, and because even non-religious lawyers will counsel and advocate in a deeply religious society.

The fact that our faculties lean decidedly to the left[81] may tempt law schools to embrace the nation's deepening political tribalism[82] and neglect to undertake the hard work of building understanding across the cultural divide. This is especially true when one's political opponents are motivated, at least in part, by religious belief. Few law schools devote significant time to

---

76 Pope Francis, *Fratelli Tutti* (Oct. 2020).

77 *Id.*

78 *Id.*

79 The admonition "Be not afraid" is found throughout scripture and Church teachings over the past two millennia, including, famously, in the pontificate of Pope John Paul II. *See, e.g.*, John Paul II Inauguration mass homily (1978) https://www.vatican.va/content/john-paul-ii/en/homilies/1978/documents/hf_jp-ii_hom_19781022_inizio-pontificato.html.

80 The First Amendment prohibits the government from "establishing" a religion and protects the "free exercise" of religion from government interference. The First Amendment does not address the myriad ways in which religious belief shapes Americans' political priorities, values, and commitments.

81 *See* James Lindgren, *Measuring Diversity: Law Faculties in 1997 and 2013*, Northwestern Pub. L. Res. Paper No. 15–17, available at SSRN: https://ssrn.com/abstract=2581675.

82 *See* EZRA KLEIN, WHY WE'RE POLARIZED (2020).

understanding the relationship between faith and law, much less recognizing and articulating instances when faith traditions have been twisted to support new political ends.

Pushing back against Christian nationalism does not require a retreat to some sort of imagined secular space—the resources for resistance are available within Christianity itself. We are, as Harold Laski put it, "bundles of hyphens,"[83] and American Christians who are lawyers and law professors should speak to this cultural moment, not only as stewards of the rule of law, but as stewards of their faith tradition. Christian nationalists are espousing a version of the faith that has profound and dangerous consequences for the rule of law. We cannot defend the rule of law by relying solely on arguments that fail to address the foundational claims from which threats emerge. Christian nationalism is one such threat, and we need to respond—as lawyers, and perhaps more importantly, as Christians.

---

83 HAROLD LASKI, THE FOUNDATIONS OF SOVEREIGNTY 170 (1921).

CHAPTER 8

THE COLOR LINE: DEMOCRACY, RACE, AND THE JANUARY 6TH INSURRECTION

Kimberly Mutcherson[1]

"[T]he problem of the twentieth century is the problem of the color line—the relation of the darker to the lighter races of men in Asia and Africa, in America and the islands of the sea."

W.E.B. DuBois, THE SOULS OF BLACK FOLK: ESSAYS & SKETCHES (1903)

At one point in 2020, I publicly declared that I was deleting the word unprecedented from my vocabulary because it had become so painfully overused that it had almost lost its meaning. And yet, I can think of few words that adequately describe the events that the United States and the world watched unfold in Washington, D.C. on January 6, 2021. On that day, as our children's children may learn in their history books, a mob of self-declared patriots attacked the U.S. Capitol. Members of that mob gleefully documented their exploits on social media as they entered the offices of members of Congress, accessed documents and technology that were not for their eyes, menaced and, in some cases, physically attacked Capitol police, and forced an hours long postponement of the traditional and Constitutionally mandated counting of electoral votes. Prior to this incident, according to the Capitol historian, the last time the Capitol was breached was during the War of 1812, making the moment even more shocking.[2] The sight of people vandalizing the offices of members of Congress, while those members cowered in fear behind barricaded doors, was truly unprecedented and deeply

---

[1] Dean & Professor of Law at Rutgers Law School. My thanks to Tess Berkowitz for her research assistance and citation wizardry and to my colleagues at Rutgers Law who are walking the walk.

[2] Amanda Holpuch, *US Capitol's Last Breach Was More Than 200 Years Ago,* THE GUARDIAN (Jan. 6, 2021, 7:59 PM), https://www.theguardian.com/us-news/2021/jan/06/us-capitol-building-washington-history-breach.

horrifying. Coupled with all that we had seen in 2020 in addition to a global pandemic—including a long overdue and painful national accounting of how race remains a defining problem for this country sparked by yet another killing of a Black man at the hands of a white police officer, this devastating beginning to 2021 felt oddly par for the course.

Unsurprisingly, many of us in the legal academy were left reeling after January 6th and thinking about the role that lawyers played in this debacle. In a message to my law school community, I described the events of January 6th as "ma[king] a mockery of our Constitutional norms and the rule of law." I continued, "That these people were egged on by a lame duck president, and his enablers, who spent weeks ceaselessly undermining the integrity of our elections with baseless allegations of widespread fraud makes what happened . . . even more repugnant." Far too many of those enablers were lawyers like Josh Hawley and Ted Cruz, both of whom offered support to the rioters in the days before and after the insurrection by feeding the lie of election fraud.[3] Lawyers like Sidney Powell who ultimately became a defendant in a defamation lawsuit resulting from her unfounded and unsupportable claims that Dominion voting machines were an essential part of an elaborate conspiracy to steal the presidential election from Donald Trump.[4] Lawyers like those at longstanding, well-heeled law firms like Jones Day and Porter Wright who pursued claims on behalf of now former President Trump and his campaign that were predicated on the flimsiest of claims and evidence and which courts quickly dismissed.[5]

For people who have dedicated their careers to training future lawyers, understanding how and why members of our profession could be so misled, so cynical, and so willing to

---

[3] Dareh Gregorian, et al., *Senate Democrats File Ethics Complaint Against Republicans Hawley, Cruz Over Roles in Capitol Riot,* NBC NEWS (Jan. 21, 2021, 6:25 PM), https://www.nbcnews.com/politics/congress/senate-dems-file-ethics-complaint-against-gop-sens-hawley-cruz-n1255228.

[4] Rebecca Davis O'Brien, *Trump Lawyers Face Rebukes Over Election Fraud Claims,* WALL ST. J. (Jan. 12, 2021, 8:31 AM), https://www.wsj.com/articles/trump-lawyers-face-rebukes-over-election-fraud-claims-11610458283.

[5] Jessica Silver-Greenberg, et al., *Growing Discomfort at Law Firms Representing Trump in Election Lawsuits,* N.Y. TIMES (Dec. 11, 2020), https://www.nytimes.com/2020/11/09/business/jones-day-trump-election-lawsuits.html.

undermine the rule of law that we should revere required us to engage in serious introspection. We have had to learn lessons from the catastrophe and consider how legal education can and should play a role in avoiding a repeat of the heinous actions of January 6. What happened on that day went beyond a simple matter of political disagreement—it was a treacherous display of ignorance and violence that called into question the very underpinnings of our political system. Choosing to actively engage or fuel this kind of brutal and unsupportable attack on our democracy deserves to be widely condemned. For my part, as I watched lawyers undermine our presidential election, I re-dedicated myself to leading my institution in a way that was in keeping with the kind of lawyers I hope will graduate from my law school.

I want Rutgers Law School graduates to enter the profession with a fundamental respect for what law is and what it can do. I want them to be steeped in substantive legal doctrine and to know how to augment their knowledge in areas where it is lacking. I want them to accept and understand the hypocrisy that we all must acknowledge was embedded in our founding documents with their lofty language about the self-evident truth that "all men are created equal" and possess "unalienable Rights" to "Life, Liberty and the pursuit of Happiness"[6] or that our Constitution exists to "promote the general Welfare, and secure the Blessings of Liberty to ourselves and our Posterity."[7] The large swaths of people not protected by these words when they were written is so obvious as to not require further elaboration. This is not to say that we must be mired in the past, but we must concede that our union has never been perfect, and making it better is an ongoing project. That project requires lawyers who understand that tearing down and rebuilding unjust systems so that they are more representative of the language that our founders used in building this country is a profoundly patriotic act. Our law schools must be spaces in which we confront tough realities, produce critical thinkers, and inculcate a respect for what law has done, good and bad, and what it can be made to do if we care enough.

---

6 THE DECLARATION OF INDEPENDENCE para. 2 (U.S. 1776).

7 U.S. CONST. pmbl.

I take the charge of producing well-trained critical thinkers as a core part of the mission of law schools and as a goal that should be shared across the political spectrum. As a Black queer woman, the first person with any of my identity categories who had ever been the dean at my law school when I got the job, my presence in law school leadership is a political act simply by virtue of being who I am and occupying a space that was not built for the likes of me.[8] I often remark that our country had a Black president before my Law School had a Black dean as a way of highlighting the slow pace of change.

Soon after becoming the Dean, I was in a conference for new deans at which some of my white male peers explained that they have a general rule of not weighing in on current events because doing so is not part of the dean role as they understand it. As a living testament to the politics and complicated realities that law deans and law schools have too often avoided confronting in their own hallways and classrooms, I am and was grateful to serve in the dean role at a high point of challenges to neutrality as an acceptable stance for the people who run the institutions that produce so many of our political leaders. I came to my role as a law school dean with an unshaking belief that law schools have a special responsibility to train lawyers to respect and protect the rule of law, obviously, but we cannot expect our graduates to do so if we do not equip them with the proper tools. One of the tools with which we must arm every law school graduate is an unflinching critique of the racist and patriarchal roots of much of the law that we teach them.

Broadly infusing antiracist teaching into our law school curriculum is one way of several to ensure that our students see law for what it is: a tool of oppression **and** a tool of justice, and wield it as the latter and not the former. The roots of the January

---

8 I am thinking here about the question posed by W.E.B. Dubois laying out the perennial struggle of being Black in America, "How Does It Feel to Be a Problem?" W.E. Burghardt DuBois, *Strivings of the Negro People*, THE ATLANTIC (August, 1897), https://www.theatlantic.com/magazine/archive/1897/08/strivings-of-the-negro-people/305446/. Being a problem is, indeed, a "strange experience." I am a law school dean who sits at the intersection of several identity categories that have faced and continue to face discrimination in the U.S. And, while the number of women and people of color and women of color who are currently law school deans is higher than it has ever been, it remains the case that we are anomalies and that our presence, especially for the many of us who are the first to have our roles, has occasioned some soul searching for us and for those around us.

6 insurrection are planted in the same soil as the roots of the waves of attacks against the 1619 Project and Critical Race Theory that are raging as of the writing of this essay. Critical Race Theory (CRT), a concept that many of its detractors are unable to describe with even a modicum of accuracy,[9] has been around for decades as a tool of legal analysis that explores the ways in which race and racism are embedded in the American legal system.[10] As one scholar described the work of critical race theorists: "[C]ritical race theory recognizes that revolutionizing a culture begins with the radical assessment of it."[11] The work of CRT scholars powerfully reminds us that race still matters in this country; that race is a social construct, not a biological fact; that racism is not just an individual act, but is deeply embedded

---

9 *See* Ron DeSantis, Governor, Florida, Address to the Florida State Board of Education Forum (Jun. 10, 2021), https://www.flgov.com/2021/06/10/governor-desantis-emphasizes-importance-of-keeping-critical-race-theory-out-of-schools-at-state-board-of-education-meeting/ (denouncing critical race theory as not factual and alleging critical race theory education is an attempt at indoctrination of political ideals); Kaylee DeWitt, *What You Need to Know About Idaho's New Critical Race Theory Law*, ABC4 NEWS (May 4, 2021, 6:44 AM), https://www.abc4.com/news/local-news/what-you-need-to-know-about-idahos-critical-race-theory-law/ (Reporting on statement from Idaho Representative Ron Nate, categorizing Critical Race Theory as rooted in Marxist thought and alleging it tries to make kids feel bad because of the color of their skin); Ian Richardson, *Iowa Gov. Kim Reynolds Signs Law Targeting Critical Race Theory, Saying She's Against 'Discriminatory Indoctrination'*, DE MOINES REG. (Jun. 9, 2021, 7:41 AM) https://www.desmoinesregister.com/story/news/politics/2021/06/08/governor-kim-reynolds-signs-law-targeting-critical-race-theory-iowa-schools-diversity-training/74898 96002/ (quoting Governor Reynolds' assertion that Critical Race Theory teaches kids to judge others based on race or other attributes rather than their character); *See also* Ben Shapiro (@benshapiro), TWITTER (Sep. 9, 2020, 12:14 PM), https://twitter.com/benshapiro/status/1303726350776188928 (describing Critical Race Theory as a philosophical movement that is directed at tearing down America while also including a link to buy his book); Stella Morabito, *Critical Race Theory is a Classic Communist Divide-and-Conquer Tactic*, THE FEDERALIST (Sep. 29, 2020), https://thefederalist.com/2020/09/29/critical-race-theory-is-a-classic-communist-divide-and-conquer-tactic/.

10 Janel George, *A Lesson on Critical Race Theory*, ABA: HUM. RTS. MAG. (Jan. 12, 2021), https://www.americanbar.org/groups/crsj/publications/human_rights_magazine_home/civil-rights-reimagining-policing/a-lesson-on-critical-race-theory/ (citing scholar Khiara Bridges' core tenants of Critical Race Theory). George explains CRT by starting with the observation from Kimberlé Crenshaw that, "CRT is not a noun, but a verb" meaning that "[i]t cannot be confined to a static and narrow definition but is considered to be an evolving and malleable practice. It critiques how the social construction of race and institutionalized racism perpetuate a racial caste system that relegates people of color to the bottom tiers. CRT also recognizes that race intersects with other identities, including sexuality, gender identity, and others. CRT recognizes that racism is not a bygone relic of the past. Instead, it acknowledges that the legacy of slavery, segregation, and the imposition of second-class citizenship on Black Americans and other people of color continue to permeate the social fabric of this nation."

11 John O. Calmore, *Critical Race Theory, Archie Shepp, and Fire Music: Securing an Authentic Intellectual Life in a Multicultural World*, 65 S. CAL. L. REV. 2129, 2145 (1990).

in many of our systems and laws, which explains its persistence; and that we cannot get past race by ignoring racism.

The 1619 Project is an incredible work of history and journalism published by the New York Times that chronicled the history of enslaved people in the Americas starting from the arrival of the first enslaved Africans in 1619.[12] The Project's explicit goal was to "reframe the country's history by placing the consequences of slavery and the contributions of [B]lack Americans at the very center of our national narrative."[13] Not surprisingly, the Project garnered many critics who found its focus on American racism and the permanent mark that slavery left in its wake, to be deceptive and un-American.[14]

In 2020, the Trump administration became concerned about diversity trainings for federal employees that purportedly involved statements that " 'virtually all White people contribute to racism' or where they are required to say that they 'benefit from racism.' According to press reports, in some cases these trainings have further claimed that there is racism embedded in the belief that America is the land of opportunity or the belief that the most qualified person should receive a job."[15] The Administration decided to tackle this supposed problem by banning any contracts for trainings that involved discussion of " 'critical race theory' or 'white privilege,' or any other training or propaganda effort that teaches or suggests either (1) that the United States is an inherently racist or evil country or (2) that any race or ethnicity is inherently racist or evil." This ban on "unAmerican propaganda training sessions" left the White House with the man who propagated it.[16]

---

12 *The 1619 Project*, N.Y. TIMES MAG. (Sep. 4, 2019) https://www.nytimes.com/interactive/2019/08/14/magazine/1619-america-slavery.html.

13 *Id.*

14 *See* Timothy Sandefur, *The 1619 Project: An Autopsy*, CATO INST. (Oct. 27, 2020), https://www.cato.org/commentary/1619-project-autopsy; The Heritage Foundation, *The 1619 Project's False Claims of America's Founding*, YOUTUBE (Dec. 10, 2020), https://www.youtube.com/watch?v=8Z01vyR6Hyk&t=27s.

15 Memorandum, Russell Vought, Director, Office of Management and Budget, Training in the Federal Government (Sep. 4, 2020), https://www.whitehouse.gov/wp-content/uploads/2020/09/M-20-34.pdf?fbclid=IwAR1r7Ej2V0gZ8pNhIEjLtHDDNlfeYvBkzEgUfbrU3cXfot7RP2XKPwnCDe4.

16 Memorandum, Robert Fairweather, Acting Director, Office of Management and Budget, Revocation of Executive Order 13950, M-20-37 and M-20-34 (Mar. 2, 2021), https://www.whitehouse.gov/wp-content/uploads/2021/03/M-21-17.pdf.

The campaign against CRT went even more mainstream in 2021 as states and localities began banning teaching CRT in public school systems. The version of CRT that these bans challenged is a version of CRT that no legitimate legal scholar would recognize. The ban proponents make claims that CRT teaches white children to be ashamed of or hate themselves, and it supposedly teaches that every white person is racist.[17] An illustrative ban from a Cincinnati school board prevents teachers from offering lessons that anyone is " 'inherently racist, sexist, or oppressive' by virtue of their own race or sex, 'whether consciously or unconsciously.' The bill also bans teachers from teaching anything that would promote 'divisions between, or resentment of 'different groups of people, like religious groups, political groups or social classes.' "[18] A statewide ban in Texas specifically forbids the teaching of the 1619 Project.[19]

These bans starkly represent the fear harbored by some about how the young people who eventually end up in our law school classrooms learn about U.S. history and the racist policies and practices that are embedded in our legal system. They display a dismissiveness toward painful truths and a desire to get beyond race by simply becoming "colorblind" and keeping race from being discussed in classrooms or public discourse in ways that create discomfort, especially for white students. Missing from this side of the discussion is any acknowledgement of how children of color feel in classrooms where these painful truths are obscured or ignored. By the time they get to us, many of our students are still in need of an education that divests them of the American myths that prevent us from tackling our nation's fatal and persistent flaws.

The importance of training new lawyers to deconstruct and critique law was only highlighted by the lawyers in Congress and out who stoked the fires of election lies centered on attempts to disenfranchise thousands of Black and Brown voters in

---

17 *See* Senator Ted Cruz, Address at Faith and Freedom Coalition Road to Majority Conference (Jun. 12, 2021).

18 Madeline Mitchell, *Why Did Gallatin County Schools Ban Critical Rach Theory? No One is 'Inherently Racist'*, CIN. ENQUIRER (Jun. 17, 2021, 4:37 PM) https://www.cincinnati.com/story/news/2021/06/17/gallatin-county-schools-superintendent-banning-critical-race-theory/7734193002/.

19 H.B. 3979, 87 Legis. (Tex. 2021).

Michigan, Georgia, and beyond.[20] Eschewing the need for evidence and scoffing at the decisions from federal courts rejecting the losing team's attempts to overturn a valid U.S. presidential election, Senators Ted Cruz of Texas and Josh Hawley of Missouri evidenced a profound lack of respect for or understanding of the rule of law and the importance of lawyers, in particular, in upholding the rule of law. An editorial in the Kansas City Star published on January 7th described Senator Hawley as "having blood on this hands."[21] Senator Mitt Romney speaking on the floor after Congress returned to session following the insurrection asked of his colleagues who fed the fires of sedition in the days leading up to the Capitol attack, "Do we weigh our own political fortunes more heavily than we weigh the strength of our Republic, the strength of our democracy and the cause of freedom? What is the weight of personal acclaim compared to the weight of conscience?"[22]

To view the January 6th insurrection as just about politics or just about a big lie of a stolen election erases a core truth of that day—racism and white supremacy were a significant impetus for the insurrection.[23] More specifically, the reality that the color line remains one of the greatest impediments to the progress of our democracy. We saw it in the strategic choices to

---

[20] *See* Ted Cruz, Senator, Texas, Joint Statement from Senators Cruz, Johnson, Lankford, Daines, Kennedy, Blackburn, Braun, Senators-Elect Lummis, Marshall, Hagerty, Tuberville (Jan. 2, 2021), https://www.cruz.senate.gov/?p=press_release&id=5541; *OAN Newsroom* (OANN television broadcast Jul. 18, 2021) https://www.oann.com/rep-matt-gaetz-warns-ariz-and-ga-audits-to-reveal-pattern-of-nationwide-election-fraud/ (interview with Rep. Matt Gaetz stating that audits in Arizona and Georgia are indicative of widespread voter fraud); *see also* Brandon Tensley, *The Racist Rhetoric Behind Accusing Largely Black Cities of Voter Fraud*, CNN (Nov. 20, 2020, 12:03 PM) https://www.cnn.com/2020/11/20/politics/trump-giuliani-black-cities-analysis/index.html (noting election fraud rhetoric from the Trump campaign is concentrated towards predominately Black cities such as Detroit, Milwaukee, Philadelphia and others).

[21] Kansas City Star Editorial Board, *Assault on Democracy: Sen. Josh Hawley Has Blood on His Hands in Capitol Coup Attempt*, KAN. CITY STAR (Jan. 6, 2021, 3:48 PM), https://www.kansascity.com/opinion/editorials/article248317375.html.

[22] Mitt Romney, U.S. Senator, Utah, Remarks on U.S. Senate Floor on Arizona Objection and Security Breach (Jan. 6, 2021), https://www.c-span.org/video/?507698-7/senator-romney-arizona-objection-security-breach; *see also* Alex Samuels & Patrick Svitek, *After Riot at the U.S. Capitol, Ted Cruz Gets Fierce Blowback for His Role in Sowing Doubts About Joe Biden's Victory*, TEX. TR. (Jan. 7, 2021, 7:00 PM), https://www.texastribune.org/2021/01/07/ted-cruz-riot-capitol/ (quoting Sen. Mitt Romney).

[23] Marcus P. Nevius, *The Legacy of Racial Hatred in the January 6 Insurrection*, JSTOR DAILY (Feb. 24, 2021), https://daily.jstor.org/the-legacy-of-racial-hatred-in-the-january-6-insurrection/.

attack the validity of votes cast in areas that were filled with Black voters.[24] We saw it in the fact that, as was true at most MAGA rallies and other events supporting then President Trump, thc insurrectionists were largely white,[25] some proudly identifying with divisive symbols of white supremacy.[26] In testimony in Congress, a Black Capitol police officer, Harry Dunn, spoke of the repeated use of the word "nigger" by white rioters as he risked his life and well-being to keep members of Congress safe.[27] Several iconic images from that day involve Capitol attackers strolling the halls of Congress proudly carrying confederate flags, an act that did not even happen during the Civil War.[28] We saw it in the makeshift gallows that protestors set up outside of Congress, evoking the painful and racist history of lynching in the United States.[29] As Aryeh Tuchman, associate director for the Anti-Defamation League's Center on Extremism told the LA Times after the insurrection, "Every time there is progress in asserting civil rights, there's a backlash. Confederate iconography is a means to reassert white supremacy when it is thought to be threatened."[30]

The attempts to downplay the January 6th insurrection, including the Senate's failure to create a commission to study what happened, followed by the House stepping into the breach

---

[24] Brandon Tensley, *supra* note 20.

[25] Fabiola Cineas & Anna North, *We Need to Talk About the White People Who Voted for Donald Trump*, VOX (Nov. 7, 2020, 9:00 AM), https://www.vox.com/2020/11/7/21551364/white-trump-voters-2020.

[26] Associated Press, *Capitol Insurrection Displayed Many of the Symbols of American Racism*, L.A. TIMES (Jan. 14, 2021, 4:29 PM), https://www.latimes.com/world-nation/story/2021-01-14/years-of-white-supremacy-threats-culminated-in-capitol-riots.

[27] Domenico Montenaro, *Capitol Police Officer Testifies To The Racism He Faced During The Jan. 6 Riot*, July 27, NPR.ORG, https://www.npr.org/2021/07/27/1021197474/capitol-police-officer-testifies-to-the-racism-he-faced-during-the-jan-6-riot.

[28] Clint Smith, *The Whole Story in a Single Photo*, THE ATLANTIC (Jan. 8, 2021), https://www.theatlantic.com/ideas/archive/2021/01/confederates-in-the-capitol/617594/.

[29] Brandon T. Jett & Allison Robinson, *The Chilling Similarities Between the Pro-Trump Mob and Lynchings a Century Ago*, WASH. POST (Jan. 15, 2021, 6:00 AM), https://www.washingtonpost.com/outlook/2021/01/15/chilling-similarities-between-pro-trump-mob-lynchings-century-ago/; *see also* Jacey Fortin, *Congress Moves to Make Lynching a Federal Crime After 120 Years of Failure*, N.Y. TIMES (Feb. 28, 2020), https://www.nytimes.com/2020/02/26/us/politics/anti-lynching-bill.html (documenting Congress's historic inability to sign federal anti-lynching bills into law, with opponents arguing in favor of states' rights on the matter and utilizing filibusters to thwart efforts).

[30] Associated Press, *supra* note 26.

and setting up its own committee to do this vital work,[31] is in stark contrast to the rhetoric that would have emerged had those protesting at the Capitol that day been largely Black and centering their cries for justice around racial equality. I doubt that Congressman Andrew S. Clyde, who infamously described what he saw in Congress on January 6th as similar to a "normal tourist visit," even as photos emerged of him helping to barricade the doors of the House chamber as rioters approached, would have offered such an innocuous reconstruction of January 6 had the protestors been Black.[32] Similarly, would Rep. Paul Gosar have described the officer who shot and killed Ashli Babbitt, one of the rioters standing on the other side of that barricaded door, as appearing "to be hiding, lying in wait and then gave no warning before killing her" if Ms. Babbitt had come to Washington to stand up for the value of Black lives?[33]

I hope that the legacy of January 6 ignites activism and insightful critique of our law schools for some time to come. As a Law School Dean in 2020, I felt privileged to serve alongside a collection of women and men who, in the wake of all that the year threw at us, used our platforms to advocate for change in our institutions, in our country, and in our world. I was especially honored to be one of five Black woman law deans who co-founded the Law Deans Antiracist Clearinghouse Project,[34] hosted by the Association of American Law Schools. This project was inspired by the killing of George Floyd and the civil unrest that followed, but a project like this was years in the making.

Law schools have, for far too long, been places that eschewed or minimized tough conversations about race, inequality, and the law in favor of "just teaching the rules" or focusing on black letter law. Many students of color and lawyers of color can

---

[31] Brian Naylor, *Senate Republicans Block a Plan for an Independent Commission on Jan. 6 Capitol Riot*, NPR (May 28, 2021, 3:31 PM), https://www.npr.org/2021/05/28/1000524897/senate-republicans-block-plan-for-independent-commission-on-jan-6-capitol-riot.

[32] C-SPAN, *"Normal Tourist Visit"*, YOUTUBE (May 13, 2021), https://www.youtube.com/watch?v=WLI0OH1ZWWc.

[33] C-SPAN, *FBI Director Christopher Wray Testifies on U.S. Capitol Attack*, C-SPAN (Jun. 15, 2021), https://www.c-span.org/video/?512552-1/fbi-director-christopher-wray-testifies-us-capitol-attack.

[34] *Law Deans Antiracist Clearinghouse Project*, ASS'N OF AMERICAN LAW SCHOOLS, https://www.aals.org/antiracist-clearinghouse/ (last visited Jul. 21, 2021).

recount stories of sitting in classrooms at PWIs and wondering how their professors could so deftly obscure the racial reality of the American legal landscape. Or we watched as race got delegated to a certain number or type of classes, which relieved the pressure on other professors and other parts of the curriculum to consider how race impacted their specific area of the law. Perhaps race mattered in constitutional law or criminal law, but no need to raise issues of race in business organizations, civil procedure, or patent law.

We know that race and racism permeate the American legal system and that the origins of the current state of our country can be found in laws that explicitly or implicitly maintained or buttressed white supremacy. Imagine the impact on 1L students if their property class involves learning about the history of redlining and how it shaped neighborhoods for decades.[35] Or a torts class that interrogates the ways in which awards for damages reify and pattern themselves after racial differences in wealth and opportunity shaped by systemic racism.[36] These moments of illumination could be deeply meaningful for students who come to law school with little or no knowledge of the racial realities that shaped and still shape much of law.

Borrowing the words of the young poet Amanda Gorman, we are "a nation that isn't broken but simply unfinished."[37] Law schools can contribute to the ongoing project that is America in a variety of ways. A criminal law class can only be made more powerful and meaningful to students if it gives insight into how the U.S. became the world leader in incarcerating its people,[38] a history that leads back to post-emancipation criminal laws, Black Codes, created to force newly freed Black people back into a Constitutionally accepted form of forced labor—prison labor.[39]

---

[35] RICHARD ROTHSTEIN, THE COLOR OF LAW, A 'FORGOTTEN HISTORY' OF HOW THE U.S. GOVERNMENT SEGREGATED AMERICA (Liveright 2017).

[36] Kimberly Yuracko & Ronen Avraham, *Valuing Black Lives: A Constitutional Challenge to the Use of Race-Based Tables in Calculating Tort Damages*, 106 CALIF. 325 (2018).

[37] AMANDA GORMAN, THE HILL WE CLIMB (2021).

[38] *Criminal Justice Facts*, SENTENCING PROJECT, https://www.sentencingproject.org/criminal-justice-facts/ (last visited Jul. 21, 2021) (citing statistics from Institute for Crime & Justice Policy Research).

[39] Ashley Mott, *Fact Check: Southern States Used Convict Leasing to Force Black People Into Unpaid Labor*, USA TODAY (Jul. 7, 2020, 11:12 AM), https://www.usatoday.com/story/news/factcheck/2020/07/07/fact-check-convict-leasing-forced-black-people-

This history fits with the fact that several Southern prisons were built on former plantations on which enslaved Black people worked and died[40] or that notorious prisons, like Parchman Farm in Mississippi, and Angola Prison in Louisiana, were run as if slavery had never been abolished.[41] There are far too many aspects of modern life treated as "just the way things are" rather than the product of choices made over decades to entrench power. "White terror" explains Clint Smith, "is as American as the Stars and Stripes. But when this is denied, it is no wonder that the events at the Capitol are read as shocking and un-American."[42]

Though January 6th and its aftermath will stand as a distressing reminder of the work still left to be done in our democracy, even that historical event cannot erase the other history making moments that 2020 and 2021 brought in the United States. Reverend Raphael Warnock won his runoff election in Georgia and became the first Black Democrat elected to the Senate from the South.[43] Hours later, Jon Ossoff became the first ever Jewish Senator from Georgia and the first Jewish person elected to the Senate from the South since the 1880s.[44] Kamala Harris became the first Black and South Asian woman to be our Vice-President.[45] Deb Haaland became Secretary of the Department of the Interior and the first Native American to serve as a Cabinet Secretary.[46] These are hard fought and

---

into-unpaid-labor/5368307002/; Evan Taparata, *The Slave-Trade Roots of U.S. Prisons*, THE WORLD (Aug. 26, 2016, 3:15 PM), https://www.pri.org/stories/2016-08-26/slave-trade-roots-us-private-prisons.

40 Evan Taparata, *supra* note 39.

41 *See* Innocence Staff, *The Lasting Legacy of Parchman Farm, the Prison Modeled After a Slave Plantation*, INNOCENCE PROJECT (May. 29, 2020), https://innocenceproject.org/parchman-farm-prison-mississippi-history/.

42 Ibram X. Kendi, *Denial Is the Heartbeat of America*, THE ATLANTIC (Jan. 11, 2021), https://www.theatlantic.com/ideas/archive/2021/01/denial-heartbeat-america/617631/.

43 *African American Senators*, UNITED STATES SENATE, https://www.senate.gov/pagelayout/history/h_multi_sections_and_teasers/Photo_Exhibit_African_American_Senators.htm (last visited Jul. 21, 2021).

44 Ben Samuels, *Ossoff's Georgia Win Will Make Jewish History*, HAARETZ (Jan. 6, 2021), https://www.haaretz.com/us-news/.premium.HIGHLIGHT-ossoff-s-expected-georgia-win-will-make-jewish-history-1.9428335.

45 *Kamala Harris*, WHITE HOUSE, https://www.whitehouse.gov/administration/vice-president-harris/ (last visited Jul. 21, 2021).

46 *Secretary Deb Haaland*, U.S. DEP'T INTERIOR, https://www.doi.gov/secretary-deb-haaland (last visited Jul. 21, 2021).

impressive victories, and are an example of what can be achieved when we embrace our history and fight to be better.

I ended the e-mail that I sent to my Law School community in the wake of the January 6th Insurrection with the following words:

> I cannot do anything about the chaos at the Capitol building today, but I can choose how to respond to what I saw, and right now I choose to focus on how this day began. After his victory, Senator-elect Warnock paid homage to his mother, Verlene, who raised him and his 11 siblings. He said, "Because this is America, the 82-year-old hands that used to pick somebody else's cotton went to the polls and picked her youngest son to be a United States senator." This is the America that I celebrate tonight. There will be plenty of time tomorrow (and in the days, weeks, and months to come) to deconstruct today's raw display of unpatriotic, undemocratic, and criminal behavior. Until then, I'll continue to think about what we do as lawyers to uphold the rule of law—whether it's Stacy Abrams fighting voter suppression in Georgia, the judges who carefully considered and then rejected lawsuits attempting to overturn the election results, or the many lawyers in Congress who went back to work as soon as they were told that it was safe to do so. This country is so much more than one man in the White House or a group of his disaffected supporters. I remain confident that our future is bright and that you are all a part of what makes it so.

I stand by those words written in the rawness of the day that followed so much striking history being made. Law school deans, like all educators, shape our country's future by shaping its future leaders. That is not a role that allows for silence or complicity. We must be bold, and we must practice the kind of brave leadership we hope to see from our students.

In her book, Their Eyes Were Watching God, Zora Neale Hurston wrote, "There are years that ask questions and years that answer."[47] May the years following the January 6th insurrection be full of answers for all of us. May those of us who have the privilege of teaching new lawyers re-dedicate ourselves to the task of allowing and encouraging them to cast a critical eye on the law, understand its origins, and strategize for change. Progress does not proceed in a straight line, but I must believe that we are ultimately moving in the right direction, and that, at the end of this journey, we will all be free.

---

47 ZORA NEALE HURSTON, THEIR EYES WERE WATCHING GOD, 53 (1937) (ebook).

CHAPTER 9

WHITE SUPREMACY'S THREAT TO U.S. DEMOCRACY

Carla D. Pratt[1]

The events of January 6, 2021 were beyond imagination for most Americans. But the attack on the Capitol was, unfortunately, an inevitable consequence of decades of mainstream denial about the expansiveness of the white power movement in the United States[2], and the failure of democratic institutions to take actions to purge white supremacists. By failing to make it clear that swearing to uphold the U.S. constitution means holding a commitment to freedom and equality for all Americans, the democratic institutions that America holds dear inadvertently have legitimated white supremacists and their cause. Before Charlottesville, many of us dismissed white supremacy as the crazy musings of a few powerless Americans on the margins of society.[3] However, for those who had been paying attention for years, like the Southern Poverty Law Center, which tracks hate groups in the United States,[4] and the FBI which had listed white supremacists as one of the primary threats to our national security,[5] white

---

[1] Dean and Professor of Law.

[2] The white power movement in the United State is comprised of many different groups. Unifying features of the movement include the belief in white supremacy, the need for a white homeland, and fear that the government will eradicate the white population. *See*, KATHLEEN BELEW, BRING THE WAR HOME: THE WHITE POWER MOVEMENT AND PARAMILITARY AMERICA 18–22 (2018).

[3] Some media outlets have tried to educate us that white supremacy has never been fringe. *See, e.g.*, https://www.npr.org/sections/codeswitch/2019/08/10/749202273/white-supremacy-isnt-emerging-from-the-fringes-its-part-of-americas-core.

[4] https://www.splcenter.org/hate-map.

[5] Prior to the insurrection and Charlottesville, the FBI warned that white supremacists pose a domestic terrorism threat. https://www.fbi.gov/news/testimony/confronting-white-supremacy.

supremacy was not merely a small group of insignificant crazies on the fringe of society.[6]

The Trump presidency emboldened white supremacists through words of adulation,[7] and provided a safe haven to the white supremacist groups that had been lurking in the shadows and building a movement premised on the worst human impulses. Particularly concerning is the extent to which those movements sought recruits among members of law enforcement and the military.[8] To understand the January 6 Insurrection, one needs to place it in the context of the through line of white supremacy that has existed in our American democracy since its founding. As lawyers, law professors, and law deans, it is imperative that we are honest about this country's roots and the continuing vestiges of its original sin.[9] Only a complete repudiation of white supremacy will empower us to build a country that actually, and finally, lives the words of our founding documents.

Legal scholars routinely cite to Justice Harlan's dissent in *Plessy v. Ferguson*[10] wherein he states that our constitution is colorblind. But the truth is that our original constitution of the United States was not colorblind. It was a very color conscious document that embraced racial hierarchy with Whites at the top and Blacks at the bottom. The original constitution refers to three racial groups of people existing in the U.S.: Whites, who are referred to as citizens[11] and "free persons"[12] who, according

---

[6] Scholars who study white supremacy also recognize that it is not an insignificant threat on the fringe of society. *See, e.g.,* KATHLEEN BELEW, BRING THE WAR HOME: THE WHITE POWER MOVEMENT AND PARAMILITARY AMERICA (2018); VEGAS TENOLD, EVERYTHING YOU LOVE WILL BURN: INSIDE THE REBIRTH OF WHITE NATIONALISM IN AMERICA (2018).

[7] After the white supremacist march at Charlottesville, then President Trump stated that there are "very fine people" on "both sides." https://www.washingtonpost.com/politics/2020/05/08/very-fine-people-charlottesville-who-were-they-2/.

[8] The FBI has released secret audio recordings that detail how white supremacist organizations recruit members of law enforcement and the military. https://www.usatoday.com/story/news/2020/10/15/splc-releases-audio-how-neo-nazi-group-recruits-military-police/3661460001/.

[9] The 1619 project seeks to educate Americans on the centrality of slavery to our nation's founding and the consequences of slavery that continue to plaque us as a nation. https://www.nytimes.com/interactive/2019/08/14/magazine/1619-america-slavery.html.

[10] 163 U.S. 537 (1896).

[11] *See, e.g.,* U.S. CONST. art. IV, § 2, cl. 1.

[12] U.S. CONST. art. I, § 2, cl. 3.

to the U.S. Supreme Court's decision in *Dred Scott*,[13] were envisioned by the drafters of the constitution to be Anglos or Caucasians who migrated to the U.S. from Europe.[14] It also refers to "Indians,"[15] who were the indigenous inhabitants of the North American territory claimed by the United States. While the constitution does not use the words "slave," "Blacks," or "Africans," it refers to the African American people who were slaves at the time of its drafting by referring to "other persons"[16] and "person[s] held to service."[17] This original founding document adopted the preexisting framework of White racial dominance that had existed in the American colonies prior to independence from England.

By the end of the seventeenth century, slavery and the law of slavery was well established in the New England colonies.[18] In the 1640s, Africans in the Virginia colony who were bound to service were bound in perpetuity.[19] By 1662, colonial law provided that in determining the status of a child as free or slave, the child would take the status of the mother, thereby ensuring that the offspring of White men who had exercised sexual dominance over African women's bodies would not be legitimated by law, but would instead be assigned the status of slave.[20] By 1670, the institution of slavery in the Virginia colony was protected by a complex system of laws,[21] and by 1715, the colony of Maryland had codified an entire body of slave law.[22] When the U.S. Supreme Court was created in 1788, the newly

---

[13] Scott v. Sandford, 60 U.S. 393 (1857).

[14] *Id.* at 421.

[15] *See, e.g.*, U.S. CONST. art. I, § 2, cl. 3.

[16] *Id.*

[17] U.S. CONST. art. IV, § 2, cl. 3.

[18] Christopher Tomlins, *Transplants and Timing: Passages in the Creation of an Anglo-American Law of Slavery*, 10 THEORETICAL INQ. L. 389, 395–96 (2009) ("The slave population of the mid-Atlantic and Southern New England . . . grew from some 1,200 in 1660 to over 5,000 by 1700, 30,000 in 1750, and 50,000 (10% of the mainland's black population) by the 1770s.").

[19] Paul Finkelman, *Exploring Southern Legal History*, 64 N.C.L. REV. 77, 90–91 (1985).

[20] Act XII, 2 LAWS OF VA. 170, 170 (Hening 1823) (enacted 1662).

[21] A. Leon Higginbotham, Jr. & Barbara K. Kopytoff, *Racial Purity and Interracial Sex in the Law of Colonial and Antebellum Virginia*, 77 GEO. L.J. 1967, 1973 (1989).

[22] *An Act Relating to Servants and Slaves*, 30 MD. ARCHIVES 283 (1715), available at https://msa.maryland.gov/megafile/msa/speccol/sc2900/sc2908/000001/000030/html/am30--283.html.

emancipated colonies had well-entrenched laws governing slavery, which had become an exclusively Black institution.[23]

Benjamin Franklin, who led the Pennsylvania Abolition Society, is reported to have spent much of his time trying to resolve America's greatest political contradiction: its promise of freedom against its practice of slavery.[24] Likewise, by the time the Constitution was ratified, the English colonists had removed many indigenous nations from the geographic boundaries of the colonies through forced removal or coerced land purchases.[25] Hence our democratic government was created in a context where White racial dominance had been manufactured for generations through African slavery and Native American conquest and removal.[26] Moreover, our constitutional democracy's governing document created an America that, according to Senators Stephen Douglas and Jefferson Davis, "was made by White men for the benefit of White men and their posterity forever."[27] From this we see that White supremacy was an underlying assumption of American democracy, and the maintenance of White racial dominance over people of color was an expectation of many founding fathers.

The Reconstruction Amendments to the U.S. Constitution sought to redeem the document from its original sin of White supremacy by prohibiting most forms of involuntary servitude,

---

[23] Stephen A. Siegel, *The Federal Government's Power to Enact Color-Conscious Laws: An Originalist Inquiry*, 92 NW. U.L. REV. 477, 494–95 (1998) ("In the Founding era almost all states permitted slavery delimited along racial lines. Between 1787 and 1791, when the nation was framing and ratifying the Constitution and the Bill of Rights, race-based slavery was legal in eleven of the fourteen states.").

[24] Paul Finkelman, *Human Liberty, Property in Human Beings, and the Pennsylvania Supreme Court*, 53 DUQ. L. REV. 453, 467 (2015).

[25] An example of this practice of colonial Indian removal arose in the case of Joint Tribal Council of Passamaquoddy Tribe v. Morton, 528 F.2d 370 (1st Cir. 1975) wherein the tribe sued the federal government asking it to bring an action against the state of Maine to recover land ceded by the tribe in 1794 without the approval of the federal government.

[26] French aristocrat Alexis de Tocqueville documented his observation of America's racial hierarchy during his visit to the United States in 1830 noting that the white man was first in power and happiness and "below him appear the Negro and the Indian. Both occupy an equally inferior position in the country that they inhabit; both experience the effects of tyranny." HARVEY C. MANSFIELD AND DELBA WINTHROP, ALEXIS DE TOCQUEVILLE, DEMOCRACY IN AMERICA at 303 (2000).

[27] Stephen Douglas, *First Joint Debate, at Ottawa, Illinois (Aug. 21, 1858)*, in 3 COMPLETE WORKS OF ABRAHAM LINCOLN 237, 255–56 (John G. Nicolay & John Hay eds., 1894). *See also* IBRAM X. KENDI, STAMPED FROM THE BEGINNING 205, 209 (2016).

making the freed slaves and their descendants citizens of the U.S., and guaranteeing all people equal protection under the law.[28] However, the project of constructing and maintaining White racial dominance was not terminated with the end of the Civil War. Whites still viewed Blacks as inferior beings and looked for other ways to regulate Blacks.[29] The mere presence of Black people in the United States following the end of slavery was viewed by Whites as a problem that was often referred to as "The Negro Problem."[30] The post-Civil War Reconstruction Amendments failed to command any "just compensation"[31] for the property of African people that was taken from them—the value of their intergenerational labor.

When President Lincoln was assassinated immediately following the end of the Civil War, Vice President Andrew Johnson became President and effectively rescinded General Sherman's order mandating that White plantation owners pay reparation to their slaves by allotting them 40 acres of land.[32] Andrew Johnson pardoned White plantation owners and returned to them the land on which 40,000 or so Black families had settled.[33] In doing so, President Johnson reiterated America's commitment to White supremacy in 1866 by stating: "This is a country for white men, and by God, as long as I am President, it shall be a government for white men."[34] A southern state convention following the Civil War proclaimed that it was a "government of White people, made and to be perpetuated for the exclusive benefit of the White Race."[35] It therefore should not be surprising that our constitutional democracy was a government that operated from its inception to create and

---

28 U.S. CONST. amends. XIII–XIV.

29 JOHN DAVID SMITH, ANTI-BLACK THOUGHT 1863–1925 at xii–xiii.

30 *Id.* at xiv–xv.

31 U.S. CONST. amend. V.

32 Adjoa A. Aiyetoro, *Formulating Reparations Litigation Through the Eyes of the Movement*, 58 N.Y.U. ANN. SURV. AM. L. 457, 459–60 (2003).

33 Kamille Wolff Dean, *Corporate Social Responsibility and Conservation: The Preservation of Ecology and Culture to Sustain the Sea Islands*, 37 WM. & MARY ENVTL. L. & POL'Y REV. 375, 382 (2013).

34 JERROLD M. PACKARD, AMERICAN NIGHTMARE: THE HISTORY OF JIM CROW 42 (2002).

35 United States v. State of Louisiana, 225 F. Supp. 353, 364 (E.D. La. 1963).

maintain the social, political, and economic dominance of White people over people of color.

Although emancipation from slavery brought a form of freedom to Black Americans, a new form of bondage replaced slavery. Even slavery era free states sought to maintain White racial dominance by participating in a new threat to freedom and democracy that became known as Jim Crow or racial segregation. Jim Crow laws existed in all previous slaveholding states and many free states including Kansas.[36] These laws mandated segregation of Black citizens from Whites and sent a clear message that the law deemed Blacks to be inferior to Whites. Jim Crow laws and customs precluded Blacks from voting, holding political office, living in certain places, being educated in elite educational institutions, and being gainfully employed in jobs that paid a living wage.[37] Racial segregation even prevented Blacks from merely existing in certain spaces; many towns were known as "Sundown Towns"[38] with ordinances that made it a crime for a Black person to simply be present in the town after sundown. The punishment for violating these cultural and legal norms were beatings, castration, torture, maiming, and lynching.[39]

The year 2021 marked the 100th Anniversary of the largest massacre of Black people in American history—the Tulsa Race Massacre.[40] Despite the fact that hundreds of innocent Black people were murdered by the hands of White Tulsans, including White law enforcement officers, no White person was ever prosecuted.[41] The few remaining African American survivors of

---

[36] Barbara Y. Welke, *Beyond Plessy: Space, Status, and Race In the Era of Jim Crow*, 2000 UTAH L. REV. 267, 268 (2000); Karl A. Cole-Frieman, *The Ghosts of Segregation Still Haunt Topeka, Kansas: A Case Study on the Role of the Federal Courts in School Desegregation*, 6 KAN. J.L. & PUB. POL'Y 23, 26 (1996).

[37] *Jim Crow Laws*, HIST. (Mar. 26, 2021), http://www.history.com/topics/early-20th-century-us/jim-crow-laws.

[38] JAMES W. LOEWEN, SUNDOWN TOWNS: A HIDDEN DIMENSION OF AMERICAN RACISM 99–105 (2d ed. 2018).

[39] *Id.* at 270–75. *See also*, SHERRILYN A. IFILL, ON THE COURTHOUSE LAWN: CONFRONTING THE LEGACY OF LYNCHING IN THE TWENTY-FIRST CENTURY (2007).

[40] 1921 TULSA RACE MASSACRE COMMISSION, https://www.tulsa2021.org/ (last visited June 23, 2021).

[41] Randy Krehbiel, *Tulsa Race Massacre: In Aftermath, No One Prosecuted for Killings, and Insurance Claims Were Rejected but Greenwood Persevered*, TULSA WORLD (June 10, 2021), https://tulsaworld.com/news/local/racemassacre/tulsa-race-massacre-in-

the Tulsa massacre have lived their lives in poverty, and as of the date of this writing have not received any compensation from the city of Tulsa for the wrongful death of their loved ones, the emotional trauma they suffered, the property they lost, or the intergenerational consequences of being a refugee in one's own nation.[42]

The promise of freedom for Black Americans would not come until the Civil Rights movement and the passage of federal civil rights laws that ended racial segregation mandated by law in public spaces and sought to enforce the constitutional right to vote for African Americans found in the Reconstruction Amendments.

Nonetheless, the Civil Rights Era did not bring true freedom to Black Americans, because the Civil Rights legislation of 1964 and 1965 banned only intentional racial discrimination that could be proven in a court of law. It did not prohibit government from acting in ways that maintained the racial dominance of Whites as a group that had been created through the laws of slavery and Jim Crow segregation. For example, Title VII of the Civil Rights Act of 1964 prohibited racial discrimination in employment but failed to offer any remedy to Blacks and other people of color for the harm imposed on them as a group due to generations of forced uncompensated labor during slavery and the denial of jobs paying a living wage during the Jim Crow era. The failure to offer a remedy for past oppression of people of color allowed white racial dominance over people of color to continue as a form of racial monopoly. Moreover, the failure to offer a remedy for past oppression ignored the reality that by 1964, white racial dominance had become locked into American democracy and its economy so that only radical government action to advance people of color could disrupt the white racial monopoly.[43]

The subordination of Blacks and other people of color in America is often hidden from view because high profile examples

---

aftermath-no-one-prosecuted-for-killings-and-insurance-claims-were-rejected/article_3ba23c3c-886d-5821-9970-02153261960a.html.

[42] *Id.*

[43] Daria Roithmayr, *Locked in Inequality: The Persistence of Discrimination* 9 MICH. J. RACE AND LAW 31 (2003).

of people of color function as proof positive that America is a nation of equal opportunity. People like Oprah Winfrey, Colin Powell, Barack and Michelle Obama, and other lawyers, doctors, politicians and engineers of color appear to many Americans to be the living proof that America is a nation built on equal opportunity. But careful examination of the data reveals that White racial dominance over people of color in America that was created by law has never been remedied. If we look beyond the high-profile examples of Black achievement, we will see the norm for Black people in America. We will see a vast wealth gap between White Americans and Black Americans that was created over time by law.[44] Although Black people make up about 13% of the US population they hold less than 3% of the nation's total wealth.[45] The median family wealth for White people is $171,000 compared to the median for Black people which is just $17,100.[46] Thirty seven percent of Black households have zero or negative net worth while only sixteen percent of White families are that poor.[47] Blacks, as subordinate members of our American polity, bear a disparate share of "negative social value" such as "substandard housing, disease, underemployment, dangerous and distasteful work, disproportionate punishment in our criminal justice system, inferior education, stigmatization, and vilification."[48]

African Americans are two and a half times more likely to be killed by police than White people.[49] The reality that people of color bear a disproportionate share of negative social value in American society is a form of White racial dominance or White supremacy that was created by slavery and Jim Crow, and that has been allowed to perpetuate into the present day. By deploying the "freedom loving" trope of democracy, along with

44 DOROTHY BROWN, THE WHITENESS OF WEALTH 17–21 (2021).

45 *Id.* at 217.

46 *Id.* at 18.

47 *Id.*

48 JIM SIDANIUS & FELICIA PRATTO, SOCIAL DOMINANCE: AN INTERGROUP THEORY OF SOCIAL HIERARCHY AND OPPRESSION 272 (1999).

49 Jeffrey Fagan & Alexis D. Campbell, *Race and Reasonableness in Police Killings*, 100 B.U.L. REV. 951, 1007 (2020).

myths of inferiority about African[50], Native[51], and Asian[52] people, our constitutional democracy has functioned as a hierarchy enhancing structure designed to position and maintain White males as the dominant group in our society.[53]

Indeed, today Black people enjoy more freedoms than ever before in American society. Nonetheless, until Black freedom on a group level is equal to White freedom on a group level, our constitutional democracy is vulnerable to attack by White supremacists who cling to America's founding belief that White racial dominance over people of color in America is justified and desirable. White supremacists believe that any threat to White dominance over people of color in America is a threat to our democracy.[54]

Many of the people who attacked the Capitol on January 6 were carrying Confederate flags[55] and donning anti-Semitic symbols in an effort to visibly support White supremacy.[56] Many of the insurrectionists were people who subscribe to the white nationalist view of America—that it is a nation created by white people for the benefit of white people. These white nationalists viewed the Trump administration as sympathetic to their White supremacy cause[57] and willing to support policies that maintain

---

50 SIDANIUS & PRATTO, *supra* note 48, at 16, 47.

51 *Id.* at 256–57.

52 *Id.* at 53.

53 *Id.* at 47.

54 Darin E.W. Johnson, *Homegrown and Global: The Rising Terror Movement*, 58 HOUS. L. REV. 1059, 1070–71 (2021).

55 The Confederate flag has a star for each of the slave-holding states that seceded from the Union in rebellion toward the federal government and a last-ditch effort to preserve slavery. It has been adopted by the white supremacy movement as a symbol of white supremacy. https://www.nationalgeographic.com/history/article/how-confederate-battle-flag-became-symbol-racism.

56 Javonte Anderson, *Capitol Riot Images Showing Confederate Flag a Reminder of Country's Darkest Past*, USA TODAY (Jan. 7, 2021 8:58 PM ET), https://www.usatoday.com/story/news/2021/01/07/capitol-riot-images-confederate-flag-terror/6588104002/.

57 Richard Spencer, a college educated alt-right white nationalist who serves as director of the National Policy Institute which promotes the "heritage, identity, and future of European people," said that Trump embodies "an unconscious vision that white people have—that their grandchildren might be a hated minority in their own country. I think that scares us. They probably aren't able to articulate it. It think it's there. I think that, to a great degree, explains the Trump phenomenon." https://www.huffpost.com/entry/donald-trump-white-supremacists_n_55dce43ee4b08cd3359dc41a; *see also*, https://www.splcenter.org/fighting-hate/extremist-files/individual/richard-bertrand-spencer-0. A leading neo-Nazi news outlet called *The Daily Stormer* endorsed Trump and said "Trump is willing to say what most Americans think: it's time to deport these

White racial dominance over people of color.[58] White supremacist podcaster, Sven Longshanks praised President Trump to his "*Daily Nationalist*" audience after Trump issued a race-baiting tweet telling four United States congresswomen of color to go back to their own countries, thereby sending the message that Black people do not belong in America.[59] White separatist, Jared Taylor who founded the magazine *American Renaissance* said that Donald Trump gave "white interests" a "voice and a reason to act."[60] The January 6 insurrectionists had high regard for President Trump and believed the former President's inaccurate statements asserting that the election and the resulting power that flows therefrom had been stolen from their preferred candidate—Trump.[61] The white power movement's distrust of government made the movement's members easy targets for the consumption of false claims asserting that the presidential election was stolen. Never before in our history had a defeated president claimed that the presidential election was not a free and fair election. Consequently that bold proclamation was a call to arms to Trump supporters, especially those who distrust government as much as white power activists do.

Many Americans seemed surprised to learn that the rioters at the Capitol included members of the military, police officers, and government officials.[62] Yet the FBI had been warning the

---

people." The news outlet also called for white men to "vote for the first time in our lives for the one man who actually represents our interests." https://www.huffpost.com/entry/donald-trump-white-supremacists_n_55dce43ee4b08cd3359dc41a.

[58] Johnson, *supra* note 54, at 1085–86 ("The Stop the Steal conspiracy theory morphed with white supremacist ideologies and QAnon conspiracy theories to cause many adherents to believe that Trump's call for followers to come to D.C. for a rally on January 6, 2021, to stop the congressional certification of the presidential election was the foretold Storm. . . . White supremacists saw the insurrection and storming of the Capitol as part of their Accelerationist ideology to bring about societal collapse.").

[59] https://www.adl.org/blog/white-supremacists-extremists-celebrate-president-trumps-latest-racist-tweets.

[60] https://www.wnycstudios.org/podcasts/otm/segments/what-white-separatist-expects-trump-administration.

[61] Johnson, *supra* note 54 at 1084 ("This big lie about election fraud radicalized his followers who believed his claims, despite the fact that over sixty judges threw out his election fraud claims on the basis that there was no evidence to support them.").

[62] Tom Dreisbach & Meg Anderson, *Nearly 1 In 5 Defendants In Capitol Riot Cases Served In The Military*, NPR (Jan. 21, 2021, 3:01 PM ET), https://www.npr.org/2021/01/21/958915267/nearly-one-in-five-defendants-in-capitol-riot-cases-served-in-the-military.

nation's leaders that White supremacist groups recruit people with military and law enforcement training.[63] Despite these warnings, state and federal government leaders have not sought to expel White supremacists from government institutions. Instead, leaders in the legal profession and all branches of government have stood firm in their commitment to protect White supremacists' First Amendment rights to believe and say things that are in opposition to the Reconstruction Amendments to the Constitution while still holding positions of power and trust throughout our government.[64] Few have condemned this privileging of First Amendment rights of Whites over the Fourteenth Amendment rights of people of color to be free from racially motivated acts of government officials.[65] The danger of using the constitution as a shield that protects the hate of White supremacists to the extent of entrusting them with positions of power in our government is that they may take over government from within. What we saw on January 6, 2021 was a warning—a call to action for all Americans who value a democracy that is committed to equality and freedom for all.

The challenge for the current generation of freedom- and equality-loving Americans is to identify and rectify ideologies, institutions, and structures that operate to infringe the freedoms of people of color and keep them, as a group, subordinate to Whites in political, social and economic power. Examples of such structures are all around us. Laws restricting voting rights will disproportionately exclude people of color from the ballot box thereby diminishing their political power to elect

---

63 *See, e.g.*, COUNTERTERRORISM DIV., FED. BUREAU OF INVESTIGATION, WHITE SUPREMACIST INFILTRATION OF LAW ENFORCEMENT 3–4 (2006); James Laporta, *Charlottesville: Alt-Right and White Supremacists Recruiting U.S. Military Veterans and Service Members*, NEWSWEEK (Aug. 11, 2018), https://www.newsweek.com/military-charlottesville-white-nationalist-neo-nazi-1069459.

64 *See, e.g.*, Johnson, *supra* note 54; Carla D. Pratt, *Should Klansmen be Lawyers?: Racism as an Ethical Barrier to the Legal Profession*, 30 FLA. ST. U.L. REV. 857 (2003); Eleanor Boatman, *The Kids Are Alt-Right: How Media and the Law Enable White Supremacist Groups to Recruit and Radicalize Emotionally Vulnerable Individuals*, 12 L. J. SOC. JUST. 2 (2019); Robin D. Barnes, *Blue by Day and White by Knight: Regulating the Political Affiliations of Law Enforcement and Military Personnel*, 81 IOWA L. REV. 1079 (1996).

65 *See, e.g.*, Pratt, *supra* note 64, at 862–63; *see generally*, OWEN FISS, LIBERALISM DIVIDED: FREEDOM OF SPEECH AND THE MANY USES OF STATE POWER (2019).

representatives that will serve their interests in Congress.[66] Another example is the enactment of laws attempting to ban the truthful teaching of history[67] that includes telling the whole truth about the horrors of slavery,[68] the century of lynching, and the contemporary consequences of racialized oppression. Political resistance to forming a bi-partisan commission to study the events of January 6 sought to pervert the narrative so that we wouldn't believe what our eyes witnessed on January 6.[69] It is only through honest analysis of our history and our present that we will understand the true threat that White racial dominance is to our democracy. White supremacy and democracy are inconsistent values. As a nation, we have to choose which one we will work to preserve and which one we will sacrifice. Let's choose democracy.

---

66 Perry Grossman, *The Case for State Attorney General Enforcement of the Voting Rights Act Against Local Governments*, 50 U. MICH. J.L. REFORM 565, 584 (2017).

67 Adrian Florido, *Teachers Say Laws Banning Critical Race Theory Are Putting a Chill on Their Lessons*, NPR (May 28, 2021, 9:04 AM ET), https://www.npr.org/2021/05/28/1000537206/teachers-laws-banning-critical-race-theory-are-leading-to-self-censorship.

68 Janel George, *A Lesson on Critical Race Theory*, AMERICAN BAR ASS'N (Jan. 12, 2021), https://www.americanbar.org/groups/crsj/publications/human_rights_magazine_home/civil-rights-reimagining-policing/a-lesson-on-critical-race-theory/.

69 Grace Segers, *Senate Republicans Block Commission on January 6 Insurrection*, CBS NEWS (May 29, 2021, 8:56 AM), https://www.cbsnews.com/news/january-6-commission-bill-capitol-riot-senate-republicans-block/. But *see*, https://www.nytimes.com/2021/06/24/us/politics/pelosi-select-committee-jan-6-capitol.html noting that House Speaker Nancy Pelosi is forming a committee to investigate the deadly attack on the Capitol on January 6.

CHAPTER 10

CAN LAW SCHOOLS HELP SAVE DEMOCRACY?

Erwin S. Chemerinsky[1]

Democracies are there until they are not. No form of government lasts forever. The events of late 2020 and early 2021 caused many to realize the fragility of American democracy and how easily it could have been lost. What if Republican election officials or Republican legislators in Georgia, Michigan, and Pennsylvania gave those states' electoral votes to Donald Trump? Or what if Mike Pence, as Vice President, had ruled in a way to make Trump the winner? The core feature of democracy—that elections decide who holds power—would have ended in the United States after 237 years.

If just 42,921 votes had changed in Arizona, Georgia, and Wisconsin, Donald Trump would have been reelected President despite losing the popular election by over seven million votes. The Republicans then would have controlled the Senate as well. It would be impossible to regard the United States as a democracy in any meaningful sense if the losing political party ruled the government yet again.

There are many heroes in this story, including the election officials, the legislators, and the Vice President who resisted pressure from the President of the United States. Among the heroes to be celebrated are the judges who heard the dozens of lawsuits that sought to overturn the results of the election. State and federal, liberal and conservative, the judges rejected the baseless assertions of voter fraud and refused to overturn the will of the people. The courts exist to uphold the rule of law and they did.

Everyone breathed a sigh of relief and there was a lot of self-congratulations about how the guardrails of democracy held. But

---

[1] Dean and Jesse H. Choper Distinguished Professor of Law, University of California, Berkeley School of Law.

I fear that all of this has caused us to overlook the real threats to democracy that have slowly developed over the course of American history. The election of 2020 must be understood as a reflection of deep problems in American democracy that remain even though Donald Trump is out of the White House.

No easy solutions exist and it is unclear whether any meaningful changes are even possible. But I believe that law schools have a critical role to play in the difficult years ahead that will determine whether the United States will remain a democracy.

In this essay, I make three points. First, deeply embedded flaws in the United States Constitution have grown worse over time and are responsible for putting American democracy in serious jeopardy. Second, American society is politically polarized and this exacerbates the threats to democracy. And third, it is important to think about what law schools can do to make a difference and to help save American democracy.

A. A DEEPLY FLAWED DOCUMENT

Our society long has exalted the Constitution.[2] But it contains flaws that are responsible for the problems seen in the American political system today.[3]

To begin with, it creates a government which is stunningly non-democratic. The Electoral College makes no sense as a way for a democracy to choose a president. During the 2020 presidential election, everyone understandably focused on the vote counts in Pennsylvania, Georgia, Arizona, and Nevada, and which candidate could get enough electoral votes to reach 270 in the Electoral College. Less attention was paid to the fact that Joe Biden decisively won the popular vote by over seven million votes.

In a democracy, the candidate with the most popular votes should win. But five times in American history, including in

---

[2] *See, e.g.*, Max Lerner, *Constitution and Court as Symbols*, 46 YALE L.J. 1290, 1294 (1937).

[3] I develop these ideas more fully in ERWIN CHEMERINSKY, BAD BONES: AMERICA'S FLAWED CONSTITUTION AND HOW TO FIX IT (work in progress, publication expected 2023).

2000 and 2016, the loser became president of the United States.[4] This anti-democratic feature of the Electoral College was intentional. Alexander Hamilton, in Federalist No. 68, explained that the "immediate election [of the president] should be made by men most capable of analyzing the qualities adapted to the station."[5] He wrote that a "small number of persons, selected by their fellow-citizens from the general mass, will be most likely to possess the information and discernment requisite to such complicated investigations."[6]

The Electoral College also was very much a product of the compromises concerning slavery that were at the core of the Constitution's drafting and ratification. Before considering the method of choosing the president, the Constitutional Convention had agreed to the "three-fifths clause," the provision in Article I of the Constitution stating that slaves counted as three-fifths of a person for the purpose of determining a state's population for allocating seats in the House of Representatives. But slaves obviously could not vote. Southern states would not get the benefit of this population in presidential elections.

The Electoral College was proposed to deal with this: electors would be allocated based on seats in Congress, meaning that slaves would count towards the number of electors each state received. If the president were directly elected by the voters, voters in the North would outnumber voters in the South because the South's half-million slaves were not voters. The Electoral College meant that each southern state could count its slaves as three-fifths of a person in its share of votes in the Electoral College. This was explicitly understood and expressed at the Constitutional Convention.[7]

But it is not just the Electoral College that is anti-democratic. Every state, regardless of population, has two

---

4 *See* Dave Roos, *5 Presidents Who Lost the Popular Vote But Won the Election*, HISTORY (Nov. 2, 2020), https://www.history.com/news/presidents-electoral-college-popular-vote (last visited Apr. 29, 2021).

5 THE FEDERALIST NO. 68 (Alexander Hamilton).

6 *Id.*

7 *See* AKHIL REED AMAR, THE CONSTITUTION TODAY: TIMELESS LESSONS FOR THE ISSUES OF OUR ERA 333 (2016) (discussing how the Electoral College "was originally much more about slavery than about a big-state, small-state balance; that in today's world, the college operates to dampen democracy; and that 'federalism' is no talismanic answer").

senators. A voter in Wyoming (population 582,000) enjoys roughly seventy times more influence in the Senate than a voter in California (population 39.5 million). When the Constitution was written, the difference between the largest and the smallest states was 12.7 to 1;[8] now it is 68 to 1.[9] Senators representing as little as 17.6% of the population can constitute a majority in the Senate.[10]

The Supreme Court and the federal judiciary also were created to be anti-democratic, with Justices and judges appointed by the president and confirmed by the Senate. Although I agree with the need to shield the judiciary from politics, the combined result of the Electoral College, the allocation of senators, and the appointment process is that a president who lost the popular vote can nominate a Justice who is confirmed by a Senate that represents a minority of the population.

This scenario is not hypothetical: Democrats have won the popular vote in seven of the last eight elections. But during this time, Republican presidents have appointed five Supreme Court Justices and Democratic presidents have appointed just two. President Trump, who lost the popular vote in 2016, appointed three Justices, all of whom were confirmed by Senators representing a distinct minority of the population. Between 1960 and 2020, there were thirty-two years with Republican presidents and twenty-eight years with Democratic presidents. But Republican presidents have named fifteen Supreme Court Justices and Democratic presidents have picked only eight.[11]

---

[8] *See 1790 Census: Return of the Whole Number of Persons Within the Several Districts of the United States*, U.S. CENSUS BUREAU, https://www.census.gov/library/publications/1793/dec/number-of-persons.html (last visited Apr. 29, 2021) (dividing the population of Virginia, 747,610, by the population of Delaware, 59,094).

[9] *See Annual Estimates of the Resident Population for the United States, Regions, States, and the District of Colombia: April 1, 2010 to July 1, 2020 (NST-EST2020)*, U.S. CENSUS BUREAU, https://www.census.gov/programs-surveys/popest/technical-documentation/research/evaluation-estimates.html (last visited Apr. 29, 2021) (dividing the population of California, 39,368,078, by the population of Wyoming, 582,328).

[10] *See id.*

[11] *See Judgeship Appointments by President*, USCOURTS.GOV, https://www.uscourts.gov/sites/default/files/apptsbypres.pdf (last visited Apr. 29, 2021). Republican Presidents appointed: Burger, Blackmun, Powell, Stevens, Rehnquist, O'Connor, Scalia, Kennedy, Thomas, Souter, Roberts, Alito, Gorsuch, Kavanaugh, and Barrett. Democratic Presidents appointed: White, Goldberg, Fortas, Marshall, Ginsburg, Breyer, Kagan, and Sotomayor.

Even the House of Representatives—which is supposed to be the most majoritarian body, with seats allocated by population—is anti-democratic because of partisan gerrymandering. In a majority of the states, the state legislature draws congressional districts and with the aid of sophisticated computer programs can ensure who will control the seats.[12] In 2018, Republican and Democratic congressional candidates in North Carolina received in total about the same number of votes.[13] But because of partisan gerrymandering, Republicans won ten of thirteen seats from North Carolina in the House of Representatives.[14] The Supreme Court ruled that the challenge to this partisan gerrymandering could not be heard by the federal courts because it is a non-justiciable political question.[15]

The greatest flaw in the Constitution is that it explicitly protected the institution of slavery and had no provision assuring equal protection of the law. Southern states simply would not have accepted a Constitution that eliminated slavery. They insisted on provisions that prevented Congress from banning the importation of slaves for twenty years (one of the only constitutional provisions exempt from the possibility of constitutional amendment), treated slaves as three-fifths of a person for purposes of apportionment (greatly benefiting slave states in the allocation of representatives in the House of Representatives and therefore the Electoral College), and required the return of an escaped slave. Nothing in the Constitution even hinted at equal protection or any limit on discrimination. The compromises made as to race and slavery are a tragic flaw that has not only haunted the country throughout its history, but continues.

---

12 Vann R. Newkirk II, *How Redistricting Became a Technological Arms Race*, THE ATLANTIC (Oct. 28, 2017), https://www.theatlantic.com/politics/archive/2017/10/gerrymandering-technology-redmap-2020/543888/ (last visited Apr. 29, 2021).

13 Maggie Astor & K.K. Rebecca Lai, *What's Stronger Than a Blue Wave? Gerrymandered Districts*, N.Y. TIMES (Nov. 29, 2018), https://www.nytimes.com/interactive/2018/11/29/us/politics/north-carolina-gerrymandering.html (last visited Apr. 29, 2021).

14 *Id.*

15 Rucho v. Common Cause, 139 S. Ct. 2484, 2508 (2019).

B. A DEEPLY POLARIZED SOCIETY

The results of the last two presidential elections paint a picture of a population almost evenly divided between sharply contrasting ideological poles. In November 2020, Joe Biden won 81,283,098 votes, or 51.3% of the votes cast.[16] Donald Trump won 74,222,958 votes, or 46.8% of the votes cast.[17] The 2016 presidential election was even closer, with Hillary Clinton beating Donald Trump by nearly three million votes.[18] Biden and Trump espoused dramatically different views and values, and they were nominated by political parties that at this time share little common ground on the issues.

Yet even that does not reflect the intensity of the divide in the country. Studies have shown that 38% of Democrats and 38% of Republicans said they would feel somewhat or very upset at the prospect of their child marrying someone from the opposite party.[19]

The divide is along racial, age, and educational lines. As Professors Gould and Pozen point out:

> Simply put, white voters favor Republicans decisively, and non-white voters favor Democrats even more decisively. In presidential elections since 2008, Republican candidates have won white voters by margins of 12% to 20%, while Democratic candidates have won Black voters by margins of 81% to 91%, Hispanic voters by margins of 36% to 44%, and Asian-American voters by margins of 27% to 47%. In recent decades, a parallel gap has opened up between increasingly Democratic-leaning younger voters and Republican-leaning senior citizens and between

---

16 James M. Lindsay, *The 2020 Election by the Numbers*, COUNCIL ON FOREIGN RELS.: THE WATER'S EDGE (Dec. 15, 2020, 5:00 PM), https://www.cfr.org/blog/2020-election-numbers (last visited Apr. 29, 2021).

17 *Id.*

18 Sarah Begley, *Hillary Clinton Leads by 2.8 Million in Final Popular Vote Count*, TIME (Dec. 20, 2016, 4:38 PM), https://time.com/4608555/hillary-clinton-popular-vote-final/ (last visited Apr. 29, 2021).

19 India Opzoomer, *America Speaks: What Do They Think About Cross-Party Marriages?*, YOUGOV (Sep. 24, 2020, 12:56 PM), https://today.yougov.com/topics/lifestyle/articles-reports/2020/09/24/america-speaks-what-do-they-think-about-cross-part (last visited Apr. 29, 2021).

increasingly Democratic-leaning women and Republican-leaning men. The contemporary partisan gap with respect to education is especially striking—highly educated voters now tend to support Democrats and less educated voters to support Republicans—in that it represents an inversion of dynamics that prevailed as recently as the early 2000s.[20]

In one sense, deep polarization is not new in the United States. For its first seventy-five years, the country was profoundly split over the issue of slavery. A civil war is the most extreme manifestation of a divided nation. The civil rights movement in the 1950s and the 1960s certainly cleaved the country. When I was in college, the country was seriously split over the Vietnam War.

But I think most would agree that the country is more divided than it has been in a very long time. There is a huge difference in values among Americans; liberals and conservatives disagree about countless basic questions. In constitutional law, this is reflected constantly on the Supreme Court. In October Term 2019, the Court decided fifty-three cases with signed opinions after briefing and oral argument.[21] Fourteen were 5–4 decisions.[22] In ten of the fourteen, the majority was Justices Roberts, Thomas, Alito, Gorsuch, and Kavanaugh, with Justices Ginsburg, Breyer, Sotomayor, and Kagan dissenting.[23] In two of the fourteen, the majority was Justice Roberts with the four liberals, Justices Ginsburg, Breyer, Sotomayor, and Kagan.[24] On all of the major constitutional issues—separation of church and state, gun control and gun rights, rights of criminal suspects and

[20] Jonathan S. Gould & David E. Pozen, *Structural Biases in Structural Constitutional Law*, 97 N.Y.U. L. REV. (forthcoming 2022) (manuscript at 21–22), https://papers.ssrn.com/sol3/papers.cfm?abstract_id=3797051 (last visited Apr. 29, 2021).

[21] *See Opinions of the Court—2019*, SUPREMECOURT.GOV, https://www.supremecourt.gov/opinions/slipopinion/19#list (last visited Apr. 29, 2021).

[22] *See* Adam Feldman, *Final Stat Pack for October Term 2019 (Updated)*, SCOTUSBLOG (Jul. 10, 2020, 7:36 PM), https://www.scotusblog.com/2020/07/final-stat-pack-for-october-term-2019/ (last visited Apr. 29, 2021) ("5–4 Cases" table). In October Term 2020, by my count there were fifty-four cases decided with signed opinion after briefing and oral argument. Twelve were decided by 6–3 margins (often reflecting six conservative justices with Barrett replacing Ginsburg) and another six by 5–4 margins.

[23] *Id.*

[24] *Id.*

defendants, death penalty, abortion rights, protection of gays and lesbians and transgender individuals from discrimination, affirmative action—there is a huge gulf between the liberal and conservative justices. This chasm mirrors the great disagreements that exist in American society on these and countless other issues.

There is an obvious and large difference between the Republican and Democratic platforms, or, in the recent election, between the views of Joe Biden and Donald Trump. The fact that 81 million people chose one and 74 million chose the other illustrates the deep disagreement in values in our country.

Donald Trump significantly increased the polarization in the United States. To be clear, he did not cause it. His election in 2016 and his campaign in 2020 reflect it. But no one can deny that in countless ways, large and small, he made it worse. His administration did not offer a semblance of efforts at bipartisanship. On nearly every major issue, he governed from the far right of the political spectrum. His style of race-baiting and insults made the divisions much worse.

Most of all, though, he squandered the opportunity that the COVID-19 pandemic offered to unify the country. A crisis uniquely offers the opportunity to bring the nation together. We saw this after 9/11. President George W. Bush, for a time, had 90% public approval ratings.[25] Unfortunately, he squandered this unity with the misguided and tragic Iraq war. I often have wondered what would have happened if he had foregone that war, saved the country a trillion dollars, and been a unifying president throughout his time in office.

COVID-19 provided another opportunity to unify the nation. What if, in the beginning of the pandemic, President Trump had said, "We're all in this together. We all must act to stop the spread of coronavirus. Everyone, wear masks. Businesses, you will need to close for a time so we can open sooner. We must follow what science and medicine tell us." If Trump had done this, it is likely that many fewer would have died. Our country

---

[25] *See Presidential Approval Ratings—George W. Bush*, GALLUP, https://news.gallup.com/poll/116500/presidential-approval-ratings-george-bush.aspx (last visited Apr. 29, 2021) (showing relatively steady decline in approval from 90% in 2001 to 34% in 2009).

could have come together. Trump likely would have easily won reelection. But that was beyond President Trump: instead, he politicized a pandemic and it increased, not lessened, the divide. Perhaps this was because he was a public official who never described the role, or apparently saw the position, as being about public service; it always seemed in his statements and actions as much more about self-aggrandizement.

To his last days in office, President Trump continued to stoke the division with his false claims of election fraud and exhorting his supporters to violence. The storming of the Capitol on January 6 reflects how deeply divided the country is and how much Trump contributed to that division. The entirely unprecedented nature of such an event in American history is a strong testament to the profound divisions that exist. Since leaving office, former President Trump has continued to falsely claim the election was decided by fraud, with 70% of Republicans and 30% of the population believing his claims that the election was stolen.

Finally, the internet and social media undoubtedly contribute to the political polarization. The internet is the most important medium for communication to be developed since the printing press. In *Packingham v. North Carolina*, the Supreme Court spoke forcefully about the importance of the internet and social media as a place for speech.[26] The Court declared unconstitutional a North Carolina law that prohibited registered sex offenders from using interactive social media where minors might be present. The Court explained that cyberspace, and social media in particular, are vitally important places for speech. Justice Kennedy, writing for the majority, explained:

> Seven in ten American adults use at least one Internet social networking service. . . . According to sources cited to the Court in this case, Facebook has 1.79 billion active users. This is about three times the population of North America.
>
> Social media offers "relatively unlimited, low-cost capacity for communication of all kinds." On Facebook, for example, users can debate religion and politics with

[26] 137 S. Ct. 1730 (2017).

> their friends and neighbors or share vacation photos. On LinkedIn, users can look for work, advertise for employees, or review tips on entrepreneurship. And on Twitter, users can petition their elected representatives and otherwise engage with them in a direct manner. Indeed, Governors in all 50 States and almost every Member of Congress have set up accounts for this purpose. In short, social media users employ these websites to engage in a wide array of protected First Amendment activity on topics "as diverse as human thought." . . .
>
> . . . .
>
> . . . While we now may be coming to the realization that the Cyber Age is a revolution of historic proportions, we cannot appreciate yet its full dimensions and vast potential to alter how we think, express ourselves, and define who we want to be. The forces and directions of the Internet are so new, so protean, and so far reaching that courts must be conscious that what they say today might be obsolete tomorrow.[27]

The internet has democratized the ability to reach a mass audience. It used to be that to reach a large audience, a person had to be rich enough to own a newspaper or to get a broadcast license. Now, though, anyone with a smartphone—or even just access to a library with public computers and WiFi—can reach a huge audience instantaneously. There are great benefits to this democratization of mass communication, but also costs.

In the twentieth century, the media played an enormous unifying function. People across the country watched the same movies, listened to the same radio programs, and saw the same television programs. Everywhere in the United States people got their news from Walter Cronkite or Huntley and Brinkley. This helped bring together a nation with enormous regional differences. Because of the internet, now, people no longer are dependent on a relatively small number of sources for news. On the other hand, people now can seek out news that not only reinforces their beliefs but also—pointedly and purposefully—

[27] *Id.* at 1735–36.

emphasizes our differences. The media is dividing, not unifying, us as a nation.

C. A ROLE FOR LAW SCHOOLS

I am not naïve and I know that the deep-seated problems that I have described defy easy solutions. Yet, I also believe that positive change is possible. I decided to go to law school because I saw law as the most powerful tool for social change. I still believe that, though certainly change is much harder than I could have imagined when I applied to law school almost 50 years ago at age 21.

Law schools can be—must be—engines for helping to solve the problems I have described in this essay. What are some of the things that law schools can and should do?

First, it is crucial that colleges and universities generally, and law schools in particular, be a place where all ideas and views can be expressed and discussed.[28] We must model civil discourse, showing our students that it is possible to disagree without being disagreeable. To say the obvious, this discourse is something desperately lacking in American society and I believe that democracy cannot survive without it.

I worry about the pressures that exist, formal and informal, to silence the messages we don't like and find offensive. I have seen that in my own law school and experience as dean. I will relate a recent example.

I loathe Ann Coulter. She is hateful and has said countless ugly things about Muslims, immigrants, racial minorities, liberals, and others. In 1998, when we were regularly guests together on a CNBC program to discuss the Clinton impeachment, I told the producer I no longer would appear when she was on the show (and I wasn't invited back). I found her rude and very unpleasant. I have adhered to that choice for over twenty years and never will appear on anything if she is present.

---

[28] I develop this more fully in ERWIN CHEMERINSKY & HOWARD GILLMAN, FREE SPEECH ON CAMPUS (2017).

But I will defend Coulter's right to speak and the right of people to listen to her. I had the occasion to do just that and have taken much grief for doing so.

On Wednesday, November 20, 2019, Coulter spoke on the Berkeley campus. A student group had invited her. She spoke without disruption. Unfortunately, though, those protesting against Coulter harassed those going to hear her. I heard from students and saw videos of those attending being spit at, doused with water, punched, and obstructed.

The next morning, I sent the following message to all of the faculty, staff, and students at Berkeley Law:

"I deeply believe that a campus should be a place where all ideas and views can be expressed. The appropriate response to speech we dislike is more speech, not disruption or harassment.

I was dismayed to learn that last night some who chose to attend Ann Coulter's speech on campus were harassed and subjected to clearly inappropriate behavior. I was relieved that this did not prevent Ms. Coulter from speaking to a large audience, but the harassment of those wanting to attend was unacceptable.

To be clear, I think it was completely appropriate to protest against Ann Coulter. But as a law school, it is important to also express support for the right to speak and to condemn those engaged in harassment and disruption."

Although some students expressed support for my message, many did not. One student angrily told me that he felt my message was a "slap to the face." Students posted on bulletin boards throughout the Law School: "Dean Chemerinsky sent an email after Ann Coulter's visit. And it wasn't in defense of students affected by hateful rhetoric."

But I strongly disagree with those who told me that I should have objected to Coulter's presence on campus. I would not invite her, but others have the right to do so and some on campus did that. I would not go listen to her, but others have the right to do so. And I believe that it is the responsibility of the university to protect her speech and the rights of those who want to hear her.

Actually, the story does not stop there. If you look on the Berkeley Law website, on a "racial justice" page, there is a statement from a group of leaders of some student affinity groups, that says: "this [law school] administration has defended the intellectual acceptability of white supremacist views citing First Amendment arguments." Of course, neither I, nor anyone in my administration, ever has defended the "intellectual acceptability" of white supremacist views. I find white supremacist views abhorrent and totally unacceptable. I recognize that hateful speakers cause real harm. Scholars like Kimberle Crenshaw, Richard Delgado, Charles Lawrence, and Mari Matsuda powerfully remind us of the injuries inflicted by hateful speech.[29] But the law of the First Amendment is clear that a public university cannot exclude speakers even when their views are deeply offensive. To say that the First Amendment protects the right to express a view in no way endorses the intellectual acceptability of that view.

I realize that this is not a popular message with some students and faculty right now. There are many who believe that campuses should prohibit hateful speech. But that is not the law and nor do I believe it should be. I do not deny that hate speech causes harm. To begin with the law, the Supreme Court has been clear that the government cannot exclude or punish speech on the grounds that it is offensive, even deeply offensive. When St. Paul, Minnesota enacted an ordinance prohibiting burning a cross or painting a swastika in a manner that would "anger, alarm, or cause resentment," the Court unanimously declared it unconstitutional.[30]

Of course, the fact that the Supreme Court says it does not make it right. But I reluctantly agree with its cases according First Amendment protection for hate speech.[31] I wish that hateful messages never would be uttered, just as I wish that Ann

---

[29] *See, e.g.,* MARI J. MATSUDA, CHARLES R. LAWRENCE III, RICHARD DELGADO, KIMBERLE WILLIAMS CRENSHAW, WORDS THAT WOUND: CRITICAL RACE THEORY, ASSAULTIVE SPEECH, AND THE FIRST AMENDMENT (1993).

[30] R.A.V. v. City of St. Paul, 505 U.S. 377 (1992).

[31] A defense of First Amendment protection for hate speech is obviously beyond the scope of this short essay. But for a careful explanation of this position, *see* NADINE STROSSEN, HATE: WHY WE SHOULD RESIST IT WITH FREE SPEECH, NOT CENSORSHIP (2018). I also explain this position in CHEMERINSKY & GILLMAN, *supra* note 28, at 82–110.

Coultor would just go away and be quiet. But I don't trust the government, including campus officials, to decide what messages to allow and which to prohibit. I know that the only way that my speech will be secure tomorrow is to protect the speech that I don't like today.

I have thought carefully about the students who were upset at the message I sent. I appreciate their being candid with me and sharing their feelings about this. But on reflection, I stand by what I said: a campus must be a place where all ideas and views can be expressed.

I am especially worried about the way in which students feel silenced if their views are different from most of their classmates. I have heard about the comments and even shaming that exist over social media. Not long ago, a student told me a story—which I verified with others—of his defending gun rights in a criminal law class. The students' social media sites were filled with criticisms and even personal attacks directed at him. He said that he then went completely off those social media sites and stopped participating in class discussions unless called upon. I also observed this in a powerful way by teaching over Zoom this past semester. In Spring 2021, I taught constitutional law to a large class (205 students) entirely online. I encouraged discussion and students could participate either by raising their hands and speaking or by writing comments in the "chat." I read every comment in the chat, but without identifying the author by name. I received vastly more comments questioning abortion rights or disagreeing with affirmative action than I have seen in class discussions. It was starkly apparent that there were strong conservative voices in the class, but they felt comfortable speaking only if they were anonymous to their classmates.

Our challenge as law schools must be to find a way for all students to feel comfortable expressing themselves and being a place where all views can be expressed. And we must lead our campuses to be places that exemplify civil discourse.

Second, law schools must play a large role in the racial reckoning, in confronting anti-Blackness, and in moving society towards greater equality. The events following the tragic death of George Floyd in May 2020 focused attention on the enormous racial inequalities that have existed in American society since its founding. To pick one example that directly involves the law: racism in policing.

Race has infected policing in the United States throughout history.[32] Statistics show that African-Americans and Hispanics are more likely to be stopped by police than whites for the same behavior, more likely to be arrested, and more likely to be subjected to police violence.[33] As President Obama explained: "A large body of research finds that, for similar offenses, members of the African American and Hispanic communities are more likely to be stopped, searched, arrested, convicted, and sentenced to harsher penalties."[34]

In 2016, Black males aged 15–34 were nine times more likely than other Americans to be killed by law enforcement officers.[35] They were also killed at four times the rate of young white men.[36] Hispanic men are nearly twice as likely to be killed by police as white men.[37] The United States Civil Rights Commission concluded that "while people of color make up fewer than 38% of the population, they make up almost 63% of unarmed people killed by police."[38] Overall, civilian deaths from shootings and other police actions are vastly higher in the United States than in other developed nations.[39]

---

[32] *See* MICHELLE ALEXANDER, THE NEW JIM CROW (2010) (describing the racism of the criminal justice system). I examine this topic in ERWIN CHEMERINSKY, PRESUMED GUILTY: HOW THE SUPREME COURT EMPOWERED THE POLICE AND SUBVERTED CIVIL RIGHTS (2021).

[33] *See* PAUL BUTLER, CHOKEHOLD (2017). For an excellent discussion of police behavior in the United States, *see* BARRY FRIEDMAN, UNWARRANTED: POLICING WITHOUT PERMISSION (2017).

[34] Barack Obama, *The President's Role in Criminal Justice Reform,* 130 HARV. L. REV. 811, 820 (2017).

[35] Jon Swaine & Ciara McCarthy, *Young Black Men Again Faced Highest Race of US Police Killings in 2016*, THE GUARDIAN (Jan. 8, 2017, 7:00 AM), https://www.theguardian.com/us-news/2017/jan/08/the-counted-police-killings-2016-young-black-men. For an excellent discussion of police shootings, *see* FRANKLIN ZIMRING, WHEN POLICE KILL (2017).

[36] *Id.*

[37] Sirry Alang, et al., *Police Brutality and Black Health,* AMERICAN JOURNAL OF PUBLIC HEALTH (May 2017) http://ajph.aphapublications.org/doi/abs/10.2105/AJPH.2017.303691.

[38] *Police Use of Force: An Examination of Modern Policing Practices,* U.S. COMMISSION ON CIVIL RIGHTS (Nov. 15, 2018), https://www.usccr.gov/pubs/2018/11-15-Police-Force.pdf.

[39] *See* FRANKLIN ZIMRING, WHEN POLICE KILL (2017).

There are seemingly endless accounts of police unnecessarily striking suspects, especially men of color, with batons, using tasers, applying chokeholds, and employing far more force than needed under the circumstances. The Center for Policing Equity found that "1 in 5 Americans interacts with law enforcement yearly. Of those encounters, 1 million result in use of force. And if you're Black, you are 2–4 times more likely to have force used than if you are White."[40] The Center's study found "that the overall mean use-of-force rate for all black residents was 273 per 100,000, which is 3.6 times higher than the rate for white residents (76 per 100,000) and 2.5 times higher than the overall rate of 108 per 100,000 for all residents. For those who were arrested, the mean rate of use of force against blacks was 46 for every 1,000 arrests, compared with 36 per 1,000 for whites."[41]

Law schools must be a force for change in this aspect of the legal system and in confronting the legacy of racism more generally. Many things must be done and these are just examples and only a beginning. We must find ways to increase the diversity of our students, faculty, and staff, with the goal of enhancing the diversity of the legal profession. We must create new courses for faculty and students to examine issues of race and the law. We must take aggressive steps to ensure equity, inclusion, and belonging for our students, faculty, and staff of color. We must create new clinics and programs to deal with racial injustices, such as those involving policing. We must encourage faculty scholarship that focuses on how to deal with police abuses and other aspects of racism. We must lead in looking for ways to make enormously overdue progress with regard to race. With regard to policing in particular, we must direct our scholarship, our classes, our clinics on this issue and help to come up with solutions.

Third, law schools must be aggressive in looking for solutions to the problems of American democracy. I argued earlier that these stem from the law, including the Constitution, and therefore the law must be integral to finding answers. The

---

[40] CENTER FOR POLICING EQUITY, https://policingequity.org/.

[41] Timothy Williams, *Study Supports Suspicion that Police Are More Likely to Use Force on Blacks*, N.Y. TIMES (July 8, 2016), https://www.nytimes.com/2016/07/08/us/study-supports-suspicion-that-police-use-of-force-is-more-likely-for-blacks.html.

tremendous talents of law professors can help to find ways to overcome the problems I discussed earlier. Conferences should focus on looking for practical solutions and ways to improve democracy.

In May 2021, the Association of American Law Schools held an online two-day conference on reforming the presidency and on voting and elections. It gathered together the most prominent professors in these fields. The discussions were superb and many ideas emerged. But a two-day conference is not nearly enough. We must create vehicles for further developing these and other ideas and most of all, for implementing them.

The internet and social media raise countless new legal issues. The legal academy must be at the forefront of finding ways to protect these essential platforms for communication, while mitigating the potential harms they can cause, such as in the rapid transmission of false information. If there are answers, they likely will need to come from law school faculty.

D. CONCLUSION

In late 2020 and early 2021, we saw the fragility of American democracy. The events reflect underlying serious problems in our society. It is urgent that we in law schools focus on them and what we can do to contribute to solutions. This time the guardrails of democracy held. If there is a next time, we might not be nearly so fortunate.

PART 3

LOOKING FORWARD/PURSUIT OF TRUTH AND SOLUTIONS

CHAPTER 11

THE RULE OF LAW AND HOW PRESIDENT TRUMP REMINDED US OF THE VALUE OF A LEGAL EDUCATION

Kevin R. Johnson[1]

A. ABSTRACT

To illustrate the meaning and importance of the rule of law, law schools traditionally teach students to studiously marshal the facts, identify the relevant legal rule, and apply it to the facts to reach a legal conclusion. To that end, law students learn about the approach known as IRAC, or Issue, Rule, Application, Conclusion, to promote reasoned decision-making and adherence to the rule of law.

Contemporary events in the United States, including what some would say represent an existential threat to democracy as we know it, should have many law school leaders thinking deeply about the fundamental nature of legal education. Making up "alternative facts" and consistently questioning the courts and, in effect, the rule of law, President Trump rejected the basic analytical approach to deciding legal problems as well as pressing public policy issues. By so doing, he undermined the very foundations of legal education. Indeed, President Trump's penchant for pronouncing alternative facts in making spurious claims, such as that the 2020 election was "stolen" from him, as well as his frequent expressions of disdain for the courts (at least those ruling against his administration), placed in question the very relevance of the law to governing.

---

[1] Kevin R. Johnson is Dean and Mabie-Apallas Professor of Public Interest Law and Chicanx Studies, University of California, Davis, School of Law. Thanks to Dean Mark Alexander for inviting me to participate in this book project, his comments on this article, and dedication to the completion of this volume. Law student Juan Dawson provided editorial assistance.

This chapter contends that the nation's experience with President Trump's approach to law and policy demonstrates the critical importance of the mission of law schools to teach rigorous factual and legal analysis as well as a commitment to the rule of law. In addition to being useful in the analysis of legal disputes, such an approach assists greatly in addressing public policy issues. Consider systemic racial injustice, which is not limited to the criminal justice system and policing, but unfortunately afflicts all aspects of U.S. social life, from education to employment to housing to health care to voting and more. Similarly, President Trump regularly discussed the challenging policy issues surrounding immigration, with racial animus obviously infecting his analysis, and frequently distorting or ignoring the facts and law. That approach resulted in policy changes that devastated communities of color.

To counter the Trump approach to policy-making, besides teaching students to engage in reasoned analysis of cases, law schools necessarily must continue to strive to educate students that many public policy issues are deeply complex and that the exercise of raw political power, and disregarding facts, laws, and reason, may allow invidious racial passions to dominate policy-making.

B. INTRODUCTION

Law school deans often spend their days thinking about rather ordinary matters, such as tuition and finances, admissions, law student job placement, *U.S. News & World Report* rankings, and bar passage rates. While such issues dominate their collective attention, law deans may have missed something extraordinary that goes to the very core of the mission of law schools. Over four tumultuous and contentious years, President Donald J. Trump's approach to governing placed in question the fundamental nature of legal education in a democratic society.

Adherence to the rule of law necessarily is a central pillar of U.S. legal education as well as the nation's courts. Indeed, it is difficult to imagine any legal system enjoying widespread public confidence and legitimacy without a steadfast commitment to the rule of law. Consistent with that approach, law schools traditionally have taught students to marshal the facts and identify the relevant legal rule before resolving a legal question. A popular framework for case analysis known as IRAC, or Issue, Rule, Application, Conclusion,[2] disciplines one to follow a sequential analysis of legal issues. IRAC, or some similar framework, is critical to "thinking like a lawyer," an overarching goal of legal education.

The election of President Trump had impacts that reverberated through law schools across the United States. For example, the early years of the Trump presidency saw the so-called "Trump Bump"[3] in the number of law school applications. A much more subtle, yet potentially far-reaching, change emerged from the chaos generated by President Trump's approach to policy-making and governing generally. Consistently playing fast and loose with the facts and law like no other modern president, the President effectively placed in question the basics of legal analysis.[4] Careful treatment of the facts and application of the law was not characteristic of the President's partisan approach to many policy issues. By misrepresenting facts and regularly questioning, if not subverting, the law and the courts, President Trump undermined the fundamentals of legal analysis and, thus, the very foundations of legal education.

President Trump's entire approach to public policy-making represented a stark repudiation of careful legal analysis. His penchant for declaring "alternative facts" in making dubious—in some instances, baseless—claims as well as his regular expressions of disdain for the law and the courts, placed in question the very relevance of the law to resolving disputes or making policy choices.[5] Moreover, all too often, the Trump administration allowed racial passions to dominate policymaking. President Trump's approach and demeanor

---

[2] *See* Clay Calvert, *Dissent, Disagreement and Doctrinal Disarray: Free Expression and the Roberts Court in 2020*, 28 WM. & MARY BILL OF RTS. J. 865, 877 (2020).

[3] *See* Stephanie Francis Ward, *The "Trump Bump" for Law School Applicants is Real and Significant, Survey Says,* ABA J. (Feb. 2, 2018), https://www.abajournal.com/news/article/the_trump_bump_for_law_school_applicants_is_real_and_significant_survey_say.

[4] *See infra* Section C.

[5] *See id.*

contrasted sharply with the studious and measured demeanor of President Barack Obama, a Harvard-trained lawyer who taught law at the University of Chicago, and strived, to sooth, not incite, the public and respectfully discussed the law and the courts.[6]

As one would expect, the Trump administration's dismissal of the facts and the law had consequences. For example, President Trump's baseless allegation that the 2020 election was somehow stolen, repeated in a speech only minutes before violence broke out, directly led to an armed insurrection by white supremacists in Washington D.C. in January 2021, which some observers characterized as an attempted coup d'état.[7]

This chapter critically examines how President Trump's crude approach to complex and controversial policy questions suggests the need for law schools to double down on teaching fundamental factual and legal analysis, as well as the central importance of the rule of law and courts in a democratic society. Besides being important to the analysis of cases, such an approach can prove useful to the analysis of pressing policy issues facing the nation. Put affirmatively, incisive analysis of the facts and law are essential ingredients to effective analysis of legal *and* public policy questions.

In addition, besides teaching students to identify and apply the applicable rule of law to the facts, law schools, as they have, must continue to educate students about the complexity of many public policy issues. Although President Trump's theatrical approach to policy-making entertained and energized his rabid political base, it did not result in significant policy successes on the most challenging issues facing the nation and, in fact, allowed for the pursuit of racist agendas that inflamed the public and deeply alienated communities of color.

To illustrate the need for rigorous policy analysis, this chapter briefly considers the nation's general reckoning with systemic racial injustice. Such injustice obviously is a concern with the modern criminal justice system and policing,

---

6 *See Barack Obama*, WHITE HOUSE BLOG, https://obamawhitehouse.archives.gov/blog/author/president-barack-obama (biography of President Obama).

7 *See* Stephanie K. Baer, *Trump Supporters Who Attempted the Coup Flaunted Racist and Hateful Symbols*, BUZZFEED NEWS (updated Jan. 7, 2021), https://www.buzzfeednews.com/article/skbaer/trump-supporters-racist-symbols-capitol-assault.

controversial issues that dominated the headlines in 2020, with police killings of African Americans crying out for immediate transformative change.[8] But, as is taught in law schools, systemic racial injustice is far from limited to the criminal law. Indeed, such injustice unfortunately is baked into all aspects of U.S. social life, from housing to education to employment to health care to voting, and more.[9] To add to the complexity, systemic racial injustice is not limited to African Americans. Racial discrimination afflicts Asian Americans, Latinx persons, indigenous peoples, Muslims, and others, who also suffer all-too-common hate violence and are denied full membership in U.S. society.[10]

To further demonstrate the importance of careful policy analysis, this chapter considers the contentious national debate over immigration. Many immigration questions do not lend themselves to easy answers and quick fixes, the touchstones of the immigration policies put into place by the Trump administration. Elevating immigration law and enforcement to a priority of the highest order, the Trump administration's approach was not even loosely tied to facts or the law but represented little more than an attempt to exercise raw political power to transform, without congressional action, the entire immigration system.[11] By so doing, President Trump sought at virtually every turn, and at almost any cost, to restrict immigration and remove increasing numbers of noncitizens from the United States.[12] In pursuit of a racially-charged immigration agenda that expressly employed unvarnished racist rhetoric, the President's single-minded policy approach had devastating impacts on noncitizens of color from the developing world.[13]

Section C considers the Trump administration's frontal attack on legal reasoning and the rule of law and his ham-

---

[8] *See generally* MICHELLE ALEXANDER, THE NEW JIM CROW: MASS INCARCERATION IN THE AGE OF COLORBLINDNESS (10th ann. ed. 2020) (analyzing the dramatic disparate impacts on African Americans of the contemporary color-blind criminal justice system).

[9] *See infra* Section D.1.

[10] *See id.*

[11] *See infra* Section D.2.

[12] *See id.*

[13] *See infra* text accompanying notes 43–47.

handed, unabashedly partisan, and insensitive, approach to complex public policy issues. Section D demonstrates how, contrary to President Trump's approach, basic tools of legal reasoning offer a logical and reasonable way to address pressing public policy problems. It briefly considers two examples, systemic racism in U.S. social life and immigration law and policy, both of which are controversial and have proven to be most challenging.

C. THE TRUMP ATTACKS ON LEGAL REASONING AND LEGAL INSTITUTIONS

Law school has been said (perhaps too many times) to teach law students to "think like a lawyer." To accomplish that mission, rigorous legal analysis long has been a staple of legal education. "Among the 'traditional structural paradigms' for analyzing a case or fact pattern is the Issue, Rule, Application, Conclusion (IRAC) formula. As one scholar rather wryly writes, 'IRAC is seen as both the bane of law student existence and as having a near-magical ability to create a successful exam outcome.' "[14] At the most fundamental level, the IRAC process requires carefully marshaling the facts and correctly identifying and applying the relevant rule of law to the case at hand to reach a legal conclusion. Besides serving as a helpful exam-taking tool, the sequential steps in the IRAC method serve to discipline the student's analysis of legal disputes. A similar analytical approach helps make rational public policy choices.

Law school, of course, is not exclusively about IRAC. The pedagogy of legal education has slowly evolved over time. Although the use of the Socratic Method by law professors teaching large classes of students dominated legal education for generations,[15] law schools have in recent years revamped instruction with skills training, experiential learning, clinical legal education, and other innovations.[16] Those pedagogical reforms generally allow students to apply legal rules and

---

[14] *See* Calvert, *supra* text note 2, at 877 (footnotes omitted).

[15] *See* ROBERT STEVENS, LAW SCHOOL: LEGAL EDUCATION IN AMERICA FROM THE 1850S TO THE 1980S, at 52–64 (1983); William Epstein, *The Classical Tradition of Dialectics and American Legal Education*, 31 J. LEGAL EDUC. 399, 399 (1981).

[16] *See* Allison Korn & Laila L. Hlass, *Assessing the Experiential (R)evolution*, 65 VILL. L. REV. 713, 716–18 (2020).

analysis taught in the classroom as a lawyer would in the practice of law. However, instructional innovation has not ended devotion to rational and rigorous legal reasoning as exemplified by the IRAC method.

As discussed in this part, President Trump and his administration refused to engage in standard analytical approaches to policy questions, or anything vaguely approaching an IRAC kind of analysis of policy challenges. In many contexts, he instead resorted to distorting and misrepresenting the facts and mangled, and often ignored, the law, approaches wholly antithetical to sound legal reasoning. The Trump administration's approach to public policy issues taught a valuable cautionary lesson: law schools should not abandon the basic emphasis on educating students to rigorously analyze the facts and identify the applicable law to reach a conclusion. Even though President Trump's brash approach to policy-making and colorful one-liners contributed to his popularity among a devoted base of supporters, it did not lead to good policy choices, especially on issues directly affecting people of color.

1. Facts and "Alternative" Facts

Facts frequently proved slippery to President Donald J. Trump. The *Washington Post* identified more than 30,000 false statements by the President in his four years in office, an incredibly large number.[17] "Alternative facts," for example, served as the foundation of President Trump's baseless claim that the 2020 election was "stolen" from him and that he in fact won in a landslide.[18] He pressed such wild allegations in the courts.[19] Other modern U.S. presidents, such as President George W. Bush, who claimed that Iraq's Saddam Hussein possessed weapons of mass destruction that justified war,[20]

---

[17] *See Trump's False or Misleading Claims Total 30,573 Over 4 Years*, WASH. POST (Jan. 24, 2021), https://www.washingtonpost.com/politics/2021/01/24/trumps-false-or-misleading-claims-total-30573-over-four-years/.

[18] *See* Marianna Spring, *"Stop the Steal": The Deep Roots of Trump's "Voter Fraud" Strategy*, BBC NEWS (Nov. 23, 2020), https://www.bbc.com/news/blogs-trending-55009950.

[19] *See, e.g.*, Trump v. Kemp, 2021 U.S. Dist. LEXIS 4185 (N.D. Ga. Jan. 5, 2021) (rejecting the President's legal challenge to the election results).

[20] *See* Sidney Blumenthal, *Bush Knew Saddam Had No Weapons of Mass Destruction*, SALON (Sept. 6, 2007), https://www.salon.com/2007/09/06/bush_wmd/.

occasionally misrepresented the facts, but none did so with the incredible frequency and zeal of President Trump.

To support many dubious positions, President Trump and his spokespersons regularly relied upon the novel concept of "alternative facts":

> Less than 24 hours after White House press secretary Sean Spicer had spouted numerous falsehoods about inauguration crowd size and more, [White House spokesperson] Kellyanne Conway went on NBC's *Meet the Press* to defend him. In the process, the counselor to President Trump coined a phrase that's now destined to follow Trump throughout his presidency—"alternative facts.". . . The Trump administration's pushback on easily verifiable facts is unprecedented and shows that the Trump we saw on the campaign trail and in debates—who was freewheeling with facts and assertions and often peddled wildly exaggerated claims—had not changed once he took the oath of office.[21]

Alternative facts, probably better characterized as falsehoods and innuendo, obviously do not serve well as the basis for effective policy-making. Fudging and distorting the facts makes the application of IRAC, or any kind of rigorous analytical tool to legal issues or policy problems, difficult, to say the least. Facts relevant to an issue may be in dispute. Resolving factual disputes is a primary function of the trial courts. Fact-findings by trial courts are generally reviewed deferentially by appellate courts.[22] In the political process, however, there is no neutral fact finder or review of factual assertions for their accuracy. Without such processes, the need for candor among political leaders is especially important. False factual assertions obviously will not likely result in good policy choices.

---

[21] Jessica Taylor & Danielle Kutzleben, *This Week in Trump's "Alternative Facts"*, NPR, Jan. 29, 2017, https://www.npr.org/2017/01/29/512068148/this-week-in-trumps-alternative-facts.

[22] *See, e.g.*, Fed. R. Civ. P. 52(a)(6) ("Findings of fact . . . must not be set aside unless clearly erroneous, and the reviewing court must give due regard to the trial court's opportunity to judge the witnesses' credibility.").

President Trump's response to the pandemic exemplifies his approach to using facts to build an argument. The President, for example, often rejected elementary scientific learning in discussing public health approaches to the pandemic. Besides the ridiculous reference to drinking bleach to fight COVID-19,[23] he often found himself in profound disagreement with scientists, including the influential and popular Dr. Anthony Fauci, about the necessary and appropriate public health and safety measures to combat the pandemic.[24] Thousands of Americans died as a result of the Trump administration's inept handling of the pandemic.[25] Besides contributing to mass death, President Trump's baseless factual assertions had other real world—and deadly—consequences. His statements, without evidence, that the 2020 election had been stolen from him undoubtedly contributed to the violence at the U.S. Capitol in January 2021.[26]

Politicians might gain from adhering to a duty of candor in discussing the facts. They also might learn from a method similar to the rigorous factual determinations made by trial courts and demanded of law students in applying IRAC. Although formal legal training is not essential for policymakers, the rational analytical tools taught in law schools can benefit the making of public policy. If nothing else, the Trump presidency taught the nation that lesson.

---

[23] *See Coronavirus: Outcry after Trump Suggests Injecting Disinfectant as Treatment*, BBC NEWS (Apr. 24, 2020), https://www.bbc.com/news/world-us-canada-52407177.

[24] *See* Curtis M. Wong, *Dr. Fauci: Trump Let "Terrible Things" Happen After Our COVID-19 Disagreements*, HUFFINGTON POST (updated Feb. 22, 2021), https://www.huffpost.com/entry/anthony-fauci-donald-trump-covid-19-conflict_n_602e780bc5b67c32961bc190.

[25] *See* Jorge L. Ortiz, *"Blood on His Hands": As US Surpasses 400,000 COVID-19 Deaths, Experts Blame Trump Administration for a "Preventable" Loss of Life*, USA TODAY (Jan. 17, 2021), https://www.usatoday.com/story/news/nation/2021/01/17/covid-19-us-400-000-deaths-experts-blame-trump-administration/6642685002/.

[26] *See* Jemima McEvoy, *Trump Claims COVID Deaths Are "Exaggerated" as U.S. Surpasses 350,000*, FORBES (Jan. 2, 2021), https://www.forbes.com/sites/jemimamcevoy/2021/01/03/trump-claims-covid-deaths-are-exaggerated-as-us-surpasses-350000/?sh=7b68e85c37b6; Steve Holland, Jeff Mason & Jonathan Landay, *Trump Summoned Supporters to "Wild" Protest, and Told Them to Fight. They Did*, REUTERS (Jan. 6, 2021), https://www.reuters.com/article/us-usa-election-protests/trump-summoned-supporters-to-wild-protest-and-told-them-to-fight-they-did-idUSKBN29B24S.

2. Courts, Law, and the Rule of Law

In addition to conjuring up alternative facts, President Trump frequently attacked judges who ruled against the positions of his administration and, by so doing, put into question the very notion of the rule of law (or the need to adhere to the law). In that vein, during his presidential campaign, Trump ruthlessly attacked a federal judge of Mexican ancestry (and U.S. citizenry) presiding over fraud lawsuits against Trump University; he

> [s]aid that U.S. District Judge Gonzalo Curiel had "an absolute conflict" in presiding over the litigation given that he was "of Mexican heritage" and a member of [a] Latino lawyer's association. Mr. Trump says the background of the judge, who was born in Indiana to Mexican immigrants, was relevant because of his campaign stance against illegal immigration and his pledge to seal the southern U.S. border.[27]

Put simply, Trump claimed that Judge Curiel's Mexican ancestry alone disqualified him from hearing a case that involved the President. Taking that logic to its conclusion, the argument would bar any judge of Mexican ancestry from hearing a case involving Donald Trump.[28]

Besides criticizing judges who ruled against the administration, President Trump regularly denigrated legal requirements and took extraordinary policy steps in violation of the law. For example, contrary to fundamental understandings that the action was unlawful, the President sent the U.S.

---

[27] Brent Kendall, *Trump Says Judge's Mexican Heritage Presents "Absolute Conflict,"* WALL ST. J. (June 3, 2016), https://www.wsj.com/articles/donald-trump-keeps-up-attacks-on-judge-gonzalo-curiel-1464911442; *see* Kevin R. Johnson, *How Political Ideology Undermines Racial and Gender Diversity in Federal Judicial Selection: The Prospects For Judicial Diversity in the Trump Years*, 2017 WIS. L. REV. 345, 362–63 (analyzing Donald Trump's attacks on Judge Curiel).

[28] Although the brashness of his attack was extraordinary, Trump's questioning of the impartiality of judges of color was not new. Years ago, Judge Leon Higginbottom Jr. famously rejected a motion, based primarily on his African American ancestry, that he remove himself from a case alleging racial discrimination against African American employees. *See* Pennsylvania v. International Union of Operating Engineers, 388 F. Supp. 155 (E.D. Pa. 1974).

military into the streets of Washington D.C. to control crowds.[29] Similarly, he took the extraordinary step—bordering on the unlawful if not downright illegal—of deploying Department of Homeland Security officers to disperse protesters in Portland, Oregon and Oakland, California.[30] Time and time again, at frequencies not seen in any other modern presidential administration, President Trump pushed policy to the limits of the law—and well beyond. Heightening racial tensions, he voiced support for white supremacists and opposed efforts to remove monuments honoring racists.[31]

In certain respects, the Trump administration levelled an all-out assault on law and the legal system. Because its policies went as far as the law would permit and, at times, beyond, the courts regularly held that his administration ran afoul of the law, including for not following appropriate legal procedures.[32] The policies in some of those cases would have been upheld if proper procedures had been followed. When the administration did not prevail in court, Trump and administration officials frequently attacked the judges.[33] Such attacks are not unheard of by a President but President Trump's frequency of making, and the gravity of, such claims was extraordinary, if not unprecedented, among modern presidents.

---

29 *See* Scott R. Anderson, Emma Broches, Eric Halliday, & Julia Solomon-Strauss, *What Made Trump's Protest Response in D.C. Unique?*, LAWFARE (June 8, 2020), https://www.lawfareblog.com/what-made-trumps-protest-response-dc-unique.

30 *See* Associated Press, *Portland Protest Groups Sue U.S. over Tear Gas, Rubber Bullets*, POLITICO (July 28, 2020), https://www.politico.com/news/2020/07/28/portland-protest-groups-sue-tear-gas-rubber-bullets-384758.

31 *See* Rosie Gray, *Trump Defends White-Nationalist Protesters: "Some Very Fine People on Both Sides,"* ATLANTIC (Aug. 15, 2017), https://www.theatlantic.com/politics/archive/2017/08/trump-defends-white-nationalist-protesters-some-very-fine-people-on-both-sides/537012/; Julia Zorthian, *President Trump Says It's "Sad" to See U.S. Culture "Ripped Apart" by Removing Confederate Statues,* TIME (Aug. 17, 2017), https://time.com/4904510/donald-trump-twitter-confederate-statues/.

32 *See, e.g.,* Dep't of Homeland Sec. v. Regents of the Univ. of Cal., 140 S. Ct. 1891 (2020) (holding that Trump administration's attempt to rescind Deferred Action for Childhood Arrivals (DACA) policy was arbitrary and capricious and violated the Administrative Procedure Act); Dep't of Commerce v. New York, 139 S. Ct. 2551 (2019) (finding that the Trump administration's decision to add a U.S. citizenship question to the 2020 Census was arbitrary and capricious); *see also* Trump v. Hawaii, 138 S. Ct. 2392, 2403–06 (2018) (reviewing first two versions of the travel ban that lower courts invalidated before the Supreme Court upheld a narrower third version of the ban).

33 *See In His Own Words: The President's Attacks on the Courts,* BRENNAN CENTER FOR JUSTICE (last updated Feb. 14, 2020), https://www.brennancenter.org/our-work/research-reports/his-own-words-presidents-attacks-courts.

In seeking to reshape the law in pursuit of his policy ends, President Trump appointed conservative judges, a number of whom the American Bar Association found to be unqualified.[34] By appointing a large number of judges, he dramatically reshaped the federal judiciary.[35] With the President primarily concerned with filling judicial seats with conservatives, pure politics, not judicial qualifications, drove his judicial selections. His appointments will affect the law, and the entire nation, for years to come. President Trump's disdain for the law led him to ignore the basic qualifications of his judicial nominees to a much greater extent than any other modern president.

By propagating alternative facts and consistently questioning the courts and in effect the rule of law, President Trump undermined the fundamentals of legal analysis and the foundations of legal education. In important respects, the President's entire approach to making decisions on public policy matters represented a repudiation of fundamental legal analysis. In his approach, facts were manipulated and law was largely irrelevant. The only law or court decisions that he unqualifiedly accepted were ones that favored the policies that the administration wanted to pursue. Raw political power, not careful legal and policy analysis, was the touchstone of the Trump approach. Put simply, President Trump's entire world view was antithetical to what law schools teach—and should teach—when it comes to legal reasoning and the rule of law.

D. EXAMPLES OF THE BENEFITS OF RIGOROUS AND FACTUAL LEGAL ANALYSIS: SYSTEMIC RACIAL INJUSTICE AND IMMIGRATION

In looking at two policy questions, this section offers a defense of basic legal analysis and the need for law schools to continue their efforts to promote critical and rigorous analysis as well as respect for the courts and the rule of law. As is the

---

34 *See* Jennifer Bendery, *Trump Keeps Picking Unqualified People To Be Lifetime Judges. Republicans Don't Care*, HUFFINGTON POST (Nov. 1, 2019), https://www.huffpost.com/entry/trump-lifetime-judges-not-qualified-senate-republicans_n_5dbc7351e4b0fffdb0f674af.

35 *See* Jonathan R. Nash, *Trump's Remaking of the Judicial System*, THE HILL (Nov. 23, 2020), https://thehill.com/opinion/judiciary/527225-trumps-remaking-of-the-judicial-system.

case today, law students must be taught about the benefits of rigorous analysis of the facts and law, the complexity of many policy issues, and the need for reasoned analysis to craft solutions.

Legal reasoning helps a lawyer analyze a case. It also assists one in reasonably approaching public policy issues. President Trump's approach to systemic racial injustice and immigration exemplify how his approach to policy analysis deviated dramatically from basic legal reasoning, as well as from the approach of any other modern president. Rather than calming racial tensions, he inflamed them by invoking racist reasoning and allowing racist passions to dominate his policies.

The Trump administration's approaches to systemic racism and immigration illustrate the importance of rigorous legal and policy analyses. As explained in this section, in these and other areas, the Trump administration often employed alternative facts and manipulated the law to achieve its own policy preferences. Both examples see racial passions—not facts or law—dominating the administration's policy decisions.

1. Systemic Racial Injustice

When it comes to racial injustice, the Trump administration was not especially attentive to the rights or sensibilities of people of color.[36] Indeed, it is likely that history will remember President Trump as one of the least thoughtful and sensitive modern Presidents on issues of race. For example, he repeatedly described COVID-19 using the terms the "Kung Flu," the "China flu," and the "Asian flu."[37] Encouraged by President Trump's statements and deeds, hate crimes escalated to frightening

---

[36] *See, e.g.*, *"Drug Dealers, Criminals, Rapists": What Trump Thinks of Mexicans*, BBC NEWS (Aug. 31, 2016), https://www.bbc.com/news/av/world-us-canada-37230916 (quoting Trump calling Mexican immigrants "criminals" and "rapists"); Eli Watkins & Abby Phillip, *Trump Decries Immigrants from "Shithole Countries" Coming to US*, CNN (Jan. 12, 2018), https://www.cnn.com/2018/01/11/politics/immigrants-shithole-countries-trump/index.html (quoting President Trump as saying that the U.S. government should not provide relief from removal to noncitizens from "shithole countries" such as Haiti and El Salvador).

[37] *See* Colby Itkowitz, *Trump Again Uses Racially Insensitive Term to Describe Coronavirus*, WASH. POST (June 23, 2020), https://www.washingtonpost.com/politics/trump-again-uses-kung-flu-to-describe-coronavirus/2020/06/23/0ab5a8d8-b5a9-11ea-aca5-ebb63d27e1ff_story.html.

levels in 2020 and 2021, with the killing of Asian women in Atlanta a stark and tragic example.[38]

President Trump's verbal attacks were not limited to Asians. He also portrayed Muslims as presumed terrorists who should be subject to "extreme vetting" before entering the country, if not outright banned from doing so.[39] "Trump kicked off his presidential bid . . . with harsh words for [Mexican immigrants] . . . 'They're bringing drugs. They're bringing crime. They're rapists. And some, I assume, are good people.' "[40] As president, "Trump specifically questioned why the U.S. would want to admit more people from Haiti. [H]e asked why more people from 'shithole countries' should be allowed into the U.S. . . . The president suggested that instead, the U.S. should allow more entrants from countries like Norway."[41] President Trump's statements about, and actions toward, African Americans, Asian Americans, Latinx persons, and others regularly offended the sensibilities of those communities. For example, invoking images of the dark days of the civil rights movement in places like Selma, Alabama, where police viciously beat civil rights protesters, President Trump threatened peaceful Black Lives Matter protesters with violence.[42]

Consistent with the President's propensity for making racist statements, the Trump administration put into place a staggering array of immigration policy initiatives with racially disparate impacts, including, but not limited to, the Muslim ban,

---

[38] *See* ASIAN AMERICAN BAR ASSOCIATION OF NEW YORK, A RISING TIDE OF HATE AND VIOLENCE AGAINST ASIAN AMERICANS IN NEW YORK DURING COVID-19: IMPACT, CAUSES, SOLUTIONS (2021), https://cdn.ymaws.com/www.aabany.org/resource/resmgr/press_releases/2021/A_Rising_Tide_of_Hate_and_Vi.pdf. Although the Atlanta killings occurred while President Biden was in office, they came after a long string of President Trump's verbal attacks on Asians.

[39] *See* Trump v. Hawaii, 138 S. Ct. 2392, 2433, 2436, 2438 (2018) (Sotomayor, J., dissenting) ("[A] reasonable observer would conclude that the [travel ban] was driven primarily by anti-Muslim animus, rather than by the Government's asserted national-security justifications.").

[40] Katie Reilly, *Here Are All the Times Donald Trump Insulted Mexico*, TIME (Aug. 31, 2016, 11:35 AM), https://time.com/4473972/donald-trump-mexico-meeting-insult/.

[41] Alan Fram & Jonathan Lemire, *Trump: Why Allow Immigrants from "Shithole Countries"?*, ASSOCIATED PRESS (Jan. 11, 2018), https://apnews.com/article/fdda2ff0b877416c8ae1c1a77a3cc425.

[42] *See* Andrew Buncombe, *Trump Threatens Protestors With "Vicious Dogs" and "Most Ominous Weapons" as Nation Braces for More Violence*, INDEPENDENT (United Kingdom) (May 30, 2020), https://www.independent.co.uk/news/world/americas/trump-george-floyd-protests-threats-violence-a9540691.html.

the infamous policy of separating migrant children from their parents and the "Remain in Mexico" policy (both that applied almost exclusively to Central Americans),[43] which required asylum seekers to wait in Mexico while their applications were being decided, immigration raids, mass detention and removals, and reducing legal immigration through virtually whatever means necessary.[44] Along those lines, President Trump championed a wall along the U.S./Mexico border, even though the evidence shows that a wall is ineffective at deterring undocumented immigration and results in increased migrant—and mostly Latinx—deaths.[45] He claimed that harsh enforcement measures, including mass immigrant detention, were needed because less than one percent of immigrants appeared at removal hearings, which was demonstrably false.[46] Undaunted and unapologetic, the Trump administration day in and day out announced tough new immigration measures that invariably injured noncitizens of color, their families, and communities. Although his base supported the tough immigration measures, some of the harshest, such as the separation of migrant children from their parents, generated a massive public backlash that resulted in a change in policy.[47]

---

[43] The Supreme Court dismissed an appeal of a challenge to the Remain in Mexico policy after the Biden administration discontinued the policy. *See* Innovation Law Lab v. Wolf, 951 F.3d 1073, 1077 (9th Cir. 2020), *vacated and remanded sub nom. as moot*, Mayorkas v. Innovation Law Lab, 141 S. Ct. 2842 (2021).

[44] *See* Muzaffar Chishti & Jessica Bolter, *The "Trump Effect" on Legal Immigration Levels: More Perception than Reality*, MIGRATION POLICY INST. (Nov. 20, 2020), https://www.migrationpolicy.org/article/trump-effect-immigration-reality.

[45] *See* Josh Marcus, *Death, Debt, and Degradation: Trump's Border Wall After Four Years*, INDEPENDENT (United Kingdom) (Oct. 30, 2020), https://www.independent.co.uk/news/world/americas/us-politics/trump-us-border-wall-native-americans-immigration-drugs-promise-b1352289.html; David J. Bier, *A Wall is an Impractical, Expensive, and Ineffective Border Plan*, CATO AT LIBERTY (Nov. 28, 2018), https://www.cato.org/blog/border-wall-impractical-expensive-ineffective-plan.

[46] *See* Ingrid Eagly & Steven Shafer, *When Trump Says Immigrants Don't Show Up for Court Hearings, He Couldn't Be More Wrong*, L.A. TIMES (Oct. 29, 2020), https://www.latimes.com/opinion/story/2020-10-29/immigration-donald-trump-joe-biden-presidential-debate; *see also* Lori Robertson, *Trump's Immigration Plan*, FACTCHECK.ORG (Aug. 20, 2015), https://www.factcheck.org/2015/08/trumps-immigration-plan/ (noting that candidate Trump's immigration plan included several statements that deviate from the known facts).

[47] *See generally* Mariela Olivares, *The Rise of Zero Tolerance and the Demise of Family*, 36 GA. ST. U. L. REV. 287 (2020) (reviewing the Trump administration's use of family separation as a tool of U.S. immigration enforcement).

Racism like that espoused by President Trump unfortunately has a lengthy pedigree in U.S. history. Critical Race Theory (CRT) has offered invaluable insights on the centrality of race historically to the law as a tool to maintain white supremacy.[48] CRT expanded analysis of racial subordination beyond the Black/white paradigm to include the subordination of Latinx persons, Asian Americans, and other racial groups.[49] It specifically has identified how race has indelibly influenced the development of the criminal justice system in the United States and its devastating impacts on communities of color.[50] Racism obviously motivated Jim Crow and institutionalized racial segregation. It rationalized the suppression of Black voters. It led to racist immigration laws. The powerful insights of CRT shed light on these racist milestones in U.S. history and brought modern attention to them. The contemporary reckoning with systemic racism has fueled efforts by law schools to incorporate racial justice and CRT into the curriculum.[51]

Despite the powerful insights of CRT, the Trump administration sought to halt efforts to incorporate the teachings of CRT on racial justice into the workings of the U.S. government. He "order[ed] the Office of Management and Budget to stop funding training on critical race theory for federal employees, calling it a 'propaganda effort.' "[52] Efforts at teaching the nation's racial history were challenged as well. The controversy sparked by President Trump led to passionate and

---

48 *See generally* RICHARD DELGADO & JEAN STEFANCIC, CRITICAL RACE THEORY: AN INTRODUCTION (3d ed. 2017).

49 *See* Juan F. Perea, *The Black/White Binary Paradigm of Race: The "Normal Science" of American Racial Thought,* 85 CAL. L. REV. 1213 (1997).

50 *See supra* note 8 (citing authority).

51 *See, e.g., UCI Law Faculty Adopts New Race and Indigeneity Curriculum Graduation Requirement,* UC IRVINE LAW (Apr. 6, 2021), https://www.law.uci.edu/news/press-releases/2021/race-indigeneity-curriculum.html.

52 Char Adams, *How Trump Ignited the Fight Over Critical Race Theory in Schools,* NBC NEWS (May 10, 2021), https://www.nbcnews.com/news/nbcblk/how-trump-ignited-fight-over-critical-race-theory-schools-n1266701; *see* Michael Crowley, *Trump Calls for "Patriotic Education" to Defend American History from the Left,* N.Y. TIMES (Sep. 17, 2020), https://www.nytimes.com/2020/09/17/us/politics/trump-patriotic-education.html; Matthew S. Schwartz, *Trump Tells Agencies to End Trainings on "White Privilege" and "Critical Race Theory,"* NPR (Sep. 5, 2020), https://www.npr.org/2020/09/05/910053496/trump-tells-agencies-to-end-trainings-on-white-privilege-and-critical-race-theor.

divisive efforts to outlaw the teaching of CRT in the public schools.[53]

As recent events made clear, systemic racial injustice is a thorny legal and policy problem that begs for remedies. Despite CRT's sustained criticism, systemic racial injustice is only now receiving widespread public attention. Rather than blame the victim and deny the existence of systemic racism, as the Trump administration did, approaches that will bring transformative change to systems of white supremacy demand more, not less, serious and meaningful government attention. Banning CRT because it addresses systemic racism in U.S. social life will not move the nation forward toward a true reckoning with that racism.

In his attack on CRT, former President Donald Trump called for the resignation of Chairman of the Joint Chief Staff General Mark Milley over his relatively mild defense of studying Critical Race Theory.[54] Trump's attack on General Milley occurred after he testified about "the importance of being well-read and his desire to understand 'white rage' in response to Republican questioning about critical race theory at a House Armed Service Committee hearing.' "[55] " 'Gen. Milley ought to resign, and be replaced with someone who is actually willing to defend our Military from the Leftist Radicals who hate our Country and our Flag,' Trump said."[56]

In a commentary, Donald Trump attacked CRT head on:

> In classrooms across the nation, students are being subjected to a new curriculum designed to brainwash them with the ridiculous left-wing dogma known as "critical race theory." The key fact about this twisted

---

[53] *See The Debate Over Critical Race Theory,* THE DAILY (podcast) (July 2, 2021), https://www.nytimes.com/2021/07/02/podcasts/the-daily/critical-race-theory-debate.html; Char Adams, Allan Smith & Aadit Tambe, *Map: See Which States Have Passed Critical Race Theory Bills,* NBC NEWS (June 17, 2021), https://www.nbcnews.com/news/nbcblk/map-see-which-states-have-passed-critical-race-theory-bills-n1271215; Fabiola Cineas, *Critical Race Theory, and Trump's War on It, Explained,* VOX (Sep. 24, 2020), https://www.vox.com/2020/9/24/21451220/critical-race-theory-diversity-training-trump.

[54] *See* Rebecca Kheel, *Trump Attacks Milley Over Critical Race Theory, Calls for Resignation,* THE HILL (July 1, 2021), https://thehill.com/policy/defense/560953-trump-attacks-milley-over-critical-race-theory-calls-for-resignation.

[55] *See id.*

[56] *Id.*

doctrine is that it is completely antithetical to everything that normal Americans of any color would wish to teach their children.

Instead of helping young people discover that America is the greatest, most tolerant, and most generous nation in history, it teaches them that America is systemically evil and that the hearts of our people are full of hatred and malice. Far from advancing the beautiful dream of the Rev. Martin Luther King Jr.—that our children should "not be judged by the color of their skin, but by the content of their character"—the left's vile new theory preached that judging people by the color of their skin is actually a good idea.[57]

President Trump's attacks wholly ignored the relevance of CRT's teachings to the analysis of systemic racism in U.S. social life. In the wake of a series of police killings of African Americans in 2020, the nation began discussions about redressing systemic racial injustice. Critical Race Theorists have long argued that law is integral to maintaining white supremacy in the criminal justice system.[58] However, rather than embrace CRT's teachings, President Trump unfortunately sought to remove any aspect of CRT from government programs. Racism fueled the attack on CRT and even the recognition of racist chapters in U.S. history.

In light of contemporary events, law schools are considering how to incorporate issues of racial justice into legal education. Integrating CRT into law school curriculum has been one focal point. After the spate of police killings in 2020, law schools accelerated efforts to incorporate racial justice into the curriculum.[59]

The events of 2020 led UC Davis School of Law to establish a Racial Justice Speaker Series,[60] with prominent civil rights

---

57 Donald Trump, *A Plan to Get Divisive and Radical Theories Out of Our Schools,* REAL CLEAR POLITICS (June 18, 2021), https://www.realclearpolitics.com/articles/2021/06/18/a_plan_to_get_divisive__radical_theories_out_of_our_schools_145946.html.

58 *See supra* note 8 (citing authority).

59 *See supra* note 51 (citing authority).

60 *See Racial Justice Speaker Series,* UC Davis School of Law, https://law.ucdavis.edu/racial-justice-speaker-series/.

scholars, public defenders, and political leaders talking about systemic racial injustice in the United States. Over the course of the year, the community heard about systemic racial injustice and possible avenues for reform and change. Hundreds of alumni, faculty, students, staff, and community members attended the events, which were held virtually because of the pandemic.

Although systemic racial injustice in the criminal justice system and the police killing of George Floyd led to mass protests in summer 2020,[61] the Racial Justice Speaker Series was not limited to analyzing racial injustice in the criminal justice system. Over the year, speakers also looked at racial injustice in family law, corporate governance, immigration, hate crimes, and related topics. The speakers also focused on the subordination of Asian Americans and Latinx people as well as African Americans, making clear that many racial groups are subject to racial subordination—and the push to maintain white supremacy—and actively engage in the contemporary struggle for civil rights for communities of color.

2. Immigration

Immigration law has proven to be a divisive issue of public debate in the United States. Racism has historically influenced the debate and continues to do so to this day.[62] As we have seen, President Trump relentlessly played on racial themes in discussing immigration. Indeed, he commenced his successful 2016 presidential bid by crudely attacking immigrants from Mexico as criminals and rapists.[63] The Trump administration subsequently took some of the most aggressive immigration measures of any President in modern U.S. history,[64] including

---

61 *How George Floyd was Killed in Police Custody*, N.Y. TIMES (May 31, 2020), https://www.nytimes.com/2020/05/31/us/george-floyd-investigation.html.

62 *See generally* ERIKA LEE, AMERICA FOR AMERICANS: A HISTORY OF XENOPHOBIA IN THE UNITED STATES (2019) (reviewing the U.S. history of xenophobia and racism directed at immigrants).

63 *See supra* text accompanying note & note 40.

64 *See* Anil Kalhan, *Revisiting the 1996 Experiment in Comprehensive Immigration Severity in the Age of Trump*, 9 DREXEL L. REV. 261, 262 (2017) ("The [Trump administration's] sweeping, high-profile immigration enforcement initiatives—along with its inflammatory anti-immigrant rhetoric—mark the ascendance of immigration restrictionism to the highest levels of the executive branch *to an extent that is entirely without modern precedent.*") (emphasis added).

an aggressive approach to immigration enforcement with devastating impacts on communities of color.[65] He did so with his use of bold and brash language about "illegals" and "Mexicans," invoking falsities masquerading as facts, and pushing to the limits—and beyond—of what the law permits.[66]

President Trump's approach to the travel ban, which barred admission into the United States of noncitizens from a group of predominately Muslim nations, teaches much about the place of the law in his analysis.[67] Exuding racism, it showed little concern with the facts and the law. The first version of the travel ban was hastily put into place in January 2017. Poorly drafted with many glaring gaps, the ban was not even clear about such basic things as whether it permitted lawful permanent residents to return to the United States. The lower courts struck down the first version of the travel ban. The same thing happened to the second somewhat narrower and improved version.[68] The Supreme Court upheld the third, much more refined version of the travel ban. In formulating various iterations of the travel ban, the Trump administration in effect took a trial and error, or hit or miss, approach to compliance with the law.

At various times, President Trump berated the law and the courts for thwarting his extreme immigration policy initiatives.[69] He did so in ways much more consistent and brash than any other modern president. That was the case even though those measures, such as the first version of the travel ban, showed little effort to comply with the law on the books. President Trump instead used the law and so-called liberal courts as political scapegoats for explaining the courts' rejection of his extreme immigration policies.

---

[65] *See* Rose Cuison Villazor & Kevin R. Johnson, *The Trump Administration and the War on Immigration Diversity*, 54 WAKE FOREST L. REV. 575, 585–94, 601–16 (2019).

[66] *See supra* text accompanying notes 43–47.

[67] Trump v. Hawaii, 138 S. Ct. 2392 (2018).

[68] *See id.* at 2403–06 (noting the invalidation of two versions of the travel ban by the lower courts before the Supreme Court upheld the third one, which was substantially narrower in scope).

[69] *See* BRENNAN CENTER FOR JUSTICE, IN HIS OWN WORDS: THE PRESIDENT'S ATTACKS ON THE COURTS (June 5, 2017), https://www.brennancenter.org/our-work/research-reports/his-own-words-presidents-attacks-courts (recounting Trump's criticism of court decisions with respect to asylum, his attempted rescission of the Deferred Action for Childhood Arrivals policy, and other immigration policy matters).

Despite the national polarization on the issue of immigration, there are opportunities for meaningful reform, including congressional action. In addition, the lack of constitutional review immigration laws and polices stems from a seminal Supreme Court decision upholding discriminatory laws barring the admission of Chinese noncitizens into the United States.[70] That and subsequent decisions remain the law even though the lack of review is more consistent with the era of Jim Crow than the civil rights revolution. Judicial elimination of the artificial restraints on constitutional review could help push Congress and the Executive Branch to act in a more moderate and balanced fashion toward immigrants.

Immigration law unfortunately is part of the mosaic of systemic racial injustice today. Moreover, the history of immigration offers insights into race relations in the United States. The exclusion of Chinese immigrants, and later all Asians, in the late 1800s was entirely consistent with widespread discrimination against the Chinese in the United States. The anti-Chinese laws influenced the development of the immigration laws, which today are employed primarily to regulate Latinx immigration to the United States.[71] Racism is baked into the overall immigration framework.

A reasoned and discerning approach to immigration is necessary to resolve some of the daunting challenges facing the nation. Simple harsh measures, or blaming others (noncitizens, the courts, etc.) for the problems, will not solve the complex public policy issues at stake. Ultimately, to bring about change, critical and meaningful analysis of the many policy issues implicated by immigration is necessary. Such analysis was missing from the Trump administration's approach to immigration. Facts and law were disregarded. Racial passions dominated immigration policymaking.

---

[70] *See* Chae Chan Ping v. United States (*The Chinese Exclusion Case*), 130 U.S. 581 (1889).

[71] *See generally* Kevin R. Johnson, *Trump's* Latinx *Repatriation*, 66 UCLA L. REV. 1442 (2019) (analyzing critically Trump administration's immigration policies and their impacts on Latinx immigrants).

E. CONCLUSION

Legal education traditionally has taught rigorous analysis of the law and the facts in a case. As the nation analyzes the recent political turmoil on pressing public policy issues, we can see the benefits of traditional tools of legal analysis, such as that exemplified by the Issue, Rule, Application, Conclusion (IRAC) method. Law schools are right to pride themselves in teaching rigorous analytical skills and in the future should continue to pursue that pedagogical goal.

The last few years have seen incredible social and racial tensions in U.S. society. Law schools are well equipped to teach the analytical skills that will help the nation to respond with policies that effectively address and calm those tensions. Although inflaming racial tensions, attacks on people of color, the courts, and the rule of law, the approach of the Trump administration did little to solve the problem, and likely made it worse.

The legal and other public policy travails of the Trump administration should reinforce the understanding that legal analysis is a sound approach not only to addressing legal problems but pressing public policy issues. For example, if we want to remedy systematic racial injustice in the United States, or create a more effective and fair immigration system, careful analysis of the facts, identification of the legal issues, and engaging in the hard work of reform and transformation of the law is necessary. Ignoring or distorting the facts and the law, as officials in the Trump administration were wont to do, simply will not suffice to bring true racial justice to U.S. society and, in fact, will move the nation away from the laudable goal of equality for all.

CHAPTER 12

CIVIC ANEMIA: LAW SCHOOLS SHOULD GIVE BOOSTERS TO COUNTER ITS EFFECTS

Anthony W. Crowell[1]

The collection of important and considered viewpoints expressed in this compendium broach only some of the most important concerns of legal scholars and educators concerning the state of our democracy in the 21st Century. These inquiries and reflections about the deadly insurrection that took place on January 6, 2021, at the United States Capitol only begin to tackle a broad range of tough questions, and of course they provoke even more of them than could ever be answered by this project.

We started talking about this project just days after the insurrection, a moment in which the effects of the unrelenting barrage of misinformation infecting the American polity, mounting threats to our democratic institutions and processes, and the upending of the core principles of the rule of law were laid bare. For me, longstanding concerns about what I term *civic anemia*, caused by the deficiency of citizenship education in the U.S., seemed like an obvious place to offer commentary. And then a political cartoon in the New York *Daily News* captured the sentiment perfectly. It depicted the Capitol, post insurrection, curtained by an iron barbed wire fence with two passers-by asserting: *"A better defense is teaching civics again."*[2]

---

1 Dean and President, Professor of Law, New York Law School.

2 Bill Bramhall, Editorial Cartoon, *A better defense is teaching civics again*, New York Daily News, February 17, 2021. Reprinted with permission.

If civic anemia is left untreated it will surely weaken and could ultimately prove fatal to the body of our democracy. Thus, the calls to revive civics education in America's schools are not new and they have been made by an impressive chorus of prominent public officials, jurists, bar leaders, and academics for several decades. Civics education in its most basic form requires students to develop the knowledge necessary to be good citizens. That means they need to understand the history of the nation's founding and development, the rule of law and principles that underly democratic ideals and values, the structure and function of government, individual rights and their limitations, political freedoms, and, capitalism and related economic freedoms.[3] The emphasis placed on civics education for American school children and adults has ebbed and flowed since World War II, reflecting the social, economic, and political imperatives and debates of various points in time. This includes the Red Scare in the 1950s to today's cultural vortex with its rising tide of American "nationalism," severe political polarization, and a sustained campaign of disinformation.

[3] This commentary aims to discuss the traditional framework of civics education, with contemporary application, in response to the insurrection and to further support law students.

Among the many things the insurrection has taught us are just how vital civics education, ethical and accountable lawyers, and legal education are to the future of the American democracy. Civics education is important because when the electorate lacks a foundational understanding of the basic structure and function of our democratic institutions and election processes, it will be ill-informed. And, an ill-informed citizenry is ill-prepared to carry-out their responsibilities as citizens and honor the outcomes of our nation's democratic mission, particularly elections.

Media reports and commentaries about the insurrection, and the individual insurrectionists themselves, point to the problem.[4] They show the clear effects of how a lack of understanding of democratic principles, and the lawful function of American government, gave rise to deep distrust in government process and an attack on the Capitol aimed to thwart both the legitimate certification of the winner of the 2020 Presidential election, and a peaceful transition of power.[5] The insurrectionists did so because they believed the disinformation that the Republican President, his lawyers, and (social) media conspiracy theorists propagated that day and in the weeks leading up to it. Namely, that there was widespread election fraud and Congress would act unlawfully to certify the election with the Democratic candidate as the winner unless Congress was stopped. This misinformation was spread by the same purveyors of other false conspiracies and narratives; those who stormed the Capitol were voracious consumers of it.[6]

Proper civics education could prevent such misbeliefs and distrust by imbuing in Americans the necessary knowledge of history, government, politics, and economics needed to make

---

[4] Caroline Anders, *A lawyer hoped history books would help her Capitol riot clients grow. She was called a traitor—and worse*, THE WASHINGTON POST, July 31, 2021, available at https://www.washingtonpost.com/dc-md-va/2021/07/31/capitol-riot-lawyer-books-defense/. *See also The Road to Insurrection*, ON THE MEDIA (2021), available at https://www.wnycstudios.org/podcasts/otm/episodes/on-the-media-road-to-insurrection (last accessed August 2, 2021).

[5] Luke Mogelson, *Among the Insurrectionists*, THE NEW YORKER, January 15, 2021, available at https://www.newyorker.com/magazine/2021/01/25/among-the-insurrectionists.

[6] Bill McCarthy, *Misinformation and the Jan. 6 insurrection: When 'patriot warriors' were fed lies*, POLITIFACT, June 30, 2021, available at https://www.politifact.com/article/2021/jun/30/misinformation-and-jan-6-insurrection-when-patriot/.

reasoned and accurate judgments about government processes and policies, and thus be able to discern fact from fiction, and truth from treachery. This would better serve our democracy and better enable citizens to hold accountable their elected leaders and government generally through constitutionally established processes, and not deadly violence like that which was resorted to by the insurrectionists. Accordingly, civics education in its purest form always has had an essential role in preserving our constitutional democracy. But only if and when it is delivered well can it be a safeguard to insulate against events like the insurrection and others that threaten the rule of law.

As the 2020 Presidential election cycle was starting, and just one year before the insurrection, U.S. Supreme Court Chief Justice John Roberts, in his *2019 Annual Report on the Federal Judiciary,* reflected on the state of our national dialogue and civics education. "[W]e have come to take democracy for granted, and civic education has fallen by the wayside. In our age, when social media can instantly spread rumor and false information on a grand scale, the public's need to understand our government, and the protections it provides, is ever more vital."[7]

Bar Association leaders support the Chief Justice's conclusion and call to action. In his 2021 Law Day remarks, New York State Bar Association President Scott Karson made several key observations on civics education specifically in relation to the insurrection. He said "[a]n antidote to the misinformation causing Americans to lose faith in the very institutions that uphold our rule of law is robust public civics education that instills the knowledge and values of our democratic republic to guard against the disrespect and wanton violence such as we witnessed on January 6th." "Students, as well as educators, and even lawyers and judges, must all become educated to apply critical thinking to what they hear and see, especially on social media." "They must learn to debate with civility, not violence." And, "lawmakers [must] provide the resources necessary to help our young people become citizens who actively participate in

---

[7] JOHN G. ROBERTS, JR., 2019 YEAR-END REPORT ON THE FEDERAL JUDICIARY (December 31, 2019), available at https://www.supremecourt.gov/publicinfo/year-end/2019year-endreport.pdf.

government and who see the value in discerning the truth and respecting the rule of law."[8]

The American Bar Association also has been forceful in attempting to instill better understanding of the law in the public domain, and also urging stronger action by policymakers to deter misinformation and protect the core right central to our democracy—voting. Last year, the House of Delegates adopted a Resolution encouraging the protection of elections, specifically from threats posed by the proliferation of misinformation.[9]

For certain, the roles of lawyers in promoting truth and respecting the rule law are not only valuable, but they are fundamental to the preservation of our democracy. In response to the insurrection, on January 12, 2021, these precepts were reinforced by 171 law deans from American Bar Association accredited law schools who signed a "Joint Statement on the 2020 Election and Events at the Capitol."[10] The joint statement reads in part:

> *The violent attack on the Capitol was an assault on our democracy and the rule of law. The effort to disrupt the certification of a free and fair election was a betrayal of the core values that undergird our Constitution. Lives were lost, the seat of our democracy was desecrated, and our country was shamed.*
>
> *Many lawyers and judges worked honestly and in good faith, often in the face of considerable political pressure, to ensure the 2020 election was free and fair. However, we recognize with dismay and sorrow that some lawyers challenged the outcome of the election with claims that they did not support with facts or evidence. This betrayed the values of our profession. Our profession*

---

[8] Scott Karson, Law Day Remarks of the New York State Bar Association President (May 1, 2021), available at https://www.nycourts.gov/whatsnew/pdf/LawDay2021transcript.pdf.

[9] American Bar Association, ABA House of Delegates Resolution 300A (2020), available at https://www.americanbar.org/content/dam/aba/administrative/news/2020/08/2020-am-resolutions/300a.pdf.

[10] Joint Statement of 171 Deans of ABA Accredited Law Schools on the 2020 Election and Events at the Capitol (January 12, 2021), available at https://law.yale.edu/sites/default/files/documents/pdf/law_deans_joint_statement_1.12.21_final.pdf (emphasis added). (The author of this chapter was one of six deans who collaborated to draft the Joint Statement adopted by individual signatories, of which he was one.)

> *demands that when lawyers pursue legal action, they must bring claims in good faith, grounded in facts and evidence, and demonstrate respect for the legal system. Only then can lawyers fulfill their responsibilities as lawyers and public citizens to promote public confidence in the rule of law and the justice system—duties that extend to all professional activities, whether lawyers are representing a client or not. The rule of law is as much a touchstone of our profession as it is of our Constitution.*
>
> *As law deans, our mission is to train the next generation of leaders to uphold the core values of our profession and sustain the rule of law. This should be a moment of reflection for legal educators and members of the legal profession. A sustained effort will be necessary to repair and preserve our precious democratic institutions. As legal educators and lawyers ourselves, we must redouble our efforts to restore faith in the rule of law and the ideals of the legal profession. We have enormous faith in the law's enduring values and in our students, who will soon lead this profession. We call upon all members of the legal profession to join us in the vital work ahead.*

Indeed, part of the vital work ahead is to ensure that, as Scott Karson suggests, law students, lawyers, and judges, have the civics education and skills to confront and navigate a world where, without it, the spread of misinformation can trigger crippling effects of civic anemia to our democratic body.

Discussions with other law deans and colleagues in the legal academy from around the country—as well with law students and from my classroom observations over more than two decades of teaching State and Local Government Law—suggest that today's students may suffer from at least some of the same civic anemia found in the general public. Today's law students have grown up entirely in the internet era, and their knowledge and sensibilities have understandably been shaped by the times into which they were born and live. Like many of their parents, many of them were potentially disadvantaged from the nation's de-emphasis of civics education over the past 60 years. They have come of age enmeshed in and contributing to the proliferation of social media that helps to shape values, priorities, and political choices. They are regular consumers of news and other important information over social media, some of which comes from unreliable sources. Some of that information is deliberate disinformation propagated by actors both domestic and foreign. Inadequate civics education may have left them, as well as others in their or their parents' generational cohorts, without a full baseline of knowledge and analytical skills to draw on and confront disinformation by asking the essential questions.

While there are generally no formal pre-requisites to enter law school, aside from completion of a bachelor's degree and the Law School Admission Test, modern American legal education from the middle of the 20th Century until today has generally assumed that law students have benefitted from a meaningful foundation in civics education laid down in primary and secondary school, followed by a liberal arts college education with substantial emphasis in history and government, political science, and economics. Indeed, the classic assumption is that most would-be law students will have majored or minored in one or more of these or closely related subjects and have internship or work experience in government or law, along with some form of community service. And while today many of them still do, many of them do not. Over the past 30 years, there are more science, technology, engineering, and math (STEM) majors applying to law school, along with a proliferation of more narrow pre-professional and interdisciplinary majors often designed and marketed as more attractive options for students than traditional pre-law subjects, or one plainly labeled "pre-law." Those developments, along with changes in undergraduate general curricular requirements that may not require instruction in American history, government, political science, or economics as a prerequisite to earning a degree, may leave today's law school bound college graduates not fully prepared for the demands of the first year of legal study and beyond.

The assumption most law professors make, and thus the assumption underlying most law school curricula, about law student civics readiness may be misplaced. Of course, while today's law students no doubt have a genuine desire to develop careers in service of others, advocate for justice and build economic opportunities, not all students have a meaningful foundation in civics as a baseline for their study of law. Students who don't have one often find themselves struggling in the early days of law school to make sense of that which others assume they know, sometimes fearful to ask questions that may reveal a lack of knowledge. But without such baseline knowledge, the learning experience can be undermined.

How did this happen? What might this mean for American legal education and today's law students? And, what can be done to counter the anemia? To begin to answer these questions, a review of post-war U.S. civics education to the present, while not a prescription for action, can provide some initial guideposts to inform a framework for response.

A. LOOKING BACK TO LOOK FORWARD

For quick perspective, look back seven decades to the end of World War II when America's educational leaders found themselves outside an iron curtain very different from the one erected around the Capitol after the insurrection. But, one whose existence also very much emphasized the need for citizenship education. Just by way of example, in 1954, the American Association of School Administrators ("AASA"), published a 394-page Yearbook entitled *Educating for American Citizenship.*[11] It was written by an AASA appointed Commission of the same name and included in its membership educational leaders from public grade and high schools, as well as higher education. It provides key insights into the fears and priorities of at least some American educators and government officials.

At the time, the United States and its allies were engaged in post-war rebuilding, while simultaneously navigating the threats of the Cold War. The Yearbook's authors framed the struggle between the Soviet regime and the "free world" as one where democratic ideals and standards would perish or survive. The Commission believed a new program of American citizenship and civics education was needed to address a world undergoing "cataclysmic" change in which post-war communist

[11] American Association of School Administrators, *Educating for American Citizenship. Thirty-Second Yearbook.* Washington, D.C. (1954).

imperialism, and "the grave danger of under-rating its power to attract intelligent people," threatened American democracy.[12] This, they stated, included the Soviet Union's "complete denial and rejection" of the principles on which western political democracy rest: "[f]reedom of the press, freedom of thought, freedom of worship, [and] freedom of enterprise," and the ridicule of the social, economic, and political institutions created to advance them.[13]

The Commission concluded that a "new appreciation for the old [American] ideals" by school children would serve as "a stable element in a shaky world," where the threat to our way of life, our freedom, and our moral values was "total." "As long as we have any citizens who believe that *autocracy* has any superiority whatsoever over democracy,. . .we have a need for citizenship education. . .that will help in the solution of [ ] civic, social, and economic problems that are so often interwoven in life."[14]

While the Commission viewed threats from foreign actors as "total," they acknowledged, though not in great detail, that contemporary threats "from within" were serious enough on their own to merit the push for changes in civics education. These internal threats included a rise in voter apathy at all levels, corruption and conflicts of interest among public officials, and racketeering, among others. The communist threat, it seems, was magnified by, and in part enabled, the profound changes in American society. The fast pace of technological development had an intense impact on occupations, industries, and institutions, and on primary face-to-face interactions in communities, leading to an increase in suspicion of citizens everywhere.

When taken together, the Yearbook is a powerful call to American public education to teach civics that "stress the difference between communist goals and methods and those of the free world as no previous program found it necessary to do."[15] The Yearbook suggested that the current world struggle made it

---

[12] *Id.* at 18.

[13] *Id.* at 16.

[14] *Id.* at 22 (emphasis added).

[15] *Id.* at 20.

clear that "that positive dynamic programs of citizenship education must be a central feature of modern education."[16]

In developing an effective program of civics education, the Commission outlined that the goals of such a program should:

- Prepare youth for intelligent participation in policy decisions in home and community, in state and nation, and in world affairs;[17]
- Concern itself with individual excellence, while equipping the individual citizen with the attitudes, sensitivities, insights, and social skills essential for membership in the home and in varied social groups and organizations that make up modern community life;[18] and
- Cultivate an understanding of the community as a form of social organization, develop competence in community leadership, and provide ample opportunity for concrete experience in decisions in the varied aspects of community life.[19]

Further, the Commission suggested that American public education was obligated to undertake the challenge "of making clear to youth and their elders the nature and meaning of democratic values, to develop a deep loyalty to these values, and to make them the touchstone of individual behavior and of public policy."[20] They recognized that while democracy "embraces free, representative political institutions," it also is "a system of moral commitments,. . .of values that govern behavior in all human relationships and in all the great social institutions of home, church, school, community, economy, and state,. . .and that seeks to make possible the release of the full potentialities of self in the life of every individual."[21]

---

[16] *Id.* at 23.

[17] *Id.* at 46.

[18] *Id.* at 47.

[19] *Id.*

[20] *Id.* at 54.

[21] *Id.* It should be noted that the Yearbook was published in February 1954, three months before the U.S. Supreme Court unanimously decided Brown v. Board of Education, 347 U.S. 483 (May 17, 1954). One might rightly expect that, had the Yearbook been published subsequent to the decision in *Brown,* the authors would have included

In articulating democratic ideals and principles, the Commission identified the following list as among that which they believed should guide a program of civics education:

- *"Worth of Persons. . .Respect for the dignity and worth of human personality is the basic concept of American Democracy."*[22]
- *"Freedom of the Individual. . .[Individuals] can be free."*[23]
- *"Government of Laws. . .[F]reedom under law is the essential condition of a free society."*[24]
- *"Sense of Justice. . .[I]n dealing with one another, [individuals] should be governed by a sense of justice, good conscience, equity, and fair dealing."*[25]
- *"Capacity for Self-Government. . .[Individuals] have the ability to govern themselves."*[26]
- *"Civic Participation. . .[Individuals] have a right to participate in decisions affecting [themselves.]"*[27]
- *"Love of Truth and Appeal to Reason. . .[Individuals] must entertain a love of truth that is supported by a rational evaluation the evidence."*[28]
- *"An Informed Citizenry. . .[C]itizens must be informed."*[29]
- *"Social Responsibility the Counterpart of Freedom. . .[T]he price of freedom is its responsible exercise."*[30]

(or at least perhaps not simply avoided) appropriate treatment of the topic of school desegregation, and the imperative of teaching constitutional history and principles of racial equality in this emerging context.

22 *Id.* at 55.

23 *Id.* at 55.

24 *Id.* at 56.

25 *Id.* at 57.

26 *Id.* at 58.

27 *Id.* at 58.

28 *Id.* at 59.

29 *Id.* at 60.

30 *Id.* at 61.

- *"Equal Opportunity. . .[E]ach individual should have equal opportunity for self-realization."*[31] *And,*
- *"The Right to be Different. . .[Individuals] have the right to be different."*[32]

The Yearbook helped foster the development of citizenship education pedagogy and programs in American public education. This is clearly seen in educational texts encouraging and responding to curricular developments in civics education around the nation. Take for example *Social Studies for Children in a Democracy,* a pedagogical text for teachers published in 1956, two years after the Yearbook's publication. It opens with the declaration that "The schools of America are dedicated to the preservation and extension of democratic ideals and to the development of the highest type of democratic citizenship on the part of each child. The discharge of this responsibility requires an education program that will develop each child's potentialities to the fullest and at the same time bring growth in the competencies essential to democratic living."[33] Citing the Yearbook, the text states "[t]he major emphasis being given to citizenship education at the present time is concrete evidence of the importance accorded this responsibility by American educators." It then goes on in detail expressing principles and prescribing curricular elements largely mirroring those identified as essential in the Yearbook.[34]

No sooner were those civics education efforts underway, than other elements of the Cold War triggered a further shift in American educational policy that took emphasis away from civics education in favor of highly important STEM subjects. In the mid-1950s, with the threat and promise of technology in plain sight, the U.S. and the Soviet Union aimed to assert their dominance over one another through their technological and military capabilities, demonstrating their global political and economic superiority. In 1957, the U.S. suffered a major political blow, giving rise to a national crisis that changed the trajectory

---

[31] *Id.* at 62.

[32] *Id.* at 64.

[33] JOHN U. MICHAELIS, SOCIAL STUDIES FOR CHILDREN IN A DEMOCRACY, 2d. Ed., Prentice Hall, Englewood Cliffs, NJ (1956), p. 1.

[34] *Id.* at pp. 1–29.

of civics education. The Soviets launched Sputnik, the first man-made satellite, into space, taking Americans by surprise and sparking the so-called "space race" between the two nations. The U.S.'s essential response was to build STEM capacity by changing educational policy and curricula and making financial investments to attract a technologically skilled workforce. The director of the American Institute of Physics, Dr. Elmer Hutchison, famously warned that, "[u]nless future generations appreciate the role of science in modern society, and understand the conditions under which science thrives, our [the American] way of life is. . .doomed to rapid extinction."[35]

In the years since then, the U.S. won the space race, ushered in an end to the Cold War, and shaped a global technological revolution. While, today, Russia still looms as a large threat to U.S. national security, so now does China. And because the U.S.'s need to compete has only grown over the years, the country has continued to invest in STEM education while investment in civics education lags far behind. A *Wall Street Journal* op-ed written by six former U.S. Department of Education secretaries, advocating for increased civics education, estimated that the U.S. spends 1,000 times more per student on STEM education than on history and civics.[36] No one can deny that the technological development realized through STEM education remains necessary and that the growth of digital technologies has paid significant returns as an outsized driver of our economic growth and global dominance.

Alternatively, and ironically, digital technologies also have played an outsized role in enabling the very foreign and domestic mischief that have served to undermine our democracy. These technologies and digital platforms have most recently made possible broad and effective sustained campaigns of political and other disinformation, manipulation of our national elections, the spread of conspiracy theories that have led to domestic political unrest, and pernicious cyber-attacks on government and

[35] Howard M. Schmeck, *Nation is Warned to Stress Science*, N.Y. TIMES, October 8, 1957.

[36] Lamar Alexander, Arne Duncan, John King, Rod Paige, Richard Riley, and Margaret Spellings, *America Needs History and Civics Education to Promote Unity*, WALL STREET JOURNAL, March 1, 2021, available at https://www.wsj.com/articles/america-needs-history-and-civics-education-to-promote-unity-11614641530.

industry causing dramatic economic and social disruption. Without a change in policy and investment in civics education to meet a changed world in which political influence is wielded most widely through digital communications, these threats will continue to undermine the stability of our democracy and national security.

The report from the Center for American Progress entitled *Strengthening Democracy With a Modern Civics Education* presents a number of important findings demonstrating the levels of investment in high school civics education, state-by-state, in 2019. The 50-state study examined high school civics curricula, course requirements for graduation, and community service requirements. Curricular content robustness "was examined by looking at materials or standards to address: (1) an explanation or comparison of democracy; (2) the U.S. Constitution and the Bill of Rights; (3) public participation; (4) information on state and local voting rules; and, (5) media literacy and the role and influence of media."[37] The results were as follows:[38]

- 26 states had curricula addressing all five subjects; another 12 states addressed some variation of 4 out of 5; and 33 addressed media literacy and the role/influence of media.
- Most states require high school students to complete some form of civics coursework to graduate: 30 states require one semester long course; 8 states require a full year course. One state requires a year and a half, and several states require a more holistic approach taken through the K–12 journey, instead of any one course.
- 20 states require students to take some sort of civics exam to demonstrate competency before graduation.

---

[37] Ashley Jeffrey & Scott Sargrad, *Strengthening Democracy With a Modern Civics Education*, CENTER FOR AMERICAN PROGRESS, December 14, 2019, https://www.americanprogress.org/issues/education-k-12/reports/2019/12/14/478750/strengthening-democracy-modern-civics-education/.

[38] *Id.*

- Community service is only required by two states, 23 in all offer some type of academic credit for it. And,
- There was no clear correlation between curricular robustness and the level of success on the Advanced Placement test in U.S. Government and Politics.

The study also reported that persistently only a fraction of students, 25%, taking the National Assessment of Educational Progress (NAEP) civics exam pass, showing an overall lack of proficiency in the subject by the test takers. Further, there are disturbing and "persistent gaps between the scores of Black and Hispanic students and those of their white peers as well as by English language learner, income, and disability status."[39] In sum, the report reveals the need for substantial progress to be made to achieve common standards, investment, and commitment to delivering holistic civics education nationally.

It is ironic that a key post-war motivator for the U.S.'s recommitment to civics education—the threat of Soviet dominance and the loss of democracy—ultimately gave rise to the disinvestment in those very curricula. This has left American students more technologically competitive on the world stage, but far less educated on the foundations and the functions of the government that sponsored these investments. Connecting these dots—the shift in educational priorities from the 1950's through the intervening decades, and now during a time of sustained disinformation, trace many paths, but arguably, one of those paths led directly from the White House to the Capitol on January 6, 2021.

What to do to re-connect those educational dots to an informed electorate is a challenge that needs to be addressed for students at all educational levels, including in America's law schools, and the public at large. Understanding the origins of civic anemia and how and why an uninformed electorate might turn to violence instead of trusting democratic process, we as law school deans, along with the profession generally, have a special duty to advocate for the return of broad-based civics education. And, we also have a duty to ensure that the future generations

---

39 *Id.*

of lawyers to come through our doors possess a strong civics foundation to support their study of law, and their work in the profession and as community leaders, so that they may fulfill their responsibilities as stewards of democracy in the 21st Century. And, while the former aspiration is not within our power, the latter duty certainly is with regard to our own students. While the democratic ideals and principles identified in the 1954 Yearbook are not a ready-made prescription for civics education required in the age of disinformation, they nonetheless reflect an enduring, and universal, set of values for American participatory democracy dating back to the nation's founding in 1776.[40] Thus, they can serve as a foundation upon which to build more contemporary instruction in civics.

B. LAW SCHOOLS SHOULD OFFER BOOSTERS TO COUNTER CIVIC ANEMIA

The American Bar Association (ABA), the Association of American Law Schools (AALS), and state bar associations, recognize the role the importance of civics education. The ABA has had a longstanding policy to foster civics education nationally through advocacy and encouraging lawyers to provide civics education in their communities. The ABA House of Delegates has adopted a dozen resolutions on civics education since 1973.[41] The ABA sponsored the former Commission on Civics Education in the Nation's Schools, and it currently offers an extensive array of electronic resources on civics education and understanding the rule of law. It conducts the annual Survey of Civic Literacy, which is often cited in popular media as revealing gaps in civics literacy among American adults, and hosts the Annual Civics and Law Academy which offers high school students an opportunity to learn from practicing lawyers as well as law student mentors.[42]

The AALS in recent years has considered how the legal profession and legal education need to forcefully engage in society's most important debates on strengthening democracy

---

[40] *See supra* notes 22–32.

[41] *See* https://www.americanbar.org/content/dam/aba/administrative/public_education/HouseResolutions.pdf.

[42] *See* https://www.americanbar.org/groups/public_education/resources/civic-literacy/.

and improving civic understanding. As then-AALS President Vicki C. Jackson described in fall 2019, "These are demands with which lawyers, law students and law professors are all familiar. We are thus well-situated (and, perhaps, professionally obligated) to play a role in enhancing a civically knowledgeable public."[43] Indeed, the AALS in its Annual Conference "themes" is clearly giving greater voice and spotlight on these issues. The themes have been titled "Building Bridges" (2019), "Pillars of Democracy: Law, Representation, and Knowledge" (2020), "The Power of Words" (2021), and, "Freedom, Equality, and the Common Good" (2022).

State bar associations are robustly engaged in supporting civics education efforts in their state and local communities. Many of the associations in the largest states have committees and standalone and multi-faceted programs. For example, the New York State Bar Association has had a "Law, Youth, and Citizenship" program since 1974 and has a Committee on Law, Youth, and Citizenship.[44] The Florida Bar has a program named "Benchmarks," a series of civic education presentations that attorneys can use then they speak to civic and community groups.[45] Lawyers can even receive CLE credit for delivering these presentations in their communities. The Florida Bar also established a standalone website to educate its citizens regarding the laws applicable to various aspects of adulthood (e.g., driving, health and wellness, housing and transactional law, citizenship, etc.), and is targeted towards young people as they become legal adults at 18 years of age.[46] The California Lawyers Association established a Committee on Access to Justice and Civic Education in 2019, and has created a Civics Engagement and Outreach Initiative, with social media campaigns.[47] And, the Illinois State Bar Association has a wide

---

[43] Vicki C. Jackson, *Law Schools and Civic Education*, AALS NEWS, 2019, available at: https://www.aals.org/about/publications/newsletters/aals-news-fall-2019/law-schools-and-civic-education/.

[44] *Law, Youth, and Citizenship*, NEW YORK STATE BAR ASSOCIATION, available at https://nysba.org/public-resources/law-youth-and-citizenship/.

[45] *Legal/Civics Education*, THE FLORIDA BAR, available at https://www.floridabar.org/public/faircts/.

[46] *Legal Survival Guide: Florida Laws You Should Know*, THE FLORIDA BAR, available at https://www.legalsurvivalguide.org/.

[47] "Civic Engagement and Outreach Initiative," California Lawyers Association, available at https://calawyers.org/initiatives/civics-engagement-and-outreach/.

array of civics resources, especially targeted at educators for K–12 students, such as lesson plans and providing lawyers to speak in classrooms.[48]

Law schools continue to occupy a unique place in educating the external communities they serve, from clients to practicing lawyers, to the general citizenry. Law professors and students at many schools have long taught civics to their surrounding communities through Street Law programs.[49] Many of these programs today are part of law school clinical and experiential learning curricula and are designed to reach local school children and teens, and other vulnerable populations. However, despite the attention paid by bar associations and law schools to promote civics education to external populations, there is little evidence to suggest that law schools have a firm grasp of the foundational civics readiness of their incoming law students and what might be needed to counteract the likely effects of civic anemia on them. Until law schools commit to ensuring their students have an appropriate baseline of civics knowledge, they cannot be assured students can navigate law school confidently, identify and dismantle disinformation, and ultimately develop the mastery of civics needed to practice law effectively as stewards of democracy in the 21st century. Statistics on civics education in the states, demographic and cultural indicators previously discussed, as well as anecdotal perspectives from law school deans, faculty members, and law students clearly suggest that many entering law students could benefit from meaningful civics reinforcements at the beginning of their law school journeys, with anticipated broader instruction as they progress.[50]

The COVID-19 pandemic, the intense political upheaval including an insurrection, campaigns of disinformation, and America's long-in-coming racial reckoning, have necessarily caused many law schools to begin revisiting their strategic

---

[48] *Civics Education,* ILLINOIS STATE BAR ASSOCIATION, available at https://www.isba.org/teachers.

[49] *See, e.g.,* Mark C. Alexander, *Law-Related Education: Hope for Today's Students,* 20 OHIO N.U. L. REV. 57 (1993), pp. 57–98.

[50] *See supra,* notes 6, 7, and 36. Also, in spring 2021, the author conducted outreach to decanal and law faculty colleagues, public school teachers, as well as law students, about the topic of civic anemia and civics education.

plans, curricula, and programs. With goals to provide more history, relevance, depth, insight, and skills development for their students, these efforts will better support and prepare students for the study and practice of law in contemporary America. Ensuring foundational civics for first-year law students should be among law schools' key priorities. Further, the ABA should encourage, and law schools should consider adopting, "mastery of civics" as a student competency in their overall programs of legal education. And it should be connected, at least in part, to other competencies related to diversity, equity, and inclusion, as well as professionalism and honoring the ethical obligations of lawyers, and, exercising leadership.

While every law school curriculum provides an array of courses where democratic institutions, principles, processes, and values are discussed in depth, not every school offers those courses to students in their first semester or first year. Those courses include Constitutional Law, Legislation and Regulation, Administrative Law, and State and Local Government Law to name a few. Law schools would be well served to assess opportunities to offer an intensive "civics booster" at new student orientation, or through special required programs in the first semester or first year within or without the formal curriculum. These opportunities would provide a concise review of foundational civics, both updating and drawing on the previous knowledge and skills developed by the students in earlier parts of their educations. It would also signal to students the issues to which they should pay close attention both in the classroom and long-term in their daily lives as they develop professionally as stewards of democracy, and personally as citizens of the nation and the world.

Most law schools would likely find it advantageous to develop their own civics booster programming to align with their particular curricula and programs, and their focus areas and institutional cultures. Some law schools, however, such as a group in a specific state, could develop a common program in collaboration with their state bar associations. Some might even consider the opportunity to develop a common program nationally in collaboration with the ABA or AALS. Programs could be delivered live in-person or synchronously, or recorded and delivered asynchronously to students to watch on their own time.

Subject matter should include the following elements. Meaningful coverage of all of them might be difficult in an introductory program, but such coverage should be an aspiration of a complete program of legal education that seeks student competency in civics. They are:

- Comparative Forms of Government.
- Founding principles and the Declaration of Independence.
- Fundamentals of the Rule of Law in a Participatory Democracy.
- U.S. Constitution and Bill of Rights.
- Separation of Powers and the Structure and Function of Government: Legislative, Executive, Judicial.
- Federalism and the Role of State and Local Governments and State Constitutions.
- Political Participation and the Responsibilities of Citizens: Representation, Elections, and Voting.
- History and Role of Race and Racism in Shaping American Law and Policy.
- History and Role of Religion in Shaping American Law and Policy.
- Capitalism and the Principles of the American and Global Economies.
- America in a Global Context: Principles of Foreign Relations, National Security, and Immigration.
- Principles of Domestic Policy, Social Welfare, and Justice.
- Information Literacy: Freedom of the Press, Freedom of Speech, and Understanding the Role and Influence of the Press and Social Media in Shaping Public Perception. And,

- Principles of Civility and Engaging in Productive Discourse.

In addition to a civics booster, law schools should assess their first-year curricula to identify opportunities where foundational civics competency can be developed. Obviously, some first-year courses will lend themselves to this end better than others, but most courses will offer at least some opportunity for reinforcement. Schools may also consider whether resequencing certain courses like Legislation and Regulation to the first semester or first year, or offering them in a shorter intensive format, could provide appropriate foundational reinforcement for entering students.

As students progress, mastery of civics competency could be developed through more in-depth or advanced coursework, with the previously suggested subject matter, much of which is already covered in required courses or existing electives. Accordingly, similar curricular assessment of upper-level courses should be undertaken to determine whether credit hours dedicated to courses such as Constitutional Law might need expansion to provide broader content coverage. Further, the growing institutional imperatives for coursework and programming in the areas of anti-racism, and diversity, equity, and inclusion, present important and unique opportunities to reinforce democratic principles and processes at the many points where issues of race and equity arise in the law school curriculum. Such efforts can provide students with new pathways and contexts to learn about, and reflect on, the evolution of the law and legal practice in the context of racism, race, and inequality, and to examine the origins and approaches to dismantling structural injustices affecting our country.

As part of the law school's upper-level curricular review, clinical programs should assess whether they can, where appropriate, integrate select elements of civics education into the provision of community based legal services. Opportunities for students to teach the fundamentals of civics in all types of settings, including through "one shot" videos or interactions using web-based technologies, should be evaluated.

Law schools also provide important continuing legal education to lawyers and serve as a hub for community civic discourse on weighty matters. The insurrection has served as a critical reminder of the importance of lawyer accountability and ethics, and continuing legal education is essential to promoting both. Law school CLE offices should consider offering ethics and professionalism, diversity and inclusion, skills and other CLE programming that also can serve as *continuing civics education* for members of the bar. As the ABA and state bar associations promote better civics education for lawyers, and seek their engagement in delivering civics education in their communities, law school partnerships through civics based CLEs, and in community program delivery, will enhance the overall effectiveness of the profession.

Finally, law faculties and law students may be uniquely situated to lend their knowledge and expertise to advocate for civics education reform and increased curricular investment. Since the insurrection there has been considerable debate and division about how to fix and fund American civics education. American legal education can work with policymakers to advocate for and shape reforms. Law faculties can work across different levels of education to help colleagues develop and implement public school and college programs and study their long-term effectiveness including among entering law students in future classes. Although, historically, civics education curricula has been the domain of historians and political scientists, law professors must be involved in these activities. What is at stake suggests that legal education must step up and take a more central role in the cure for civic anemia.

C. CONCLUSION

Indeed, civic anemia has been a difficult challenge for our nation for decades. But, in the wake of the insurrection at the Capitol on January 6, 2021, it has become a profound threat to our democracy. While many institutions, experts, and policymakers have made diagnoses of the causes, and proposed solutions, legal education itself can and must take greater responsibility. Implementing curricular and programmatic changes to address deficits in foundational civics knowledge early on in our students' education will vastly improve their understanding of their roles as lawyers and stewards of democracy, and in turn, help further their impact once they return to their communities as new lawyers. By seriously reexamining our roles, all societal institutions together can substantially improve the health of our body politic and reverse the pernicious and corrosive effects that have accelerated civic anemia and helped create our current crisis of democracy.

CHAPTER 13

ELECTION LAW, DEMOCRACY, AND LEGAL EDUCATION

Daniel P. Tokaji[1]

The events of January 6, 2021 exposed the deterioration of American democracy like nothing before. It was not simply the insurrection aimed at stopping the sacred process through which the nation's chief executive is selected, but the actions leading up to and following it that have raised serious questions about democracy's future. Even as the sights and sounds of that day recede in our memory, the cancer within our republic continues to metastasize.

The first step to recovery is admitting you have a problem. So before considering what law schools can do to improve American democracy, its maladies must first be examined and diagnosed. For years, starting long before Donald Trump first ran for President, the symptoms of decay have become more and more visible. Our country is deeply divided along partisan lines. The problem is not the existence of divergent beliefs about everything from race and policing to guns and abortion. Impassioned disagreement is endemic to a free society, something to be celebrated rather than condemned. No, the problem is that Americans do not see themselves bound together by a set of common values like liberty, equality, and democracy, but rather as mortal enemies. Democrats and Republicans view the opposing camp with mutual disdain or even contempt, a phenomenon political scientists call "affective polarization."[2] Racial resentment, always an undercurrent of our politics, increasingly fuels partisan polarization. We have abundant evidence that President Trump won in 2016 by appealing to white voters' feelings of fear and insecurity, making race an even

---

[1] Fred W. & Vi Miller Dean and Professor of Law, University of Wisconsin Law School.

[2] *See infra* notes 55–61 and accompanying text.

more central component of our politics.[3] So much for the fantasy of a post-racial society. And no wonder that the losers of our quadrennial presidential elections see defeat as Armageddon.

Yet there are hopeful signs too. Dispiriting as President Trump's attacks on the integrity of our elections were, the system held up remarkably well to the unprecedented challenges it faced, much better than breathless commentators on the right and the left would have us believe. The public servants who have labored in the trenches of my primary field of election law for the past two decades deserve a pat on the back. The 2020 election represents a triumph of the reforms that have been adopted in the two decades since the contested Bush versus Gore presidential election, which gave rise to the Supreme Court decision of that name. Despite a global pandemic and worries about vote suppression, turnout was astonishingly high. Election officials demonstrated an admirable professionalism amid a sea-change in how people exercise their fundamental right to vote, and the courts (with some notable exceptions) generally performed their job of ensuring that elections conform to rules prescribed in advance of voting.

While the 2020 election showcased laudable improvements in the United States's electoral infrastructure, it also exposed the deterioration of our democracy. These two things may seem incongruous, but they aren't. As well as the election system performed this cycle, the people who run elections are under greater stress than ever. They now face not only the strain of running elections in a hyperpolarized environment, but also threats to their personal safety that are causing some to quit. And though it didn't happen in 2020, there is an increased risk of elected officials—a Governor, a Secretary of State, a state legislature, or even Congress—overturning the expressed preferences of the polity. As many times as Trump repeated The Big Lie that the election was stolen from him, he didn't persuade these officials to reject the will of the people. We may not be so fortunate next time. Looking deeper, the fact that most Republicans believe that the election was rigged bespeaks an abandonment of the methods for discerning truth upon which a

---

3 *See infra* notes 62–67 and accompanying text.

well-functioning democracy depends.[4] The concoction of misinformation, hyperpolarization, racism, and violence that exploded on January 6 should be a call to action for those concerned about the future of American democracy.

Election law reforms can address some worst-case scenarios, but they cannot solve the deeper problems in our democracy. This chapter argues that legal education can be an antidote. Three attributes of the American legal method are especially salient, all of which go to the heart of the truth-finding aspirations of our profession. The first is a commitment to airing opposing perspectives. A hallmark of our legal system is that it allows disputants to present their evidence, make their arguments, and have their day in court. This willingness to hear divergent perspectives is essential to a well-functioning political discourse. The second characteristic of the legal method is its insistence that factual claims be backed up with evidence. Lawyers can't just make stuff up and hope to win. Rudy Giuliani and his co-counsel found that out the hard way during their ill-fated attempts to reverse the 2020 election results, when even conservative jurists laughed them out of court.[5] Third and finally, the legal method depends upon faithful adherence to laws and legal precedents. We as lawyers often disagree on how the law—especially our highest law, the U.S. Constitution—should be interpreted. But whatever our politics, we as lawyers share a fidelity to certain interpretive norms and guiding principles, which courts mostly adhered to in their 2020 election decisions.

U.S. law schools should not settle for teaching the legal method to our existing students. We should strive to democratize legal education by actively seeking a wider audience for it. Although the law's complexity may intimidate outsiders, not to mention first-year law students, there is nothing about the legal method that should be so mysterious. Expanding our teaching of the legal method would go a long way toward undoing the damage that American democracy has suffered in recent years

---

4 *See* Daniel P. Tokaji, *Truth, Democracy, and the Limits of Law*, 64 ST. L. U. L.J. 569 (2020).

5 *See infra* notes 30–35 and accompanying text.

and in building a reverence for the rule of law and a more constructive democratic discourse for future generations.

This chapter begins with my primary field of election law, documenting that the system held up well to the enormous stresses 2020 presented, while also showing systemic vulnerabilities. It proceeds to disentangle the intertwined strands of misinformation, hyperpolarization, racism, and violence that came together on January 6. Finally, I consider the role that law schools should play in reversing the deterioration of American democracy, arguing that teaching the legal method can help address the disdain for truth that lies at the root of these problems.

A. THE TRIUMPH OF ELECTION REFORM

Let's start with the good news: the U.S. conducted an incredibly successful election, marked by high voter turnout and skilled election administration, under exceptionally difficult circumstances. The 2020 election was the culmination of twenty years of professionalizing election management. While debates over vote suppression and electoral fraud have gotten much of the attention, the hard work of election administrators was largely overlooked—particularly after Trump's Big Lie and the reaction it caused. That's unfortunate, given what an extraordinary job election officials did in 2020.

Conducting a successful election amid the unprecedented turnout was no small miracle.[6] Millions of people who have previously voted in person chose to vote absentee instead. And by and large, election officials showed exceptional adaptability in response. More impressive is that they did their jobs under a microscope, in an unforgiving environment filled with partisans ready to pounce on any mistake as evidence of fraud or manipulation.[7]

There were good reasons to worry about how well the election system would function in 2020, especially after a primary season that coincided with the emergence of the COVID-19 pandemic. In Ohio, the state's public-health director

---

6 *See* Nathaniel Persily & Charles Stewart III, *The Miracle and Tragedy of the 2020 Election*, 32 J. DEMOCRACY 159 (2021).

7 *Id.* at 170–75.

ordered polling places closed right before they were to open, leading the state to pivot rapidly to an almost-all-mail election conducted.[8] Things were even more chaotic in Wisconsin, where 1) the Governor issued an executive order suspending in-person voting, 2) the state supreme court blocked that order, and 3) the U.S. Supreme Court stayed a federal-court injunction allowing ballots to be returned after election day—all the day before the election.[9] These late-breaking events compelled Wisconsinites to choose between risking their health by coming to the polls and giving up their right to vote.[10] People of color were disproportionately affected, with their turnout around 20 points less than that of white voters.[11]

Despite these snafus, the system generally held up well to the challenges that the pandemic posed in 2020. The last-minute changes in the Ohio and Wisconsin primaries sent a warning to other states, which shifted to mostly-mail voting for the remainder of the primary season.[12] This proved to be excellent preparation for the general election, which saw a dramatic shift away from in-person voting on election day and toward absentee voting. Most states—a total of 29 in all, plus D.C.—adopted changes to their laws aimed at making voting easier.[13] At least 34 states had no-excuse absentee voting in 2020, meaning that people could avoid the polls on election day without having to provide a reason why they needed to do so.[14] The results were a dramatic shift in how Americans voted. According to one survey, the percentage of people voting by mail more than doubled (going

---

[8] *Id.* at 160.

[9] Republican National Committee v. Democratic National Committee, 140 S. Ct. 1205 (2020); Amy Gardner, Elise Viebeck & Dan Simmons, *Wisconsin Supreme Court Blocks Order by Governor to Stop Tuesday's Election in State's Latest Whipsaw*, WASH. POST (Apr. 7, 2020), https://www.washingtonpost.com/politics/wisconsin-governor-suspends-in-person-voting-in-tuesdays-elections-amid-escalating-coronavirus-fears/2020/04/06/9d658e2a-781c-11ea-b6ff-597f170df8f8_story.html.

[10] *Wisconsin Primary Recap: Voters Forced to Choose Between Their Health and Their Civic Duty*, N.Y. TIMES (Apr. 7, 2020), https://www.nytimes.com/2020/04/07/us/politics/wisconsin-primary-election.html.

[11] Persily & Stewart, *supra* note 6, at 161.

[12] *Id.*

[13] *Id.* at 163.

[14] National Conference of State Legislators, *Voting Outside the Polling Place Report*, Table 1: States with No-Excuse Absentee Voting (May 1, 2020), https://www.ncsl.org/research/elections-and-campaigns/vopp-table-1-states-with-no-excuse-absentee-voting.aspx.

from 21% to 46%) while the percentage voting in person on election days decreased by more than half (going from 60% to 28%).[15]

Most encouraging, voter turnout reached its highest level in well over a century. Some 160 million people exercised their right to vote in 2020. That's two-thirds of all eligible citizens, the highest level since 1904.[16] The greater availability of mail ballots helped. Liberalized voter registration rules also made a difference. Before the 2020 general election, there were reasons to be concerned that—with traditional means of registration, like motor vehicle offices, closed—many would-be voters would not have the opportunity to register or update their registrations before election day.[17] A countervailing factor was the expansion of opportunities for simultaneous registration and voting in many states. The largest jumps occurred in states that were highly competitive or ones that instituted election-day registration after 2016.[18] As with every election, there were some administrative problems. The most serious was the long lines that some voters seeking to vote in person faced, which increased to levels not seen since 2008.[19]

Still, the banner headline of 2020 is—or at least should be—that more Americans successfully exercised their right to vote than ever before. The high turnout is largely attributable to the fact that this was a high-stakes, competitive election conducted against a backdrop of pressing issues of racial and social justice that generate profound disagreement. But the fact that our system managed to handle this record number of voters so well is attributable to the legislators who adjusted state election laws, the thousands of public officials and poll workers who did the thankless work of running our election system, and the millions of eligible citizens determined to exercise their

---

15 Charles Stewart III, *How We Voted in 2020: A Topical Look at the Survey of the Performance of American Elections* 6 (March 2021), http://electionlab.mit.edu/sites/default/files/2021-03/HowWeVotedIn2020-March2021.pdf.

16 Persily & Stewart, *supra* note 6, at 165.

17 Daniel Tokaji, *Voter Registration in a Pandemic*, U. CHI. L. REV. ONLINE (2020), https://lawreviewblog.uchicago.edu/2020/06/26/pandemic-tokaji/.

18 Persily & Stewart, *supra* note 6, at 165.

19 *Id.* at 169.

fundamental right to vote. That all this happened in the middle of an unprecedented global pandemic was genuinely miraculous.

All this stands in marked contrast to the contested election two decades ago, which we law professors remember even if most of our current students don't. Like the 2020 election, the 2000 election was the subject of intense public scrutiny. That's mainly because it was so close, with only a few hundred votes separating candidates George W. Bush and Al Gore in the decisive State of Florida. Bush won that election, of course, thanks partly to the decision in *Bush v. Gore*[20] that effectively ended the recount and led to Gore's concession. After the election, a raft of reports took a close look at the U.S. system of elections. That close look revealed a system with deep flaws, not only in the voting equipment that attracted so much unfavorable attention, but also in voter registration and polling place operations. A widely respected report from the Caltech/MIT Voting Technology Project found that some 4–6 million votes were lost in 2000, with voter registration rather than technology probably the most common reason.[21]

The 2000 election was also remarkable for the partisanship demonstrated by state election officials, particularly Republican Secretary of State Katherine Harris and other officials in Florida who seemed to be making decisions motivated by their political preferences. Though many other problems have been addressed over the past 20 years, the partisan attachments of election officials are a lingering problem.[22] Most state chief election officials (typically the Secretary of State) are elected as nominees of one or the other major political party. This creates an inherent conflict of interest between their duty to administer election laws impartially and their loyalty to their political party and its candidates.[23] Even when officials attempt to discharge their duties conscientiously and evenhandedly—as they usually do—there is a risk that the perception of partisan manipulation will

[20] 531 U.S. 98 (2000).

[21] Caltech/MIT Voting Technology Project, *What Is, What Could Be* (2001), https://vote.caltech.edu/documents/153/voting_what_is_what_could_be.pdf.

[22] *See* Daniel P. Tokaji, *Comparative Election Administration: A Legal Perspective on Electoral Institutions*, in COMPARATIVE ELECTION LAW (forthcoming 2022), https://papers.ssrn.com/sol3/papers.cfm?abstract_id=3500868.

[23] *Id.*

taint the election results. Though election officials generally resisted partisan pressure in 2020, as described below, the risks inherent in partisan election administration are more apparent than ever.

These persistent conflicts of interest shouldn't cloud the fact that we've seen great improvements in election administration over the past twenty years. The contrasting behavior of state election officials in 2020, compared with 2000, is particularly noteworthy. Republican-affiliated election officials, in particular, faced intense pressure from President Trump and his allies to accept their unwarranted assertions of fraud and reverse the result. The most conspicuous example was Georgia Secretary of State Brad Raffensperger, whom the President called asking that he "find 11,780 votes" that would allow him to reverse the declared result and take the state.[24] To his credit, Secretary of State Raffensperger did not buckle, though he has since faced a backlash in the form of a censure from the Georgia Republican Party and he may lose his bid for reelection as a result[25]—a harbinger of bigger problems addressed in the next section. Yet despite the inherent conflict of interest that elected election officials face, the vast majority of them performed admirably under the intense pressure of conducting an election under hyperpolarized political conditions in the midst of a global pandemic.

The courts likewise did an exemplary job of handling the many election cases that came their way in 2020. While there are always a large number of cases in a presidential election year, 2020 was extraordinary even by that yardstick. The Stanford/MIT Healthy Elections Project counted over 500 cases and appeals in 46 states and D.C., many of them arising from the new legal issues that the pandemic raised.[26] This gives the

---

[24] Amy Gardner, *'I Just Want to Find 11,780 Votes': In Extraordinary Hour-Long Call, Trump Pressures Georgia Secretary of State to Recalculate the Vote in His Favor*, WASH. POST (Jan. 3, 2021), https://www.washingtonpost.com/politics/trump-raffensperger-call-georgia-vote/2021/01/03/d45acb92-4dc4-11eb-bda4-615aaefd0555_story.html.

[25] Russell Berman, *Trump's Revenge Begins in Georgia*, THE ATLANTIC (July 12, 2021), https://www.theatlantic.com/politics/archive/2021/07/trumps-revenge-brad-raffensperger-georgia/619407/.

[26] Stanford-MIT Healthy Elections Project, *COVID-Related Election Litigation Tracker*, https://healthyelections-case-tracker.stanford.edu/search.

2020 election the distinction of being "the most litigious in modern history."[27] While some people might view the quantity of litigation as a bad thing, the reality is that courts have an especially important role to play when conflicts arise under dynamic conditions. Some of the 2020 cases were brought by Democrats and their allies, generally seeking relief in the weeks and months leading up to the election that would make it easier to vote.[28] Others were brought by Republicans and their allies, challenging the liberalization of voting rules and ultimately the results of the election in some states.[29]

The conduct of Republican-appointed or affiliated judges, who overwhelmingly resisted the President's repeated attacks on the integrity of elections, bears honorable mention. The Trump Campaign and its allies brought a raft of cases after election day, seeking to challenge or cast doubt on the results—and by implication on the integrity of the electoral system. Those cases did not fare well. Out of 73 post-election lawsuits brought by pro-Trump plaintiffs, only two minor ones were successful: one to extend polling hours in some Nevada precincts and other to limit the period in which Pennsylvania voters could provide proof of identification.[30] The bigger and more prominent cases that the Trump campaign and its allies brought, alleging widespread irregularities that tainted the result in key swing states that Biden one, uniformly met with ignominious rejection. That included the so-called "Kraken" cases, the term used by Trump supporter Sidney Powell drawing on a mythical many-tentacled sea creature to which she compared lawsuits in Michigan, Wisconsin, Georgia, and Arizona.[31]

Pennsylvania was the biggest target of Trump's attacks, with his campaign or its allies bringing seven cases on or after election day.[32] In one of those cases, *Donald J. Trump for*

---

[27] Jacob Kovacs-Goodman, *Post-Election Litigation Analysis and Summaries*, STANFORD-MIT HEALTHY ELECTIONS PROJECT (Mar. 10, 2021), https://healthyelections.org/sites/default/files/2021-04/Post-Election_Litigation_Analysis.pdf.

[28] DANIEL HAYS LOWENSTEIN, RICHARD L. HASEN, DANIEL P. TOKAJI & NICHOLAS STEPHANOPOULOS, ELECTION LAW CASES AND MATERIALS: 2021 SUPPLEMENT 55–56 (2021).

[29] *Id.* at 56.

[30] Kovacs-Goodman, *supra* note 27, at 3.

[31] *Id.* at 6.

[32] *Id.* at 4.

President v. Secretary Commonwealth of Pennsylvania,[33] the campaign sued Pennsylvania's chief election official and county boards of election, seeking to invalidate millions of votes cast in 2020 based on vague and tenuous claims of procedural irregularities. In an opinion authored by Judge Stephanos Bibas (a Trump appointee) and joined by two judges appointed by President George W. Bush, the Third Circuit affirmed the district court's decision not to let the Trump campaign amend its complaint and declined to issue an injunction undoing the certified vote in Pennsylvania. As Judge Bibas explained at the start of the court's opinion:

> Free, fair elections are the lifeblood of our democracy. Charges of unfairness are serious. But calling an election unfair does not make it so. Charges require specific allegations and then proof. We have neither here.[34]

The U.S. Supreme Court likewise resisted the Trump campaign's attempt to subvert the election result. In separate litigation arising in state court, the U.S. Supreme Court declined to reverse a Pennsylvania Supreme Court decision allowing absentee and mail-in ballots received after election day to be counted, over the dissents of Justices Alito and Thomas (joined by Gorsuch).[35] The Supreme Court later rejected for lack of standing—this time unanimously—a case brought by the State of Texas, seeking to invalidate the election result in Pennsylvania and three others states the Biden won.[36]

That said, the Court's handling of 2020 election cases deserves some criticism. Especially problematic is the Court's hardening of the *Purcell v. Gonzalez*[37] doctrine, which has devolved into a virtual prohibition against lower federal courts issuing injunctions to protect the right to vote close to an election.[38] This has the unfortunate effect of making it more

---

33 830 Fed. Appx. 377 (3d Cir. 2020).

34 *Id.* at 381.

35 Republican Party of Pennsylvania v. DeGraffenreid, 141 S. Ct. 732 (2021).

36 Texas v. Pennsylvania, 141 S. Ct. 1230 (2020).

37 549 U.S. 1 (2006) (per curiam).

38 *See* Democratic National Committee v. Wisconsin State Legislature, 141 S. Ct. 28 (2020) (affirming stay of district court injunction based on perceived risk of

difficult to protect voting rights through pre-election litigation, thus channeling conflicts toward post-election litigation where the stakes are higher and the risks to electoral integrity greater. Still, the Court did the right thing when it mattered most, rejecting the Trump campaign's spurious attempt to overturn the results.

In sum, we witnessed the triumph of election reform in 2020, the culmination of two decades of efforts to improve the infrastructure of American elections. Election officials did an incredibly effective job in handling the many disruptive changes that the pandemic threw into their laps, and in conducting a successful election in which turnout increased to its highest level in well over a century. Those officials not only managed the massive shift from in-person to mostly-mail voting, but also withstood a barrage of pressures and threats aimed at undermining their integrity. The courts did their jobs promptly and skillfully, rejecting Trump and his allies' attempts to subvert the election result. While the U.S. Supreme Court has made things more difficult through its repeated reversals of injunctions protecting the right to vote, it too stood up to the Trump campaign's scorched earth litigation tactics.

This is very good news for our election system. But for our democracy? Not so much. For all the improvements in the administration of American elections over the past two decades, the condition of American democracy is more perilous than ever. The events following the election, including but not limited to the January 6 insurrection, leave no doubt of that.

B. THREATS TO DEMOCRACY

Elections are to democracy what sex is to marriage. It's hard for the latter to thrive without the former. But well-run elections aren't enough to make a democracy strong, any more than sex alone makes for a strong marriage. These are perilous times for democracy, in the U.S. and around the world. The reasons for this are complex but, as in marriage, dishonesty is deadly.

The paradox of 2020 is that, despite an extraordinarily well-run election, the vulnerabilities of our democracy became more

disruption). For criticism of the Court's reliance on *Purcell, see* Wilfred U. Codrington III, Purcell *in Pandemic*, 96 NYU L. REV. 941 (2021).

glaring than ever. President Trump's propagation of The Big Lie didn't persuade the courts or change the election result, but he did manage to convince most of his supporters. According to a poll conducted in May 2021, 56% of Republicans believe that the election was rigged or the result of illegal voting, while 53% believe that Trump is the "true President."[39]

One response to this lack of confidence in the election system is to consider ways in which election laws and institutions can be improved. Although that would help, there are much deeper problems. Trump's success in propagating The Big Lie demonstrates a disdain for truth—more precisely, for the established methods of discerning truth. The flight from truth is poisonous to democracy, especially when combined with the hyperpolarization, racial resentment, and violence that came to a head on January 6.

To untangle this web, let's return to election law. Since the 2020 general election, scholars in the field have focused on the risk of election subversion—the possibility that election officials or elected officials might reject the will of the people, expressed through their votes, and overturn an election result. That's exactly what Trump tried to do through his pressure on Georgia's Secretary of State, as well as state legislators who he hoped might enact legislation to overturn the result in Pennsylvania and other states.[40] Trump and his allies even tried to assemble a group of "alternative electors," whose vote totals might be sent to Washington, D.C. and be counted on January 6, the day of the electoral count.[41] When all that failed, Trump gave a provocative speech to his supporters that began just before noon that day, claiming that the election had been "rigged" and urging his supporters to "fight like hell" and "walk down

---

[39] Ipsos/Reuters, *The Big Lie: Over Half of Republicans Believe Donald Trump Is the Actual President of the United States* 1, 2, 6 (May 21, 2021), https://www.ipsos.com/sites/default/files/ct/news/documents/2021-05/Ipsos%20Reuters%20Topline%20Write%20up-%20The%20Big%20Lie%20-%2017%20May%20thru%2019%20May%202021.pdf.

[40] Kyle Cheney, *Trump Calls on GOP State Legislatures to Overturn Election Results*, POLITICO (Nov. 21, 2020), https://www.politico.com/news/2020/11/21/trump-state-legislatures-overturn-election-results-439031.

[41] Nicholas Riccardi, *Why Trump's Latest Electoral College Ploy Is Doomed to Fail*, AP (Dec. 14, 2020), https://apnews.com/article/election-2020-joe-biden-donald-trump-elections-electoral-college-ab4452c5e54dc55b5e45bbe737ae66ee.

Pennsylvania Avenue . . . to the Capitol."[42] That led to a mob of Trump supporters breaching, occupying, and looting the Capitol, assaulting police officers and reporters along their way. After the Capitol was cleared and Congress reassembled, Senate Majority Leader Mitch McConnell called this series of events a "failed insurrection."[43] Early the next morning, Congress finally finished counting the electoral votes and certified Joe Biden and Kamala Harris as the new President and Vice President.

Although Trump's strenuous efforts to subvert the 2020 election failed, they revealed some vulnerabilities, particularly in presidential elections.[44] There are multiple ways in which a losing candidate might try to overturn the will of the people:

- Persuading state or local election officials to alter the official vote tally prior to certification.
- Persuading state court judges, most of whom are subject to elections and many of whom are chosen through partisan elections, to change the result.
- Persuading the state legislature to enact legislation overriding the result declaring the losing candidate the winner.
- Persuading a state's chief election official—typically a Secretary of State, elected on a partisan basis—to certify the losing candidate as the winner.
- Persuading a state's Governor to send a false Certificate of Ascertainment, one that identifies the losing candidates' electors as the ones that should be counted in Congress.
- Persuading Congress to reject some of the electoral votes presented and instead to use its counting authority to declare that the loser won.

---

[42] THE WALL STREET JOURNAL, *Trump's Full Speech at D.C. Rally on Jan. 6*, at 70:45 (Feb. 7, 2021), https://www.wsj.com/video/trump-full-speech-at-dc-rally-on-jan-6/E4E7BBBF-23B1-4401-ADCE-7D4432D07030.html.

[43] Matthew Choi, *'They Failed': McConnell Condemns Rioters Who Stormed the Capitol*, POLITICO (Jan. 6, 2021), https://www.politico.com/news/2021/01/06/mcconnell-condemns-rioters-in-congress-as-failed-insurrection-455660.

[44] For an overview of the electoral count process, *see* Congressional Research Service, *Counting Electoral Votes: An Overview of Procedures at the Joint Session, Including Objections by Members of Congress* (Dec. 8, 2020).

- Persuading the Vice President, in his role as Senate president, to intervene in the electoral count.
- Persuading the U.S. Supreme Court to intervene at some point in this process, to overturn the electoral result.

Each of these topics warrants a law review article of its own, and many will no doubt be written in the months and years to come. An especially important question is how state and local election officials can be insulated from partisan pressure so that they can execute their duties impartially. The U.S. remains an outlier among democratic countries, in the extent to which the people running our elections are affiliated with one major party or the other—the most common model is for the state's chief election officials to be elected to office as the nominee of a political party.[45] The conflicts of interest to which state and local election officials are subject makes it very difficult for them to do their job of running elections without favoritism toward the party with which they're affiliated. Impartial election administration should be a top priority of election reformers.[46]

The threats to the impartiality of election officials have only grown since the 2020 election concluded. Republicans in Arizona and other states have pursued "audits" of state election systems. Although Arizona's process did not meet the standards of a fair and genuine audit (including transparency, objectivity, competence, and security), it still found no proof of systemic fraud.[47] Trump loyalists in other states have nevertheless contemplated their own inquiries, to the chagrin of the Republican political establishment. Former Congressman Charlie Dent, for example, calls the possibility of conducting an

---

[45] National Conference of State Legislatures, *Election Administration at State and Local Levels* (Feb. 3, 2020), https://www.ncsl.org/research/elections-and-campaigns/election-administration-at-state-and-local-levels.aspx.

[46] Daniel P. Tokaji, *The Future of Election Reform: From Rules to Institutions*, 28 YALE L. & POL'Y REV. 125, 126–27 (2009). *See also* Tokaji, *supra* note 22 (arguing that the functional impartiality of election administrators is more important than their formal independence).

[47] Michael Waldman, *Phony Audits=Real Threats to the Vote,* BRENNAN CENTER FOR JUSTICE (July 13, 2021), https://www.brennancenter.org/our-work/analysis-opinion/phony-audits-real-threats-vote; Bob Christie & Christina A. Cassidy, *GOP Review Finds No Proof Arizona Election Stolen from Trump,* AP (Sept. 24, 2021), https://apnews.com/article/donald-trump-elections-arizona-phoenix-conspiracy-theories-d38321441bcd6cea58421f6871b4f74e.

Arizona-style audit in Pennsylvania "a blunder of epic proportions" and asks: "Why bring the Arizona clown show to Pennsylvania?"[48] Still, many Republican election officials and candidates have joined the chorus of calls for phony audits, which are becoming a test of loyalty to the former President and a pledge of allegiance to his false claim that the 2020 election was stolen.

Attacks on the impartiality of election administrators don't stop there. We're also seeing efforts to strip state and local election officials of their authority, giving it instead to Republican-controlled state legislatures. A recent report found 216 bills in 41 states to give state legislatures more power over election officials, 24 of which have already been enacted into law.[49] Many election officials have received threats of physical violence as well. Some have retired or quit, possibly to be replaced by Trump loyalists who embrace The Big Lie.[50] Those who remain will face ever-growing pressure to bow to partisan interests rather than doing their jobs of running election impartially.[51]

When one looks deeper, the threats to constitutional democracy become even more frightening. Aziz Huq and Tom Ginsburg have identified three essential attributes of a well-functioning constitutional democracy: competitive elections, free speech and association, and the rule of law.[52] All three are at risk. Election subversion is a much greater danger than we thought before 2020, with multiple ways in which a losing presidential candidate can seek to undo the result. Freedom of

---

[48] Marc Levy, *Pennsylvania Election Audit Gets GOP Campaign Trail Embrace*, AP (July 18, 2021), https://apnews.com/article/government-and-politics-elections-pennsylvania-campaigns-senate-elections-ce34efb5201d89392653002fafd49cf3. *See also* Miles Park, *Experts Call It A 'Clown Show' But Arizona 'Audit' Is A Disinformation Blueprint*, NPR (June 3, 2021), https://www.npr.org/2021/06/03/1000954549/experts-call-it-a-clown-show-but-arizona-audit-is-a-disinformation-blueprint.

[49] Nick Corasaniti & Reid J. Epstein, *How Republican States Are Expanding Their Power Over Elections*, N.Y. TIMES (June 19, 2021), https://www.nytimes.com/2021/06/19/us/politics/republican-states.html.

[50] Michael Wines, *After a Nightmare Year, Election Officials Are Quitting*, N.Y. TIMES (July 2, 2021), https://www.nytimes.com/news-event/2020-election.

[51] *Election Officials Under Attack*, BRENNAN CENTER FOR JUSTICE (June 16, 2021), https://www.brennancenter.org/our-work/policy-solutions/election-officials-under-attack.

[52] Aziz Huq & Tom Ginsburg, *How to Lose a Constitutional Democracy*, 65 UCLA L. REV. 78, 80 (2018).

expression is under pressure from both the left and the right.[53] And though the rule of law held up well to the challenges that it faced in 2020, it too is under greater strain than ever. Particularly problematic was the effort of Trump and his allies to persuade election officials, legislators, and judges to disregard both the law and the facts by declaring him the victor in key swing states he lost. This was an assault on the administrative and adjudicative rule of law, one that poses great dangers for future elections.

The hyperpolarization of America lies at the root of these threats to democracy.[54] The ideological divide among Republicans and Democrats in Congress is wider than at any point in the last century.[55] It's not just politicians but also the polity who have developed strong negative feelings toward those on the other side of the political spectrum.[56] Democrats and Republicans look on members of the other party with distrust and even contempt, seeing them as hypocritical, selfish, and close-minded, a phenomenon that political scientists call "affective polarization."[57] Increasingly, we Americans want nothing to do with those on the other side of the political fence—we don't want to talk with them, we don't want to socialize them, and we certainly don't want them marrying our children.[58] Part of the explanation can be found in the fact that, more than ever, our political views are essential components of our social identities.[59] The divergent viewpoints reflected in the information we consume, including through news and social media, may also be a factor. Although the empirical research on that question is mixed, there is some evidence that partisan

---

[53] Harry Bruinius, *Why Free Speech Is under Attack from Right and Left*, CHRIST. SCI. MON. (July 1, 2021). I address challenges to freedom of speech from the left *infra* notes 80–86 and accompanying text.

[54] *See* Daniel P. Tokaji, *Vote Dissociation*, 127 YALE L.J. FORUM 761, 771 & nn. 64–67 (citing sources on polarization).

[55] *See* Alan I. Abramowitz & Steven Webster, *The Rise of Negative Partisanship and the Nationalization of U.S. Elections in the 21st Century*, 41 ELECTORAL STUDIES 12 (2016).

[56] *See Id.*; *see also* Alan I. Abramowitz & Steven Webster, *Negative Partisanship: Why Americans Dislike Parties but Behave Like Rabid Partisans*, 39 POL. PSYCH. 119, 119–20 (2018).

[57] Shanto Iyegar, *The Origins and Consequences of Affective Polarization in the United States*, 22 ANN. REV. POL. SCI. 129, 130 (2019).

[58] *Id.* at 132.

[59] *Id.* at 134; *see also* EZRA KLEIN, WHY WE'RE POLARIZED (2020).

media and social networks may exacerbate affective polarization.[60] Whatever the role of divergent media in fomenting polarization, there is little doubt that that the polarization of electorate makes people more susceptible to believing misinformation spread through social media and other dubious sources.[61]

What's beyond dispute is that partisan polarization in the U.S. is closely connected with race, including not just our racial identities but also our views on race matters. Trump's appeals to racial resentment in 2016 attracted strong support among non-college-educated white voters, while causing him to lose support among those with a college degree.[62] This isn't a new development. The U.S. political system has experienced a dramatic realignment over the past several decades, with non-white voters flocking toward the Democratic Party and non-college-educated whites shifting Republican.[63] These changes are closely connected to racial attitudes. Since the 1990s, white voters have exhibited a marked increase in their level of "racial resentment," a scale based on survey questions like whether Blacks should work their way up "without special favors" or whether discrimination creates conditions that makes it difficult for them to do so.[64] The correlation between racial resentment and Republican voting has risen sharply over the years, to the point that it was *six times* stronger in 2016 than in 1988.[65] While political scientists are still exploring the relationship between race and voting in 2020, the early data suggest that—even though more people of color supported Trump than in 2016—the relationship between racial *attitudes* and candidate choice was

---

[60] Iyegar, *supra* note 57, at 134–36.

[61] *See* Michael Hameleers & Toni G.L.A. van der Meer, *Misinformation and Polarization in a High-Choice Media Environment: How Effective Are Political Fact-Checkers?*, 47 COMMUNICATION RES. 227, 228 (2020); Mathias Osmundsen, Michael Bang Peterson & Alexander Bor, *How Political Polarization Drives the Spread of Fake News*, BROOKINGS TECH STREAM (May 13, 2021).

[62] *See* Alan Abramowitz & Jennifer McCoy, *United States: Racial Resentment, Negative Partisanship, and Polarization in Trump's America*, 681 ANNALS AM. ACAD. POL & SOC. SCI. 137 (2019).

[63] Abramowitz & Webster, *supra* note 56, at 123–24.

[64] *Id.* at 125–26.

[65] *Id.* at 126; *see also* Brian F. Schaffner, Matthew MacWilliams & Tatishe Nteta, *Understanding White Polarization in the 2016 Vote for President: The Sobering Role of Racism and Sexism*, 133 POL. SCI Q. 9, 10 (2018) (finding attitudes on race and sex strongly correlated with support for Trump).

even stronger.[66] With the proliferation of white identity politics, it's no surprise that racism was so prominent on January 6.[67]

Perhaps most disconcerting is the disdain for truth. Democracy depends on our shared commitment to truth. Conversely, a contempt for truth is a hallmark of tyrants around the world.[68] As historian Timothy Snyder puts it: "To abandon facts is to abandon freedom. If nothing is true, then no one can criticize power, because there is no basis upon which to do so."[69] To be more precise, democracy depends on our agreement on certain *ways of knowing* what is true. It depends, in other words, on our commitment to widely accepted methods of distinguishing truth from falsity. Truth can't be just what the President or anyone else says it is.

The widespread belief in The Big Lie both reflects and exacerbates a weakening commitment to truth. President Trump bears considerable responsibility. Commentator Matt Yglesias has called Trump the "Bullshitter-in-Chief," because he so often seems oblivious to whether what he says is true or false.[70] This draws on philosopher Harry Frankfurt's famous distinction between lies and bullshit:[71] that lying is saying something you know to be untrue, while bullshitting is making factual claims without knowing or caring whether they are true. To borrow the terms of the Supreme Court's landmark First Amendment decision *New York Times v. Sullivan*,[72] it's the difference between saying something you know is false and making statements with reckless disregard for whether they are

---

66 Perry Bacon, Jr., *American Politics Now Has Two Big Racial Divides*, FIVETHIRTYEIGHT (May 3, 2021), https://fivethirtyeight.com/features/american-politics-now-has-two-big-racial-divides/.

67 *See* Aaron Morrison, *Racism of Rioters Takes Center Stage in Jan. 6 Hearing*, AP (July 28, 2021), https://apnews.com/article/joe-biden-government-and-politics-riots-race-and-ethnicity-capitol-siege-51e7098111e221b88e3b64d476f241c8. For a deeper exploration of the racial divide in American politics, *see* ASHLEY JARDINA, WHITE IDENTITY POLITICS (2019).

68 TIMOTHY SNYDER, ON TYRANNY: TWENTY LESSONS FROM THE TWENTIETH CENTURY (2017).

69 *Id.* at 65; *see also* STEPHEN LEVITSKY & DANIEL ZIBLATT, HOW DEMOCRACIES DIE 198–99 (2018) (shared belief in truth is essential to democracy).

70 Matthew Yglesias, *The Bullshitter-in-Chief*, VOX (May 30, 2017).

71 HARRY FRANKFURT, ON BULLSHIT 5 (2005).

72 376 U.S. 254, 279–80 (1964).

true or false.[73] It's often hard to tell whether Trump is lying or bullshitting—whether he is knowingly making false statements or simply indifferent to whether what he's saying is actually true or false. In the end, it doesn't much matter. Either way, the consequence is a diminished reverence for truth among Trump's followers. And because Trump still holds the allegiance of most Republican voters, if not party elites, the GOP is at risk of becoming not just the anti-Democratic party but the anti-democratic party.

There is method to Trump's seeming madness. Repeating things he wants people to believe, without regard for whether they're true, serves his political interests while also weakening the fidelity to truth upon which democracy depends. More precisely, it weakens our collective commitment to what Jonathan Rauch calls the "The Constitution of Knowledge."[74] This term describes the set of community norms that affirm our collective commitment to truth. Like many other learned commentators, Rauch is concerned about the disregard for truth—and the attendant increase in lies and bullshit—that we've seen in recent years.[75] His distinctive contribution is to identify a set of *methods* that define "the reality-based community."[76] That community encompasses people who are genuinely committed to truth-seeking, as opposed to those for whom "factual" claims are simply a means to other ends (e.g., Trump's Big Lie).[77]

As Rauch explains, the methods of the reality-based community include professional scholarship, journalism, government research, and law. Each of these fields has a set of norms designed to distinguish truth from falsehood.[78] People within a field often disagree on what the facts are, of course, but they share a commitment to a *process* for discovering truth.[79] These processes—including the legal method—are under more

---

[73] Tokaji, *supra* note 4, at 573.

[74] JONATHAN RAUCH, THE CONSTITUTION OF KNOWLEDGE: A DEFENSE OF TRUTH (2021).

[75] *Id.* at 5–8, 107–08, 169–73.

[76] *Id.* at 4.

[77] *Id.* at 172–73.

[78] *Id.* at 100–02.

[79] *Id.* at 116.

serious and frequent attacks than ever. And on January 6, they turned into a literal attack on the citadel of American democracy at the very moment when the electoral votes to choose our next President were being counted. Rauch's focus on the methods of truth-seeking thus dovetail nicely with Huq and Ginsburg's concern with the rule of law. Both recognize that the legal method itself is essential to the sustenance of democracy.

Disdain for truth. Hyperpolarization. Racial resentment. Political violence. Each of these developments is harmful by itself, but they combined to create an especially lethal concoction, which exploded on January 6, 2021. The problems run much deeper than our 45th President. Saving our democracy will require that we address this web of mutually reinforcing pathologies.

To this point, I've focused on the political right, and for good reason. On the national stage, that's where the construction of a fact-free reality and attendant receptivity to violence is most evident. But there are worrying signs on the left too, including the pressure toward ideological conformity evident on some college and university campuses. It is easy to exaggerate the prevalence of "cancel culture" and "wokeness" among students. But if we are to be honest, we must acknowledge a kernel of truth to the hyperbolic claims so regularly made on Fox News and other right-leaning media. Call-out campaigns and pressure to disinvite[80]—or to avoid inviting in the first place—controversial speakers have become more common. To take an extreme example, Heather MacDonald of the Manhattan Institute was effectively blocked from speaking at Claremont McKenna in 2017, by students who thought her views on policing racist.[81] Not content to merely protest and engage in counter-speech, students prevented others from entering and pounded on the glass of the ground-level lecture hall, forcing her evacuation.[82] There have even been a few scattered incidents of

[80] *Id.* at 220; FIRE, *Disinvitation Database*, https://www.thefire.org/research/disinvitation-database/#home/?view_2_sort=field_6|desc&view_2_page=1&view_2_per_page=500.

[81] GREG LUKIANOFF & JONATHAN HAIDT, THE CODDLING OF THE AMERICAN MIND: HOW GOOD INTENTIONS AND BAD IDEAS ARE SETTING UP A GENERATION FOR FAILURE 88–89 (2018).

[82] *Id.* To its credit, the University disciplined those responsible. Scott Jaschik, *5 Suspended for Blocking Speech*, INSIDE HIGHER ED (July 18, 2017), https://www.inside

violence.[83] Although such incidents are rare, the more common problem isn't so much censorship as censoriousness, which Rauch characterizes as "a combination of conformity and intimidation."[84]

The problems on the left and right are not identical, but there is an uncomfortable resemblance when it comes to their relation to truth. At both ends of the spectrum, we see a willingness to unquestioningly accept factual claims that conform to one's ideological views, while aggressively rejecting–or even trying to suppress–evidence and arguments that cut in the opposite direction. On the left, this sometimes takes the form of an expansive concept of "safety," to encompass not just physical safety and being protected from harassment and bullying, but also freedom from *ideas* claimed to threaten emotional harm.[85] These are worrisome trends, that threaten to imperil our collective commitment to truth and the health of our democracy.

The pursuit of truth is essential to our universities as well as our democracy. Truth-seeking depends in turn on viewpoint diversity, which cannot thrive in an environment of coercive conformity. At the national level, the proliferation of falsehood has been a much bigger problem on the right edge of the political spectrum. But there have been cases of misinformation campaigns, typically inflamed by social media, on the left as well.[86] To be clear, my point here isn't to suggest a moral equivalency between campus call-outs on the one hand, and the violence of January 6 on the other. There is none to be found. The point is that some worrisome social practices—antithetical to the search for truth and the functioning of democracy—have developed at both ends of the ideological spectrum. In the next section, I consider what we as lawyers and legal educators can do to counteract them.

---

highered.com/news/2017/07/18/claremont-mckenna-suspends-5-students-blocking-speech.

[83] LUKIANOFF & HAIDT, *supra* note 81, at 81–90.

[84] RAUCH, *supra* note 74, at 12; *see also* LUKIANOFF & HAIDT, *supra* note 81, at 96–97 (quoting Van Jones on the dangers of emotional safetyism).

[85] RAUCH, *supra* note 74, at 203–09.

[86] *See id.* at 211–12 (providing example of a philosopher whose unorthodox views on transracialism were mischaracterized).

C. LEGAL EDUCATION AS ANTIDOTE

I now turn to the question of what law schools can do to improve American democracy. As I have argued, an essential part of the solution is to confront the waning commitment to truth evident in contemporary political debates. Democrats and Republicans today inhabit different factual universes. Shouting matches about what we believe to be true won't accomplish anything. A better approach is to reenforce established *methods* for discerning truth from falsity. As Rauch explains, one of those key truth-seeking processes is the legal method.[87] It channels disagreement toward reasoned resolution, requiring that opposing parties have a chance to make their arguments, that factfinding be based on evidence, and that a settled body of doctrine be applied to those facts.

Law schools can help improve American democracy by broadening and strengthening our collective commitment to the legal method, which can be a formidable counterweight to the anti-democratic movement. An understanding of the legal method should not be the exclusive province of those privileged to pursue a J.D. or LL.M. degree. Legal educators should consider how we might democratize legal education, teaching the legal method to those who will never practice law but who would benefit from understanding this process and its underlying methodological commitment to truth-seeking.

But what exactly *is* the legal method? While there are many books on legal methods or "thinking like a lawyer,"[88] I'm not sure that there's consensus among lawyers or law professors on what we mean we use this term. I understand it to encompass three essential characteristics of the U.S. legal system that are entwined with its commitment to discerning truth from falsity: hearing opposing perspectives, evidence-based factfinding, and principled application of law to facts. These are well-established norms of our profession, ones that we teach law students from

---

87 RAUCH, *supra* note 74, at 102.

88 *See, e.g.,* TIMOTHY P. TERRELL, THE DIMENSIONS OF LEGAL REASONING: DEVELOPING ANALYTICAL ACUITY FROM LAW SCHOOL TO LAW PRACTICE (2016); KENNETH J. VANDERVELDE, THINKING LIKE A LAWYER: AN INTRODUCTION TO LEGAL REASONING (2d ed. 2011); FREDERICK SCHAUER, THINKING LIKE A LAWYER: A NEW INTRODUCTION TO LEGAL REASONING (2009).

the moment they step in first-year classes. Let's consider each in turn:

1. *Airing Opposing Perspectives.* A bedrock of our system of justice is the idea that lawyers for disputants should have the opportunity to present their factual claims and legal arguments to an impartial decisionmaker.[89] Of course, the adversarial process—in which advocates argue their clients' positions, often quite forcefully—fuels the popular perception that lawyers have an appetite for conflict. But the reality is that conflict and disagreement are inevitable in a free society.[90] As the 2020 election reminded us, our society is deeply polarized upon partisan and racial lines. It's unrealistic to expect that these partisan divisions will disappear anytime soon. Rather than trying to end polarization, our energies would be more productively engaged in determining how best to channel it more constructively.

The legal process provides a worthy model of how this can be done, one that's vastly preferable to what we commonly see in the political arena. Particularly in Congress, there is little room for compromise. Both sides see each legislative battle as an opportunity for their side to score points that might help in the next election.[91] The legal process functions differently, channeling disagreement toward a reasoned resolution. It gives opposing parties the opportunity to present evidence and make arguments—to have their day in court.

A hallmark of the American legal system is that courts hear evidence and arguments from both sides (or all sides in a multiparty dispute) before judgment is rendered. Underlying this basic feature of our legal process is the idea that it is essential to entertain and understand opposing perspectives before making decisions. It helps develop critical thinking skills, the ability to assess those competing arguments and arrive at a reasoned conclusion.[92] These skills are especially essential in a

---

[89] *See* Ellen E. Sward, *Values, Ideology, and the Evolution of the Adversary System*, 64 INDIANA L.J. 301, 301–02 (1989).

[90] *See* TERRELL, *supra* note 88, at 5 ("the controversies and difficulties lawyers encounter preceded them—discord and friction were already and always there").

[91] FRANCES E. LEE, INSECURE MAJORITIES (2016).

[92] For discussion of the role of legal education in developing critical thinking skills that may have democracy-enhancing effects, *see* Guido Pincione, *Critical Thinking and*

diverse society, which includes people who embody a wide range of identities, backgrounds, experiences, and perspectives.

To be clear, my claim isn't that every societal conflict should be resolved through litigation, nor that litigation inevitably produces fair results. Rather, it's that the legal process—particularly the core idea of hearing from opposing parties before a decision is made—is a salutary model, one that people who will never become lawyers would benefit from learning. At the heart of this process is the idea that the discovery of truth depends on listening to opposing perspectives and taking them seriously. Familiar as this idea is to us lawyers, we should not take its existence for granted among other would-be participants in democracy, particularly in an era where partisans on both sides are so reluctant to listen to perspectives with which they disagree.

2. *Evidence-Based Factfinding*. Another premise of the U.S. legal system is that factual allegations should be based upon evidence. The brick wall that Trump and his allies ran into, when trying to overturn the results of the 2020 election in court, is a glowing example of our judicial system's fidelity to evidence-based factfinding.

In the real world, lawyers won't get far making up facts. Our legal system instead requires that allegations be supported by evidence.[93] It has elaborate rules designed to accomplish just that, including rules of procedure that define the process for discovering information and rules of evidence that are designed to determine what information the trier of fact may consider.[94]

Legal Culture, 0 RATIONALITY, MARKETS & MORALS 373, 378, 388 (2009). Interestingly, the empirical research is mixed on whether *college* education enhances the ability to develop critical thinking skills. Christopher R. Huber & Nathan R. Kuncel, *Does College Teach Critical Thinking? A Meta-Analysis*, 86 REV. EDUC. RES. 431 (2016).

[93] *See* SCHAUER, *supra* note 88, at 206–18 (describing the factfinding process in which courts engage); HENRY M. HART, JR. & ALBERT M. SACKS, THE LEGAL PROCESS: BASIC PROBLEMS IN THE MAKING AND APPLICATION OF LAW (William N. Eskridge, Jr. & Philip P. Frickey, eds. 1994) (separating the problems "of accurately finding what happened in a case and of justly determining what should be the legal consequences of the happenings").

[94] *See, e.g.*, RICHARD D. FREER, CIVIL PROCEDURE 361 (2d ed. 2009) (discovery process allows each party to learn relevant information from the other, "promot[ing] the search for truth and . . . provid[ing] a 'reality check' for the parties"); CHRISTOPHER B. MUELLER & LAIRD C. KIRKPATRICK, EVIDENCE 2 (3d ed. 2003)("accurate factfinding" is a core purpose of the law of evidence).

Attorneys are subject to sanctions for making false or unsubstantiated factual claims.[95] When I was a first-year student, I recall my Torts professor telling us that although it's called "law school," it should really be "fact school" as well. Seeking out evidence and determining how to best present are core tasks for practicing lawyers. Four years later, when I became a civil rights litigator, I discovered how true that was. Even as an ACLU attorney, where most of our cases hinged on questions of law rather than fact, much of my time was spent on factfinding: interviewing clients, tracking down witnesses, drafting discovery requests, taking depositions, reviewing documents, and otherwise gathering evidence that we might use to support our factual allegations.

An essential characteristic of the legal method is that you can't just make stuff up. Factual claims must be based on evidence, on pain of sanctions and potential discipline.[96] This stands in marked contrast to contemporary political discourse. Some of our most successful politicians have made their careers out of making stuff up. Of course, no matter how good our rules of evidence might be, it's often hard to distinguish truth from falsity. Judges and juries acting in good faith sometimes get the facts wrong. This too is essential for our students to understand, as it should help them make them more skeptical consumers of information—less likely to blindly accept claims that conform to their ideological views, or to reject ones that cut in the opposite direction.

3. *Principled Application of Law to Facts.* A distinct practice governs the interpretation and application of laws to the facts found. Here too, judges aren't free simply to make things up. A well-established set of norms governs the process for interpreting and applying the law, including constitutions, statutes, regulations, and common law rules. Among the most important constraints is precedent,[97] embodied in the doctrine of

---

95 *See* FED. R. CIV. P. 11.

96 Alison Durkee, *Pro-Trump Attorneys Sanctioned in Colorado Over Election Lawsuit—'One Enormous Conspiracy Theory,' Judge Fumes*, FORBES (Aug. 4, 2021); *see also* Andrew M. Perlman, *The Legal Ethics of Lying about American Democracy* (Chapter 1 of this volume) (explaining the circumstances under which false statements by lawyers might be subject to discipline).

97 *See* SCHAUER, *supra* note 88, at 36–60 (explaining the role of precedent in legal reasoning).

stare decisis.[98] Lawyers and judges are generally expected to follow interpretations of the law laid down in previously published decisions. Judicial decisions interpreting written laws thus become part of the law itself. A related presumption is that laws and judicial interpretations of the law should be publicly available, so that lawyers and parties can read it and make principled argues about how it should be interpreted.[99] To us lawyers, these are basic concepts, ones that we internalize very early in our careers as law students.[100] They are so basic to how we do our work that to articulate them explicitly, as I just have, feels almost weird. We must remember, however, that the idea of following written law and relying on precedent isn't intuitively part of how everyone—including first-year law students—sees the world. This is a set of analytic tools that must be learned.

As legal educators, we should help our students see the connection between the method of factfinding and lawmaking they learn and the sustenance of our democracy. We should teach them not only that they have a responsibility as future lawyers and leaders to make our democracy work better, but also that there's a connection between the method that they learn and their fulfillment of this responsibility. For too many law students, that connection isn't clear. A recent study by sociologist Kathyrne M. Young, for example, finds that law students perceive a disconnect between what they learn in law school and the pressing issues of racial and social justice that they see in the world around them.[101] That can lead to career dissatisfaction and even depression. Professor Young explains:

> This dynamic forces students into one kind of separation between different selves: their selves as people who care about the world and their law student selves. Such a separation can hinder role integration,

---

98 JANE C. GINSBURG, LEGAL METHODS: CASES AND MATERIALS 2–3 (1996).

99 Dakota Rudesill, *Coming to Terms with Secret Law*, 7 HARV. NAT'L SEC. J. 241, 252 (2015).

100 ROBERT N. COVINGTON, ET AL., CASES AND MATERIALS FOR A COURSE ON LEGAL METHODS 5–7 (1969)(describing the basic mechanics of the case method).

101 Kathyrne M. Young, *Understanding the Social and Cognitive Problems in Law School That Create Unhealthy Lawyers*, 89 FORDHAM L. REV. 2575 (2021).

which is a crucial process for young professionals' identity development.[102]

We should help our students understand that the tools they learn to master aren't just for serving your clients and winning cases. They're essential to our collective commitment to truth, upon which the sustenance of constitutional democracy depends. We as lawyers must take responsibility for furthering justice and the rule of law. One way we do that is affirming the value of the truth-seeking norms that guide our profession. At the same time, we should also recognize the limitations of this or any other system for distinguishing truth from falsity. No system is perfect. Understanding the weaknesses of our system for finding facts and resolving disputes will help our students become better clinical thinkers—and, in the end, better advocates for justice.

While law schools can do a better job of connecting the methodological practices we teach to lawyers' responsibility to help make democracy better, we shouldn't stop there. Instead, we should consider how law school might teach the legal method to the vast majority of people who will never become lawyers.[103] Non-lawyers too should have a basic understanding of the legal system's commitment to airing opposing perspectives, evidence-based factfinding, and the reasoned application of law to fact. There's nothing about these concepts that should be particularly mysterious. Students who will never become lawyers can learn them as well, not just law students but college students. The basics of the legal method might even be taught in our public schools.[104]

I close with a story to illustrate this point. Like many parents, I spent some extra time attending to my children's learning during the pandemic. To supplement what my 12-year-old daughter was (or wasn't) learning via Zoom, I had her read a few of my favorite Supreme Court cases, such as *Brown v. Board of Education* and *Loving v. Virginia,* and then write short essays

[102] *Id.* at 2582.

[103] Carol A. Parker, *Legal Education for All (or More Than Just Lawyers)*, CHRON. HIGHER. EDUC. (Sept. 9, 2013), https://www.chronicle.com/article/legal-education-for-all-or-more-than-just-lawyers/.

[104] This might be paired with better civics education, which many commentators have suggested as a way of improving democracy. *See* Anthony Crowell, *Civic Anemia: Law Schools Should Give Boosters to Counter Its Effects* (Chapter 12 of this volume).

on them. I asked her to describe the facts of the case, who the opposing parties were, what the Court rules, and what its reasoning was. And I asked her to consider how that reasoning might apply to other situations—for example, whether the *Harper v. Virginia Board of Elections* decision declaring the poll tax unconstitutional could be applied to invalidate strict voter ID laws. In short, my daughter learned the basics of the legal method. Now, my daughter is pretty sharp for a sixth grader, but that isn't the point of this anecdote. The point is that the analytic tools we teach in law school need not be the exclusive province of those seeking a J.D. or LL.M degree. We can teach them to people who are much younger. And our democracy would benefit from more people gaining exposure to the norms of truth-finding that are integral to the legal profession.[105]

D. CONCLUSION

The January 6 insurrection, along with the events that precipitated and followed it, leave no doubt that our democracy needs saving. But it is not beyond hope. For all the attacks that Trump and his allies levelled, our election system held up remarkably well to the formidable challenges that it faced in 2020. That includes both election administrators and judges across the ideological spectrum, who courageously rebuffed attacks on their impartiality and integrity. Still, for as well as our election system withstood the pressure, American constitutional democracy is in big trouble. The toxic brew of misinformation, hyperpolarization, racism, and violence, which has been simmering for decades, boiled over with the attack on the Capitol. To address this set of problems, we must redouble our commitment to truth—and more specifically, to established methods for finding truth. Prominent among them are the legal method, particularly its norms of adversarial decision-making, evidence-based factfinding, and the principled application of law to facts. We should help our existing students understand the relationship between these commitments and their responsibility to improve our democracy. And we should

[105] It would also be helpful to conduct empirical research on whether learning the legal method enhances the capacity to distinguish truth from falsehood, and thus to have the democracy-enhancing effects I postulate.

democratize legal education, seeking new ways of teaching the legal method to the next generation of servant-leaders.

CHAPTER 14

THE ASSAULT ON AMERICAN DEMOCRACY AND A PATH FORWARD

Mark C. Alexander[1]

We are at a crucial point in our nation's history, where we are drifting. In some ways, we can see this moment as analogous to being pulled by a riptide in the ocean. This strong current moves us away from the safety of the shores of our democracy, running out to an endless, dangerous sea. Swimmers caught in the riptide may not even realize what is happening, and then suddenly the shore is far away. Swimming back becomes difficult, perhaps impossible, and the shore—our democracy—is out of reach. The swimmer may try hard, panic, and even exhaust him or herself by trying to swim against the tide, just to be caught up endlessly adrift and drowning. We are in danger of such a fate in our nation.

The Preamble to the Constitution provides:

> We the People of the United States, in Order to form a more perfect Union, establish Justice, insure domestic Tranquility, provide for the common defence, promote the general Welfare, and secure the Blessings of Liberty to ourselves and our Posterity, do ordain and establish this Constitution for the United States of America.

This established an aspirational nation, always working to become more perfect—we can never achieve utopian perfection, but we can always strive. In these dangerous and difficult times, we must rededicate ourselves to a commitment to the

---

[1] Mark C. Alexander, Arthur J. Kania Dean and Professor of Law, Villanova University Charles Widger School of Law. Sincere thanks to my co-authors for their commitment to this book and for their collegiality and dedication. I am deeply grateful for the hard work and keen insights of Research Assistants, Olivia Arasim, Juan Dawson, and Madelyn VanDorpe. I very much appreciate the many contributions of my Villanova Law faculty colleagues. Above all, I thank my family, who have instilled and reinforced in me a love of and dedication to country. The opinions here are mine.

Constitution and customs of democracy, including open and honest debate and discussion (protected by the First Amendment), and seeking common ground and universal values. In these pages, I will look at the January 6th Insurrection and related events, with an eye through these lenses. That day's events showed a failure, of systems and of individuals, and prompted a need to confront those failures and move forward toward a more perfect Union.

The events of January 6th, 2021 stained our nation's history, as insurrectionists tried to subvert the peaceful transition of power after a duly held, free and fair election. Hundreds (perhaps thousands) of individuals formed a mob that attacked the Capitol; they were gathered and encouraged by many people, including the President, Senators, and Members of Congress. Their actions were, in large part, inspired by, and in service to, The Big Lie. We must search out ways to move forward, to pursue our more perfect Union, with certain truths and commitments at the core of public discourse. Relentlessly pursuing truth on the important issues of that day will help us succeed. We must commit to a full, robust, wide-open, uninhibited debate going forward, in order to protect against such insurrection again—or any attempts to subvert and destroy our American democracy. Returning to the riptide analogy, such a process and commitment to democratic dialogue will allow us to return safely to shore.

A. THE JANUARY 6TH INSURRECTION—WHAT HAPPENED

We hear so much discussion about The Big Lie, what happened on January 6th, 2021, and what occurred before and after that fateful day. There are numerous important truths to consider. First, it is unassailably true—the numbers prove it—that Joe Biden was duly elected President, and that Donald Trump was not re-elected. Just as Donald Trump beat Hillary Clinton four years before, and just as we have done for over two centuries, the United States held an election for President, the votes were counted in the states and then in the Electoral College, and the process yielded a conclusive winner. In some sense, The Big Lie perpetrated by Donald Trump and those who attacked the Capitol on January 6th, 2021 is about disregarding that truth. But there is much more.

The country is bigger than any one person, and the Insurrection is about more than the thousands of individuals in Washington and at the Capitol on that day. In the 2020 presidential election, one major candidate won and the other lost, and that is a verifiable fact. Donald Trump's arguments to the contrary are indeed central to The Big Lie. As damaging as his lies are, they can obscure a bigger reality: the insurrectionists—and all who supported and encouraged them before January 6th, and all who embolden them going forward—pose a threat to our nation, and their words and deeds could tear down our government. The efforts of countless individuals have been dedicated to disregarding and destroying the rules, the facts, the customs and norms, and the institutions of our government. These individuals are slowly undermining the American system of government—a death by a thousand cuts. Some articulated and acted upon a clear desire to overthrow the government on that day. Many others took actions that are just as damaging to our country in the long run. We saw forces seek to undermine and erode the legitimacy of our government, in order to install Donald Trump as the leader for an indefinite period; that would have brought about a totalitarian dictatorship, whether or not called by that name. He was not re-elected, so to re-install him as president would be profoundly anti-democratic. What happened is akin to, and dangerously close to, civil war, and a sort of culture war. The danger is real, by whatever label is affixed.

Beyond the Trump vs. Biden specific election results, there is a bigger truth we need to confront regarding the civic values of our democracy. The truth is not about one politician or one election alone, but about preserving and defending the Constitution and government of the United States from those who would disregard our norms and destroy our form of government. Those who attacked the Capitol on January 6th tried to stop the proper functioning of our system of government, while Members of Congress were fulfilling their solemn constitutional duty. They attempted a coup: a sudden, violent overthrow of our government. It was an insurrection, attacking and revolting against our duly established government and its actors. While we may have survived this moment of rebellion, the forces at work have not abandoned the call to arms, whether violent or otherwise.[2]

How did we get here? It started *at least* as far back as 2016, with Donald Trump boasting that he would win the primaries and become the Republican nominee for president, and that he would lose only if the primaries were rigged.[3] He then extended

---

[2] Admittedly, Donald Trump's supporters in Washington on January 6th, and the people who stormed the Capitol on that day, formed a complicated collection of individuals. Some people were inspired by trying to help Donald Trump, in a form of almost cult-like hero-worship; some were looking for an excuse to do damage to the building in their fit of rage; some wanted to hurt or kill people; some wanted to disrupt Congress; some stayed outside to protest; others rallied but did not march on the Capitol. Many people strongly believed they were pursuing the Truth (as falsely told to them by Donald Trump); some certainly knew better; and some probably didn't even care what the truth was. Not everyone who supported Donald Trump or who participated in protests on January 6th was trying to overthrow the government or knew The Big Lie was not the truth. While each individual's specific motivation and action varied, together these individuals and their actions came together in a traitorous insurrection. But whoever acted with whatever motivation, as much as I disdain the acts, in this chapter I extend myself to those individuals, as we try to form a more perfect Union. Each person can find their way to understanding these events and working to support our democratic system. This work requires metaphorically building bridges large and small, all across the nation.

[3] This is not the first or last time that we have faced a contested election. Democrats and Republicans alike have made claims of unfairness, election-rigging, and more, but never in the way, or to the extent exhibited here, and certainly not by the president himself. While we are focusing on the 2020 election and Donald Trump, this problem began before he entered the political sphere, aided by the advent of many media outlets and social media, which allows disinformation to proliferate within minutes. Donald Trump, however, took the problem to a whole new level. Although past presidents have certainly lied, they've never done so with such frequency and ease; *The Washington Post* documented that Donald Trump lied more than 30,000 times while in office. "What is especially striking is how the tsunami of untruths kept rising the longer he served as president and became increasingly unmoored from the truth. Trump averaged about six claims a day in his first year as president, 16 claims day in his second year, 22 claims day in this third year—and 39 claims a day in his final year. Put another way, it took him 27 months to reach 10,000 claims and an additional 14 months to reach 20,000. He then exceeded the 30,000 mark less than five months later." *See* Glenn Kessler, *Trump's false or misleading claims total 30,573 over 4 years*, THE WASHINGTON POST (Jan. 24, 2021), https://www.washingtonpost.com/politics/2021/01/24/trumps-false-or-misleading-claims-total-30573-over-four-years/. *See also* John Santucci and Candace Smith, *Trump Says He's 'Afraid the Election Is Going to be Rigged'*, ABC NEWS (Aug. 1, 2016, 4:57 PM), https://abcnews.go.com/Politics/trump-afraid-election-rigged/story?id=41050425 (reporting that Donald Trump stated " 'First of all, it [the primary season] was rigged, and I'm afraid the election is going to be rigged. I have to be honest. Because I think my side was rigged.").

Thus, I fear that one of Donald Trump's legacies is a societal desensitization to falsehoods, a problem which has arguably allowed the biggest lies of all regarding the election and its aftermath to be generally accepted by one of the two major political parties, and a large percentage of the American people.

his claim as a general election candidate, never promising to honor the results if he wasn't the winner.[4] In 2016, Donald Trump's claims were disturbing, but they were often brushed off as the rhetoric of someone who had never been a public servant, had never run for office, and had never exchanged in the customs of politics. But these customs matter, for their symbolism is a signal of our respect for the rule of law and the functioning of the electoral system.[5] Donald Trump's abandonment of political custom continued throughout his presidency. He peddled in conspiracy theories, during everyday events and briefings and through major moments, like impeachment. Donald Trump told Americans to follow him, and that anyone who opposed him was evil, corrupt, or an enemy of the people.[6] Not only did Donald Trump say these things, but countless politicians, media personnel, and millions of individuals on social media departed from the customs and values addressed in these pages.

The 2020 election cycle became another opportunity for Donald Trump to recite and to promote his conspiracy theories and to inflame his supporters. Even though *he* was the chief executive of the national government, he claimed that the election could be stolen from him and that the government and system were rigged against him by forces unseen and unknown. This assault on the system was a further assault on custom, which is essential to the rule of law. In this context, the question may not be whether someone violated a specific law, but did they undercut the customs and norms that hold our society together. The Constitution calls on us to honor and respect elections. A democracy requires us to hold elections regularly and to honor the results. Neither the Constitution nor any law declares that the losing candidate must publicly concede defeat, but that is

---

4 *See Trump won't accept election results if he loses as Clinton expands campaign into red states*, PBS (Oct. 21, 2016), https://www.pbs.org/weta/washingtonweek/episode/trump-wont-accept-election-results-if-he-loses-clinton-expands-campaign-red-states.

5 The Delaware "burying the hatchet" tradition post-election is but one example of our outward manifestation of respect for the system. *See Trail to the Voting Booth, An Exploration of Political Ephemera: Return Day: A Delaware Tradition*, UNIVERSITY OF DELAWARE LIBRARY, MUSEUMS AND PRESS ONLINE EXHIBITIONS, https://exhibitions.lib.udel.edu/trail-to-the-voting-booth/return-day/ (last visited July 25, 2021).

6 *See* Jordan Fabian, *Trump calls impeachment efforts 'evil' and 'corrupt' as he claims win over Democrats*, NATIONAL POST (Feb. 6, 2020), https://nationalpost.com/news/world/trump-calls-impeachment-efforts-evil-and-corrupt-as-he-claims-win-over-democrats. Trump said that the impeachment (and, relatedly, those conducting it), "[W]as evil, it was corrupt, it was dirty cops, it was leakers and liars. . . ."

what we do. It signals adherence to the rule of law; it is a norm that enforces our broader values.

The results became clear by the Saturday after Election Day 2020: Joe Biden had received the majority of votes in enough states to give him a clear and convincing win in the Electoral College. Within a week, we knew that Joe Biden won (perhaps ironically) by the exact same count as had carried Donald Trump over Hillary Clinton just four years earlier.[7] For two months following Election Day, ballots were counted and recounted, consistent with law and custom. Donald Trump and his lawyers went to court over sixty times, as allowed by law, and they were rejected every time but one (and the one time did not alter the results at all). There were no merits to their complaints. The judges who heard the Trump campaign's claims had been appointed by Democrats and Republicans (including Trump appointees) and served in a wide variety of states, in both state and federal courts. Every judge, sworn to uphold the Constitution and laws, ruled in favor of the legitimacy of this free and fair election.

But Donald Trump argued and screamed every step along the way, as did his lawyers. At one point he stated, "IF YOU COUNT THE LEGAL VOTES, I EASILY WIN THE ELECTION! IF YOU COUNT THE ILLEGAL AND LATE VOTES, THEY CAN STEAL THE ELECTION FROM US."[8] For the two months between the election and January 6th, Donald Trump continued to escalate his rhetoric, with an extended screed and tantrum against the nation that did not re-elect him. He rejected our nation's time-honored custom of conceding

---

[7] In discussing the process two days after the election, Joe Biden wisely counseled patience through the process. " 'It is the will of the voters, no one, not anything else, that chooses the president of the United States of America,' he said. 'So, each ballot must be counted, and that's what we're going to see going through now. And that's how it should be.' In brief remarks to reporters in Wilmington, Delaware, Mr. Biden continued: 'Democracy is sometimes messy. It sometimes requires a little patience as well. But that patience has been rewarded now for more than 240 years with a system of governance that's been the envy of the world.' " Thomas Kaplan and Katie Glueck, *Democracy 'sometimes requires a little patience,' Biden says*, THE NEW YORK TIMES (Nov. 6, 2020), https://www.nytimes.com/2020/11/06/us/elections/democracy-sometimes-requires-a-little-patience-biden-says.html.

[8] *See* Jemima McEvoy, *Here Are The (Debunked) Voter Fraud Claims Trump And His Supporters Are Spreading*, FORBES (Nov. 5, 2020, 7:00 PM), https://www.forbes.com/sites/jemimamcevoy/2020/11/05/here-are-the-debunked-voter-fraud-claims-trump-and-his-supporters-are-spreading/?sh=24a149331fca.

defeat.[9] Instead, he chose to promote himself and his personal grievance over the proper functioning of our American democracy. To tens of millions of Americans, that self-serving approach signaled that they should not trust the results. That Trump-centric approach undercut norms and the rule of law. The result is far bigger than the one man and his grievance, to the detriment of the American electoral system and our democracy as a whole.

Consequently, we need to open ourselves to a conversation about truths, to honest dialogue and debate, and ultimately, to our national commitment to protect our always-evolving Union. Seeking truth is essential, growing from the Constitution and customs, the First Amendment, and universal values espoused in religion and in secular society. We share values and customs as a country which can—and must—unite us in the wake of the January 6th Insurrection. We must live out a faithfulness to the Constitution, the rule of law, and customs that hold us together in our pursuit of a more perfect Union. Nothing can be more important as we seek to preserve our nation and grow as fifty states, united, with a citizenry committed to country.

B. A MORE PERFECT UNION, THE CONSTITUTION, AND THE FIRST AMENDMENT

Our constitutional structure and the protection of free speech envision a people engaged, together, in the process of self-governance. The Constitution's Preamble contains a remarkable premise, committing our nation to constantly engage in self-governance, in its call "to form a more perfect Union." The American experiment is aspirational, as it envisions our never-ending work: we were not perfect then, and we are not today. But we are committed to being *more perfect.* As Ben Franklin purportedly replied, when asked if we had a monarchy or a republic: "A republic, if you can keep it."[10] That quest requires

---

[9] Donald Trump also did not attend Joe Biden's inauguration, again bucking an important symbolic custom of American democracy.

[10] *See* Richard R. Beeman, Ph.D., *Perspectives on the Constitution: A Republic, If You can Keep It,* NATIONAL CONSTITUTION CENTER, https://constitutioncenter.org/learn/educational-resources/historical-documents/perspectives-on-the-constitution-a-republic-if-you-can-keep-it (last visited July 25, 2021).

daily work[11] and a commitment to shared civic values; participation in American self-governance also depends on adherence to customs and norms for engagement. The founders had a vision that is an aspirational clarion call, framed in few words in the Constitution, but not detailed in the great document or laws. Instead, we have developed, maintained, and enforced customs and norms that serve our democracy, through our commitment to democratic dialogue.

Free speech and open, honest, and respectful debate are central to our nation's commitment to self-governance. We the people are committed to a system of government that allows (and maybe even expects) us all to participate in governance, free from government regulation of ideas. As Justice Brennan wrote in *NY Times v. Sullivan* in 1964, we have "a profound national commitment to the principle that debate on public issues should be uninhibited, robust, and wide-open, and that it may well include vehement, caustic, and sometimes unpleasantly sharp attacks on government and public officials."[12] The First Amendment protects the right of the people to speak up and to speak out on policies and politicians, and it prohibits the president or any government official from impeding our self-governance.[13]

In addition, allowing free speech serves as a sort of safety valve, to release any pressure that may build up among the people. They will have a chance to express themselves and vent steam. Political speech is protected to allow for the people to advance ideas and support or oppose candidates and elected officials. As a result, the people can move government officials in

---

[11] *Id.* "If there is a lesson in all of this it is that our Constitution is neither a self-actuating nor a self-correcting document. It requires the constant attention and devotion of all citizens. There is a story, often told, that upon exiting the Constitutional Convention Benjamin Franklin was approached by a group of citizens asking what sort of government the delegates had created. His answer was: 'A republic, if you can keep it.' The brevity of that response should not cause us to under-value its essential meaning: democratic republics are not merely founded upon the consent of the people, they are also absolutely dependent upon the active and informed involvement of the people for their continued good health."

[12] New York Times Co. v. Sullivan, 376 U.S. 254, 270 (1964).

[13] *See* U.S. CONST. amend. I. The First Amendment states: "Congress shall make no law respecting an establishment of religion, or prohibiting the free exercise thereof; or abridging the freedom of speech, or of the press; or the right of the people peaceably to assemble, and to petition the Government for a redress of grievances."

or out, through peaceful means, not violence; we let the political process work. Likewise, we debate policy proposals, bills, and laws publicly and openly, in pursuit of our more perfect Union. Letting those processes of democracy work also means accepting that when the debate is over and the votes are counted, we must move on. That norm is an essential feature of American democracy—we participate in an open dialogue about the important matters of the day, and we respect differences and disagreements. So, we hold political speech in highest regard.[14] That also requires honesty, truth, and a commitment to facts; we cannot have a meaningful debate on important matters of the day if a speaker is lying. We cannot pursue truth via public debate if one side distorts and denies the truth. Free speech protection was designed to protect all kinds of ideas, whether popular or not, but not to provide unlimited privilege to lies and falsehoods. To the extent that free expression furthers democracy, it feeds on truth. We are committed to democracy, not autocracy or mob rule.

The First Amendment guarantees a mechanism for our democratic republic's work to form a more perfect Union, and it involves risks as well as rewards. It manifests a commitment to the aspirational republic, as free expression serves to keep the people engaged and informed in public debate. A brief look at First Amendment doctrine[15] reflects the basic principle that we must protect free expression as a requisite condition for a strong, healthy society. Why do we protect (even exalt) speech in this country? The First Amendment is essential to the pursuit of truth in a marketplace of ideas. The government is not allowed to interfere with this market, so that good ideas can rise and fall on their merits. By allowing all of us to speak with minimal

---

[14] *See* Citizens United v. Federal Election Comm'n, 558 U.S. 310, 339–40 (2010) (stating that "Speech is an essential mechanism of democracy, for it is the means to hold officials accountable to the people. . . . The right of citizens to inquire, to hear, to speak, and to use information to reach consensus is a precondition to enlightened self-government and a necessary means to protect it. . . . For these reasons, political speech must prevail against laws that would suppress it, whether by design or inadvertence. Laws that burden political speech are 'subject to strict scrutiny.' . . .").

[15] This chapter's brief discussion of First Amendment principles is designed to be limited in scope, illustrative but hardly exhaustive or definitive.

constraints, the marketplace of ideas sorts out debates on key issues and subjects.[16]

Not all speech or expression is protected. While we protect words for their importance in our democratic society, words also have the power to incite or to instigate real harm. So, if using certain words in speech crosses the line, the speech effectively loses its First Amendment protection. For one familiar example, in 1919, Justice Oliver Wendell Holmes memorably wrote, "the most stringent protection of free speech would not protect a man in falsely shouting fire in a theater and causing a panic."[17] Our aspirational Constitution and the First Amendment exalt dialogue and not force—the mighty pen is preferred to the sword. Speech or fighting words that cause serious violence, harm, riots, or unlawful activity, may be limited. These fighting words are verbal provocations that generate violence; they can be punished or banned in order to protect against such violence (akin to incitement theory),[18] but are not punishable simply because they are *offensive* words. A fighting words analysis focuses on the danger of violence and retaliation. Intimidation and threats via name-calling or use of symbolic speech may lose protection depending on how far it leads toward physical violence. In the incitement and fighting words context, we draw a line at violence. Specifically, you do not have the right to use words that are "directed to inciting or producing imminent unlawful action and [which are] likely to incite or achieve such action."[19] This means that words are protected, but sometimes expressive activity crosses a dangerous line, and if so, it loses its First Amendment shield. Inciting a crowd to ransack the Capitol, for example, is not protected speech. The First Amendment does not

---

16 Admittedly, the marketplace of ideas is more complicated than ever in this day and age of social media and Big Tech. The implications of our ability to reach hundreds, thousands, or even millions with just a few keystrokes has a dramatic impact on the wide-open public debate, both enhancing and skewing conversations; that is certainly a topic for another chapter or article, but at least worth noting here.

17 Schenck v. United States, 249 U.S. 47, 52 (1919).

18 Virginia v. Black, 538 U.S. 343 (2003), is consistent with this theory. The Court permitted prosecution of cross-burning *only* where the intent to intimidate was proven. Stated differently, the crime was the combined effect of criminal intent and intimidation of the victim.

19 Brandenburg v. Ohio, 395 U.S. 444, 447 (1969).

and cannot protect words designed to—and likely to—cause heat, not light, proverbially speaking.

Free speech is essential to promoting our democratic values of resolving matters through debate, discussion, and votes, not through violence or brute force. Words that incite a crowd to violence lose First Amendment protection. We are free to speak to persuade, to express, and to vent, but not to provoke violent action.[20] In the marketplace of ideas, we allow all speakers, including very unhappy ones, to speak out, and the engaged citizenry can accept those ideas that are worthy. But when advocacy moves to likely violence or lawbreaking, it loses constitutional protection. The law says no; customs and norms say no as well. We allow heated conversation, but not such as to incite violent lawless behavior.

This brief glance at some First Amendment doctrine emphasizes the commitment to allowing free speech of honest nature, and not speech designed to spark violence and physical harm.[21] But at the same time, the First Amendment doesn't prohibit lying *per se*. It doesn't prohibit a man from saying he won an election when he lost.[22] But our aspirational commitment

---

[20] In *Brandenburg v. Ohio,* the Court held that the First Amendment does not protect words that are directly connected to harmful action. In that context, speech is *not* protected if the speaker has the intent to (the speech is directed to) cause dangerous or criminal behavior (inciting or producing unlawful action); the harm is present (at least imminent) and likely to occur.

[21] As another example, in commercial speech doctrine, the advertisement or commercial speech at issue must not be misleading. The first prong of the *Central Hudson* test for analyzing regulation of commercial speech provides that in order to receive protection from state regulation, commercial speech must not be misleading. Central Hudson Gas & Elec. Corp. v. Public Serv. Comm'n of New York, 447 U.S. 557, 566 (1980). Truth is protected; known falsehoods are not; they have no value in an attempt to ascertain the truth in the marketplace of ideas. One last example of how the First Amendment is designed to further the pursuit of truth comes in the context of slander and libel. The First Amendment may not protect individuals who engage in such speech when they display actual malice and knowingly publish false information or publish information "with reckless disregard for the truth." New York Times Co. v. Sullivan, 376 U.S. 254, 280 (1964).

[22] *See* United States v. Alvarez, 567 U.S. 709, 723 (2012) (holding that the Stolen Valor Act constituted a content-based restriction on free speech, in violation of the First Amendment) "Permitting the government to decree this speech to be a criminal offense, whether shouted from the rooftops or made in a barely audible whisper, would endorse government authority to compile a list of subjects about which false statements are punishable. That governmental power has no clear limiting principle. Our constitutional tradition stands against the idea that we need Oceania's Ministry of Truth. *See* G. ORWELL, NINETEEN EIGHTY-FOUR (1949) (Centennial ed. 2003). Were this law to be sustained, there could be an endless list of subjects the National Government or the States could single out. Where false claims are made to [a]ffect a fraud or secure moneys

to form a more perfect Union through robust public debate relies on truth and honesty. More than two centuries of tradition protect our system, as we engage in debate on the important issues of the day. An open and honest debate requires good faith adherence to the truth, and not making up "alternative facts" to fit the argument. With a common ground of facts, we can debate opinions and solutions. And we should expect our leaders to engage in the highest standards of ethical behavior, and to conduct themselves with honesty in the public arena. The First Amendment and norms on political debate require a commitment to truth and to promoting and protecting country first, ahead of self. In sum, the Constitution's aspiration for a more perfect Union is made possible through our robust public debate, protected by the First Amendment. Our aspiration demands our participation in honest, truthful, and respectful dialogue.

C. VALUES AND A GREATER PURSUIT

My concern in these pages is our pursuit of a more perfect Union, and a stronger national community. In addition to the tenets and principles of our American democracy enshrined in the Constitution, each of us can find guidance from our own personal, religious, and often universal values.[23] I speak from my individual perspective as the dean of the law school at Villanova University, an Augustinian Catholic university. From that perspective I see lessons that reinforce a commitment to truth and aspiration for our community. I further posit that our

---

or other valuable considerations, say offers of employment, it is well established that the Government may restrict speech without affronting the First Amendment. *See, e.g.*, Virginia Bd. of Pharmacy, 425 U.S. 771 (noting that fraudulent speech generally falls outside the protections of the First Amendment). But the Stolen Valor Act is not so limited in its reach. Were the Court to hold that the interest in truthful discourse alone is sufficient to sustain a ban on speech, absent any evidence that the speech was used to gain a material advantage, it would give government a broad censorial power unprecedented in this Court's cases or in our constitutional tradition. The mere potential for the exercise of that power casts a chill, a chill the First Amendment cannot permit if free speech, thought, and discourse are to remain a foundation of our freedom."

[23] Tapping into universal values is not an exercise that is unique to organized religion. The values I address here are notably *not* unique to religions. Humanists, atheists, agnostics, secularists, and more give voice to universal values in their own ways. There is no one religion to which all Americans subscribe—quite the opposite in our pluralistic nation that enshrines freedom of religion. But with as many different organized religions and belief systems as we may have, there are often universal truths and values that run through all of our lives.

nation derives strength from traditional Augustinian values as we aspire to be a more perfect Union. St. Augustine wrote "our hearts are restless until they rest in You"[24] and urged each person to "become what you are not yet."[25] These words remind us that as a community, whether secular or religious, we remain always aspirational. Both our nation's commitment to self-governance through peaceful expression and Villanova University's commitment to our Augustinian heritage speak to that aspiration.

Saint Augustine had a dynamic vision of people living in community, united in mind and heart in the ardent search of wisdom and the divine truth. For Augustine, every heart is restless in this quest. All people pursue universal wisdom and truth through open, intelligent, responsible, and mutually respectful interaction of differing points of view.

When I welcome speakers to our community (especially controversial ones), I often invoke Villanova University's motto—*Veritas Unitas Caritas*, which we translate as *Truth Unity Love*. We seek our direction from those words every day, and they can point the way forward in times of great challenge in any community, whether a few members of a nuclear family, the hundreds in our Charles Widger School of Law, the 11,000 students at Villanova, a whole city, a state, or even our entire nation. It admittedly becomes harder to work out these principles in larger groups, but it is possible. We must start somewhere. So how do those three words translate into actions and deeds?

As an institution of higher learning, we are in the business of ideas, in a constant pursuit of truth (*Veritas*). As such, we welcome a diversity of ideas, whether we agree with them or not.

---

[24] *See* Villanova University, *Division of Student Life, Be Informed: Office of the Vice President*, VILLANOVA UNIVERSITY, https://www1.villanova.edu/villanova/studentlife/be_informed/vicepresident.html (last visited Aug. 14, 2021); Villanova University, *Mission & Ministry: University Heritage, History and Tradition: Augustinian Tradition*, VILLANOVA UNIVERSITY, https://www1.villanova.edu/villanova/mission/heritage.html (last visited Aug. 14, 2021). *See also Article #15: Our Hearts are Restless*, CHRISTIAN HISTORY INSTITUTE, https://christianhistoryinstitute.org/incontext/article/augustine (last visited July 25, 2021).

[25] *See* Villanova University, *Office of University Communication and Marketing: The Nation's Augustinian Catholic University*, VILLANOVA UNIVERSITY, https://www1.villanova.edu/villanova/unicommunication/nations_augustinian_catholic_university.html (last visited Aug. 14, 2021).

And sometimes we grow the most by confronting the ideas which challenge us the most, and then by responding. We educate ourselves as we listen to speakers and their perspectives. We are seeking ideas and information to develop our ultimate understanding of facts, opinions, and ideas—our pursuit of truth. We place truth as a premium value toward the development of each student, all members of our community, and those with whom we interact outside of Villanova.

In that context, we confront varying perspectives. We have hosted speakers with whom I vigorously disagree. As dean, I welcome them to share their ideas, and I urge those who agree to speak up, and those who disagree to speak up as well. To speak with clarity of conviction. To speak with passion. To speak from knowledge. And always to speak with respect. Why respect? Because that is essential to our community—that's the *Unitas* part. At Villanova Law, we rise and fall as a community, unified in our commitment to the study of law. We are brothers and sisters in this venture. Bound by the spirit of Villanova University. Bound by a commitment to each other. And bound by our own love, care, and concern for each other. And that is the *Caritas* part. I offer myself as a brother, with love for each and every member of the Villanova Law community. And whenever people come into our community, we need to offer our best selves and our respect. All are welcome. I expect speakers to come with respect and with care and concern for the individuals in the Villanova Law community, and I expect us to show a reciprocal respect to the outside speaker. At the end of it all, we all will grow if we can come with love and respect, committed to open and honest debate about ideas. I require no political or religious litmus test. I demand no specific oath. But each person is invited to engage in our discourse. It may be hard sometimes, and that is our own unique struggle. With that understanding, I welcome everyone to Villanova Law, and I ask all present to approach conversations with a commitment to truth, unity, and love.

I also see consistency between the teachings of St. Augustine, our First Amendment doctrine and theory, and our national pursuit of a more perfect Union. The First Amendment and our secular ideology of democracy calls on us to have a robust public debate on the key issues of the day, as part of our grand experiment and exercise in self-government. I believe that the spirit of the Constitution forcefully requires us to *engage* in the spirit of St. Augustine's insights. We must come to the constitutional self-governance conversation with an open heart and an open mind. Only by approaching our difficult conversations this way can we make progress toward a more perfect Union. If we only state our own opinions and refuse to listen to others, we will not succeed in our secular, national mission of self-government. If we engage, we will move forward.

Thus, we have a shared commitment in our religious and secular roots. As an Augustinian Catholic school with a mission, and as a country formed and guided by an aspirational constitution, we are committed to (1) freedom to speak, with parameters and expectations on how we speak, and (2) the pursuit of truth through examination and engagement. With that commitment, the Constitution and Augustinian values merge. While the Constitution enshrines a right to free expression and debate, the Augustinian tradition provides guidance about how to approach expression and debate—to speak from the heart and to carry a similar commitment to help our community strive to become what it is not yet—a more perfect Union.

In so concluding, I have drawn upon the words of St. Augustine and Villanova University's 180-year-old Augustinian Catholic heritage. But I am convinced that these values are universal. Catholics, Protestants, Jews, Muslims, Buddhists, atheists, agnostics, secularists, and more are all finding some way to seek truth through conversation, dialogue, and introspection. Different cultures, communities, faiths, and families may provide different specific words, actions, and traditions. But in the end, who opposes Truth, Unity, and Love? At the core, as we all seek to become who we are not yet, both as individuals and as a more perfect Union, we must maintain a commitment to these ideals and principles. To me, our national commitment—as expressed in the constitutional structure, the First Amendment, and beyond—reflects universal values.[26]

---

[26] This analogy is not perfect, as Villanova is a voluntary association with an articulable mission. Our country is a place where 300+ million people live, many/most through no choice of their own. I assert that our Constitution (which functions, in

D. THE ROOTS OF INSURRECTION—DISREGARD AND DESTRUCTION

With that said, we return to the specific subject of this book: the January 6th, 2021 Insurrection. For years, both before and during his presidency, Donald Trump and his supporters disregarded norms, the truth, facts, political and social customs, and more. That laid the groundwork for the Insurrection on January 6th, 2021. There are myriad examples of what Donald Trump and his devotees did and said to divide this country during this time.

For example, starting on Day 1, White House Press Secretary Sean Spicer made demonstrably false statements about the attendance numbers at the inauguration.[27] On January 22, 2017, on Meet the Press, Counselor to the President Kellyanne Conway sought to defend Spicer's falsehoods, famously saying that he was providing "alternative facts."[28] The show's host, Chuck Todd, responded, "Look, alternative facts are not facts. They're falsehoods."[29] Everyone is entitled to an opinion, but not to their own facts.[30] Providing and discussing different facts and perspectives is a natural part of democracy and free debate. The problem here was that the people making these statements knew they were untrue and lacked any basis

significant part, as a restraint on government power) calls us to approach every communication with an open heart and an open mind. My vision is aspirational, perhaps hopelessly so. I am an incurable, hope-filled optimist, and I think that these values must be imbued in our civic conversation, every day. It is incumbent on *we the people* to act, and to speak up in this unique representative democracy. I seek to build bridges to that more perfect Union.

[27] *See* Politico Staff, *Transcript of White House press secretary statement to the media*, POLITICO (Jan. 21, 2017, 7:23 PM), https://www.politico.com/story/2017/01/transcript-press-secretary-sean-spicer-media-233979; Rachel Chason, *Sean Spicer says he 'absolutely' regrets crowd-size briefing*, THE WASHINGTON POST (Sept. 19, 2017), https://www.washingtonpost.com/news/the-fix/wp/2017/09/18/sean-spicer-says-he-absolutely-regrets-crowd-size-briefing/.

[28] *See* Alexandra Jaffe, *Kellyanne Conway: WH Spokesman Gave 'Alternative Facts' on Inauguration Crowd*, NBC NEWS (Jan. 22, 2017, 9:59 AM, updated 8:29 PM), https://www.nbcnews.com/storyline/meet-the-press-70-years/wh-spokesman-gave-alternative-facts-inauguration-crowd-n710466.

[29] *See* Ben Zimmer, *A Clash of 'Alternative' and 'Facts'*, THE WALL STREET JOURNAL (Jan. 26, 2017, 1:18 PM), https://www.wsj.com/articles/a-clash-of-alternative-and-facts-1485454691.

[30] *See ForbesQuotes: Thoughts on the Business of Life*, FORBES, https://www.forbes.com/quotes/1164/ (attributing a slightly different version of this quote, "Every man has a right to his opinion, but no man has a right to be wrong in his facts," to Bernard M. Baruch).

in verifiable truth—these were bad faith statements. Statements and facts presented in public debate on matters of importance must be supported, not baseless assertions unsubstantiated by anything but bald assertion. If we are to engage in the robust public debate that is protected by the First Amendment in our aspirational pursuit of a more perfect Union, we cannot tolerate "alternative facts," but that's just what Donald Trump and others promoted. In that context, they were not breaking a law, but they were disregarding customs and norms and flaunting the spirit and essence of our participatory democracy. Disregard for those norms became a new norm, and the truth was placed in the corner, with a corrosive impact on our robust public debate.

Donald Trump also effectively, and without pointing to any verifiable facts, assailed the press throughout his presidency. It is well-established that the Fourth Estate is essential to the functioning of our democracy, and the freedom of the press is guaranteed in the First Amendment.[31] The press is essential to the dissemination of factual information to inform us all as we engage in our democratic dialogue. These attacks on the press are collateral attacks on the truth and informed debate. Yet in April 2019, in one of his more famous attacks, "President Trump said . . . that the press is 'truly the enemy of the people,' ratcheting up his use of the derisive label to attack the news media. 'The press is doing everything within their power to fight the magnificence of the phrase, MAKE AMERICA GREAT AGAIN!' Trump tweeted. 'They can't stand the fact that this Administration has done more than virtually any other Administration in its first 2yrs,' he continued. 'They are truly the ENEMY OF THE PEOPLE!' "[32]

Donald Trump also disregarded other institutions of government—the pillars of our system. Beyond just disagreeing with opinions and outcomes he didn't like—as was the custom over the centuries—Donald Trump attacked the courts and judges personally, to undercut their legitimacy. In one notable

---

[31] U.S. CONST. amend. I. "Congress shall make no law . . . abridging the freedom . . . of the press."

[32] *See* Brett Samuels, *Trump ramps up rhetoric on media, calls press 'the enemy of the people'*, THE HILL (Apr. 5, 2019, 2:21 PM), https://thehill.com/homenews/administration/437610-trump-calls-press-the-enemy-of-the-people.

example, Donald Trump attacked a federal judge who was born in Indiana, whose parents had immigrated to the United States from Mexico a generation earlier. Trump claimed that the "Mexican judge" couldn't rule impartially on his case, because of Trump's campaign call to build a border wall and make Mexico pay for it.[33] This claim clearly attacked the notion and importance of an independent judiciary, and it was personal—going far beyond previous norms.

Donald Trump's rhetoric shifted into high gear during the 2020 election cycle, when he frequently said that the only way he would lose was if his enemies and opponents rigged the election.[34] He refused to say that he would concede.[35] And when confronted on the use of violence and intimidation against those who didn't support him, Donald Trump flouted all norms of civility and decency. At the September 29, 2020 presidential debate, Donald Trump famously egged on the violent Proud Boys movement:

> Debate moderator Chris Wallace asked Trump if he was willing to condemn white supremacists and militia groups and tell them to "stand down" and not add to violence during recent protests in U.S. cities such as Portland, Oregon, and Kenosha, Wisconsin.
>
> Trump agreed to do that, asking, "Who would you like me to condemn?" Biden interjected: "The Proud Boys."

---

[33] *See* Nina Totenberg, *Who Is Judge Gonzalo Curiel, The Man Trump Attacked For His Mexican Ancestry?*, NPR (June 7, 2016, 7:20 PM), https://www.npr.org/2016/06/07/481140881/who-is-judge-gonzalo-curiel-the-man-trump-attacked-for-his-mexican-ancestry.

[34] *See* Morgan Chalfant, *Trump: 'The only way we're going to lose this election is if the election is rigged'*, THE HILL (Aug. 17, 2020, 7:22 PM), https://thehill.com/homenews/administration/512424-trump-the-only-way-we-are-going-to-lose-this-election-is-if-the; Greg Sargent, *Opinion: Trump just repeated his ugliest claim about the election. Why isn't it bigger news?*, THE WASHINGTON POST (Sept. 15, 2020, 10:46 AM), https://www.washingtonpost.com/opinions/2020/09/15/trump-just-repeated-his-ugliest-claim-about-election-why-isnt-it-bigger-news/; William Cummings, Joey Garrison and Jim Sergent, *By the numbers: President Donald Trump's failed efforts to overturn the election*, USA TODAY (Jan. 6, 2021, 5:01 AM, updated at 10:50 AM), https://www.usatoday.com/in-depth/news/politics/elections/2021/01/06/trumps-failed-efforts-overturn-election-numbers/4130307001/.

[35] *See* Franco Ordoñez and Roberta Rampton, *Trump Is In No Mood to Concede, But Says Will Leave White House*, NPR (Nov. 26, 2020, 8:37 PM), https://www.npr.org/sections/biden-transition-updates/2020/11/26/939386434/trump-is-in-no-mood-to-concede-but-says-will-leave-white-house.

> Trump then urged the Proud Boys to "stand back and stand by."[36]

Not surprisingly, the Proud Boys joyfully took this remark as a sort of endorsement.[37] In effect, Donald Trump and many of his supporters promoted violence and intimidation at the expense of open, honest debate and deliberation. That violence undermined our commitment to the debate and discussion that form the underpinnings of our democracy.[38]

Another example of Donald Trump's divisive tactics occurred during the 2020 presidential campaign: a video went viral, showing a caravan of his supporters harassing a Biden campaign bus, and effectively running it off the road. Instead of condemning violence in his name, Donald Trump doubled down and retweeted the video itself, with approval, stating: "I LOVE

---

[36] *See* Ted Hesson and Kristina Cooke, *Explainer: President Trump asked the Proud Boys to 'stand by.' Who are they?*, REUTERS (Sept. 30, 2020, 5:00 PM), https://www.reuters.com/article/us-usa-election-extremists-explainer/explainer-president-trump-asked-the-proud-boys-to-stand-by-who-are-they-idUSKBN26L3Q1.

[37] *See* Ben Collins and Brandy Zadrozny, *Proud Boys celebrate after Trump's debate callout*, NBC NEWS (Sept. 30, 2020, 8:34 AM), https://www.nbcnews.com/tech/tech-news/proud-boys-celebrate-after-trump-s-debate-call-out-n1241512.

[38] We saw a similar problem in the context of Charlottesville, where Donald Trump declared that there were "very fine people on both sides." *See* Katie Reilly, *President Trump Again Blames 'Both Sides' for Charlottesville Violence*, TIME (Aug. 14, 2017, 5:18 PM), https://time.com/4902129/president-donald-trump-both-sides-charlottesville/. His comments inflamed passions and divided our nation and were rebuked on both sides of the political aisle. This is one of the conundrums of my argument. We must tolerate people with different ideas, but we need standards. I am not a White Supremacist, but I will let them say what they believe, confident that my position will prevail, and theirs will not. As Dr. Martin Luther King, Jr. said, "The arc of the moral universe is long, but it bends toward justice." Dr. Martin Luther King, Jr., *Remaining Awake Through a Great Revolution*, March 31, 1968. But what happened in Charlottesville does not suggest very fine people who came to that event with an open mind and an open heart. They came laden with hostility to others, armed with torches, ready and desiring to fight, but not open to learning and sharing ideas. These people seemed determined to start a riot, and as a result, many were hurt, and one person lost her life to senseless, hateful violence. All good people should condemn that as inconsistent with our commitment to peaceful, respectful debate on the important issues of the day.

In addition, I think it is clear that if you are marching with violent individuals and neo-Nazis, saluting and chanting along the lines of Hitler's brigades, it's time to make a choice. Good people dedicated to our country do not march alongside that. As Senator Orrin Hatch said, "We should call evil by its name. My brother didn't give his life fighting Hitler for Nazi ideas to go unchallenged here at home." *See The Latest: Trump's remarks on clashes draw strong reactions*, AP NEWS (Aug. 12, 2017), https://apnews.com/article/ec099d3d41be44cb988e3b3484f4b76c. In that sense, we must stand up for right, against wrong, in a way that follows the constitutional and Augustinian teaching.

TEXAS!"[39] Another norm shattered. Another rejection of unity. Another day in which the commitment to form a more perfect Union was subverted by thugs and violence.

We saw more of this same disregard of truth and norms during the post-election period, as every day, Donald Trump, his lawyers, and his supporters tried to undermine the election results and the entire electoral system. At certain points, they seemed to be following the established processes for such challenges in court. But every time a court ruled against Team Trump, their response was not gracious acceptance of defeat, but a diatribe against those courts and judges. Jenna Ellis, one of Trump's attorneys, tweeted: "The activist judicial machinery in Pennsylvania continues to cover up the allegations of massive fraud. . . . On to SCOTUS!"[40]

These are but a few examples of what could fill volumes. The point is that this approach caused damage. Team Trump's escalating disregard of institutions, persistent lies, and flaunting of norms over four years slowly eroded our republic. It intensified during the 2020 election cycle and spiraled out of control from Election Day 2020 to January 6th, 2021. Sadly, it culminated in an angry mob attempting an insurrection by storming the Capitol on January 6th, 2021.

E. A PATH FORWARD?

Some believed Donald Trump was a good president, and he was the right choice for four more years. Others thought he was not a good president or thought Joe Biden would make a better president. Presumably the former voted for Donald Trump and the latter voted for Joe Biden. People on each side had their opinions, and we should protect their reasonable speech throughout the campaign process. But when the voting was done, the *verifiable fact* remains that Joe Biden won more votes in the Electoral College than Donald Trump, making Joe Biden the freely and fairly chosen President of the United States. No

---

[39] *See* Matthew S. Schwartz, *Trump Speaks Fondly of Supporters Surrounding Biden Bus in Texas*, NPR (Nov. 1, 2020, 3:52 PM), https://www.npr.org/2020/11/01/930083915/trump-speaks-fondly-of-supporters-protecting-biden-bus-in-texas.

[40] *See* Tucker Higgins, *Trump says his election challenges probably won't make it to the Supreme Court*, CNBC (Nov. 29, 2020), https://www.cnbc.com/2020/11/29/trump-acknowledges-the-supreme-court-.html.

matter how strongly anyone wanted Donald Trump to win a second term, he simply didn't earn enough votes in enough states to make it so.

But Donald Trump and his adherents constantly spouted The Big Lie, claiming that the election was somehow fraudulent or stolen. That claim is demonstrably false.[41] American elections, held at regular intervals, with open access to eligible voters, are remarkable and a point of national pride. They should be. Team Trump changed that in the 2020 election.

There can be no sugar-coating these truths: Donald Trump lied. Rudy Giuliani lied. Sydney Powell lied. Countless others, including Senators like Josh Hawley, Ted Cruz, and Ron Johnson, further perpetrated The Big Lie. And above all, they never admitted the biggest truth: that their agenda encompassed more than one man and his petulant grievances, but it was instead an attempted coup. Regular elections and the peaceful transition of power are the hallmarks of our democracy; on January 6th, the insurrectionists attempted to stop the Electoral College count and effectively overthrow our system of government. The relentless disregard of (and consequent destruction of) norms made this possible. We can make it out by turning to these universal values as we re-commit to the hard work of forming a more perfect Union. That is truly difficult, and the nation is at an historic point of inflection.

Donald Trump and his acolytes spent years elevating one man over the system that we built painstakingly, through revolution, Civil War, and more, since the 18th century. They toed the line of what was explicitly legal, pushed boundaries of democratic norms and customs, and lied about verifiable facts that were inconvenient to their world view. That four-year assault on the democratic institutions we hold dear became the bridge to an explosive, culminating event on January 6th, where

---

[41] Despite the pandemic, social unrest, and more, our great country once again held a free and fair presidential election. *See* Kaitlin Collins and Paul LeBlanc, *Trump fires director of Homeland Security agency who had rejected President's election conspiracy theories*, CNN (Nov. 18, 2020, updated 4:55 AM), https://www.cnn.com/2020/11/17/politics/chris-krebs-fired-by-trump/index.html. Christopher Krebs, director of the Cybersecurity and Infrastructure Security Agency, emphasized the election's security, stating that there "[was] no evidence that any voting system deleted or lost votes, changed votes, or was in any way compromised." Director Krebs was subsequently fired by Donald Trump for his statement.

thugs broke the law itself and stormed the Capitol, attempting to stop the counting of the Electoral College votes; they looted, killed, and vandalized. Their rampage shocked our nation and the world and laid bare the ultimate truth.

The actions of Donald Trump undermined our democracy in a singular fashion. Donald Trump has been castigated through the constitutionally-defined impeachment process, becoming the only President of the United States to have been impeached twice (and only the third in history to have been impeached at all). He does not appear to have learned a lesson, even in light of 57 of the 100 senators voting to convict (this majority fell short of the two-thirds required for conviction). The criminals who stormed the Capitol on his behalf broke countless laws. Individual lawbreakers can be prosecuted and punished, and the January 6th insurrectionists are experiencing a measure of justice through their criminal records, imprisonment, and monetary fines. At the same time, we cannot be distracted by just these individuals, for they pose a larger threat, representing a much bigger erosion of respect for laws and norms that sustain our entire system and are a mere embodiment of a greater danger, due to the shifts that have taken place over these important four years.

F. CONCLUSION

As we close out this discussion, I return to my analogy of a riptide in the ocean. The currents have indeed taken us far from our shores. Misinformation, distortion, and disregard of Constitution and custom have emboldened some individuals to take action that is tantamount to an assault on democracy. As that riptide carried countless Americans, and specifically thousands of rioters and insurrectionists on January 6th, we all felt the pull out and away from the safety of the shores of our democracy. So many of us had no sense of what was happening, and January 6th was a wakeup call, warning us that the shore is far away. Throughout this book, we have wondered if swimming back to safety is possible, and if so, how. Is the shore out of reach? I think not, but it will be hard work, and we are just getting started on the way back. We can—and must—fight the riptide daily, steadily working our way back. The tide is powerful, and the specific actions of January 6th represent just part of the dangerous and powerful tide. Now is the time to act and not panic or tire as we swim back.

The Preamble of our founding document says that we established the Constitution *in order to form a more perfect Union.* Let us be true to that commitment by engaging in the hard conversations, with a commitment to making ours a better country through dialog, engagement, and respectful disagreement. That is our big challenge on campuses across the country. Let us come to our neighbors, classmates, teammates, and friends with an open heart and an open mind. Let us love one another as sisters and brothers. Let the First Amendment be more than forty-five words written on a page. And let St. Augustine's spirit and articulation of what are not only Catholic, but also universal, values illuminate our path.

With this major problem laid out, the solution is to return to the aspirational commitment to dialogue, to norms that not only permit (and elevate) discussion and debate but require respect. Start with the principle that we are united as a community. We each can start locally, in our universities, companies, towns, and neighborhoods, and build from there. The Constitution aspires to our becoming a more perfect Union. The First Amendment protects a wide-open, robust public debate. And time-honored values of truth, unity, and love—expressed throughout and across societies over time—can carry us there. It requires a radical re-commitment to where we are going. It requires re-establishing norms of civility and decency and respect. It requires adherence to civic values and actual facts. Keep in mind, one man or one terrible day is not the only problem. The continual, intentional, and systematic disregard and destruction of customs, laws, and facts have undermined our democracy in the most sinister way. Punishing the insurrectionists is a necessary first step on the road back. This is just the beginning. The harder work of re-committing our nation will take much longer, and the battle for the soul and future of our American republic is still ongoing. It is a republic. Can we keep it?

ABOUT THE AUTHORS

Mark C. Alexander is the Arthur J. Kania Dean and Professor of Law at the Villanova University Charles Widger School of Law. He was a faculty member at Seton Hall University School of Law for twenty years prior to becoming dean at Villanova Law. His teaching and scholarship focus primarily on the areas of constitutional law, the First Amendment, and election law.

Michèle Alexandre has served and taught in higher education for twenty years. Alexandre is currently Dean of Stetson University College of Law, Professor of Law and Counsel to the president of Stetson University for Strategic Initiatives and Operations. Alexandre's scholarly and teaching areas include constitutional law, international law, civil rights law, disability law, critical race theory, human rights, and gender. They are the author of two books: The New Frontiers of Civil Rights Litigation (2019) and Sexploitation: Sexual Profiling and the Illusion of Gender (2014).

Erwin S. Chemerinsky is Dean and Jesse H. Choper Distinguished Professor of Law, University of California, Berkeley School of Law. He has been a law professor since 1980 and specializes in constitutional law. He is the author of 15 books and over 200 law review articles.

Danielle M. Conway is Dean and Donald J. Farage Professor of Law at Penn State Dickinson Law. She has been in academia for 25 years. Her teaching and scholarship are in the fields of government contract law, intellectual property licensing law, and indigenous peoples' rights. She is a veteran of the U.S. Army.

Anthony W. Crowell is Dean and President, and Professor of Law, at New York Law School. He has served in this role since 2012. His area of focus is State and Local Government Law. Previously, he was Counselor to New York City Mayor Michael Bloomberg for more than a decade where he spearheaded numerous reforms to improve the City's election and civic engagement processes. Dean Crowell is member of several non-profit boards that promote democracy, civic engagement, and leadership.

Garry W. Jenkins is Dean and William S. Pattee Professor of Law at the University of Minnesota Law School. He joined the academy in 2004 after serving as chief operating officer and general counsel of a large corporate foundation in New York City. His research and teaching interests are in law and philanthropy, leadership studies, corporate governance, and civil rights law.

Kevin R. Johnson is Dean and Mabie/Apallas Professor of Public Interest Law and Chicana/o Studies at the University of California, Davis School of Law. He has been dean since 2008 and served as Associate Dean for Academic Affairs for ten years before that. His primary area of scholarship is immigration law and civil rights.

Jennifer L. Mnookin is Dean and Ralph and Shirley Professor of Law at UCLA School of Law. She is also the co-founder and faculty director of PULSE@UCLA Law (the Program on Understanding Law, Science and Evidence). Her scholarship primarily focuses on evidence, especially expert and scientific evidence, and, more generally, the relationship between law, science, and knowledge. She is currently in her seventh year as dean and her 24th year in legal academia.

Kimberly Mutcherson is Dean and Professor of Law at Rutgers Law School in Camden. Dean Mutcherson writes on issues related to reproductive justice with a focus on assisted reproduction, abortion, and maternal-fetal decision-making.

Andrew M. Perlman is Dean and Professor of Law at Suffolk University Law School. During his more than 20 years in academia, his teaching and scholarship have focused on the fields of civil procedure and professional responsibility.

Prior to her current appointment, Carla D. Pratt served as the Nancy J. LaMont Faculty Scholar and Professor of Law at Penn State Dickinson Law where she taught constitutional law, federal Indian law, and race and American law, and produced scholarship at the intersection of those areas.

Theodore W. Ruger is Dean and Bernard G. Segal Professor at the University of Pennsylvania Carey Law School. He is a scholar of constitutional law, specializing in the study of judicial authority, and an expert on health law, pharmaceutical regulation, and legal ethics. He has been on the Penn Carey Law faculty since 2004 and dean since 2015.

Daniel P. Tokaji is the Fred W. & Vi Miller Dean and Professor of Law at the University of Wisconsin Law School. Dean Tokaji has published over 50 articles and scholarly papers on voting rights, free speech, and democratic inclusion and is co-author of *Election Law: Cases and Materials.*

Robert K. Vischer is Dean and holds the Mengler Chair in Law at the University of St. Thomas School of Law in Minneapolis. He has published two books with Cambridge University Press—*Conscience and the Common Good: Reclaiming the Space Between Person and State* and *Martin Luther King Jr. and the Morality of Legal Practice: Lessons in Love & Justice*—as well as more than three dozen law review articles and book chapters.

TABLE OF CASES